CW01475033

Improving Conflict-Phase Access

Identifying U.S. Policy Levers

BRYAN FREDERICK, KRISTEN GUNNESS, GABRIELLE TARINI,
ANDREW STRAVERS, MICHAEL J. MAZARR, EMILY ELLINGER,
JONAH BLANK, SHAWN COCHRAN, JEFFREY W. HORNUNG,
LYLE J. MORRIS, JORDAN ERNSTSEN, LYDIA GREK,
HOWARD WANG, LEV NAVARRE CHAO

Prepared for the Department of the Air Force
Approved for public release; distribution is unlimited.

RAND PROJECT AIR FORCE

For more information on this publication, visit **www.rand.org/t/RRA1742-1**.

About RAND

The RAND Corporation is a research organization that develops solutions to public policy challenges to help make communities throughout the world safer and more secure, healthier and more prosperous. RAND is nonprofit, nonpartisan, and committed to the public interest. To learn more about RAND, visit www.rand.org.

Research Integrity

Our mission to help improve policy and decisionmaking through research and analysis is enabled through our core values of quality and objectivity and our unwavering commitment to the highest level of integrity and ethical behavior. To help ensure our research and analysis are rigorous, objective, and nonpartisan, we subject our research publications to a robust and exacting quality-assurance process; avoid both the appearance and reality of financial and other conflicts of interest through staff training, project screening, and a policy of mandatory disclosure; and pursue transparency in our research engagements through our commitment to the open publication of our research findings and recommendations, disclosure of the source of funding of published research, and policies to ensure intellectual independence. For more information, visit www.rand.org/about/research-integrity.

RAND's publications do not necessarily reflect the opinions of its research clients and sponsors.

Published by the RAND Corporation, Santa Monica, Calif.
© 2023 RAND Corporation
RAND® is a registered trademark.

Library of Congress Cataloging-in-Publication Data is available for this publication.

ISBN: 978-1-9774-1251-5

Cover: Tuna salmon/Adobe Stock, Senior Airman Jessi Roth/U.S. Air Force.

Limited Print and Electronic Distribution Rights

About This Report

The ability of the U.S. Air Force (USAF) to deter aggression from the People's Republic of China in the Indo-Pacific rests in large part on gaining access to the territory and airspace of U.S. allies and partners during any potential regional conflict. This report explores how U.S. allies and partners are likely to make decisions about granting the U.S. conflict-phase access requests and what policies the United States may be able to adopt during peacetime to shift partners' calculations.

RAND Project AIR FORCE

The research reported here was commissioned by Pacific Air Forces (PACAF) and conducted within the Strategy and Doctrine Program of RAND Project AIR FORCE as part of a fiscal year 2022 project, "Defining Victory for Phase 0 Competition."

RAND Project AIR FORCE (PAF), a division of the RAND Corporation, is the Department of the Air Force's (DAF's) federally funded research and development center for studies and analyses, supporting both the United States Air Force and the United States Space Force. PAF provides the DAF with independent analyses of policy alternatives affecting the development, employment, combat readiness, and support of current and future air, space, and cyber forces. Research is conducted in four programs: Strategy and Doctrine; Force Modernization and Employment; Workforce, Development and Health; and Resource Management. The research reported here was prepared under contract FA7014-22-D-0001.

Additional information about PAF is available on our website: www.rand.org/paf/.

This report documents work originally shared with the DAF on September 14, 2022. The draft report, dated September 2022, was reviewed by formal peer reviewers and DAF subject-matter experts.

Acknowledgments

The authors wish to thank the sponsor of this work, Brig Gen Christopher J. Niemi of Pacific Air Forces, who provided essential feedback in shaping this research. We are also greatly indebted to other members of the PACAF team, including Capt Jovan Popovich, for their insights and help with coordination. This report also benefited from the insights of several U.S. government and outside experts with whom we held discussions but who have asked not to be named. At RAND, we are indebted to Raphael S. Cohen, Director of the Strategy and Doctrine Program within Project AIR FORCE, and to Laura Poole, who provided invaluable administrative and logistical support. Satu Limaye of the East-West Center and Timothy R. Heath at RAND provided invaluable reviews that improved the document.

Summary

Ensuring access to the territory of allies and partners in the Indo-Pacific in the event of a future conflict with China is a critical concern for U.S. policymakers. The physical and political geography of the region sharply limits U.S. options for access to such an extent that some allied and partner decisions regarding providing access could determine the outcome of a conflict. A clearer understanding of how and why U.S. allies and partners are likely to make conflict-phase access decisions, and what U.S. policymakers can do to affect the decisions ahead of time, is therefore essential.

Approach

This report addresses the questions of how U.S. allies and partners are likely to make conflict-phase access decisions and what the United States and the U.S. Air Force (USAF) may be able to do to affect these decisions ahead of time through a detailed investigation of the decisionmaking processes of U.S. allies and partners. It begins with a review of prior literature on these questions and a survey of relevant historical case studies of conflict-phase access decisions to develop a framework that summarizes how states consider conflict-phase access requests. The authors then adapt this general framework to five specific U.S. allies and partners in the Indo-Pacific region—Japan, the Philippines, Singapore, Indonesia, and India—through a deep-dive investigation of their strategic outlooks, internal politics, and economic incentives. Next, the authors develop a typology of the full range of potential policy levers that the United States might use to shift allied and partner decisionmaking, then consider the levers in this typology in light of the key factors identified in the country-specific deep-dive analyses to identify those that would be most promising for affecting allied and partner decisionmaking.

Key Findings

- U.S. policymakers and planners should limit their expectations for how much U.S. peacetime policies, and USAF policies in particular, may be able to shift the conflict-phase access decisionmaking of U.S. allies and partners. The specific characteristics of the future conflict, as well as the broader geopolitical alignment decisions of states that are difficult to influence absent large shifts in U.S. policy, are likely to affect these decisions more.
- For some allies or partners, there is potential for lower-level access, such as overflight and logistics, granted during peacetime to increase the likelihood that similar requests will be granted during conflict. However, the ally's or partner's leadership will carefully

scrutinize higher-level access requests, most notably including the ability to conduct combat operations from ally or partner territory, according to the specific characteristics of the future contingency. These likely cannot be routinized in advance.

- All the U.S. allies and partners we investigated viewed the United States as having a critically important role in the region to balance against Chinese power and potential aggression. This desire to see the United States retain its strong role in the region and avoid a military defeat at the hands of China was one of the main factors that could motivate allies and partners to approve U.S. conflict-phase access requests.
- Several U.S. allies and partners continue to be concerned about whether the United States is firmly committed to their defense, and addressing these concerns is likely to be essential for increasing the likelihood of conflict-phase access in these countries.
- The degree of regional and international consensus on the importance of opposing aggression from the People's Republic of China and the potential for a collective response to that aggression are likely to have a large influence on U.S. ally and partner conflict-phase access decisions.

Recommendations

- For the U.S. government
  - Consider clarifying or expanding security guarantees for allies and partners uncertain of U.S. defense commitments.
  - Expand U.S. economic engagement in the Indo-Pacific to provide a credible regional economic counterweight to China.
  - Expand efforts to build regional consensus against Chinese aggression.
- For the U.S. Department of Defense
  - Expand high-level discussions with allies and partners about likely U.S. access requests in a future contingency.
  - Regularize requests to allies and partners for lower-level access anticipated to be relied on in a future contingency.
  - Increase intelligence-sharing, information resilience, and cyber cooperation with allies and partners to underline the U.S. commitment and enhance awareness of aggression from the People's Republic of China.
- For the USAF
  - Increase the frequency and regularity of USAF requests for lower-level but operationally essential allied and partner access.
  - Focus USAF activities in the Indo-Pacific on demonstrating U.S. commitment and enhancing capabilities for combined operations with allies and partners rather than building independent allied or partner capabilities.
  - Prepare to cooperate with allies and partners on their defense against a wider range of contingencies.

Contents

Figures and Tables

Figures

Tables

CHAPTER 1

Introduction

The U.S. Department of Defense (DoD) focus on deterring aggression from the People's Republic of China (PRC) in the Indo-Pacific has highlighted the central role that U.S. allies and partners would play in any potential regional conflict. Not only would allies and partners bring important capabilities of their own to any conflict centered on defending their own territories, but access to their territories, airspace, and waters would be vital for the U.S. prosecution of any such conflict in the region. This is particularly the case for the U.S. Air Force (USAF), which would likely rely on access to allied and partner airspace and bases in the region to counter the PRC.

The USAF, and DoD more broadly, has invested substantial time and effort in increasing its access to allied and partner territory in the Indo-Pacific region during peacetime, but the extent to which this peacetime access will translate into access during a potential future conflict or crisis has received less attention. Can U.S. allies and partners that provide peacetime access to U.S. military forces be relied on to provide similar access in a future conflict? Would other states that might be hesitant to provide peacetime access change their approach in a future contingency, offering new options for U.S. operational planners? And what steps, if any, can the United States take now to increase the likelihood that allies and partners will approve access requests during a potential future conflict? This report focuses on these questions.

Background

Current U.S. force posture in the Indo-Pacific relies on a network of formal main operating bases and informal places where the United States regularly deploys forces for exercises or on a rotational basis with a host country. Japan is the clear center of activity for U.S. forces in the region. U.S. Forces Japan facilities include air bases in Kadena, Yokota, and Misawa and Marine Corps air stations at Futenma and Iwakuni.[1] The United States also maintains main operating bases in Korea, including air bases at Kunsan and Osan.[2] The remaining perma-

---

[1] International Institute for Strategic Studies, *The Military Balance 2022*, February 2022, pp. 61–62.

[2] International Institute for Strategic Studies, 2022, p. 62.

nent U.S. facilities closest to China are on Guam, located nearly 3,000 km from strategically important areas, such as the Taiwan Strait.

In addition to formal bases, U.S. forces frequently deploy to conduct joint operations and exercises with other partner countries in the Indo-Pacific. Although fewer than 200 active-duty U.S. personnel are permanently stationed in the Philippines, the two countries share a legal architecture that allows U.S. forces to rotate through five Philippine military bases, including four air bases.[3] U.S. and Philippine forces also conduct an annual exercise, for which as many as 6,500 U.S. active-duty personnel have deployed to the Philippines.[4] Similarly, the United States and Singapore have a formal agreement granting U.S. forces access to Singaporean air and naval bases, which the United States has used to rotationally deploy combat and surveillance aircraft.[5]

But whether the peacetime military access DoD enjoys will convert to conflict-phase access in a crisis or conflict remains uncertain. There are numerous historical examples of U.S. allies and partners in other theaters refusing to allow conflict-phase access despite close peacetime levels of military cooperation. For example, U.S. peacetime access to Qatari airspace did not convert into conflict-phase access for airstrikes against Islamic State forces in 2014, and all but one North Atlantic Treaty Organization (NATO) ally denied the United States base access to provide supplies to Israel during the 1973 Arab-Israeli War.[6] The authors of a prior RAND Corporation report found that challenges to U.S. conflict-phase access "have occurred regularly."[7]

Whether and how DoD and the USAF will maintain military access to partner countries in the Indo-Pacific has urgent implications for operational limits during a prospective crisis or conflict with China. U.S. conflict-phase access beyond its formal bases is particularly pressing. The People's Liberation Army's (PLA's) decades-long modernization program has included the development of an anti-access, area-denial threat envelope that may potentially hold U.S. forces at risk within the Second Island Chain (see Figure 1.1).[8] These capabilities

---

[3] U.S. Department of State, "Joint Vision for a 21st Century United States-Philippines Partnership," press release, November 16, 2021c; Ben Werner, "Philippines Freezes Pull-Out From Visiting U.S. Forces Agreement," USNI News, June 8, 2020; Gregory Poling and Conor Cronin, "The Dangers of Allowing U.S.-Philippine Defense Cooperation to Languish," War on the Rocks, May 17, 2018.

[4] Matthew Bragg, "31st Iteration of Balikatan Kicks Off," U.S. Indo-Pacific Command, April 20, 2015.

[5] Ministry of Defence, Singapore, "Singapore and the US Renew Memorandum of Understanding," press release, September 24, 2019b.

[6] Renanah M. Joyce and Becca Wasser, "All About Access: Solving America's Force Posture Puzzle," *Washington Quarterly*, Vol. 44, No. 3, September 2021; Andrew Yeo and Stacie Pettyjohn, "Bases of Empire? The Logic of Overseas U.S. Military Base Expansion, 1870–2016," *Comparative Strategy*, Vol. 40, No. 1, January 2021.

[7] Stacie L. Pettyjohn and Jennifer Kavanagh, *Access Granted: Political Challenges to U.S. Overseas Military Presence, 1945–2014*, RAND Corporation, RR-1339-AF, 2016, p. 143.

[8] U.S. Department of Defense, *Military and Security Developments Involving the People's Republic of China 2021: Annual Report to Congress*, November 3, 2021, pp. 77–81.

FIGURE 1.1

Chinese Missile Threats to U.S. Forces in the Second Island Chain

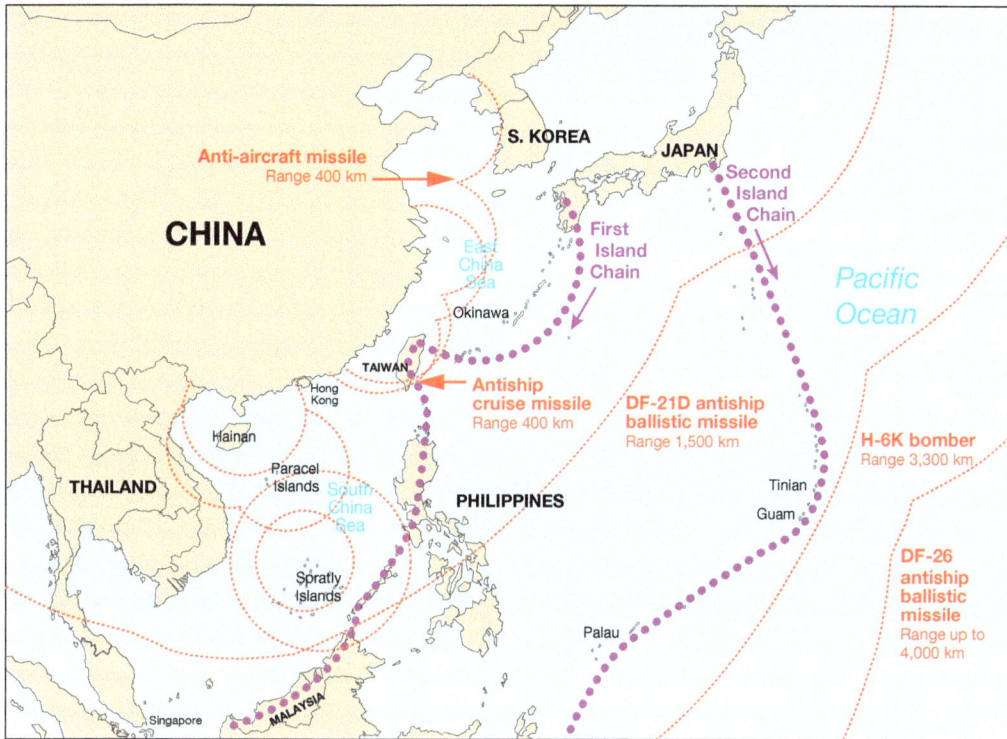

SOURCE: Features information from Carl Rehberg and Mark Gunzinger, *Air and Missile Defense at a Crossroads: New Concepts and Technologies to Defend America's Overseas Bases*, Center for Strategic and Budgetary Assessments, 2018; DoD; and "America's Top Brass Responds to the Threat of China in the Pacific," *The Economist*, March 7, 2021.

pose threats to U.S. bases in Japan and Korea, on which the United States would "undoubtedly have to rely" as "key locations from which to maneuver" in a conflict with China. according to the deputy commander of Pacific Air Forces in 2022, Lt Gen John Thomas, USAF (Ret.).[9]

To address these and other challenges, DoD and the USAF introduced the Agile Combat Employment operational concept to generate combat power while increasing survivability by operating from a network of dispersed locations rather than centrally located infrastructure that an adversary can target and strike more easily.[10] Given the Indo-Pacific's maritime geog-

---

[9] John T. Thomas, "Bases, Places, and Faces: Operational Maneuver and Sustainment in the Indo-Pacific Region," *Journal of Indo-Pacific Affairs*, April 8, 2021. A 2017 report assessed that Chinese missile forces already had the capability to strike "almost every major fixed headquarters and logistical facility" and "almost every U.S. ship in port in Japan," crater "every runway and runway-length taxiway at all major U.S. air bases in Japan," and destroy over 200 U.S. aircraft on the ground (Thomas Shugart and Javier Gonzalez, *First Strike: China's Missile Threat to U.S. Bases in Asia*, Center for a New American Security, 2017, p. 13).

[10] Air Force Doctrine Note 1-21, *Agile Combat Employment*, Curtis E. Lemay Center for Doctrine Development and Education, December 1, 2022, pp. 1–3.

raphy, the spaces most suitable for such a network of dispersed locations are in U.S. allied and partner countries along China's periphery. Maximizing Agile Combat Employment's operational effectiveness requires taking advantage of ally and partner-nation locations, including conflict-phase access to a broad range of airfields in potential host countries.[11]

The existing open-source literature discussing which countries would likely provide the United States with conflict-phase access for operations against China is divided and tends to be specific to a Taiwan scenario. Experts generally consider Japan and Australia the most likely to grant conflict-phase access in a war over Taiwan and present a range of lower-confidence assessments about the access decisions of other countries in the Indo-Pacific.[12]

Experts generally describe three drivers for the potential host countries' decisions for granting the United States conflict-phase access in a war over Taiwan. First, one group of experts argues that the power disparity between China and potential host countries, compounded with the countries' fear of Chinese retaliation, makes such countries as Korea, the Philippines, Singapore, and Thailand likely to grant only severely restricted conflict-phase access or to deny the U.S. request altogether.[13] Second, other experts adopt a model in which the decision to grant conflict-phase access depends on how well a potential host country's values, interests, and threat perceptions align with those of the United States. In this model, countries concerned about China's growing power, such as India and Vietnam, may grow to develop sufficient common interests with the United States to grant conflict-phase access, but only long-standing treaty allies, such as Japan, Australia, and the United Kingdom, are likely to grant such access.[14] Third, another expert has cited historical precedent as a potential driver for granting conflict-phase access, noting that countries today are likely to grant such access because "since 1945, more than 90 percent of U.S. requests for contingency base access have been granted," even without preexisting bases or the country's direct involvement in the relevant conflict.[15]

Public U.S. government documents and statements infrequently address military access in host countries and may suggest low confidence in securing broad conflict-phase access in the Indo-Pacific region. For example, although former Secretary of Defense Mark Esper pub-

---

[11] Air Force Doctrine Note 1-21, 2022, p. 6.

[12] Bonny Lin, "U.S. Allied and Partner Support for Taiwan: Responses to a Chinese Attack on Taiwan and Potential U.S. Taiwan Policy Changes," testimony presented before the U.S.-China Economic and Security Review Commission on February 18, 2021, RAND Corporation, CT-A1194-1, 2021, p. 2; Zack Cooper and Sheena Greitens, "What to Expect from Japan and Korea in a Taiwan Contingency," in Henry D. Sokolski, ed., *New Frontiers for Security Cooperation with Seoul and Tokyo, 2021*, Nonproliferation Policy Education Center, 2021, p. 18; Renanah M. Joyce and Brian Blankenship, "Access Denied? The Future of U.S. Basing in a Contested World," War on the Rocks, February 1, 2021.

[13] Cooper and Greitens, 2021; Daljit Singh, *Southeast Asia's Uneasy Position in America's Indo-Pacific Strategy*, ISEAS–Yusof Ishak Institute, November 28, 2018, pp. 3-4.

[14] Joyce and Blankenship, 2021.

[15] Michael Beckley, "The Emerging Military Balance in East Asia: How China's Neighbors Can Check Chinese Naval Expansion," *International Security*, Vol. 42, No. 2, November 2017, p. 106.

licly called for "looking at how we expand our basing locations" in the Indo-Pacific region, neither he nor DoD publicly specified where new bases or new access to existing bases might be established.[16] Similarly, in a 2022 speech, Assistant Secretary of Defense for Indo-Pacific Security Affairs Ely Ratner only referenced engagements with such countries as Japan and the United Kingdom (UK) when describing U.S. forward operations in the Indo-Pacific, while his mentions of such countries as the Philippines and Thailand remained focused on capacity-building and considering frameworks for negotiating reciprocal access.[17]

Research Approach

This report addresses the questions of how U.S. allies and partners are likely to make conflict-phase access decisions and what the United States and the USAF may be able to do to affect these decisions through a detailed investigation of the decisionmaking processes of U.S. allies and partners. It begins with a review of prior literature on these questions and a survey of relevant historical case studies of conflict-phase access decisions to develop a framework that summarizes how states generally consider conflict-phase access requests. This framework and the evidence underlying it are presented in Chapter 2. The report then adapts this general framework to five specific U.S. allies and partners in the Indo-Pacific region through deep-dive investigations of their strategic outlooks, internal politics, and economic incentives. Each deep dive concludes by identifying the key factors that are likely to be most influential for the conflict-phase access decisionmaking of each assessed U.S. ally or partner.

The five countries chosen for these investigations were selected because of their potential relevance for U.S. operations in the Indo-Pacific and to ensure diversity in geography and likely access challenges, with the final selections made by the project sponsor. The five countries selected were Japan, the Philippines, Singapore, Indonesia, and India; the deep-dive analyses for each are presented in Chapters 3 through 7, respectively. Each deep-dive chapter incorporates an extensive literature review of both Western and local-language literature relevant to access decisionmaking in that country. The chapters also include analysis from our discussions with a variety of subject-matter experts (SMEs). We conducted four to seven interviews for each country that included current and former U.S. government and military officials, U.S.-based SMEs, and local former officials and SMEs residing in the host nations. In all, we conducted 28 interviews. We spoke with 14 current U.S. government and DoD officials, five U.S.-based SMEs, and nine local experts and former officials in the deep-dive countries.[18]

---

[16] Aaron Mehta, "Esper Calls for New Basing Investments in the Pacific," *Defense News,* August 27, 2019.

[17] C. Todd Lopez, "Building Asymmetric Advantage in Indo-Pacific Part of DOD Approach to Chinese Aggression," press release, U.S. Department of Defense, July 27, 2022.

[18] For the Japan deep-dive analysis, we also incorporated a number of interviews from prior RAND research.

Chapter 8 then turns to the question of how the United States, and the USAF in particular, may be able to improve the likelihood that allies and partners will approve future U.S. conflict-phase access requests. It begins by developing a typology of the full range of potential policy levers that the United States might use to shift allied and partner decisionmaking, based on a review of both ongoing U.S. government activities and prior historical efforts to improve U.S. influence in allies and partners in other contexts. We then consider the levers in this typology in light of the key factors identified in the country-specific deep-dive analyses to identify the levers that would be the most promising for affecting allied and partner decisionmaking. Chapter 9 summarizes the analysis and highlights recommendations for the U.S. government, DoD, and the USAF.

CHAPTER 2

Framework for Conflict-Phase Access Decisions

What process do leaders go through when making decisions related to basing and access for outside powers during conflicts? Scholars and policymakers have explored this question in theoretical pieces, empirical work, and reviews of historical episodes over time, but a holistic framework of leadership decisionmaking processes has yet to be put forward. Such a framework would bring together the various strands of previous literature to look at such questions through the eyes of a country's leadership during a crisis. This chapter presents that framework by highlighting five key heuristic questions that guide leadership decisionmaking over access and basing in a crisis: Would granting conflict-phase access

1. affect the leader or regime's political survival?
2. affect the country's direct security, including risk of retaliation?
3. affect the outcome of the conflict?
4. be reciprocated by other regional states?
5. affect the country's economy?

A country's leadership does not, of course, consider these questions in a vacuum: The characteristics of the conflict itself and the type of access the United States is requesting are critical considerations for anticipating how leaders are likely to answer each of these questions. Careful consideration of these issues represents an important part of any application of the framework, as we will discuss in greater detail later in this chapter.

These five questions emerged from the international relations literature and historical work on access considerations over the past century. In many cases, this literature focuses on peacetime access considerations, which differ in important ways from conflict-phase access. Therefore, in some cases, we also evaluate how or whether that work may or may not apply to the conflict phase, given the differential circumstances that tend to prevail in conflict determinations.

Numerous considerations are at play in access decisions, but these five questions combine the dozens of individual lower-level issues that are identified in the theoretical and historical literatures, such as arms sales, security guarantees, trade deals, and aid packages, into higher-order questions that leaders consider in a conflict. Organizing our understanding of conflict-phase access decisionmaking this way also allows a better understanding of how leadership considers categories of issues and how these considerations might be aggregated together rather than being a simple list of considerations that have historically or theoretically been associated with access. Leaders often consider these lower-level considerations as a set of heuristic questions that are shortcuts to weighing these other issues against each other. In the end, our list of questions provides a framework for understanding how leaders make decisions and, thus, how the United States might be able to influence them in its favor during a crisis.

This list also does not imply that these considerations are all equal or mutually exclusive. For instance, the state of the country's economy affects the leader and regime's ability to stay in office and to build a military capable of protecting the country's sovereign territory. The answers to these questions also must be balanced against each other in light of the issues that are most important to the regime or leader, which—as will be discussed in subsequent chapters—is likely to vary by country. In the end, this framework provides a usable way forward in understanding the likely calculations of national decisionmakers in deciding whether to grant the United States conflict-phase access. Subsequent chapters will discuss how this framework can be adapted and used to identify how the United States might be able to use this information to favorably influence this decisionmaking process.

Before delving into an explanation of the considerations themselves, it is important to note that the decisionmaking process surrounding conflict-phase access is heavily contextualized by the status quo in peacetime. Large divergences from the peacetime status quo depend on the nature of the crisis and, in turn, how strongly the factors emerging from the crisis weigh into each of these questions. For instance, crises that directly threaten the political survival of leaders, the territory of the country, or the economic prosperity of the people are likely to see larger divergences from the state of peacetime access than crises that do not fundamentally change these calculations. Within the shifts in the considerations that can take place during a crisis, the United States and allies can add specific incentive structures to potentially tip the balance for a country's decisionmaking.

The following sections review each of the five key questions and describe the theory behind how these questions affect conflict-phase access decisionmaking for states in general. In doing so, it also clarifies prior research, academic and policy literature, and historical examples or case studies on which these assessments are based.

Question 1: Would Granting Conflict-Phase Access Affect the Leader or Regime's Political Survival?

Perhaps the first rule of political decisionmaking is that leaders act in their own self-interest, including—often—a desire to remain in their positions of responsibility or power. They seek to stay in office for two main reasons. First, their ability to enact their agendas is likely to be substantially greater if they maintain power, so survival often supersedes individual policy questions. A loss for the leader in terms of a policy may be short-lived if leadership is maintained and the policy can be reversed later.[1] This dynamic can also occur beyond a single leader and apply to broader governmental structures, such as coalitional governments. In many cases, these types of coalitions put pressure on leaders to adopt a certain policy to keep the governing coalition together. This has occurred multiple times in past considerations of conflict-phase access for the United States. For example, during operations in the Balkans, the Bulgarian Parliament denied the transportation of ground forces through Bulgarian territory because of the need to compromise with portions of the coalition government that were opposed to the NATO mission in Kosovo altogether and threatened to bring down the government.[2] In Italy, the Communist members of the government publicly threatened to withdraw from the government if NATO used ground forces in Kosovo.[3] A decade prior, the Italian government collapsed over the prime minister's approval of an American access request during the *Achille Lauro* hijacking.[4] Even further back in history, King Constantine I of Greece sought to maintain neutrality between belligerents in World War I in an attempt to maintain power.[5] His concerns over his own political survival were exacerbated by the Greek prime minister's interest in allowing Entente access, a decision that would eventually lead to a major schism in Greek politics and the abdication of the king.[6]

Second, especially in nondemocracies, the punishment for losing office can be particularly harsh; the outcomes of losing the position can include exile, imprisonment, and death. Leaders in nondemocracies often cling to power more fiercely than those in democracies, especially democracies with term-limited officeholders.[7] Thus, losing power is the ultimate fate that nondemocratic leaders look to avoid. While democratic leaders also seek to stay in power, there are often institutional or partisan considerations that supersede that desire because the consequences of losing power in a democracy are typically much more benign for the individual.

---

[1] Bruce Bueno De Mesquita, Alastair Smith, Randolph M. Siverson, and James D. Morrow, *The Logic of Political Survival*, MIT Press, 2005.

[2] Karen Donfried, *Kosovo: International Reactions to NATO Air Strikes*, Congressional Research Service, RL30114, April 21, 1999; Kostadin Grozev, "Bulgaria in the Post-Kosovo Era," *Wilson Center: Insight and Analysis*, January 19, 2000.

[3] Donfried, 1999.

[4] "Regime in Italy Falls Amid Furor," United Press International via *South Florida Sun Sentinel*, October 18, 1985; Indro Montanelli and Mario Cervi, *Italy of the Years of Mud*, Rizzoli, 1993.

[5] Foreign Office, "Greece," collected papers, British National Archives, FO 800/63, 1915

[6] George Kaloudis, "Greece and the Road to World War I: To What End?" *International Journal on World Peace*, Vol. 31, No. 4, December 2014.

[7] Giacomo Chiozza and Hein Erich Goemans, *Leaders and International Conflict*, Cambridge University Press, 2011; Giacomo Chiozza and Hein E. Goemans, "Peace Through Insecurity: Tenure and International Conflict," *Journal of Conflict Resolution*, Vol. 47, No. 4, 2003.

Threats to a leader or regime's position in office can come from multiple sources. First, leaders and regimes worry about internal threats. Leaders in authoritarian states follow various strategies to "coup proof" their regimes to maximize their survival in office.[8] Leaders act in their own interests to preserve power, and this often takes the form of moving to sideline or disempower other powerful groups in society, including domestic out-groups and threats. Basing and access decisions can help leaders do this in a variety of ways. Regimes often exclude ethnic groups from coalitions when the groups are perceived to be a threat to the regime.[9] This exclusion can, in turn, lead to civil conflict, with the out-group acting against the government. When this conflict threatens a regime's hold on power, regime leadership is more likely to allow foreign basing and access to bolster its own security position.[10] Playing into these calculations is that terrorist attacks have an ability to destabilize regimes, particularly in nondemocracies, and an outside military force that provides security and empowers the regime may help it stay in power.[11]

These types of threat-reduction steps can also come in the form of reduced support for democratization in the partner state and other types of guarantees from the state requesting access. When the United States is not actively supporting regime opponents, simply entering into such an agreement with the United States can provide the regime with legitimacy that may have been lacking. In such a contract, the world's leading power recognizes the country's leadership as the legitimate authority in the country, which can help entrench a government in power against domestic threats.[12] Access deals with the United States can, therefore, be a tempting option for autocratic leaders who seek to enhance their legitimacy and potentially head off U.S. support for a democratic opposition by making the regime's support indispensable to a U.S. strategic calculation.

Of course, while leaders have an overriding concern to stay in office, this impulse is not divorced from their actual performance in office but is an overriding concern in any situ-

---

[8] Jun Koga Sudduth, "Coup Risk, Coup-Proofing and Leader Survival," *Journal of Peace Research*, Vol. 54, No. 1, January 2017; James T. Quinlivan, "Coup-Proofing: Its Practice and Consequences in the Middle East," *International Security*, Vol. 24, No. 2, Fall 1999.

[9] Janina Beiser-McGrath and Nils W. Metternich, "Ethnic Coalitions and the Logic of Political Survival in Authoritarian Regimes," *Comparative Political Studies*, Vol. 54, No. 1, 2021; Nils-Christian Bormann, "Uncertainty, Cleavages, and Ethnic Coalitions," *Journal of Politics*, Vol. 81, No. 2, April 2019.

[10] J. Wellington Brown and Dean C. Dulay, "Barracks and Barricades: How Internal Security Threats Affect Foreign Basing Access in the Philippines," *Asian Security*, Vol. 17, No. 3, 2021; Christopher E. Diehl, *Small Allies, Big Challenges: The International Politics of Military Access*, thesis, Villanova University, 2009.

[11] Johann Park and Valentina Bali, "International Terrorism and the Political Survival of Leaders," *Journal of Conflict Resolution*, Vol. 61, No. 7, 2017; Andrew Stravers and Dana El Kurd, "Strategic Autocracy: American Military Forces and Regime Type," *Journal of Global Security Studies*, Vol. 5, No. 3, July 2020.

[12] David A. Lake, "Legitimating Power: The Domestic Politics of US International Hierarchy," *International Security*, Vol. 38, No. 2, Fall 2013; Alexander Cooley, *Base Politics: Democratic Change and the US Military Overseas*, Cornell University Press, 2012.

ation.[13] Leaders manipulate their chances of losing office to gain bargaining advantages in international exchanges, in signals to other leaders who have the same incentives to stay in office.[14] Leaders also attempt to orient the domestic context in a way that best maximizes their survival in office, such as acquiring more government revenue through such things as oil profits rather than through mechanisms that require labor. Such methods are thus subject to more domestic pushback.[15] Leaders can gain access to this type of revenue through foreign aid from outside powers as well, which acts as a free resource, much like oil, that does not rely on the domestic public.[16]

Several historical examples show this dynamic in action. First, late in World War II and in the years following, the government in Greece faced a communist insurgency. Because the insurgency threatened the continued rule of the royal family, it allowed access to American forces and brought in American military aid.[17] These steps not only helped defeat communist insurgents but also assisted in building functional institutions within the state, including the development of a postal system that helped soldiers communicate with their families while they were deployed.[18] Thus, American assistance from the outside bolstered the Greek government both by defeating its enemy and in demonstrating competence, although both were more possible because of infusions of resources from the outside. Similarly, U.S. access in the Philippines has closely tracked internal threats to the regime, with U.S. forces both providing direct security and assisting the development of greater state capacity to secure the support of the citizenry.[19]

Leadership must weigh these benefits against the potential for a public backlash that reduces its hold on power. To entrench itself in office, the regime may use the resource infusion from an outside military force, but there is a limit to the extent of public discontent over a decision to allow foreign military access, particularly during a conflict, that a regime is capable of withstanding. The level of public outcry about a basing or access relationship that

---

[13] Bruce Bueno De Mesquita, James D. Morrow, Randolph M. Siverson, and Alastair Smith, "Policy Failure and Political Survival: The Contribution of Political Institutions," *Journal of Conflict Resolution*, Vol. 43, No. 2, 1999.

[14] James D. Fearon, "Domestic Political Audiences and the Escalation of International Disputes," *American Political Science Review*, Vol. 88, No. 3, September 1994.

[15] Bruce Bueno De Mesquita and Alastair Smith, Political Survival and Endogenous Institutional Change," *Comparative Political Studies*, Vol. 42, No. 2, 2009; Jørgen Juel Andersen and Silje Aslaksen, "Oil and Political Survival," *Journal of Development Economics*, Vol. 100, No. 1, 2013.

[16] Amanda A. Licht, "Coming into Money: The Impact of Foreign Aid on Leader Survival," *Journal of Conflict Resolution*, Vol. 54, No. 1, February 2010.

[17] Richard G. Davis, *The U.S. Army and Irregular Warfare 1775–2007: Selected Papers from the 2007 Conference of Army Historians: Selected Papers from the 2007 Conference of Army Historians*, Center of Military History, U.S. Army, 2010.

[18] Davis, 2010.

[19] Brown and Dulay, 2021; John P. McLaurin III, *US Use of Philippine Military Bases*, Army War College, 1990.

can threaten the leadership's position depends partially on the regime type, with nondemocracies generally being able to withstand more widespread public outcry, as long as the discontent does not extend to critical regime officials.[20] In democracies, public discontent that exists among key stakeholders (important racial, religious, gender, or economic groups in the society) plays a similar role and jeopardizes the leadership's position in office and, therefore, the basing relationship.[21]

What determines the level of public discontent with a decision to grant foreign basing access during a conflict that can then lead to regime vulnerability? Much of the work done on why basing and access create public discontent is done in a peacetime context. However, two main factors determine the public's view in that context, which we would expect to carry over into conflict-phase access. First, general views of the state being granted access and that state's relationship to the host state matter a great deal. For instance, the vast majority of the Pakistani public expressed unfavorable views of the United States even before access was granted to support operations in Afghanistan in the early 2000s.[22] Such pervasive views among the population contributed to a great deal of instability in Pakistan in the early years of conflict and counterinsurgency in Afghanistan.[23] This instability included multiple assassination attempts on General Pervez Musharraf, the leader who allowed American access.[24]

Second, it is also clear that the purposes for which access is being granted matter to the public. Public opposition in Libya to U.S. involvement in the 1967 Arab-Israeli conflict led to a series of civil disturbances around the country.[25] The United States had maintained a presence at Libya's Wheelus Air Base near Tripoli since World War II without much incident. However, amid rumors that the base was being used to transit supplies to Israeli forces, military dependents were forced to flee their off-base homes to the base for protection. In the end, more than 7,000 people were evacuated to Europe and back to the United States because of the dangers resulting from public opposition to the purpose for which the U.S. access was being used.[26] Less than two years later, King Idris' government was overthrown by Muammar Gaddafi, forcing the United States to withdraw from Wheelus Air Base entirely.

This level of discontent can also greatly depend on whether allowing basing access fits with the leadership's wider international strategy and comports with various groups' views of the state and whether outside access would constitute a fundamental violation of the coun-

---

[20] Lake, 2013; Stravers and El Kurd, 2020.

[21] Andrew Yeo, *Activists, Alliances, and Anti-US Base Protests*, Cambridge University Press, 2011.

[22] Pew Research Center for the People and the Press, *What the World Thinks in 2002*, December 4, 2002.

[23] Anita Singh, "Pakistan's Stability/Instability Complex: The Politics and Reverberations of the 2007 November Emergency," *Strategic Studies Quarterly*, Vol. 3, No. 4, Winter 2009.

[24] "Assassination Attempts Against Pakistan's Musharraf," Reuters, July 6, 2007.

[25] Daniel Lee Haulman, *The United States Air Force and Humanitarian Airlift Operations, 1947–1994*, U.S. Government Printing Office, 1998.

[26] Haulman, 1998.

try's sovereignty.[27] In some cases, a state negotiating away a portion of its sovereignty for a U.S. military presence that may enhance its security is a deal worth making. In others, the presence of foreign forces themselves (even for the purposes of protection from another threat) is seen as too high a price to pay. This is, again, often tied back to the type of access the U.S. requests and whether it provides simple defensive protection or conducts offensive operations that may be seen as going beyond the security needs of the country. For instance, the population in the Philippines began to oppose the presence of U.S. forces in the 1980s as threats from internal insurgents waned, and no external threats were currently present.[28] U.S. bases therefore constituted a violation of sovereignty rather than protection from threats to it.[29] Similarly, in the aftermath of the Gulf War, American forces in Saudi Arabia were seen as a violation of sovereignty rather than protection against Iraq.[30]

In these cases, attempts to strengthen the regime against domestic audiences and enhance its position against potential public discontent with various forms of side payments to leadership from the state seeking access played an important role in the decision to allow basing access.[31] These payments often form a critical mechanism that serves the leadership's interest in staying in office, particularly in nondemocracies. Such mechanisms have played a key role in past access decisions, forming the basis for much of the appeal of American access in Central Asian states after September 11, 2001. These side payments enhance the leadership's position against the public even as they can turn the larger population away from both the regime and the United States. They also bolster the leadership's position relative to other elites, who often do not have access to such infusions of cash.

Question 2: Would Granting Conflict-Phase Access Affect the Country's Direct Security, Including Risk of Retaliation?

One of the primary considerations that leaders take into account is the protection of the country's national security and territorial integrity.[32] Leaders take security considerations into account in multiple ways. First, leaders calculate to what degree it is possible to obtain security via an outside power, considering both the capabilities of the requesting state and

---

[27] Catherine Lutz and Cynthia Enloe, *The Bases of Empire: The Global Struggle Against US Military Posts*, NYU Press, 2009; Cooley, 2012.

[28] Brown and Dulay, 2021.

[29] Brown and Dulay, 2021.

[30] Sharon Otterman, "Saudi Arabia: Withdrawal of U.S. Forces," Council on Foreign Relations, February 7, 2005.

[31] Alexander Cooley, "U.S. Bases and Democratization in Central Asia," *Orbis*, Vol. 52, No. 1, 2008; Stravers and El Kurd, 2020.

[32] Elizabeth N. Saunders, *Leaders at War: How Presidents Shape Military Interventions*, Cornell University Press, 2011.

the domestic population's appetite for relying on another country for security. As we will explain, gaining security from an outside power still comes at the cost of a level of sovereignty, and some leaders and publics will be unwilling to bear this cost. Second, the immediate security concerns in a crisis are not the only considerations that leaders make. Instead, they also incorporate how access decisions will affect their long-term security interests, given the potential for reprisals from the opposing party in the conflict or even after the conflict is over. Third, leaders also consider that assisting the requesting state may leave the host state more vulnerable to other regional actors as a result of power vacuums that may emerge or refugee flows that may result. Thus, leaders consider security threats in both the short and long terms and from multiple different actors (some of whom may not even be party to the conflict) in making determinations about the security wisdom of granting access.[33]

Leaders often care about security issues out of concern for the national interest, but over time, leaders have also fostered fierce belief in territorial sovereignty as a way to buttress their own political survival against foreign enemies.[34] Because of this dynamic from below, leaders must also take into account the fact that populations generally react intensely to perceived sovereignty violations. A failure to protect the country's security may be fatal to the leader's prospects of staying in office because of a negative reaction from their own public, before a foreign military ever comes close to challenging the leader directly.[35]

When the country is unable to protect its own sovereignty, leaders can seek to contract out security via outside powers.[36] Such a contract with an external power can take the form of an alliance, basing and military access for an outside power, or both. In exchange for this provision of security by an outside power, partner states can gain some degree of control over how that security is provided, where, and for what purpose. Thus, to limit the degree of sovereignty costs incurred by allowing an outside power military access, countries can tailor that access to the specific direct security concerns that it has.

For instance, Saudi Arabia provided military access to the United States during the Gulf War, reversing its prior hesitation to do so because of the acute perceived threat from Iraq.

---

[33] The evidence on what level of military capabilities makes states more likely to host outside military forces is mixed. The two main pieces of evidence come from Michael Anthony Allen, *Military Basing Abroad: Bargaining, Expectations, and Deployment*, dissertation, Binghamton University, State University of New York, 2011, which shows that states with *higher* degrees of power are more likely to accept new U.S. bases. Alternatively, Andrew Stravers, "Pork, Parties, and Priorities: Partisan Politics and Overseas Military Deployments," *Conflict Management and Peace Science*, Vol. 38, No. 2, 2021, shows no relationship between host military capabilities and U.S. military presence.

[34] Burak Kadercan, "Military Competition and the Emergence of Nationalism: Putting the Logic of Political Survival Into Historical Context," *International Studies Review*, Vol. 14, No. 3, September 2012.

[35] Jaroslav Tir, "Territorial Diversion: Diversionary Theory of War and Territorial Conflict," *Journal of Politics*, Vol. 72, No. 2, April 2010.

[36] Anessa L. Kimball, *Alliances from the Inside Out: A Theory of Domestic Politics and Alliance Behavior*, dissertation, Binghamton University, State University of New York, 2006; David A. Lake, *Entangling Relations: American Foreign Policy in Its Century*, Princeton University Press, 2020.

However, after the war, the Saudi government imposed a set of restrictions on the U.S. deployment of forces from Saudi Arabia to address security concerns from Iraq.[37] These restrictions included requiring the United States to get permission from the Saudi Defense Minister for every flight aimed at enforcing the no-fly zone over Iraq during the 1990s. Later, the Saudi government also saw little threat from Iraq in the run-up to U.S. operations in 2003, so U.S. forces were not allowed to use Saudi territory for the invasion.[38] The level of threat seen by the partner nation will be reflected in the amount of access given and the restrictions on how that access can be used, with the partner state maintaining the ability to push back against the outside power if it exceeds the authority given to it.[39] For example, when the United States used its access to Thailand without the permission of the Thai government in the 1975 Mayaguez crisis, the government responded by forcing the removal of the entire U.S. military contingent from the country.[40] If the security threat is severe, the partner state is more likely to be willing to give carte blanche to an outside force, as the Saudis largely did during the 1991 Gulf War. If the threat is less severe or more confined to a specific issue, an outside state may be given access only related to that realm.

Beyond the direct role that perceptions of the external threat can play, previous work shows that arms sales can also play a critical role in the access and basing contract.[41] Arms sales often have the dual purpose of enhancing the country's direct security position and empowering the regime against domestic opponents by bolstering its coercive power.[42] Through these dual mechanisms, arms sales become very attractive to leadership because they help prevent direct security threats, support its ability to deal with both internal and external security threats as they arise, and reinforces its power in the domestic context. Such was the case in Central Asia during the opening days of operations in Afghanistan, where U.S. arms sales could nominally be used to protect against spillover from Afghanistan and against domestic rivals and insurgent groups.[43]

---

[37] W. Eric Herr, "Operation Vigilant Warrior: Conventional Deterrence Theory Doctrine, and Practice," thesis, Air University, School of Advanced Airpower Studies, 1996.

[38] Herr, 1996.

[39] Kitti Prasirtsuk, "An Ally at the Crossroads: Thailand in the US Alliance System," in Michael Wesley, ed., *Global Allies: Comparing US Alliances in the 21st Century*, Australian National University Press, 2017.

[40] R. Sean Randolph, *The United States and Thailand: Alliance Dynamics, 1950–1985*, Institute of East Asian Studies, University of California, Berkeley, 1986.

[41] Robert E. Harkavy, *Bases Abroad: The Global Foreign Military Presence*, Oxford University Press, 1989; Robert E. Harkavy, *Great Power Competition for Overseas Bases: The Geopolitics of Access Diplomacy*, Elsevier, 1982; James R. Blaker, *United States Overseas Basing: An Anatomy of the Dilemma*, Praeger, 1990; Kent E. Calder, *Embattled Garrisons*, Princeton University Press, 2008; Alexander Cooley and Daniel H. Nexon, "The Bases of Empire: Globalization and the Politics of US Overseas Basing," NUPI, 2007.

[42] Stravers and El Kurd, 2020.

[43] Cooley and Nexon, 2007.

While security considerations over conflict access are often based on the immediate threats the country is confronting, leaders also consider how basing and access will affect their long-term security concerns. Basing and access agreements often come with larger defense-cooperation agreements; defense guarantees; and, sometimes, full alliances.[44] These longer-term alliances can guard against direct security threats well into the future after the shorter-term threat is over and can lay a firmer foundation for the country's security structure after the crisis is over.[45] This was one of the considerations Bulgaria made when entering World War I, when only one coalition (the Central Powers) was capable of assisting Bulgaria's attempt to take Balkan territory that it considered indispensable to its long-term security.[46] These agreements can bind the outside power to the host state's security interests and ensure that, if basing and access incur retaliation, the outside power will be militarily responsible for the protection of the basing state.[47]

Such guarantees can alleviate some of the concerns of the potential host state when it comes to reprisals from a regional rival but cannot overcome all potential dangers. Because of geographic vulnerability, weakness of the country's armed forces relative to those of the rival, or the inability of an outside force to bring enough power to bear in the situation to fully address the security concerns, some security concerns may remain.

Such a situation occurred with Romania's entry into World War I on the side of the Entente. Promised support could not be provided because of geographic difficulties and needs elsewhere.[48] Similarly, such considerations helped keep Spain neutral during World War II; a decision to throw the country's support fully in either direction risked invasion from the other.[49] Likewise, prior to operations in Iraq in 2003, the significant economic incentives that the United States offered Turkey were insufficient to overcome such concerns. Then, Turkey saw a threat from potential Kurdish autonomy and statehood that it feared could emerge from the U.S. invasion of Iraq.[50] In these negotiations, Turkey's position was that it be allowed to deploy troops to block refugees from Iraq into Turkey, fight against the Kurdistan Worker's Party inside Iraq, and prevent the establishment of a Kurdish state. Because of the potential

---

[44] Sean D. Murphy, "The Role of Bilateral Defense Agreements in Maintaining the European Security Equilibrium," *Cornell International Law Journal*, Vol. 24, No. 3, 1991; Stephan Frühling, "Is ANZUS Really an Alliance? Aligning the US and Australia," *Survival*, Vol. 60, No. 5, 2018.

[45] Jae-Jeok Park, "A Comparative Case Study of the US-Philippines Alliance in the 1990s and the US-South Korea Alliance Between 1998 and 2008: Alliance (Dis) Continuation," *Asian Survey*, Vol. 51, No. 2, March/April 2011.

[46] Sean McMeekin, *July 1914: Countdown to War*, Basic Books, 2013.

[47] Diehl, 2009.

[48] Glenn E. Torrey, *Romania and World War I: A Collection of Studies*, Histria Books, 1998; McMeekin, 2013.

[49] Wayne H. Bowen, *Spain During World War II*, University of Missouri Press, 2006.

[50] Ramazan Gözen, "Causes and Consequences of Turkey's Out-of-War Position in the Iraq War of 2003," *Turkish Yearbook of International Relations*, Vol. 36, 2005.

to spark a wider conflict between Kurds and Turkey, the United States did not agree to these terms.[51] For Turkey, no plausible monetary incentives could overcome a perceived inability to secure its long-term interests in regard to the Kurds in Iraq.[52] These positions are all consistent with the view that the 1991 Gulf War had been harmful to Turkey's long-term security interests because the war encouraged the growth of groups that Turkey viewed as terrorists and hurt the Turkish economy through the imposition of sanctions.[53] Thus, the Turkish leadership sought to resolve these concerns during the negotiations with the United States over U.S. requests for conflict-phase access in the lead-up to the 2003 invasion, but were unable to do so.

In some cases, preexisting military alliances are also not enough to overcome these considerations; states may seek to find ways to exit the alliance rather than succumb to a larger vulnerability. Turkey, for instance, signed onto an alliance with Britain and France in 1939 but quickly denounced it after the fall of France in 1940 in reaction to fear of vulnerability in the face of German pressure. In this way, Turkey's short-term security interests took precedence over any long-term strategy about its security position.[54] Rather than seeing the policy through and working toward an Allied victory and the potential spoils it would bring, Turkey hedged and opted out of the alliance with France and Britain early. In doing so, Turkey hoped to avoid being on the losing side of a war once again, as it had been in World War I.

In World War II, Sweden was geographically vulnerable to German attack. If Swedish public opinion had driven the country's policies, alignment with the Allies would have been a near certainty because the public was "overwhelmingly favorable to the Allied cause" despite a "long tradition of sympathy between Sweden and Germany particularly in military matters."[55] For a while, the Allies believed Sweden might provide robust support against the Axis powers, because of the robust public support for the Allies and the personal alignment of Swedish leaders to the Allied cause.[56] In addition, reports of aggressive German maritime activities led British analysts to believe that Sweden would likely be receptive to the Allies.[57]

---

[51] Gözen, 2005.

[52] Yola Habif, "The Future of Iraq," *Turkish Policy Quarterly*, Vol. 1, No. 4, 2002.

[53] Solmaz Unaydin, "Turkey's Policy Towards the Middle East and the Question of Iraq," *Turkish Policy Quarterly*, Vol. 1, No. 4, Winter 2002; Jean-Christophe Peuch, "Turkey: U.S. Plan to Oust Saddam Leaves Ankara Between Iraq and a Hard Place," Radio Free Europe/Radio Liberty, August 8, 2002.

[54] William Hale, "Turkey and Britain in World War II: Origins and Results of the Tripartite Alliance, 1935–40," *Journal of Balkan and Near Eastern Studies*, Vol. 23, No. 6, 2021.

[55] Foreign Office, *Annual Report: Political Survey of Sweden for 1939*, British National Archives, FO 188/351, 1940.

[56] Foreign Office, 1940.

[57] There was a report that Germans had been machine-gunning merchant vessels from the air and, on December 14, 1939, a report that Germany had sunk three ships in three days in neutral waters. It was later determined that two of the ships had actually been sunk in Norwegian waters. Furthermore, Germany had shot and sunk a Swedish vessel; in the opinion of British analysts, that would enrage Sweden and show that

However, according to other descriptions from British diplomats, the Swedish geographic position placed it in "a trial of strength between two fears," with a credible likelihood of reprisal from the Soviet Union, Germany, or both.[58] Swedish concerns about Germany in particular had to take precedence because of Germany's ability to "inflict immediate damage."[59] Hermann Göring made such threats explicit, telling Swedish officials that Germany "would be compelled to take action if troops were sent to Finland," let alone if Sweden provided open support to the Allies.[60] The Allies had a much lower ability to bring forces to bear in a way that would prevent such a German reprisal.[61] British analysts believed that, even if Sweden granted full access, Allied forces attempting to keep control of the iron ore mines would be unable to hold off a German offensive.[62] Moreover, once Germany invaded Norway in 1940, there was no longer any plausible path for the introduction or withdrawal of Allied forces from Sweden.[63] So, despite Swedish public opinion being opposed to Nazi Germany, the country steered a neutral course because the likelihood of reprisal for siding with the Allies was too high.[64] Because of these considerations, Sweden's government calculated that its best way forward was to steer a neutral course, privately assist the Allies, and occasionally make public demonstrations of resistance to Allied pressure.[65]

Besides the situations in which a state is caught in the middle between two powers, its leaders might see a threat from the country requesting access. The leadership can also use basing and access negotiations to bolster the state's security by negotiating ways to help reduce this perceived threat. During the Cold War, the United States maintained access to Portugal by promising to withdraw support for rebels fighting against Portuguese colonialism in Africa.[66] In World War II, a similar situation occurred when it came to German attempts to lure Spain onto the side of the Axis powers and to gain access to Spanish territory. Spanish suspicion of German intentions was part of the calculation Francisco Franco made in staying

---

Germany did not care about Swedish lives. See J. R. M. Butler, *History of the Second World War: Grand Strategy*: Vol. II, *September 1939–June 1941*, Her Majesty's Stationery Office, 1957; Foreign Office, 1940.

[58] Bernard Kelly, "Drifting Towards War: The British Chiefs of Staff, the USSR and the Winter War, November 1939–March 1940," *Contemporary British History*, Vol. 23, No. 3, 2009.

[59] Butler, 1957.

[60] Foreign Office, 1940.

[61] M. Gunnar Hagglof, "A Test of Neutrality: Sweden in the Second World War," *International Affairs*, Vol. 36, No. 2, April 1960.

[62] War Cabinet, Chiefs of Staff Committee, COS Secret Series of Memoranda, 271(S)–319(S), British National Archives, CAB 80/105, March 31–May 3, 1940a.

[63] War Cabinet, Chiefs of Staff Committee, Plan R.4: Postponement. Note by the Secretary, British National Archives, CAB 80/105/3, April 3, 1940b.

[64] Hagglof, 1960.

[65] Foreign Office, 1940.

[66] Cooley and Nexon, 2007.

neutral throughout the conflict, with British intelligence even determining that Germany planned to invade Spain if Franco did not join the Axis powers outright.[67] Given that Spain may have seen a similar move from the Allies if it joined the Axis, Franco pursued a policy of ambiguous neutrality and foot-dragging. Prior to the war in Iraq, Turkey also had a similar view, with 71 percent of respondents in a poll saying that they saw the United State itself as a threat.[68]

Overall, states are wary that they may be taken advantage of by the largest coalition partner in the aftermath of a conflict in a variety of ways. Larger states can create security issues for the smaller state directly and can sign onto peace agreements that leave smaller states worse off.[69] Of course, a larger state can also do this in the absence of the smaller state joining the larger state's coalition. However, joining a coalition and being left vulnerable from a disadvantageous peace deal may be worse than refraining from joining the coalition altogether. Joining the coalition by providing access may single out the smaller state for future retribution from the opposing party in the conflict, but the smaller state may be free of such retribution if it denies access in the conflict.

In these ways, allowing basing access into a country involves a variety of direct security concerns, ranging from immediate security considerations emanating from the conflict itself to the long-term strategic security of the country overall. Scholarship has shown time and again that leaders care about the security of the country, independent of concerns about staying in office, and their calculations on how best to maximize that security bring in a host of factors included here.

Question 3: Would Granting Conflict-Phase Access Affect the Outcome of the Conflict?

Given the security, economic, and leadership consequences that can emanate from granting basing and access, a state is likely to carefully consider whether granting access is likely to make victory more likely for their preferred side. The literature on whether access and basing decisions affect the outcome of a conflict is scant. However, in many instances, granting basing and access is the most militarily valuable thing a country can offer the United States, especially if its own military is not necessarily capable of taking the offensive itself. If the potential host nation shares the goals or strategic outlook of the United States for the conflict, it may be strongly motivated to provide potentially valuable assistance of this type. On

---

[67] Bowen, 2006; Jeff Hemmer, "The Third Reich and Spain," paper, Cultiv—Gesellschaft für internationale Kulturprojekte, 2004; Carlton J. H. Hayes, *Wartime Mission in Spain, 1942–1945*, Hassle Street Press, 2016.

[68] Gözen, 2005.

[69] R. Harrison Wagner, "Bargaining, War, and Alliances," *Conflict Management and Peace Science*, Vol. 21, No. 3, 2004; Darren Filson and Suzanne Werner, A Bargaining Model of War and Peace: Anticipating the Onset, Duration, and Outcome of War," *American Journal of Political Science*, Vol. 46, No. 4, October 2002.

the other hand, from the perspective of the opposing side in the conflict, granting basing or access is likely to be viewed very negatively. If the opposing side lost the conflict, its ability to retaliate might be more limited. However, winning might improve the opposing side's position to retaliate. Because of the potential costs and the benefits, assessing whether granting conflict-phase access is likely to affect the outcome of the conflict can be a critical consideration for the host nation.

In past conflicts, granting access has sometimes made the opposing side perceive the host state as a member of the U.S. coalition, even if the host's forces are not actively engaged in the fighting.[70] In other examples, such as Spain and France in the El Dorado Canyon operation, states denied overflight to the United States because of a credible fear of retaliation and because of the perception that they would be seen as supporting the operation if they granted overflight, while remaining confident that their access decisions would not ultimately affect the outcome.[71] Thus, if a state assesses that granting access to the United States is unlikely to affect the course of the conflict, it may be more inclined to refuse access and avoid these potential costs. If, instead, the state assesses that granting access to its territory would be essential for its preferred side to win the conflict, it may be more willing to take on the potential direct costs of granting access to help ensure this outcome.

Especially in relation to any potential future crisis involving China, both China and third-party states would likely consider providing access to the United States as a form of picking a side, as they have in past crises. Although many states have preexisting access and alliance relationships with the United States in peacetime, granting access in a conflict itself would likely be seen as a new and separate decision. And regardless of the state's prewar relations with the United States, any adversary harmed by the decision to grant access to U.S. forces is likely to consider retaliation. While not a direct example of this phenomenon, a peacetime example illustrates this point. While the United States already has a robust military presence in South Korea, China treated the deployment of the Terminal High-Altitude Area Defense (THAAD) missile system to the country as a new development, which led to immediate sanctions from the Chinese.[72] China imposed these sanctions because it perceived the deployment of THAAD as being particularly useful against China. So, even though this deployment was part of a wider military relationship, China perceived the move as providing additional material support for the United States in case of a conflict and, thus, worthy of repercussions.

There is no extensive literature on leadership decisions over whether access and basing decisions will affect the outcome of a conflict. However, there is a robust literature on

---

[70] Roger Dingman, "The Dagger and the Gift: The Impact of the Korean War on Japan," *Journal of American-East Asian Relations*, Vol. 2, No. 1, Spring 1993; Peter Lowe, *The Origins of the Korean War*, Routledge, 1997; Wada Haruki, *The Korean War: An International History*, Rowman & Littlefield, 2018.

[71] Gregory L. Trebon, *Libyan State Sponsored Terrorism—What Did Operation El Dorado Canyon Accomplish?* Air Command and Staff College, 1988.

[72] Matt Stiles, "Upset over a U.S. Missile Defense System, China Hits South Korea Where It Hurts—in the Wallet," *Los Angeles Times*, February 28, 2018.

coalition-joining behavior and the calculations leaders make about the likelihood that join-ing a coalition will determine the outcome of a conflict. Even in peacetime, both China and third-party states currently view granting military basing and access to the United States as a measure of alignment, which would likely only be heightened in a conflict.[73] Thus, what we know about general coalition-joining behavior is relevant because the key players in such a conflict are likely to view granting basing or access as tantamount to picking a side in the conflict.

Prior research on the behavior of states in deciding whether to join a conflict shows that the probability of victory for a chosen side increases in proportion to the capabilities that the joining party brings to bear.[74] Say, for instance, that a joining party can increase the probabil-ity of a U.S. victory by providing simple overflight access that allows fighters and bombers a more direct route to their targets. Without a direct route, the demand for tankers to redirect around a country's territory taxes American tanker capacity or may slow the sortie genera-tion rate to the point that it reduces the operational effectiveness of U.S. airpower. Because a decision to allow access and mitigate these limitations can make a U.S. victory in the conflict more likely, the opposing side in the conflict would likely look on the host nation quite nega-tively, which could produce severe consequences for the access-granting state.

This possible outcome must be balanced against the potential benefits of a U.S. victory, which could, for example, produce a regional security architecture that ensures such elements as maritime rights to shipping lanes, island territories, and undersea natural resources. Other potential benefits include freedom from coercion by more powerful states, a fair international commercial system, and the general rules-based order. Possible benefits of a U.S. victory lie along the lines of each question presented here, from the retention of self-determination and national sovereignty to the ability to define the nation's own economic and diplomatic desti-nies. Often, the benefits of a U.S. victory may lie along a different dimension than the benefits of a Chinese victory. For instance, a U.S. victory may come with greater long-term security, while a Chinese victory may come with greater commercial benefits. Because these benefits come along such different dimensions, the costs and benefits can be exceedingly difficult to weigh against each other. Therefore, and as we will examine in greater detail in ensuing chapters, the United States can seek to minimize the potential benefits of an American defeat, enhance the potential benefits of an American victory, and shield the host nation from the potential negative consequences of supporting the United States. By doing so, the United States can maximize the desire of a potential partner to provide support because of the out-sized benefits to the country's interests than an American victory would have. In tipping the

---

[73] Bonny Lin, Michael S. Chase, Jonah Blank, Cortez A. Cooper III, Derek Grossman, Scott W. Harold, Jennifer D. P. Moroney, Lyle J. Morris, Logan Ma, Paul Orner, Alice Shih, and Soo Kim, *Regional Responses to U.S.-China Competition in the Indo-Pacific: Study Overview and Conclusions*, RAND Corporation, RR-4412-AF, 2020.

[74] Mancur Olson and Richard Zeckhauser, ""An Economic Theory of Alliances," *Review of Economics and Statistics*, Vol. 48, No. 3, August 1966; Wagner, 2004.

calculation of future benefits further in favor of the United States, even a small possibility that a country could have an impact on the final outcome will come with higher payoffs for partners and increase the likelihood that they will provide basing or access.[75]

These consequences can come in four forms, as shown in Table 2.1. If the third party joins and provides access, the chosen side can win or lose; if the third party does not provide access, the preferred outcome can emerge or not. Whether providing access or not, the potential granter of access must determine whether the potential beneficial outcome creates returns either in the short term or in the future that warrant the cost relative to the likely negative consequences of the preferred party losing. In addition, the outcome may be positive even if the cost is not paid, in which case states may wish to stay on the sidelines to avoid the cost. The last is likely the main possibility that looser U.S. partners may consider because it is a consistent behavior of states in the international system that is called *free-riding*. How likely are states to be able to realize the benefits of a victory for their preferred side without accruing the costs? This is the key question that states will ask themselves because they would prefer to stay on the sidelines if their preferred outcome is assured without participation.

The basis of the concept of free-riding is the collective action problem—the idea that it is more beneficial to receive a benefit without doing the work than to accrue the costs of contributing to the effort. Significant work in international relations and foreign policy identifies collective action problems as central to cooperation failures. States will generally seek to pass the buck to others for difficult tasks in the hopes of gaining the benefits without paying the costs.[76] This occurs in issues as diffuse as economics, climate policy, and defense. A classic example of free-riding is Britain in World War I, which hoped to contribute "the smallest

TABLE 2.1

Potential Outcomes for Access-Granting States to Consider

	Preferred Side Wins	Preferred Side Loses
Provides access	Receive benefits of victory while paying direct costs from adversary	Do not receive benefits of victory while also paying costs from adversary
Does not provide access	Receive benefits of victory while paying no direct costs from adversary	Do not receive benefits of victory but do not pay costs from adversary

NOTE: Preference ordering will depend on the size of the potential benefits and costs. All else equal, states will generally seek the outcome on the bottom left, which receives the benefits of victory without paying the costs. However, depending on how strongly states prefer victory or how strongly they wish to avoid facing retaliation, they may prefer different options.

---

[75] Randall L. Schweller, "Bandwagoning for Profit: Bringing the Revisionist State Back In," *International Security*, Vol. 19, No. 1, Summer 1994; Eric J. Labs, "Do Weak States Bandwagon?" *Security Studies*, Vol. 1, No. 3, 1992; David C. Kang, "Between Balancing and Bandwagoning: South Korea's Response to China," *Journal of East Asian Studies*, Vol. 9, No. 1, 2009. While Schweller theorizes that greater future profit can lead to *bandwagoning* (revisionist) behavior, the application in this instance is simply in terms of calculations of future benefits, not that the state offering access would be revisionist.

[76] Carla Norrlof and William C. Wohlforth, "Is U.S. Grand Strategy Self-Defeating? Deep Engagement, Military Spending and Sovereign Debt," *Conflict Management and Peace Science*, Vol. 36, No. 3, 2019; Mette Eilstrup-Sangiovanni, "The End of Balance-of-Power Theory? A Comment on Wohlforth et al.'s Testing

amount of money and the smallest number of men with which we may hope, some day, to win the war."[77] Britain's hope was to stave off German victory primarily through French casualties while making fewer sacrifices of its own forces so that it would have the strongest military at the end of the war and be able to dictate the terms of the peace. Only when it appeared that France was on the verge of exhaustion did Britain devote its full resources to the war instead of continuing the initial strategy of "limited liability."[78] States in the region of a potential conflict between the United States and China may seek to do the same thing, minimizing their own contributions while hoping that their desired outcome will come to fruition nonetheless. If their desired outcome looks to be at risk, however, they may be more likely to reconsider and lend more active support to the preferred side.

The United States can alter the preference ordering involved in Table 2.1 by manipulating both the costs and benefits involved in the calculations. For instance, states that do not provide access could be cut off from some of the benefits of victory. However, this risks states siding with the opposing side in the conflict. An alternative is to maximize the benefits of victory for each participating state while shielding it from the costs, which encourages participating in the U.S. coalition by providing access. On the likelihood-of-victory side, a partner that believes the United States may lose may choose to sit on the sidelines in hopes of minimizing both the short-term and long-term consequences emanating from the opposing state. For instance, this was the crux of the disagreement between Prime Minister Eleftherios Venizelos and King Constantine I in Greece during World War I. The prime minister pushed to side with the Entente in the hopes of gaining spoils from the collapsing Ottoman Empire after the war. The king did not think such potential spoils were worth the risk of retaliation.[79] Throughout the literature on alliance formation, balancing, and bandwagoning, both the likely future benefits that may accrue from victory and the likelihood of victory play prominent roles.[80] The United States can encourage access through manipulation of these costs and benefits in ways that we will detail further in Chapter 8.

A key additional consideration that leaders will weigh when it comes to free-riding is whether the requesting state has other options that make victory possible without drawing the potential host nation into the conflict. Given all the potential downsides of offering access, incentives to free ride in these situations will be high, especially if the United States has other options available. In such a case, it may appear to the requested state that it will

---

Balance-of-Power Theory in World History,'" *European Journal of International Relations*, Vol. 15, No. 2, 2009; Thomas J. Christensen and Jack Snyder, "Chain Gangs and Passed Bucks: Predicting Alliance Patterns in Multipolarity," *International Organization*, Vol. 44, No. 2, Spring 1990.

[77] David French, *British Strategy & War Aims: 1914–1916*, Routledge, 2014, p. 247.

[78] French, 2014, pp. 200–201.

[79] Greece, 1915.

[80] Schweller, 1994; Randall L. Schweller, "Unanswered Threats: A Neoclassical Realist Theory of Underbalancing," *International Security*, Vol. 29, No. 2, Fall 2004; Robert G. Kaufman, "'To Balance or to Bandwagon?' Alignment Decisions in 1930s Europe," *Security Studies*, Vol. 1, No. 3, Spring 1992.

likely see the benefits of victory without having to bear the potential direct costs, although it would, of course, also forgo additional benefits the United States might wish to provide to states that assisted it in the conflict. States that stay on the sidelines will likely not be subject to either economic or military reprisals from adversaries and may not be singled out for further repercussions after the conflict is over. In addition, if other options are available to the United States, a country would also be unlikely to see significant repercussions come its way in American policy.

For instance, Morocco opted to remove the American military presence from its soil in the 1960s and 1970s.[81] U.S. installations in Spain and Portugal, intercontinental ballistic missiles, along with satellites in space, had rendered the basing arrangement unnecessary.[82] The government in Morocco was also unwilling to bear the continued political cost of hosting American forces after the U.S. intervention in Lebanon in 1958 brought mass demonstrations into the streets.[83] Moroccan officials thus began to determine that a U.S. presence in Morocco was unnecessary to win in a conflict against the Soviet Union and unhelpful in Morocco's desire to stay in power. Similarly, after the Gulf War, Saudi Arabia paid a heavy political cost for continuing to host U.S. personnel. As the United States developed other options in the Gulf region, Saudi Arabia was able to negotiate the removal of American forces because neither country saw the U.S. presence on Saudi territory as necessary any longer.[84]

Particularly in the absence of victory, any negative security or economic consequences of granting access may linger into the long term, thereby weakening a country's position well after the conflict. These considerations also depend on the type of conflict that is occurring because the long-term outcomes may not resolve underlying security concerns for states granting access. In addition, the defeated power may conduct ongoing economic reprisals even if victory is gained in the short term.[85] Given Chinese reliance on economic pressure in the past, the potential for such retaliation may be particularly acute in any U.S.-China conflict, as we will discuss in more detail later, under Question 5. In this case, the cost of granting access will continue over the long term even though victory was gained in the short term.

For instance, conflict with a regional power may only result in a return to the status quo rather than lead to regime change or policy alterations that would alleviate long-term security or economic concerns. As a result, a victory in the conflict may help alleviate the security threat in the short term, but the consequences of joining the regional rival's adversary may continue as punishment for granting access in the conflict. Thus, states considering granting

---

[81] Claudia Wright, "Journey to Marrakesh: US-Moroccan Security Relations," *International Security*, Vol. 7, No. 4, Spring 1983.

[82] Wright, 1983.

[83] Wright, 1983.

[84] Otterman, 2005.

[85] Filson and Werner, 2002; Branislav L. Slantchev, "How Initiators End Their Wars: The Duration of Warfare and the Terms of Peace," *American Journal of Political Science*, Vol. 48, No. 4, October 2004.

access to the United States will not only consider whether doing so will affect the outcome of the conflict but also calculate what victory will look like for them over the long term. States will generally seek to realize the benefits of the preferred outcome without paying costs, when possible. To grant access, states will need to believe that their contribution will assist in assuring victory and that the victory will be beneficial to them over the long term.[86]

Question 4: Would Granting Conflict-Phase Access Be Reciprocated by Other Regional States?

States are always sensitive to the size of a coalition, especially in relation to the stances of their neighbors. Larger coalitions are more likely to emerge victorious from a conflict because of the likely power differential that will emerge between the powerful coalition and its target.[87] States are more likely to join existing powerful coalitions rather than coalitions that are more evenly matched with the adversary. Because coalitions become more powerful with each additional member, individual countries are more likely to bandwagon once others join rather than be the first mover. Being the first to join a weaker coalitions risks losing in the conflict and not being reciprocated by neighbors, which could single out the joiner for more-severe consequences from the opposing side in the conflict or even from other neighbors. While work in this area is not directly aimed at access and basing considerations, this is a reasonable corollary. Often, a state's geography may be the most valuable thing a state has to contribute to an American military effort, and so granting it may be tantamount to fully joining a U.S. coalition.

States joining larger and more-powerful coalitions that consist of neighboring states are less likely to be singled out for punishment by the opposing side in a conflict. The costs of punishing (either militarily or economically) those participating in a coalition increase as more members participate, which makes repercussions for each additional coalition member lower and the likelihood of victory higher. The behavior of Central Asian states during U.S. operations in Afghanistan is an example of this as well, where multiple states provided forms of access to the United States. Acting as a part of a bloc allowed each to reduce the individual risk that they took on that could come from Russia, terrorists, or opposition elements within their own societies.[88]

There are also normative considerations to joining a larger coalition. Larger coalitions tend to come with legitimation from international bodies, such as the United Nations (UN),

---

[86] Scott Wolford, "Power, Preferences, and Balancing: The Durability of Coalitions and the Expansion of Conflict," *International Studies Quarterly*, Vol. 58, No. 1, March 2014.

[87] Daniel S. Morey, "Military Coalitions and the Outcome of Interstate Wars," *Foreign Policy Analysis*, Vol. 12, No. 4, October 2016; Slantchev, 2004; Wolford, 2014.

[88] Cooley, 2008.

which provide normative justification for an operation.[89] While approval from international bodies provides moral justification, it also reduces the likelihood that states will see repercussions for their participation from other elements of the international community. While the prospect of UN support is unlikely in a conflict involving China, given the PRC's permanent membership on the UN Security Council, the same dynamic is also true of regional organizations, such as NATO, the Arab League, and the Association of Southeast Asian Nations (ASEAN).[90] Support from the organization makes punishment from individual neighbors less likely. States take cues from these international bodies about the punishment they may be likely to receive for taking an action, with less approval from the bodies indicating a higher degree of future repercussions.[91]

States are also more likely to join coalitions with more-reliable or more-capable allies. For many, this includes their neighbors, with whom they have a persistent and long-term relationship and with whom they share similar incentives, threats, and opportunities.[92] Joining a coalition by providing basing and access with a larger and more distant state presents a series of risks for smaller states closer to a conflict. For instance, the more-remote states often deal with less risk than smaller states closer to the conflict, which may see larger and more devastating military and economic consequences. As a result, more-powerful, and more-distant states may be less sensitive to the risks that a nearby state may face in granting access and less likely to provide protection equivalent to the risk that the nearby state is assuming as a result.[93] A coalition that includes many of a state's immediate neighbors, by contrast, may be seen as generating fewer risks, and some states may refuse to join a coalition in its absence. An example of this comes from World War I, when Romania contemplated joining the Entente powers in exchange for a promise of military forces from the Entente. However, Romania calculated that the promised military forces were insufficient to meet the danger that a move into the Entente camp would raise because Romania's neighbors would be hostile to such a move. The Entente also determined that its own forces were needed in areas of higher risk for their own security.[94] For this and other reasons related to mistrust and misalignment among

---

[89] Atsushi Tago, "Why Do States Join US-Led Military Coalitions? The Compulsion of the Coalition's Missions and Legitimacy," *International Relations of the Asia-Pacific*, Vol. 7, No. 2, 2007.

[90] ASEAN is the grouping of the ten most economically and diplomatically powerful nations in the region: Indonesia, Malaysia, Singapore, Thailand, Vietnam, the Philippines, Cambodia, Myanmar, Laos, and Brunei.

[91] Terrence L. Chapman, "International Security Institutions, Domestic Politics, and Institutional Legitimacy," *Journal of Conflict Resolution*, Vol. 51, No. 1, 2007.

[92] Brett Ashley Leeds, "Alliance Reliability in Times of War: Explaining State Decisions to Violate Treaties," *International Organization*, Vol. 57, No. 4, Autumn 2003b; Erik Gartzke and Kristian Skrede Gleditsch, "Why Democracies May Actually Be Less Reliable Allies," *American Journal of Political Science*, Vol. 48, No. 4, October 2004.

[93] Slantchev, 2004.

[94] Vladen N. Vinogradov, "Romania in the First World War: The Years of Neutrality, 1914–1916," *International History Review*, Vol. 14, No. 3, August 1992.

the Entente, Romania, and its neighbors, Romania remained neutral for the first two years of World War I.[95]

A regional bloc of smaller states joining a coalition together, for example by all providing access, may be more able to balance the power of more risk-acceptant states that may be further from the conflict zone and may lead the coalition to make more cautious or de-escalatory decisions, reducing the likelihood that the smaller states will be drawn further into a more costly conflict. Countries may therefore see multiple advantages in providing basing and access only when accompanied by a critical mass of neighbors that also support the actions of the United States in the conflict.

Question 5: Would Granting Conflict-Phase Access Affect the Country's Economy?

Leaders also care deeply about the state of the country's economy. First, because economic power undergirds military power, a strong economy allows countries to better withstand security threats in both the short and long terms. Leaders will therefore take the security implications of economic impacts into account. Second, a country's people care about the state of the economy. In both democracies and nondemocracies, the state of the economy is directly tied to leadership survival in office.[96] Third, leaders consider economic factors on their own, outside their impact on political survival and military might. Economic growth and development are seen as independently good for the nation, along with the nation's prestige and long-term success. Fourth, while not directly related to the country's economy, side payments to leaders mentioned earlier are seen as a positive benefit of a basing relationship for the good of the leader or regime outside the context of the ability to stay in office.

First, a country's economy undergirds its ability to produce the military power necessary for its protection.[97] Any country that allows basing and access in a way that harms its economy, in both the short and long terms, will be reducing the country's security because economic success and military power are inextricably linked. A short-term gain in security from an American presence may seem wise under some circumstances, but if the long-term economic consequences from such a decision are too great, the long-term security consequences may also be too great. Thus, in some situations, there may be a security-prosperity trade-off.

---

[95] Marcel Mitrasca, *Moldova: A Romanian Province Under Russian Rule: Diplomatic History from the Archives of the Great Powers*, Algora Publishing, 2002; Laurenţiu-Cristian Dumitru, "Preliminaries of Romania's Entering the World War I," *Bulletin of "Carol I" National Defence University*, No. 1, 2012.

[96] Paul J. Burke, "Economic Growth and Political Survival," *BE Journal of Macroeconomics*, Vol. 12, No. 1, 2012.

[97] Lloyd J. Dumas, "Economic Power, Military Power, and National Security," *Journal of Economic Issues*, Vol. 24, No. 2, 1990; Joseph S. Nye, Jr., "The Changing Nature of World Power," *Political Science Quarterly*, Vol. 105, No. 2, Summer 1990; Robert J. Art, "To What Ends Military Power?" *International Security*, Vol. 4, No. 4, 1980.

This is especially true if other powers may economically punish a country for providing basing and access, as was threatened in the World War II examples of both Sweden and Spain. For instance, the Allies threatened to blacklist the products of Swedish companies that continued to supply the Germans. The Swedish circumvented these threats by providing materials to the Allies at a discount, shown to be 74 percent of the price the Germans paid in 1938 and 68 percent by 1943.[98] Some of the trade preferences Sweden offered the Allies increased over time because Germany continued to threaten Swedish shipping and occasionally sank Swedish ships.[99] Thus, the Allies' respect for the integrity of Swedish shipping and refraining to use the available coercive pressure assisted the Allied cause with Sweden over the long term. For Spain, the Allies threatened to cut off exports of products critical to the Spanish economy, such as petroleum and fertilizer, if Spain went beyond a minimum level of exports to the Axis.[100] The Allies had the capability to severely undermine the Swedish and Spanish economies if the Allies did not receive significant concessions in return that either capped Axis capabilities or expanded Allied ones. The lack of Allied action to do so compared with occasional Axis violence increased the economic tilt of the neutral countries over time.

States will consider whether economic retaliation from adversaries or regional actors may not be worth the benefits received from allowing basing and access. In some cases, states may hope to soften the blow of economic retaliation through aid payments from the United States and its allies, through the economic infusions that come from a basing presence, or through the security that may come from military aid. However, larger trade relationships will be difficult to replace with these mitigation strategies, which tend to include smaller sums.

Second, a country's economic performance affects the ability of leaders to stay in office. Economic infusions from a basing-and-access relationship can come in multiple forms. Often, outside powers will send aid payments to the host state as part of the basing bargain. Such aid can help the country achieve its overall development goals beyond what would be possible in the absence of a basing relationship. For instance, Central Asian states received billions of dollars in aid payments as part of their basing packages during American operations in Afghanistan.[101] The presence of American forces also comes with direct economic infusions into the communities in which they operate. The American military purchases local goods,

---

[98] Eric B. Golson, "Did Swedish Ball Bearings Keep the Second World War Going? Re-Evaluating Neutral Sweden's Role," *Scandinavian Economic History Review*, Vol. 60, No. 2, 2012; Peter Hedberg and Lars Karlsson, "Neutral Trade in Time of War: The Case of Sweden, 1838–1960," *International Journal of Maritime History*, Vol. 27, No. 1, 2015; Bowen, 2006.

[99] One such attack, on December 3, 1939, occurred when a German U-boat hit the Swedish merchant vessel *Rudolf*, which was carrying 2,760 tons of coal. Nine Swedish sailors were killed ("Rudolf: Swedish Steam Merchant," webpage, uboat.net, 2022).

[100] Bowen, 2006.

[101] Cooley and Nexon, 2007.

employs local citizens, and constructs infrastructure.[102] In some cases, the financial flows that come with an American military presence's direct economic activity can be in the billions of dollars, which can have a significant impact on local economies.

This dynamic is demonstrated by occasions when the United States has decided to leave a location, and the community surrounding the base, fearing economic loss, has protested against the withdrawal.[103] In some cases, leaders can also use economic infusions that arise from basing and access agreements to substitute for a country's own spending on social welfare programs in these areas and, in other cases, use the potential savings from relying on American security forces to bolster spending on social welfare programs nationwide.[104] Using basing rents and the economic activity that comes with an American presence this way can help a leader stay in office.

Third, leaders consider the economic well-being of the country as an independent factor in calculating whether to provide basing and access. For instance, in the Sweden case mentioned earlier, granting access to either the Axis or Allies during World War II would have likely ended in a cutoff in trade with the others, which would have had severe negative consequences for the Swedish economy.[105] Other countries have made similar determinations over time in their decisions to stay neutral during conflicts.[106] Spain made an equivalent decision in World War II because its economy was inextricably tied to that of Portugal. The British held considerable sway over Portuguese foreign policy and would have been able to exact serious economic pain on the Spanish economy through Portugal. In addition, the British followed a policy of tying the Spanish economy *even more* to Portugal than before the war, to increase the weight of this factor in Spanish calculations.[107] Portugal's economic state was much healthier than Spain's at the time, usually having a current account surplus and plentiful options for foreign supply.[108] Spain's devastation after its civil war, along with its lack of outside options for these economic considerations meant that Spain had little choice but to pursue a neutral path rather than the preferred choice of siding with a coalition of fellow

---

[102] Michael A. Allen, Michael E. Flynn, Carla Martinez Machain, and Andrew Stravers, "Outside the Wire: U.S. Military Deployments and Public Opinion in Host States," *American Political Science Review*, Vol. 114, No. 2, 2020.

[103] Elsa Rassbach, Protesting U.S. Military Bases in Germany," *Peace Review*, Vol. 22, No. 2, 2010.

[104] Bruce Russett, "Defense Expenditures and National Well-Being," *American Political Science Review*, Vol. 76, No. 4, December 1982; Alex Mintz and Chi Huang, "Guns Versus Butter: The Indirect Link," *American Journal of Political Science*, Vol. 35, No. 3, August 1991.

[105] Golson, 2012.

[106] Hedberg and Karlsson, 2015.

[107] Antonio Marquina, "The Spanish Neutrality During the Second World War," *American University International Law Review*, Vol. 14, No. 1, 1998.

[108] Eric Solsten, *Portugal: A Country Study*, ed., Library of Congress, U.S. Government Printing Office, 1993.

fascists.[109] Another example is Greece in World War I, which had an extremely dire financial situation following the Balkan Wars the previous year. In describing Greece, British soldiers noted that "food and accommodation are at famine prices," and Greek Prince Nicholas lamented that the country had only enough funds to mobilize the Greek Army for three days.[110] The financial concern for Greek stakeholders was that they could not afford a foreign military presence because it would divert already scarce supplies from citizens.

Fourth, side payments to leaders may not be good for the country's economy but are a factor leaders consider when calculating the costs and benefits of granting basing and access. For instance, in Central Asia during operations in Afghanistan, the basing contract in Kyrgyzstan necessitated that the United States purchase fuel from two entities, one of which was owned by then-President Ascar Akayev's son-in-law.[111] Lease payments were also made to Manas International Airport, which was owned and operated by a company in which the president's son was part owner. The Federal Bureau of Investigation discovered that the president's family had gained tens of millions of dollars from basing contracts.[112] While these side payments to the president and his family did not entrench his position in office to the extent that he could withstand the Tulip Revolution in 2005, it did enrich the family and create an economic incentive for it to allow basing and access during operations in Afghanistan.

Conclusion

As this chapter illustrates, various internal and external considerations inform decisions about the level and type of access leaders may be willing to offer an outside power during a conflict. In this chapter, we have organized these considerations into a set of five heuristic questions that combine the dozens of individual issues that have played historical roles in access decisions or that scholarly work has pointed to as likely being critical. The answers to these questions are likely to determine how leaders will respond to access requests from the United States during a potential future conflict.

This chapter has provided an overview of these key heuristic questions for states in general, drawing on a wealth of literature and examples across the globe and throughout history. This report, however, focuses on the conflict-phase access decisions of states likely to be of interest to U.S. defense planners in a potential future conflict with China. Further, the chapter illustrates how the characteristics of the conflict and the type of access the United States

---

[109] Eric Solsten, and Sandra W. Meditz, eds., *Spain: A Country Study*, Library of Congress, U.S. Government Printing Office, 1990; Hemmer, 2004.

[110] War Office, Patrol and Road Reports: Usambara Railway, British National Archives, WO 158/455, 1914–1916; H. M. The King [George V] and Queen Alexandra, collected papers, British National Archives, Folios 621–630, 636–639, 645–647, 649, and 670, 1915.

[111] Cooley, 2008.

[112] Cooley, 2008.

requests are critical considerations for anticipating how country leaders are likely to view each of the five questions in any particular circumstance. The following chapters explore how the general framework developed in this chapter should be adapted to better understand the decisionmaking of a series of specific states in the Indo-Pacific and the conflict and access request characteristics on which their decisions will likely depend.

CHAPTER 3

Adapting the Conflict-Phase Access Framework to Japan

For many reasons, Japan is the most important U.S. ally in terms of supporting Indo-Pacific contingencies. Japan has the world's third-largest economy, after the United States and China, and has the most powerful armed forces in the region after those two major powers. It appears to have committed to significant increases in defense spending,[1] a broader regional security profile, and expanded defense cooperation with the United States, which together represent an evolution in the country's traditionally restrained approach to security affairs. In its diplomatic engagements with such countries as India, Australia, and ASEAN members, Japan is taking an increasingly forward-leaning role in counteracting Chinese influence in the region.[2]

Japan is arguably even more important to the United States in terms of access to facilities essential for military operations, in peace or war. As host to the largest U.S. permanent presence in the Indo-Pacific, it is home to the Navy's Seventh Fleet and the world's only forward-stationed carrier strike group; the Marine Corps' III Marine Expeditionary Force; and a sizable USAF presence, including the 18th Air Wing, the largest combat wing in the USAF.[3] U.S. forces in Japan possess by far the most elaborate set of basing facilities of any country in the region. The only country that comes close—South Korea—is unlikely to be involved in off peninsula military contingencies and, therefore, may be much less likely to grant conflict-phase access for contingencies that do not involve North Korea. Japan's southernmost islands represent the closest land masses to Taiwan and, thus, could be critical in a contingency involving Chinese aggression against that island.

In the event of a crisis or war, Japan's decisions on access may also set precedents. Japan granting access to U.S. forces quickly and comprehensively might help persuade other regional

---

[1] Ken Moriyasu, "Abe Leads Charge for Japan to Boost Defense Spending to 2% of GDP," *NikkeiAsia*, April 22, 2022.

[2] Scott W. Harold, Derek Grossman, Brian Harding, Jeffrey W. Hornung, Gregory Poling, Jeffrey Smith, and Meagan L. Smith, *The Thickening Web of Asian Security Cooperation: Deepening Defense Ties Among U.S. Allies and Partners in the Indo-Pacific*, RAND Corporation, RR-3125-MCF, 2019, pp. 19–70.

[3] Jeffrey W. Hornung, *Managing the U.S.-Japan Alliance: An Examination of Structural Linkages in the Security Relationship*, 2nd ed., Sasakawa USA, 2019, p. 4.

countries to grant access as well. If Tokyo were to stand aside from a conflict and either deny conflict access to U.S. forces or impose various domestic constraints on that access, other countries would have a ready excuse to do the same, given regional perceptions of the close relationship between the United States and Japan.

The broader context of Japanese thinking and security policy would seem to be increasingly supportive of positive conflict-phase access decisions, at least ones likely to involve direct attacks of some kind on some Japanese territories. (Japanese access decisions on more distant, third-party conflicts are another matter.) Japan is a hyper–status quo power with respect to its strong commitments to the international order and the alliance.[4] Current prime minister Kishida Fumio follows his predecessors in seeking not just to maintain the alliance with the United States but to strengthen it. This includes modernizing Japan's own capabilities and strengthening "joint capabilities by fully aligning strategies and prioritizing goals together, to address evolving security challenges in an ever more integrated manner, with partners and across all instruments of national power, domains, and the full spectrum of situations."[5] Through these efforts, Japan and the United States are in synch in their resolve "to ensure alignment of Alliance visions and priorities."[6] Tokyo is also on the same strategic page as Washington in regional concerns about Chinese provocations in the East China Sea (ECS) and South China Sea (SCS) and activities in Hong Kong and Xinjiang, of the importance of peace and stability of the Taiwan Strait, of North Korea's nuclear and missile issues, and of Russia's actions against Ukraine.[7]

The Kishida administration, like its predecessors, is in agreement with Washington about the importance of its efforts to strengthen the international order. In his January summit with President Joseph Biden, Kishida agreed on the need for the alliance to "work together and deepen cooperation with like-minded countries" to promote and achieve a free and open Indo-Pacific.[8] This concept was created by the Abe Shinzō administration, was adopted by the Trump and Biden administrations, and continues to play a guiding role in how Japan and the United States approach the region.[9] Additionally, the Kishida administration seeks to strengthen relationships with key U.S. allies and partners. This includes participating in

---

[4] Jeffrey W. Hornung, "Resolved: Japan-China Rapprochement Will Fail," *Debating Japan*, Vol. 1, No. 2, December 6, 2018.

[5] U.S. Department of State, "Joint Statement of the U.S.-Japan Security Consultative Committee ('2+2')," press release, January 6, 2022a.

[6] U.S. Department of State, 2022a.

[7] Prime Minister of Japan [Kishida Fumio], "Press Conference by the Prime Minister Regarding Japan-U.S. Video Conference Summit Meeting," Speeches and Statements by the Prime Minister, webpage, January 21, 2022.

[8] Prime Minister of Japan, 2022.

[9] Jeffrey W. Hornung, "Abe Shinzō's Lasting Impact: Proactive Contributions to Japan's Security and Foreign Policies," *Asia-Pacific Review*, Vol. 28, No. 1, May 2021a; U.S. Department of State, 2022a.

smaller multilateral formats, such as the Quadrilateral Strategic Dialogue (Quad),[10] and tri-lateral formats with the United States and other countries (such as Australia, India, and South Korea); maintaining an institutional relationship with NATO; and participating bilateral for-mats with several like-minded U.S. partners and allies, including key NATO members, such as the United Kingdom and France. Japan has also been in lockstep with G-7 countries, not just in criticizing Russia's invasion of Ukraine but in taking unprecedented steps to punish Russia.[11] Most broadly, Japanese officials know that, in a truly major contingency touching on Japan—such as an unprovoked Chinese attack on Taiwan—to deny U.S. access would be to put the U.S.-Japan alliance at risk, thus imperiling Japan's security.

Therefore, if there is one country in the Indo-Pacific whose access decisions will most critically affect U.S. military operations in the event of conflict, it is likely Japan. This chapter explores the five major questions developed in the project framework to offer an assessment of the factors likely to govern that decision. Its primary purpose is not to forecast Japan's choices but to identify the strongest influences on them. Nonetheless, in the conclusion, we do offer some insights about the trend of Japanese thinking and the likelihood of access under different circumstances.

The History of U.S. Access in Japan

U.S. military posture in Japan has a long post–World War II history and has been important to the conduct of multiple regional contingencies, including the Korean and Vietnam wars. From the standpoint of access decisions, the critical history relates not so much to the facili-ties themselves—their number or composition—as it does to the formal bilateral agreements that underpin the posture and provide the basis for potential access discussions in the future.

In this context, the foundational document is the 1960 Treaty of Mutual Cooperation and Security, commonly referred to as the Japan-U.S. Security Treaty.[12] This lays out each part-ner's essential rights and obligations in the alliance. Article 4 of the treaty requires the parties to consult "whenever the security of Japan or international peace and security in the Far East is threatened." Article 5 is, in many ways, the centerpiece of the treaty, requiring that the two countries "act to meet the common danger" of an "armed attack against either Party in the territories under the administration of Japan."[13]

---

[10] The Quad is a four-nation minilateral group of the United States, India, Japan, and Australia.

[11] Ministry of Foreign Affairs of Japan, "G7 Leaders' Statement," Berlin, Germany, March 11, 2022. See also Michael J. Green, "Will Japan Fight? Assessing the Scenarios for Conflict on China's Maritime Periphery," testimony before the U.S.-China Economic and Security Review Commission, April 13, 2017, p. 9.

[12] Treaty of Mutual Cooperation and Security Between Japan and the United States of America, January 19, 1960.

[13] Emma Chanlett-Avery and Caitlin Campbell, "The U.S.-Japan Alliance," Congressional Research Ser-vice, RL33740, June 13, 2019, p. 24.

From the standpoint of access for contingencies that do not involve the defense of Japan, however, the key component of the treaty is Article 6, which provides U.S. forces the use of "facilities and areas in Japan" for both Article 5 responsibilities (i.e., defense of Japan) and the U.S. responsibility for "the maintenance of international peace and security in the Far East."[14] To further clarify U.S. responsibilities regarding Article 6, a separate 1960 Exchange of Notes requires the United States to engage in "prior consultation" with the Japanese government regarding major changes in the deployment into Japan of U.S. armed forces, major changes in equipment, and the use of facilities and areas in Japan as bases for military combat operations to be undertaken from Japan other than those conducted under Article V.[15] While the exact form this consultation would take is not clarified, it is likely to occur at the level of senior officials from the U.S. government approaching the Japanese government before U.S. combat operations involving Japanese bases are undertaken. This ensures that the Japanese leadership has an opportunity to consent to or voice concerns about U.S. intentions before operations from Japanese territory commence. Some officials even see this as an opportunity to veto U.S. requests.

The roles and missions of the allies that are included in these foundational agreements have been further elaborated in a series of "Guidelines for U.S.-Japan Defense Cooperation," first agreed to in 1978 and updated in 1997 and 2015.[16] These guidelines lay out specific scenarios for U.S.-Japan consultation and cooperation in peace and war that provide one piece of the context in which future access decisions will be made. The most recent iteration in 2015 discusses scenarios involving a direct attack on Japan and attacks against third countries and calls out a number of particular areas for collaboration, including noncombatant evacuation operations, missile defense, search and rescue operations, minesweeping and maritime escort operations, and logistic support.[17]

The Biden administration has accelerated defense planning with Japan in various areas, including preparing for regional contingencies. While nothing has been officially confirmed by either government, a series of reporting discussed new agreements about the movement of U.S. Marines to Japan's southwest islands (Nansei Shotō) in the event of a conflict, with the reports citing operational plans that have been drafted for a joint operation. These reports say that, at

> the initial stage of a Taiwan emergency, the U.S. Marine Corps would set up temporary
> bases on the Nansei island chain, which stretches southwest [from the southern tip of

---

[14] Japan-U.S. Security Treaty, 1960.

[15] Ministry of Foreign Affairs of Japan, "Exchange of Notes on the Implementation of Article VI of the Treaty" ["条約第六条の実施に関する交換公文"], January 19, 1960. See also Jeffrey W. Hornung, *Japan's Potential Contributions in an East China Sea Contingency*, RAND Corporation, RR-A314-1, 2020, pp. 91–92.

[16] Hornung, 2020, p. 89; Japan and the United States of America, "The Guidelines for Japan-U.S. Defense Cooperation," April 27, 2015.

[17] Hornung, 2020, p. 89.

Kyūshū all the way] toward Taiwan. Japan's armed forces would reportedly provide logistical support in such areas as fuel and ammunition.[18]

Table 3.1 lays out the major U.S. forces and facilities in Japan as of this writing. One important fact is that this posture is essential not just to executing a rapid operation at the onset of hostilities but also to setting the theater for the inflow of U.S. forces from outside the theater. This is true for the USAF and other services in areas ranging from reception, staging, onward movement, and integration to the role of Japan-based logistical capabilities in supporting regional operations. In the process, the participation of Japan's SDF is essential to the fulfillment of U.S. operations: In the event of crisis or war, U.S. forces will rely on Japanese support in several areas, such as infrastructure, logistics, and base defense.[19] Japan, in turn,

TABLE 3.1
Selected U.S. Military Posture in Japan, 2021

Categories of Forces or Facilities	Specific Examples
Air bases and air facilities	Misawa, Yokota, and Kadena Air Bases, Naval Air Facility Atsugi, Marine Corps Air Stations Iwakuni and Futenma
Communication facilities	Fuchu and Tokorozawa Communication Stations, Owada, Yugi, Yaedake, Kyogamisaki, Sofu, and numerous other communication sites
Training ranges	Tori Shima, Idesuna Jima, and Kume Jima ranges; multiple ranges on Okinawa
Ports and naval facilities	Yokohama, Naha, Sasebo, and Tategami Basin port facilities
Ground and general bases and facilities	Camp Zama, Camp Shields, Camp Schwab, Camp Hansen and other camps on Okinawa
Supply and storage facilities	Akizuki, Kawakami, and Hiro ammunition depots; numerous petroleum, oil, and lubricant depots; Azuma storage area
Major combat formations	III Marine Expeditionary Force, U.S. 7th Fleet, 5th Air Force, U.S. Army Japan and I Corps (Forward)

SOURCES: U.S. Forces Japan, homepage, undated; 5th Air Force, homepage, undated; Commander, U.S. 7th Fleet, homepage, undated; U.S. Army Japan, homepage, undated; III Marine Expeditionary Force, homepage, undated.

---

[18] Joe Gould, "US, Japan Agree to Two Defense Pacts Amid China Worries," *Defense News*, January 7, 2022. See also "Japan and U.S. Draft Operation Plan for Taiwan Contingency," *Japan Times*, December 23, 2021, which added:

> The condition under which the U.S. military will set up a temporary base is when the Japanese government judges that conflict between the Chinese and Taiwanese militaries will undermine the peace and security of Japan, if left as is, the sources said.

> In such a scenario, the U.S. military will deploy its high mobility artillery rocket system to a temporary base location while the SDF [Self-Defense Forces] will be tasked with logistical support by providing ammunition and fuel. To prevent coming under attack, U.S. Marines will change base locations, the sources added.

[19] Jeffrey W. Hornung, "Taiwan and Six Potential New Year's Resolutions for the U.S.-Japanese Alliance," War on the Rocks, January 5, 2022; Jeffrey W. Hornung, "What the United States Wants from Japan in Taiwan," *Foreign Policy*, May 10, 2021b.

will rely on U.S. forces to fulfill its obligations, as set out in the Japan-U.S. Security Treaty. This mutual dependence creates a very specific context for conflict-phase access decisions, in which Japanese agreement will be essential to the successful preparation for and prosecution of any regional contingencies. For example, the "United States would find it nearly impossible to respond promptly and effectively to Chinese aggression against Taiwan without being able to call on these assets and facilities."[20]

Evaluating the Framework for Conflict-Phase Access Decisions in Japan

The core of this assessment involved an analysis of the five major questions that senior decisionmakers are likely to take into account when considering conflict-phase access decisions (see Chapter 2). Each of the following subsections addresses one of these questions and describes several factors likely to be decisive in answering it.

It is critical to clarify what is, and is not, at stake for the United States in terms of access to its facilities in Japan. If a contingency involves the direct defense of Japan, U.S. access can safely be assumed. If the United States is conducting peaceful military missions, such as intelligence, surveillance, and reconnaissance (ISR) flights from bases in Japan, the United States can claim the right to conduct such missions without permission under current alliance agreements. In theory, Japan does not have the right to limit access to U.S. bases. The question we have examined is narrower: the U.S. ability to access its bases, or other locations in Japan, for operations during a conflict that *may not directly involve Japan's defense*, at least initially. Under almost any other conditions, U.S. access to its bases in Japan will face few constraints.

In that narrow and more challenging scenario, however, the choice for Japan—whether to allow the United States to essentially wage war partially from Japanese territory as part of a contingency that does not threaten Japan's own survival—will be much more difficult. Japan will face the tremendous costs and risks of any decision to grant the United States substantial access for combat operations during a conflict that does not directly involve the defense of Japan. Japan's leaders may well decide that its dependence on the United States for security and growing concern about Chinese power leave them no choice but to agree.

Question 1: Would Granting the United States Conflict-Phase Access Affect the Leader or the Regime's Political Survival?

Our analysis suggests that three primary factors will affect the political implications of conflict-phase access for Japanese governments:

---

[20] David Sacks, *Enhancing U.S.-Japan Coordination for a Taiwan Conflict*, Council on Foreign Relations, Center for Preventative Action, January 18, 2022, p. 10.

1. the potential for Chinese economic punishment of Japan and the resulting effects on Japanese economic performance
2. public attitudes toward China and a potential conflict
3. the political resilience of the Japanese government in power at the time.

Economic Dependence

One major factor governing Japanese conflict-phase access decisions may be the extensive economic relationship between Japan and China and the potential negative ramifications for Japan of a Chinese decision to punish Japanese access choices with severe economic sanctions. We summarize economic risks to Japan in the fifth question in the framework.

Japanese Public Opinion

A second political factor influencing Japanese decisions on U.S. wartime access will be public opinion. One aspect of public opinion is support for the U.S. alliance, which remains strong. According to Cabinet Office polls, the public overwhelmingly supports the United States, with 88.5 percent having an affinity toward the United States; 91.3 percent believing that U.S.-Japan relations are good; and 98.2 percent believing that developments between the two countries are important for themselves and the Indo-Pacific region.[21] Similarly, 77.5 percent of the people believe that the U.S.-Japan alliance plays a role for Japan's peace and stability.[22]

Yet that support is counterbalanced by a public that remains reluctant to engage in any type of use of force. For example, public polling by the *Asahi* newspaper shows no majority in favor of having the SDF engage in collective self-defense operations, which—while they go beyond granting access to U.S. forces—could be the relevant operations asked of Japan, if the United States came to Taiwan's defense.[23] Some polls show that small percentages of the

---

[21] Government of Japan, "Relations Between Japan and Other Countries/Regions" ["日本と諸外国・地域との関係"], webpage, undated. The latest Pew survey found similar results: 70 percent of Japanese have a favorable opinion of the United States, more than most U.S. NATO allies; and 76 percent of Japanese say that the United States is a somewhat or very reliable partner (although the proportion saying "very reliable" is lower than in some other U.S. partners and allies). Attitudes toward China have declined: Only 9 percent have confidence in Xi Jinping as a leader (compared with more than 60 percent having confidence in presidents Biden and Emmanuel Macron). See Richard Wike, Janell Fetterolf, Moira Fagan, and Sneha Gubbala, *International Attitudes Toward the U.S., NATO and Russia in a Time of Crisis*, Pew Research Center, 2022.

[22] The Cabinet Office, "Public Opinion Surveys on Self-Defense Forces and Defense Issues ["自衛隊・防衛問題に関する世論調査"], 世論調査 [Opinion Polls], Government of Japan, 2017, Figure 15.

[23] In response to a question about whether people support or oppose the law that expanded the SDF's overseas activities to include the use of collective self-defense, *Asahi* found that 46 percent supported it, and 33 percent were opposed ("Participation in the Nuclear Ban Treaty Greatly Exceeds Non-Participation by 59%" ["核禁条約参加を、59% 不参加を大きく上回る"], *Asahi Shimbun*, November 17, 2020, p. 4). As one CRS report concluded, the shift of Japanese public opinion toward a more hawkish acceptance of military roles

> has been largely incremental rather than fundamental. Observers caution that there is still deep-seated reluctance among the public to shift away from the tenets of the "peace constitution." Even as Japan's

Japanese public even show skepticism about using force if the country were directly attacked, although no Japanese government would be likely to follow these views.[24] Without a population that supports the use of force for collective defense missions of other states not involving a direct attack on Japan, Tokyo could find it difficult to translate political will into action to grant access to the United States. Allowing U.S. access to facilities for wartime operations for contingencies not viewed as an existential threat to Japan could be perceived as tantamount to joining the war itself, which could draw significant public opposition or the possibility that the U.S. adversary would directly threaten Japan. If an adversary were to directly attack Japan, however, the country's response—and U.S. access to facilities in Japan to support that response—would likely be to proactively support U.S. operations. But for collective defense scenarios in which the aggressor has not brought Japan more directly into the war, Japanese governments will face conflicting pressures from public opinion.

Japanese Political Situation

The third factor likely to shape Japanese access decisions on allowing U.S. access of its bases for combat operations that are not directly tied to the defense of Japan is its domestic political context more generally, including both institutional and political party issues.

One basic political challenge involving access is the associated procedure needed for Japan to define what type of situation an unfolding crisis is. For Japan to engage its SDF in conflict, a prime minister must decide what type of scenario is occurring, which, in turn, defines the maximum range of responses possible.[25] These decisions are largely political but have the potential not just to limit what Japan can do for any specific scenario but to take time, delaying responses. Japanese politics is famously slow to react, and the natural difficulty in getting rapid action may constrain Japan's responses to U.S. access requests in a crisis.[26] The specific character of the crisis will, of course, affect how quickly Japan can respond; if the threat to Japan itself is immediate, the response will likely be more rapid.

Beyond the structures of Japanese politics, the political context at the time of a conflict will also have tremendous implications for access decisions. In periods with a very strong prime minister, such as during the Abe Shinzō administration (2012–2020), a prime minister could feel emboldened by public support to find ways to broaden the role for SDF participation and could act swiftly and decisively, including acquiescing to U.S. requests. On the other hand, if the balance in the Diet is less favorable and public support is weak, the government

---

defense establishment moves to become more "normal," in the sense of shedding limitations on military activities, it is unclear whether the Japanese people are comfortable with these developments. (Congressional Research Service, June 13, 2019, p. 10.)

[24] According to the Cabinet Office, 19.6 percent would resist without engaging in force, and 6.6 percent would not even resist; another 10.6 percent answered that they do not know what they would do (The Cabinet Office, 2017, Figure 13).

[25] Hornung, 2020.

[26] Cooper and Greitens, 2021.

may feel more constrained and less willing to act. Similar dynamics within the Liberal Democratic Party could affect access decisions: A prime minister with unquestioned authority over the party may be able to convince an otherwise recalcitrant party of the need to support the United States for the sake of Japan's security. A prime minister facing intraparty conflicts, however, may find it difficult to get a majority of his or her own party to support the government's intentions.

What Factors Specific to the Conflict Might Shape the Decisions?

One aspect of the way a conflict begins and unfolds will be critical to determining the political effects in Japan of its access decisions: whether Japan determines that the scope and reach of a conflict make it an existential threat to Japan itself. If so, it would cross the threshold for authorizing the SDF to use force and would make access decisions for U.S. forces almost a formality. The obvious threshold for meeting that criterion would be direct attacks on Japan, but, since 2015, Tokyo has made clear that it could see wars that do not directly involve its homeland as existential issues as well.

Question 2: Would Granting the United States Conflict-Phase Access Affect the Country's Direct Security Position?

In the case of Japan, this question will bear heavily on any decision to grant the United States access to facilities for operations during a conflict that does not directly involve the defense of Japan because of the significant possibility that such a choice would place Japan in the crosshairs of the U.S. adversary. But that risk is not the only security-related factor at work; as in all areas, there is a complex mix of influences.

Japan's Reliance on the U.S. Security Partnership

The first and most important factor related to Japan's security position that might govern its access decisions is the crucial role of the U.S. alliance, and broader U.S.-led international order, to Japan. Japan sees its security as tightly interwoven with that of the postwar international order, especially with its relationship to the United States. As one RAND report concluded, "The most fundamental aspect of Japan's security strategy is its reliance on and support for the postwar international order. Japan accepts the fact that the order was U.S.-built and is U.S.-led. Japanese leaders often credit the United States for its efforts."[27]

This reliance on U.S. power and a U.S.-led order would make it more difficult for Japan to deny U.S. access requests in a crisis or war that Japanese leadership believed could fundamentally threaten Japan's survival. Japan would be deeply concerned about the military and economic risks of allowing U.S. access and potentially inviting military strikes on Japanese

---

[27] Michael J. Mazarr, Jonah Blank, Samuel Charap, Benjamin N. Harris, Timothy R. Heath, Niklas Helwig, Jeffrey W. Hornung, Lyle J. Morris, Ashley L. Rhoades, Ariane M. Tabatabai, and Sean M. Zeigler, *Understanding the Emerging Era of International Competition Through the Eyes of Others: Country Perspectives*, RAND Corporation, RR-2726/1-AF, 2022, p. 50.

territory if that conflict did not already directly involve Japan, but the whole weight of its postwar strategic posture leans in the other direction, creating what will be a powerful sense of obligation to support the United States.[28]

Japan's Decisions About Its Own Use of Force

A second factor related to Japan's security position that will affect Tokyo's decision is how Japan views the conflict in the context of its own criteria for the use of force. These decisions are distinct from the choice to grant the United States access, but the considerations involved in this choice shed important light on access choices and are worth examining on their own terms. A Japan that had decided to employ force would be almost certain to grant the United States full access for wartime operations; a Japan resisting that choice would be more reluctant to grant access.

These criteria changed in 2015. Previously, Japan's SDF was allowed to respond only to direct attacks on the homeland, but now the multiple tiers of potential contingencies allow various levels of Japanese response. Following an expansion of alliance responsibilities in 1997 that allowed Japan to respond to situations in areas surrounding Japan, "legislation enacted in Japan since 2001 has allowed Japanese forces to take on more active noncombat roles, including in Iraq and in the Indian Ocean, under the category of international peace cooperation activities."[29] Then, in 2015, Japan passed a suite of security bills that clarified and expanded Japan's authorities into essentially three distinct categories. The first, unchanged from before, is a direct attack on Japan. The second refers to situations that "have an important influence on Japan's peace and security" (重要影響事態), which do not involve an armed attack on Japan but could lead to one if left unaddressed.[30] The third refers to a threat to Japan's survival (存立危機事態), which, as with a direct attack on Japan, would allow the SDF to use force.

The two new situational categories have distinct implications for Japan's use of force. When a situation is categorized as having only "important influence" on Japan, the SDF's ability to participate in any operational activities will be limited; they will not be authorized to use force. Moreover, Japan's support for U.S. forces, as a recent RAND report explained, would be limited to "noncombat, rear-area support activities that can be conducted either in Japanese territory/waters/airspace or on the high-seas," such as "logistic support, provision of supplies, repair and medical services, and [noncombat] search and rescue operations." This support would also include ammunition but exclude the weapons themselves. Another constraint is that this support cannot extend into areas "where combat activities are actually occurring" and cannot violate a more general prohibition on the "integration with the use of

---

[28] "Japan is also not unrealistic. If a contingency erupted between the United States and China, and Japan refused the U.S. use of its bases, officials admit the 'alliance will be finished.'. . . Realistically, it is difficult to imagine Japan opposing a U.S. request to use its bases if a regional conflict erupts." Hornung, 2020, p. 93.

[29] Chanlett-Avery and Campbell, 2019, p. 31.

[30] Hornung, 2020, pp. 96–97.

force with another military" (武力行使との一体化).[31] If a situation is categorized as a threat to Japan's survival, however, the wider spectrum of roles and missions opens up, including the use of force and activities in combat zones.

In terms of the contingency of most concern to the United States—a potential Chinese invasion of Taiwan—significant shifts in Japan's public positioning have occurred since 2020, which some analysts have interpreted as potentially indicating a change in Japanese support for possible U.S. efforts in a Taiwan contingency. In December 2020, for example, Japan's then–Deputy Minister of Defense Nakayama Yasuhide, in his personal capacity at an English-language think-tank event, referred to Taiwan security as a redline for Japan, appearing to place it into the category of threats that could potentially justify SDF involvement.[32] The following April, however, Prime Minister Suga Yoshihide visited the White House and issued an official joint statement with President Biden announcing a shared interest in the "importance of peace and stability across the Taiwan Strait" and "the peaceful resolution of cross-Strait issues."[33] While nowhere close to the type of language used by Nakayama, this was the first time in half a century that a U.S.-Japan joint leader statement had mentioned Taiwan. However, demonstrating that Japan's position had not changed, Suga was quick to clarify a week later that this statement did "not presuppose military involvement" in parliamentary debate.[34]

The following year saw many additional statements from Japanese leaders—but none in their official capacity—that tended to reinforce a general trend of Japanese officials speaking more vocally about Taiwan. As one recent analysis describes,

> Japan's senior policymakers have gone even further in subsequent months. In June [2021], Defense Minister Nobuo Kishi stated that ["]the peace and stability of Taiwan is directly connected to Japan," seeming to imply that Japan could respond to an attack on Taiwan within its current constitutional framework. Nakayama then explicitly stated "we have to protect Taiwan as a democratic country." In July, Japan released its annual defense white paper, which spoke of Taiwan in an unprecedented manner, asserting that "stabilizing the situation surrounding Taiwan is important for Japan's security and the stability of the international community. Therefore, it is necessary that we pay close attention to the situation with a sense of crisis more than ever before." . . .
>
> Also in July, Japanese Deputy Prime Minister Taro Aso stated that if a major problem took place in Taiwan, ["]it would not be too much to say that it could relate to a survival-

---

[31] Hornung, 2020, p. 97.

[32] Sacks, 2022, pp. 8-9.

[33] Joseph R. Biden, Jr., and Suga Yoshihide, "U.S.-Japan Joint Leaders Statement: 'U.S.–Japan Global Partnership for a New Era,'" April 16, 2021.

[34] Hornung, 2021b.

threatening situation," an assessment that would enable Japan to exercise collective self-defense.[35]

Yet, as public as these statements have been, these changes should not be misinterpreted. As Suga's backtracking suggests, no Japanese official has gone as far as formally indicating that a Taiwan contingency would automatically justify the employment of force by Japan. Thus, Japan has not said in any fashion that it would defend Taiwan or even support the United States in the defense of Taiwan. As East Asia scholar Adam Liff rightly concluded, "Japan's government has never made an explicit commitment to defend Taiwan or to necessarily assist a possible U.S. military response if a cross-strait conflict occurs. . . . [R]ecent developments do not indicate a major change in Japan's official posture toward the Taiwan Strait." Japan does not sell arms to Taiwan or regularly criticize China for cross-strait tensions. In terms of the Suga-Biden statement, Liff stated that, "Though this single sentence in the 2,100-word statement is historically significant . . . it is also relatively anodyne. Unlike numerous U.S. unilateral statements or last year's U.S.-Australia ministerial statement, it contains no explicit reference to Taiwan itself."[36] In sum, Japanese officials have hinted at some greater willingness to participate in this scenario, but the country's official position has not changed.

Japan's ultimate determination of the status of any regional contingency—does it "threaten Japan's survival" or merely contain the potential for "important influence" on it—cannot be predicted in advance. As the recent vocal statements of Japanese officials on Taiwan make clear, Japan is, thinking more about regional security in ways than it has heretofore—and being public about it—but this does not presuppose any choice when a crisis emerges. Still, the argument here is that any such decision will be a critical factor—perhaps the single essential variable—determining Japan's conflict-phase access decisions.

The Risk of Direct Attack on Japan

The third security-related factor is the danger that granting U.S. access to facilities for combat operations that do not directly involve the defense of Japan would invite direct attacks in retaliation on the Japanese homeland, even if Japan had not yet decided to enter the conflict. This factor is, of course, closely intertwined with the previous one: If Japan were to decide to enter a Taiwan contingency, for example, it would have chosen to accept the risks of possible retaliation. If it did not, however, such an action would increase the risk of possible retaliation. This factor will therefore mostly apply in a relatively narrow set of circumstances: when a major contingency is underway that the United States is engaged in but that does not directly involve Japan and that Japanese leadership has determined does *not* meet the criteria as a threat to Japan's survival. (This could be, for example, a distant flare-up with China over

---

[35] Sacks, 2022, pp. 8-9.

[36] Adam P. Liff, "Has Japan's Policy Toward the Taiwan Strait Changed?" Brookings Institution, August 23, 2021.

territorial claims in the SCS.) In such a case, granting access would pose serious security risks in the form of inviting adversary strikes on U.S. and possibly Japanese facilities and drawing Japan into a war it had decided to avoid.

For this factor, the type of access requested might influence the likelihood of Japan granting access in a conflict if Japanese leaders perceived that granting lower-level access, such as logistical and ISR support, would reduce the risk of Chinese retaliation while still signaling support for the United States. However, as we will discuss, given Japan's critical role for the U.S. military in a regional contingency, assessing the risk of Chinese retaliation for the different types of access is difficult because China might choose to retaliate in some manner, regardless of the level of access Japan grants.

What Factors Specific to the Conflict Might Shape the Decisions?

We have already largely outlined the factors specific to the conflict that would influence the decision. The primary factor is whether the contingency is one that triggers a Japanese decision that its own survival is directly or indirectly at stake and, therefore, that it has the political basis to approve SDF participation in the use of force. Such a top-level political and strategic decision would override more discrete security concerns. If the contingency is one that does not produce such a Japanese decision because it is distant or secondary but is nevertheless viewed as one that could have an important influence on Japan's security, any access decision would come with significant security risks for Japan.

Decisions do not depend entirely on objective factors but also on political perceptions and the prevailing political views. It is thus not the objective factors specific to the conflict that will make the difference but the perceptions of senior Japanese officials in power at the time. A Taiwan contingency, for example, could fall into either category—generating a Japanese judgment that its survival is threatened or simply that the situation will have an important influence, leading to a Japanese decision to stay out of the war.

A related aspect of the conflict that may have some effect on Japan's decision is the way that any conflict begins. In a possible conflict over Taiwan, for example, if Taiwan (and perhaps the United States) are perceived to have brought about Chinese action with unnecessarily provocative actions regarding such issues as independence claims and U.S.-Taiwan security cooperation, this could reduce the perceived legitimacy of the war in Japanese eyes and intensify Japanese desire to remain distant from its risks and costs. If, on the other hand, China's aggression is entirely unprovoked and viewed as a Ukraine-like act of reckless adventurism, one that might hint at future aggression that could threaten Japan, this could strengthen views in Japan that it had a strategic obligation to help support U.S. efforts to defeat the attack.

Question 3: Would Granting Conflict-Phase Access Affect the Outcome of the Conflict?

This question will bear on Japanese decisions on access, but it is largely a subset of other criteria. As noted earlier, U.S. facilities in Japan are essential to theater combat operations and to the logistical and sustainment efforts to support combat operations. A U.S. joint force denied access to facilities in Japan in prosecuting a contingency, such as Taiwan, would be operationally hamstrung. The U.S. dependence on Japan is even deeper than that, in fact, because U.S. logistical and supply operations in Japan are critically dependent on Japanese contractors, civilian facilities, and SDF support for specific functions.[37]

Japanese officials appreciate these factors and understand that their access decision could be the one variable that causes the United States to fail in a conflict with China. We highlighted this factor earlier under political and strategic considerations for Japan. Simply put, Japan's security is dependent on the U.S. relationship and the larger international order that the United States has sponsored, and access to facilities in Japan will be required for the United States to succeed in a regional contingency. While any Japanese leader will face internal political pressure to keep Japan out of a war that does not directly involve it, Japan's dependence on the United States lies at the very core of Japan's security. Thus, any U.S. request for access will create immense pressure for Japan to accede. Whether that pressure is decisive, however, cannot be known in advance.

What Factors Specific to the Conflict Might Shape the Decisions?

The nature of the conflict that could affect this criterion most would be its overall importance and centrality to Japanese security. A distant and less regionally significant crisis or localized conflict—a narrow battle over a very discrete SCS feature, for example—would likely produce less-intense demands on Japan to grant access, particularly if the Japanese viewed the conflict as simply having an important influence on Japan or chose to not categorize the situation at all. This would be both because it is far enough away that U.S. facilities in Japan might be less central and because the Japanese and U.S. interests at stake would be less vital. Meanwhile, a Taiwan contingency that seemed to threaten the Japanese home islands, whether through direct Chinese attacks or the risk of escalation, would pose a much higher risk to Japan's security and, thus, would create much stronger demands for the United States to use facilities in Japan.

Question 4: Would Granting the United States Conflict-Phase Access Affect—or Be Affected by—Regional Decisions Regarding Granting Similar Access?

The decisions of other countries about granting the United States access during a conflict are not likely to be dominant influences on Japan's decision. The core political and strategic concerns, especially the factors related to Japan's security and the U.S. alliance, will be primary. But the regional and world reactions to a potential contingency will create an important part of the context for Japan's choices. This is true in two primary ways: The general degree of consensus in countering the adversary's aggression, and the weight that regional security partnerships will carry in Japanese thinking.

---

[37] Hornung, 2021b.

The Emergence of a Regional and Global Consensus

The first factor related to this question is the degree to which the access decisions of other countries—both regionally and globally—create a powerful, widely shared agreement on the illegitimacy of China's aggression and the need to respond to it. Because of Japan's continuing constraints on an expeditionary security policy, its more active support for or even participation in any U.S.-led military actions will be significantly eased if it sees itself as joining a powerful global consensus, particularly if the UN supports that consensus. While full UN Security Council endorsement of any conflict involving China is implausible given Beijing's veto, consensus statements of support in the UN General Assembly or other forums could be influential. This will be most important within the region—for the Japanese public and other regional actors to perceive that whatever actions Japan takes, these actions are in support of the consensus of the dominant majority of other countries.

The Views of Other Close Japanese Partners

The second important factor bearing on this criterion is the evolution of Japan's security partnerships with other countries in the region.[38] These are establishing deeper bilateral relations that could create more sensitivity in Japan to third-party choices about a contingency. A critical mass of Japan's security partners joining the United States in a regional contingency—or, on the contrary, a vast majority studiously avoiding involvement—could have some influence on Japan's decisionmaking over granting the United States conflict-phase access. Japan has been steadily building its security relations with countries throughout the region, including Australia, India, South Korea, the Philippines, Vietnam, and Indonesia.

These ties could have an important effect on Tokyo's decisions in any crisis or war involving China. If the target of Chinese aggression is a close Japanese partner or if a critical mass of regional countries at least strongly condemns China's action (and, in some cases, grants access to U.S. operations), Japan's existing ties with these countries will play an important role in drawing Japan into certain choices about conflict-phase access. Japanese officials may also see the credibility of their regional position at stake: If Japan stands aside during a major conflict that will shape the region's future, countries that had begun to view it as a leader in regional security networks might question that perception. This is especially likely if some of their leading partners and regional powers take firm positions in support of the United States in the conflict and, perhaps, become involved in it.

While Japan is expanding ties with many countries in the region, several key states would likely have more influence over Japan's access decisions in a conflict. The first, and arguably the most influential, is Australia. Australia is now Japan's closest security partner after the United States.[39] According to the Australian Embassy in Tokyo: "The Australia-Japan part-

---

[38] Jeffrey W. Hornung, "Japan's Growing Hard Hedge Against China," *Asian Security*, Vol. 10, No. 2, 2014; Jeffrey Hornung, "Japan's Pushback of China," *Washington Quarterly*, Vol. 38, No. 1, 2015.

[39] Harold, Grossman, Harding, Hornung, Poling, Smith, and Smith, 2019, pp. 30–31.

nership is our closest and most mature in Asia."[40] Japan and Australia, both part of the Quad and founding members of the Comprehensive and Progressive Trans-Pacific Partnership (TPP) agreement, share a close defense relationship. The two countries engage in high-level exchanges (2+2 ministerial dialogues and annual defense and foreign minister meetings)[41]; regularly participate in naval, ground, and air force exercises; and have signed an acquisition and cross-servicing agreement (ACSA).[42] In 2014, Tokyo and Canberra began negotiating a reciprocal access agreement, which is Tokyo's first.[43] A growing consensus in both countries about the growing security challenge of China has added impetus to closer bilateral relations.[44] Australia is also the other country in the region most likely to support U.S. military operations in a future contingency. Its decisions may end up influencing Japan's, given their increased bilateral ties: Australia quickly and boldly offering access to the United States (and, perhaps, even commits its own military to the conflict) could pressure Japan to match the commitment as a like-minded democratic ally.

Japan's deepening security relationship with the Philippines might also influence its access decisions in a regional contingency, particularly in an SCS conflict. The Philippines and Japan established a strategic partnership in 2011 over shared concern about Chinese maritime aggression. Since then, Tokyo has provided aid, grants, training, education, and other maritime assistance programs to Manila.[45] Further, Japan supported the Philippines' lawsuit against China in the SCS at the International Tribunal on the Law of the Sea.[46] In 2020, Japan agreed to sell a warning and control radar system to the Philippines—representing the first export of finished defense equipment since Japan lifted its ban on transfers in 2014 and the first-ever defense equipment sale to Southeast Asia.[47] In 2022, Tokyo and Manila upgraded their meetings to formal 2+2 ministerial dialogues, the second of such agreements Tokyo has

---

[40] Australian Embassy, Tokyo, "Strategic Partnership," webpage, undated.

[41] A *2+2 ministerial dialogue* is a meeting between the U.S. secretaries of State and Defense with their foreign counterparts.

[42] Harold, Grossman, Harding, Hornung, Poling, Smith, and Smith, 2019, pp. 34–36; Ministry of Foreign Affairs of Japan, "The Signing of the Japan-Australia Acquisition and Cross-Servicing Agreement (ACSA)," webpage, May 19, 2010.

[43] Agreement Between Australia and Japan Concerning the Facilitation of Reciprocal Access and Cooperation Between the Self-Defense Forces of Japan and the Australian Defence Force, January 6, 2022; Mike Yeo, "Australia and Japan to Strengthen Defence Cooperation," *Australian Defence Magazine*, December 2, 2021.

[44] Jeffrey W. Hornung and Hayley Channer, "Russia's Invasion of Ukraine May Harden US Indo-Pacific Allies," *The Hill*, May 26, 2022.

[45] Embassy of Japan in the Philippines, "Japan's Development Cooperation in the Philippines: Proactive Support for Inclusive and Sustainable Growth," May 5, 2022.

[46] Ministry of Foreign Affairs of Japan, "Japan-Philippines Summit Meeting," June 4, 2015.

[47] Daishe Abe, "Philippines Radar Deal Marks Japan's First Arms Exports, Nikkei Asia, August 29, 2020; Sebastian Strangio, "Japan, Philippines Agree to Boost Security Cooperation," *The Diplomat*, April 8, 2022c.

with Southeast Asian countries.[48] Japan views the Philippines as providing important support for regional efforts to counterbalance China's power and maintain the status quo in the region, which is likely the reason it has prioritized building bilateral defense ties. It is possible that this bilateral defense relationship will continue to deepen, which could lead to a situation in which Japan might feel obliged to assist the Philippines in the event of Chinese aggression against Philippine interests or territory by supporting U.S. forces engaged in combat operations or if the Philippines grants U.S. forces access in a contingency over Taiwan.

Japan has also increased defense ties with South Korea, India, Vietnam, and Indonesia, although to a lesser extent than Australia and the Philippines. These relationships would likely carry less weight for Japanese decisionmakers on access decisions in a conflict. However, they would still factor into Japanese decisionmakers' views on whether there is a regional consensus against China and/or regional support for the United States in a conflict. For example, a close U.S. ally, such as South Korea, offering U.S. forces even noncombat access in a Taiwan contingency would likely pressure Japan to offer access as well to signal support for the U.S. and Japan's regional partners and bolster Japan's status as a regional power. Similarly, Japan's leadership would view India strongly condemning China in a conflict as a signal of regional support for U.S. operations against China, which might increase the likelihood of Japan granting access.

What Factors Specific to the Conflict Might Shape the Decisions?

The aspects of the conflict likely to affect this criterion are similar to those that will affect the others. If the conflict results from crude, unprovoked Chinese aggression, the regional reaction is likely to be more vigorous, and Japan would feel more compelled to strongly support efforts to oppose the aggression, including granting access to the United States. This will be particularly so if that conflict is closer to Japan and, thus, is perceived as a threat to its survival. If a contingency is more distant, less significant, or central to regional balances of power and/or more ambiguous in its origins, Japan's relationships with other regional actors and their positions on the conflict will be less affected. And of course, as discussed earlier, the stronger the regional consensus in support of the United States during the conflict, particularly as reflected in access decisions, the greater the likelihood that Japan may feel some additional pressure to provide access to the United States as well.

Question 5: Would Granting the United States Conflict-Phase Access Affect the Economic Prosperity of the Country?

The final question in the framework focuses on the economic implications of access decisions for Japan and on how Japanese officials perceive the implications. At least two specific aspects of this issue are likely to weigh on Japanese decisions.

---

[48] Elaine Lies and Sam Nussey, "Japan, Philippines Eye Further Defence Cooperation at First 2+2 Meeting," Reuters, April 9, 2022. Japan's first such 2+2 agreement in Southeast Asia was with Indonesia.

The first is a sense of the regional and global economic effects of any major war. While there is little direct evidence available on this point, our sense from discussions with Japanese officials and scholars is that they will generally assess economic impacts in terms of the larger effects of the war itself rather than access choices. A massive regional conflict, whether it involves Japan directly or not, would have profound implications for Japan's economy. But this more general economic effect is a function of the war itself and not Japan's access choices and, thus, is unlikely to be decisive in shaping such choices.

The second economic factor could have more direct ramifications for Japan's choices: the perception of China's ability to punish Japan in targeted economic ways for allowing U.S. access in wartime. China has a history of using economic coercion to punish countries for actions it finds unacceptable. Beijing has executed these punishments at least 13 times since 2010 in the form of boycotts and restrictions on imported products, restrictions of Chinese tourism, suspension of trade, and fees on commodity imports (Table 3.2). If Japan granted the United States access to its bases, Beijing might retaliate using economic coercion.

Japan's economic dependence on China makes it especially vulnerable to such coercion. China has long been Japan's top trade partner; as of 2021, China constituted 26.1 percent (US$165.9 billion) of Japan's total trade imports and 32.1 percent of its total trade exports (US$106.1 billion), making it very economically vulnerable to China.[49] In making access decisions, Japanese officials have to consider the possibility that a decision to join a conflict against China or to grant the United States extensive use of facilities in Japan for wartime operations would almost certainly trigger substantial Chinese economic sanctions with profound ramifications for the Japanese economy. Table 3.3 summarizes the overall scale of Japan's economic dependence on China. While the United States, Taiwan, and close U.S. allies also provide a substantial (and indeed larger) share of Japanese trade than China, the Chinese share remains sufficient to dramatically affect the Japanese economy and could have outsized effects on more specific goods or industries (see Table 3.4).

A good example of such vulnerability is Japan's dependence on China for rare-earth elements (REEs). Japanese imported goods are very China-dependent as well. As of 2019, China was reported to have at least a 50-percent share in 23.5 percent of all categories of imported goods. This is more than twice the amount of U.S. dependence on Chinese imported goods.[50] Of these categories, electronic equipment and machinery are consistently the top imported categories, amounting to $32.35 billion and $26.72 billion in 2020, respectively.[51] This is primarily due to China's strong position in REEs, which are necessary to produce such products as smartphones, plasma screens, batteries, and engines (see Table 3.5). Further, many products rely on several REEs to function. The Apple iPhone, for example, requires neodymium

---

[49] Ministry of Foreign Affairs of Japan, "Japan-China Relations (Basic Data)," webpage, February 24, 2022; UN Statistics Division, undated.

[50] Nohara, 2022.

[51] OEC, undated-d.

TABLE 3.2

Chinese Economic and Political Coercion, 2010–2022

Country	Year	Action	Punishment
Norway	2010	Liu Xiaobo granted Nobel Peace Prize	Restricted salmon imports
Japan	2010	Chinese fishing captain arrested in Senkaku Islands dispute	Blocked exports of rare-earth mineral
Philippines	2012	Scarborough Shoal confrontation	Blocked imports of fruit, restricted tourism
Mongolia	2016	Dalai Lama visit	Fees on commodity imports
South Korea	2016	THAAD deployment	Boycott on South Korean products
Taiwan	2016	Rejecting "one China"	Restricted tourism, boycott on fruit
Australia	2017–present	Campaign on interference, fifth-generation technology (5G) policy, investigations of coronavirus disease 2019 (COVID-19) origins	Limited imports on coal, wine, barley, copper, sugar, timber, lobster
Canada	2018	Meng Wenzhou's arrest	Ban on some agricultural goods
New Zealand	2019	Ban on Huawei 5G	China–New Zealand year of tourism postponed
Czech Republic	2019	Prague signs sister-city deal with Taipei	Shanghai cuts Prague as sister city and ends official contacts
UK	2020	Official support for Hong Kong protesters	Suspension of Shanghai-London stock connection
Sweden	2021–present	Ban on Huawei 5G	Reduced share in Ericsson
Lithuania	2021–present	Opening of Taipei office in Vilnius	Stopped trade, suspended rail freight

for its speakers, europium for its LED screen, and cerium for the phone's final polish.[52] Therefore, it is difficult for Japan to become more independent from China by just focusing on identifying alternative supplies for one or two elements.

China has already proved its ability and willingness to punish Japan economically through restrictions on REEs. In 2010, the Japan Coast Guard arrested and detained—under Japanese law—a Chinese captain of a fishing trawler in the waters surrounding the Senkaku Islands after he rammed two Japan Coast Guard boats. In protest over the dispute, the Chinese government blocked exports of REEs to Japan.[53] Although the ban was brief, the threat

[52] Jay Greene, "Digging for Rare Earths: The Mines Where iPhones Are Born," CNET, September 26, 2012.

[53] Keith Brasher, "Amid Tension, China Blocks Vital Exports to Japan," *New York Times*, September 22, 2010.

TABLE 3.3
Japan's Economic Dependence on China

	Value
Trade, imports (2021)	
US$ billions	165.9
% of total	26.1
Trade, export (2021)	
US$ billions	206.2
% of total	32.1
Foreign direct investment (FDI), inflow (2020)	
US$ billions	0.5
% of total	4.9
Tourism (2020)	
US$ millions	1.07
% of total	26
Tourism consumption (2020)	
US$ billions	2.14[a]
% of total	34.1
China-dependent imported goods (2019)	
Amount (out of ~5,000 categories of goods	1,133
% of total value	23.3
Laptops and tablets imported from China (2019)	
% of total imported laptops and tablets	98.8
Cellphones imported from China (2019)	
% of total imported cellphones	85.7[b]
Rare-earth minerals imported from China (2022)	
Metric tons	645.34[c]
Rare-earth minerals imported from China (2020)	
US$ millions	118
% of total rare-earth imports	54

SOURCES: Ministry of Foreign Affairs of Japan, 2022; UN Statistics Division, undated; UN Conference on Trade and Development, "General Profile: Japan," webpage, UNCTADSTAT, October 20, 2022b; Yoshiaki Nohara, "Japan Flags Vulnerability to China Supply Chain Constraints," Bloomberg, February 3, 2022; "China's Exports of Rare-Earth Compounds Increased by 90.05% Annually, as of in October 2021" ["中国2021年10月份稀土化合物出口量同比上升90.05%"], Sohu, March 2, 2022; TrendEconomy, "Japan | Imports and Exports | World | Compounds of Rare-Earth Metals, of Tritium or of Scandium or of Mixtures of These Metals," webpage, November 14, 2021.

[a] Converted from 253.6 billion yen.

[b] Up from 69.1 percent in 2009.

[c] Up 4.12 percent from 552.1 metric tons in 2021.

TABLE 3.4
Japan's Total Bilateral Trade, by Country

Year	China	United States	Australia	Taiwan	Republic of Korea	Germany	UK	France
2012	376.7	220.3	74.9	67.6	103.2	50.2	14.9	19.6
2013	351.6	206.5	68.0	62.4	94.7	48.6	14.5	18.1
2014	349.5	203.8	62.3	61.6	86.0	47.7	13.3	17.5
2015	307.2	194.7	47.6	58.0	71.4	41.2	12.7	14.7
2016	306.2	199.8	44.5	60.1	71.8	44.5	15.4	16.0
2017	334.6	208.9	55.0	62.5	81.9	48.0	17.8	16.7
2018	354.9	224.2	62.8	67.0	85.1	52.1	18.9	18.1
2019	340.0	221.7	60.0	67.3	76.0	49.9	19.4	18.9
2020	339.1	187.6	47.9	71.1	71.1	44.3	15.0	14.9
2021	387.3	216.6	67.5	88.2	84.7	49.3	15.3	18.3

SOURCES: Observatory of Economic Complexity (OEC), "Japan/China," undated-d; U.S. Census Bureau, "U.S. Trade in Goods by Country," webpage, undated; World Bank, "World Integrated Trade Solution," database, undated-c; Japan External Trade Organization (JETRO), "Japanese Trade and Investment Statistics: Japan's International Trade in Goods (Yearly)," various years; Australian Government, Department of Foreign Affairs and Trade, "Trade Statistical Pivot Tables," undated; Bureau of Foreign Trade, Taiwan, "Bureau of Trade—Trade Statistics: Export/Import Value (by Country)," webpage, undated; Korea Customs Service, Trade Statistics," webpage, undated, for export/import by country; German Federal Statistics Office, "Exports and Imports (Foreign Trade)," 2022; Office for National Statistics, "UK Trade: Monthly Trade in Goods," database, September 2022; UN, "UN Comtrade Database," webpage, undated, trade data for Japan.

NOTE: Amounts in billions of U.S. dollars. China includes data for Mainland China, Macau, and Hong Kong.

of destruction of the Japanese economy was powerful enough to encourage Japan to diversify its suppliers of the elements.[54]

The 2010 incident sparked new concern in Japan about this vulnerability, and since then it has both reduced its dependence on China for REEs and increased reserve stockpiles. Tokyo undertook a global effort to diversify its sources of REEs, led by the Japan Oil, Gas and Metals National Corporation, known as Jogmec.[55] Its dependence on China's REEs has dropped from a peak of 99.8 percent in 1999 to 74 percent in 2022.[56] The goal is to reduce this to less than 50 percent by 2025. That will still leave the country heavily dependent on China, however, and vulnerable to another REE embargo in time of war.

[54] Yuko Inoue, "China Lifts Rare Earth Export Ban to Japan: Trader," Reuters, September 28, 2010.

[55] Mary Hui, "Japan's Global Rare Earths Quest Holds Lessons for the US and Europe," *Quartz*, April 23, 2021.

[56] Nabeel A. Mancheri and Tomoo Marukawa, "Rare-Earth Elements: China and Japan in Industry, Trade and Value Chain," ISS Contemporary Chinese Research Series, No. 17, February 2008, p. 65; TrendEconomy, 2021.

TABLE 3.5

China's Exports of Rare-Earth Elements to Japan

REE Name	Uses	2019	2018	2017
Cerium	Catalytic converters, liquid-crystal display (LCD) and plasma screens, oil refining, rechargeable batteries, smartphones	8.12 (1.1%)	12.8 (1.7%)	10.4 (1.5%)
Dysprosium	Lasers, missile guidance, nuclear reactor control rods, permanent magnets, wind turbines	22.4 (3.1%)	26.0 (3.5%)	32.7 (4.7%)
Europium	Energy efficient light bulbs, lasers, LCD and plasma screens	0.581 (0.01%)	0.667 (0.01%)	0.659 (0.01%)
Lanthanum	Catalytic converters, hybrid vehicles, oil refining, rechargeable batteries, smartphones	16.1 (2.2%)	16.3 (2.2%)	15.3 (2.2%)
Neodymium	Catalytic converters, computer hard drives, missile guidance, permanent magnets, smartphones, wind turbines	30.2 (4.2%)	65.8 (8.8%)	29.5 (4.2%)
Praseodymium	Aircraft engines, catalytic converters, missile guidance, permanent magnets, smartphones, wind turbines	3.11 (0.4%)	7.23 (1.0%)	6.83 (1.0%)
Terbium	LCD and plasma screens, missile guidance, permanent magnets, solid-state electronics, sonar systems	49.9 (6.9%)	36.0 (4.8%)	29.0 (4.2%)
Yttrium	Energy efficient light bulbs, lasers, LCD and plasma screens	5.22 (0.7%)	5.78 (0.8%)	4.24 (1.0%)
Other elements		$70.2 (9.7%)	$65.1 (8.7%)	$56.9 (8.1%)

SOURCES: China Power Project, "Does China Pose a Threat to Global Rare Earth Supply Chains?" Center for Strategic and International Studies, May 12, 2021; World Bank, undated-c.

NOTE: Amounts in millions of U.S. dollars and the percentage of Japan's total imports (parentheses).

What Factors Specific to the Conflict Might Shape the Decisions?

The nature of the conflict would be largely irrelevant to the question of economic effects on Japan, and the resulting influence on Japan's decisionmaking. Key issues are the degree of economic chaos caused by a war and the degree of Chinese coercive pressure. Smaller contingencies are obviously less likely to generate large economic effects, and bigger and more fundamental contingencies—such as a war over Taiwan—would raise more fundamental issues of economic coercion. Other than this simple distinction, the nature of the conflict is not a critical driver of this criterion.

How Might Japan's Decisions Vary Depending on the Types of Access Requested?

It is not clear that there can be significant differences in Japanese decisions based on the type of access required. This is true for two reasons. First, the United States not only enjoys a wide spectrum of capability options already based in Japan but will also be dependent on both U.S. and Japanese facilities—including repair facilities—and will be hard-pressed to limit its request to specific types of access or to a small set of locations. The access requested—at least for support and logistics functions—is likely to be comprehensive and include facilities across the Japanese archipelago. Second, Japan would likely be concerned that China would see a Japanese decision to support the United States as a binary question: Japan supporting U.S. efforts to wage war in the region would be likely to trigger many of the punishments outlined earlier, although, as previously noted, retaliatory actions can range from more to less severe. Trying to calibrate the degree of access allowed to fit underneath some Chinese threshold of retaliation is likely to be very difficult, if not impossible, for Japanese leaders.

That said, the type of access requested might matter if Japan perceives that granting lower levels of access could reduce the risk of Chinese retaliation. U.S. forces requesting access to Japan for strictly nonkinetic support and logistics operations, for example, might result in less Japanese concern over significant retaliation than would Japan's granting access to conduct active combat operations directly launched from its territory. Japanese leaders would likely view the latter as leading China to see Japan as a cobelligerent, triggering Chinese attacks on the Japanese homeland. In practice, however, while Japanese leadership may want to draw lines between nonkinetic rear-area support and frontline combat support, it may be difficult to publicly distinguish between these operations in a way that does not result in similar levels of Chinese retaliation. However, at least in theory, a nonkinetic support-only form of access could pose fewer risks and, thus, be more palatable to Japanese leaders in certain circumstances.

Summary

Table 3.6 summarizes the findings of this analysis. The most fundamental conclusion is that, in approaching conflict-phase access decisions for a contingency that has not already involved aggression against Japan, Japanese leaders and officials will be primarily influenced by a fundamental dilemma. On the one hand, vital security interests—in the U.S. alliance and the norms of the post-1945 order—will create powerful incentives to grant the United States almost any access it asks for. On the other hand, such a decision will come with tremendous risks of economic and, perhaps, military retaliation by China and would challenge Japan's long-standing emphasis on ensuring Japan's security.

One factor that could help Japan resolve this contradiction is if it were to decide that a given contingency met the threshold for the use of force by Japan itself. If Japan were attacked

TABLE 3.6

Summary of Adaptation of Conflict-Phase Access Decisionmaking Framework for Japan

Framework Question	Key Factors That Affect Leaders' Calculation	Conflict Characteristics on Which Assessment Depends
Would granting the United States conflict-phase access affect the leader or the regime's political survival?	• Degree of economic dependence on China • Public opinion • Japanese political situation • Nature of the contingency's threat to Japan as formally defined by the Japanese government	• Degree to which Japanese government determines the contingency as posing an existential threat to their nation
Would granting the United States conflict-phase access affect the country's direct security position?	• Reliance on U.S. security umbrella • Formal definition of the type of contingency under Japanese constitution and the resulting decision about Japan's own use of force (role of SDF) • Risk of direct attack on Japan	• Whether contingency poses survival threat to Japan • How it begins: degree of unquestioned Chinese aggression
Would granting conflict-phase access affect the outcome of the conflict?	• U.S. dependence on Japanese bases for most regional contingencies	• Location of the conflict • Intensity of the conflict
Would granting the United States conflict-phase access affect—or be affected by—regional decisions regarding granting similar access?	• Perception of regional and/ or global consensus on response to contingency • Weight of Japan's accumulating regional security relationships	• Origins of the conflict and how it begins; degree of perceived Chinese aggression • Degree of regional and global consensus in support of the United States
Would granting the United States conflict-phase access affect the economic prosperity of the country?	• Perception of threats inherent in economic dependence • Perception of economic risks of conflict, including the distinction between participating and not	• Potential economic impact of the contingency

or if Tokyo were to classify a given contingency as a threat to Japan's survival, leadership could authorize the SDF to use force in self-defense. Once that threshold has been crossed, granting access to the United States not only becomes an easy decision, it becomes essential to provide support to Japan's own defense effort. As noted earlier, Japanese officials have been increasingly signaling that Tokyo may view a Taiwan scenario in this way, but these remain hints rather than official policy. And taking this decision does not remove concern for the potential costs noted earlier or decisions made about the types of access to grant; it would merely indicate that Japan has chosen to accept them.

Another broad finding of this analysis is that many complex, interrelated, and uncertain variables are at work on this issue for Japan. The answer to the question will only be resolved at a specific moment, in a specific set of circumstances (including the character of the conflict), under a specific set of pressures. Planning for future contingencies should, therefore, take into account the varied pressures Japan could face and the varied responses Tokyo could give as a result.

CHAPTER 4

Adapting the Conflict-Phase Access Framework to the Philippines

The U.S. alliance with the Philippines, having weathered several challenges and adjustments during the post–Cold War period, remains a pillar of the overall U.S. security and diplomatic presence in Southeast Asia. The alliance continues to enjoy strong support from the Philippine population and most political and military elites in the Philippines. The relationship has been strained, however, by President Rodrigo Duterte's desire to pursue an "independent foreign policy" and form "open alliances" with China since his election in 2016.[1] Like most countries in Southeast Asia, China has emerged as one of the Philippines' most important sources of trade and investment, encouraging Manila to strike a balance between closer economic cooperation with Beijing and a deep security partnership with the United States. However, the Philippines' perception of China as more of a threat than a partner, driven by ongoing tensions with Beijing over territorial disputes and past incidents of economic coercion by China, will likely continue, creating opportunities for further strengthening of the U.S.-Philippine alliance in the future.[2]

Overall, we found that the Philippine leadership would be more likely to grant U.S. access requests for nonkinetic or lower-end capabilities, such as ISR, overflight, and logistics, because of a perception that this type of access would invite less risk of kinetic retaliatory attack from China. In addition, this type of access would be supported by the Philippine public, given its positive views toward the U.S.-Philippine security alliance, and some of the capabilities, such as logistics and prepositioning, are already part of the Enhanced Defense Cooperation Agreement (EDCA) and could be expanded on.[3] Philippine leadership responses to U.S. access requests for higher-end kinetic capabilities, such as long-range fires and direct combat operations from Philippine soil, would likely depend on whether Philip-

---

[1] Renato Cruz De Castro, "The Duterte Administration's Foreign Policy: Unravelling the Aquino Administration's Balancing Agenda on an Emergent China," *Journal of Current Southeast Asian Affairs*, Vol. 35, No. 3, 2016.

[2] Michael J. Green and Gregory B. Poling, "The U.S. Alliance with the Philippines," *Hard Choices: Memos to the President*, Center for Strategic and International Studies, December 3, 2020.

[3] Green and Poling, 2020; Agreement Between the Government of the United States of America and the Government of the Republic of the Philippines on Enhanced Defense Cooperation, April 28, 2014.

pine interests are directly involved or threatened—such as Philippine territorial interests in the SCS. The Philippine leadership might also be more willing to grant access for higher-end capabilities if they are supportive of the U.S.-Philippine security alliance and to offer assistance if the conflict were leading to significant U.S. and allied casualties. In this case, the leadership would likely want to support U.S. operations and might be more willing to grant access for that reason. Whether the Philippine leadership perceives that the United States is providing enough in economic compensation or security benefits to offset the increased risk of Chinese retaliation would also likely factor into the decision.

History of U.S. Access in the Philippines

For much of the Cold War, the United States relied on access to military facilitates in the Philippines to support military operations in the Indo-Pacific region.[4] The combination of airfields, ports, and army bases throughout the country has provided crucial logistics; repair and maintenance; training; and command, control, computers, and intelligence support for U.S. Indo-Pacific Command's (USINDOPACOM's) peacetime and wartime operational needs. The country's strategic importance for U.S. access in wartime contingencies, therefore, remains of keen interest to U.S. military planners. While the failure to negotiate renewal of the 1951 mutual defense treaty in 1991 and subsequent expulsion of U.S. troops from Subic Bay dealt a blow to U.S. access opportunities, the EDCA provides the legal basis for the United States to continue to access military installations in the Philippines.[5]

The EDCA, alongside the visiting forces agreement (VFA),[6] provides the legal and operational foundation for U.S. access in the Philippines. The EDCA allows the United States to build and operate facilities on Philippine military bases for the rotational deployment of U.S. troops and equipment and "to upgrade agreed-upon Philippine military bases in exchange for rotational access with the intent of increasing U.S. power projection over the SCS and deterring Chinese use of force against the Philippines," in five locations.[7] The agreement enables the United States to develop tactics, techniques, and procedures with Philippine armed forces

---

[4] F. A. Mediansky, "The U.S. Military Facilities in the Philippines," *Contemporary Southeast Asia*, Vol. 8, No. 4, March 1987.

[5] Agreement Between the Government of the United States of America and the Government of the Republic of the Philippines, 2014. Only one facility has been built since EDCA was signed in 2014—a storage warehouse at Cesar Basa Air Base. See Priam Nepomuceno, "EDCA to Allow PH, US to Respond to Regional Security Challenges," Philippine News Agency, April 18, 2018.

[6] Agreement Between the Government of the Republic of the Philippines and the Government of the United States of America Regarding the Treatment of United States Armed Forces Visiting the Philippines, February 10, 1998.

[7] Green and Poling, 2020. The five locations are Cesar Basa Air Base, Fort Magsaysay Military Reservation, Lumbia Air Base, Antonio Bautista Air Base, and Mactan Benito Ebuen Air Base.

and local civilian contractors to enhance joint interoperability capabilities.[8] Such capabilities would invariably be used in an actual contingency in the region. The agreement also allows the U.S. military to leave behind defense articles on completion of operations from EDCA bases, which would facilitate the prepositioning of material in the event of a contingency in the area.[9]

However, there are limitations to how much EDCA can facilitate rapid access to the U.S. military in a conflict. For example, the Philippine government still has to sign off on any U.S. government request for use of an EDCA facility, which can be time-consuming.[10] Second, most of the EDCA sites are not equipped with the kind of supporting infrastructure necessary to enable most types of high-intensity U.S. military operations.[11] Therefore, while EDCA offers sites and capabilities that would otherwise not be available to the U.S. military, there are constraints on their rapid and efficient use.

Finally, the Philippines has, in the past, offered its bases and ports to U.S. military personnel to support regional operations. Philippine bases have been used as logistic hubs for refueling, transport, and maintenance of U.S. military assets during the Vietnam War and during humanitarian assistance and disaster relief (HA/DR) contingencies in Southeast Asia. For example, bases in the Philippines were used for multinational relief efforts after the 2004 Indian Ocean tsunami and the 2013 Typhoon Haiyan.[12]

Evaluating the Framework for Conflict-Phase Access Decisions in the Philippines

Question 1: Would Granting the United States Conflict-Phase Access Affect the Leader or the Regime's Political Survival?

Three key factors would likely play a role in Philippine conflict-phase access decisions related to this question:

1. Philippine domestic public opinion on the U.S.-Philippines security alliance
2. the public's views of China
3. the leadership's preferences on the balance between the U.S. and China.

On the first factor, the Philippine leadership would likely consider the public's opinion on the U.S.-Philippine security alliance and on existing U.S. military presence or security cooperation activities. Historically, the Philippine public has held a very positive view of the

---

[8] Interview with U.S. government official, April 31, 2022.

[9] Interview with U.S. SME on the Philippines, April 31, 2022.

[10] Interview with U.S. government official, May 19, 2022.

[11] Interview with U.S. government official, May 19, 2022.

[12] Dan Lamothe, "Everyone Hates U.S. Bases in Asia—Until Disaster Strikes," *Foreign Policy*, November 12, 2013.

United States in general. As Table 4.1 illustrates, polls consistently show highly favorable views of the United States, compared with those of the PRC.

The Philippine public is also generally supportive of U.S. military presence in the country. A Pew Research Center survey in 2017 found that the majority (75 percent) supported a U.S. military presence in the Philippines and that the United States would (68 percent) and should (58 percent) come to the country's aid in the event of a serious military conflict with China.[13] As shown in Table 4.2, another survey conducted annually from 2018 to 2020 found similar results about views of the U.S. military presence in the Philippines, although with slightly less positive views of the U.S. government and the American people in general. That same survey found views of the Chinese government to be at even lower levels than the Pew survey did.[14] Additionally, the Philippine armed forces have a more traditional, pro-American stance and would likely support increased American military presence and cooperation.[15] Strong public support for the U.S. military and positive views of the U.S.-Philippines security alliance suggest the potential for the public to support U.S. military access if a regional conflict erupted, particularly one that might threaten Philippine territory.

TABLE 4.1

Philippines Favorability Ratings of the United States and China, 2013, 2018

	Favorable Views (2013)	Favorable Views (2018)	Unfavorable Views (2018)	Unfavorable Views (2018)
United States (%)	85	78	13	18
China (%)	48	55	48	40

SOURCE: Poushter and Bishop, 2017.

TABLE 4.2

Philippine Favorability Ratings of the United States and China, 2018–2020

Favorable views of	2018	2019	2020
U.S. military presence (%)	76	76	70
U.S. government (%)	60	62	56
U.S. people (%)	62	64	61
Chinese government (%)	33	20	17

SOURCE: Allen et al., undated.

---

[13] Jacob Poushter and Caldwell Bishop, "People in the Philippines Still Favor U.S. Over China, but Gap Is Narrowing," Pew Research Center, September 21, 2017.

[14] Michael Allen, Michael E. Flynn, Carla Martinez Machain, and Andrew Stravers, "Survey on the Political, Economic, and Social Effects of the United States' Overseas Military Presence, 2018–2020," webpage, Minerva Research Initiative Project, undated.

[15] Harold et al., 2019, p. 295.

However, it is also possible that the level of public support for U.S. military access might vary by the type of access the U.S. military requests. Several interviewees noted that the Philippine population and leadership might support U.S. access requests that involve capabilities that would assist the U.S. and Philippine military in countering China in the areas that directly affect Philippine territory—such as the SCS. However, U.S. access for combat operations for other contingencies not directly involving Philippine interests, such as Taiwan, would likely not enjoy the same level of public support because this type of access would increase the risk to the Philippines of Chinese retaliatory attacks.[16] One interviewee hypothesized that, in a Taiwan contingency, the Philippines might initially grant overflight access but would wait to see how the conflict unfolded before granting further access.[17]

The second factor is the Philippine public's views of China. The public in general holds negative views about China's role in regional affairs and views China as a potential threat to Philippine territory and security interests. The public's perspective that China is a possible threat to Philippine security interests appears to stem largely from China's coercive behavior toward the Philippines over the territorial disputes in the SCS.[18] For example, in polling by the ISEAS–Yusof Ishak Institute in Singapore in 2021, 87 percent of Filipinos considered Chinese encroachments in the Philippines' exclusive economic zone (EEZ) to be their top security concern in the SCS.[19] Given a hypothetical requirement to ally with either the United States or China in a SCS conflict, the same percentage chose the United States.[20] Furthermore, three recent RAND reports on regional perceptions of China found that the population of the Philippines has historically harbored negative views of China and the Chinese Communist Party.[21] In addition to China's coercive behavior in the SCS, such negative views also originate in the historical context of China's support of communist insurgencies in the Philippines during the Cold War. These negative views remain today among most Filipinos.[22]

The negative views of China might also play a role in the Philippine public's expectations for its leadership to act if Philippine territory is threatened in the SCS in a conflict. For

---

[16] Interview with U.S. government official, May 19, 2022; interview with U.S. SME on the Philippines, April 1, 2022.

[17] Interview with U.S. government official, April 29, 2022.

[18] Joshua Kurlantzick, "Duterte's Ingratiating Approach to China Has Been a Bust," Council on Foreign Relations, June 16, 2021; Consuelo Marquez, "Most Pinoys Do Not Agree Chinese Gov't Has Good Intentions for PH," Inquirer.net, April 5, 2019.

[19] Marquez, 2019.

[20] Marquez, 2019.

[21] See, for example, Michael J. Mazarr, Derek Grossman, Jeffrey W. Hornung, Jennifer D. P. Moroney, Shawn Cochran, Ashley L. Rhoades, and Andrew Stravers, *U.S. Major Combat Operations in the Indo-Pacific: Partner and Ally Views*, RAND Corporation, RR-A967-2, 2023; Lin et al., 2020; Harold et al., 2019, pp. 298–299.

[22] Nick Aspinwall, "'We Are Filipinos, and We Hate China': China's Influence in the Philippines, and Backlash Against Tsinoys," China Project, June 6, 2019.

example, given negative views among most Filipinos toward China, if the Philippine president decided not to grant the United States access in a contingency with China, resulting in China taking over Philippine territory in the SCS or threatening other security interests, the political blowback might be strong enough to affect his or her political standing and future reelection prospects.

The third factor that might be influential in Philippine leaders' decisionmaking on access for this question is the leadership's historical preference to balance between the United States and China, attempting to protect Philippine interests while not choosing sides—a position that has been harder to maintain with increased U.S.-China competition in the region and increased Chinese coercion in the SCS.[23] The rise in U.S.-China tensions and in Chinese assertiveness in the SCS territorial disputes has made how the Philippine leadership approaches relations with the United States and China a politically fraught issue.[24] For example, during the past six years of his administration, President Duterte attempted to pivot away from the United States toward China. However, his approach ultimately failed to reduce tensions in the SCS or result in the influx of investment for infrastructure projects to the Philippines that China promised.[25]

Given the lack of results, Duterte came under domestic political pressure to back away from the China pivot, resulting in him reinstating the VFA, which he had previously threatened to revoke.[26] President Ferdinand Marcos, Jr., who took office in June 2020, faces a similar political balancing act, and has so far sought to protect Philippine security and economic interests through the diplomatic relationship with China, while also pushing back on Chinese coerciveness in the SCS where feasible. For example, in May 2023, Philippines and Chinese leaders discussed fishing rights in the SCS, and Marcos pushed for a direct communication line with China to help prevent a conflict.[27] In June 2023, Marcos stated that the Philippines will continue to build ties with China and that Manila is not shifting away from Beijing toward the United States—highlighting his efforts to balance Philippine relations with the United States and China.[28]

Elite preferences can also play a role in how Philippine leaders approach China and whether they support the U.S.-Philippine alliance. Many Philippine leaders have, or have had, personal and business ties to China and the Chinese Communist Party—including President

[23] International Crisis Group, *The Philippines' Dilemma: How to Manage Tensions in the South China Sea*, Asia Report, No. 316, December 2, 2021b, p. 1.

[24] Julius Cesar Trajano, "US-Philippines: Resetting the Security Alliance?" commentary, S. Rajaratnam School of International Studies, February 24, 2021.

[25] Yen Nee Lee, "Philippine President Duterte's China Pivot Hasn't Reduced Tensions in the South China Sea," CNBC, December 26, 2021.

[26] Cliff Venzon, "Duterte Struggles to Sell His China Pivot at Home" Nikkei Asia, October 9, 2019.

[27] "Philippines, China to Discuss Fishing Rights in South China Sea, Marcos Says," Reuters, May 1, 2023.

[28] Andreo Calonzo, "Philippines Isn't Shifting Away from China, Marcos Says," Bloomberg, June 8, 2023.

Marcos.[29] If, for example, several key cabinet members of the Philippines, or the family of the sitting Philippine president, had significant personal business ties with Chinese businesses during the period of conflict between China and the United States, there might be voices within the Philippine government advocating not to involve the Philippines further in a conflict with China by opening up Philippine bases to the U.S. military.[30] However, despite these elite preferences, it is likely that public opinion, as discussed earlier, would continue to constrain the leadership's approach to either country.

What factors specific to the conflict might shape the decisions? Beyond the three components discussed earlier, the Philippine leadership might also consider specific conflict characteristics that would affect leaders' political standing if they granted or refused U.S. access in conflict. For example, a conflict that specifically threatens Philippine territorial interests in the SCS, which is a top issue for the Philippine public according to opinion polls, might increase the likelihood of Manila granting the United States access.[31]

The willingness of the Philippines to support U.S. operations in a regional conflict will also likely depend on the scale of Chinese attacks against the United States and its allies and partners. A conflict that has a high number of U.S. casualties, for example, might place political pressure to grant access on a Philippine leader who has forged closer ties to the United States and emphasized the importance of the U.S.-Philippine security alliance to other leaders and the Philippine public.[32] Refusing to grant access in this case might reflect poorly on Philippine leaders' intentions and priorities for the U.S.-Philippine security alliance and might also affect Philippine regional standing.

Question 2: Would Granting the United States Conflict-Phase Access Affect the Country's Direct Security Position?

Three factors would likely inform Philippine leadership assessments of this question:

1. the Philippine leadership's assessment of its national security interests and how U.S. capabilities or access might help it in defending these interests
2. the relative weakness of the Philippine military and lack of domestic defense capabilities if China retaliated

---

[29] David Engel, "How Far Will Bongbong Marcos Tilt the Philippines Towards China?" ASPI Strategist, May 20, 2022.

[30] Interview with U.S. government official, April 29, 2022. For one scenario on how China cultivates personal ties with Philippine political elites, see Alvin Camba, "China's Bet on Sara Duterte Pays Off," Nikkei Asia, May 15, 2022.

[31] Brenda Tan, "Friend or Foe? Explaining the Philippines' China Policy in the South China Sea," E-International Relations, August 10, 2020.

[32] The point about a highly kinetic conflict resulting in high numbers of U.S. and allied casualties was emphasized by SMEs and U.S. government officials RAND spoke with (interview with U.S. SME on the Philippines, March 25, 2022; interview with U.S. government official, May 19, 2022).

3. the Philippine leadership's assessment of the risk-benefit calculus of maintaining a security alliance with the United States with the retaliatory risk from an increasingly militarily capable China.

On the first factor, official Philippine documents, such as the National Defense Strategy, published in 2019, indicate the Philippines' primary national security interests to be: "1) safeguard and preserve national sovereignty and territorial integrity; 2) ensure maritime and airspace security; and 3) strengthen international relations."[33] The National Defense Strategy also discusses the importance of three mission sets within these interests, including a focus on maritime and air defense, cybersecurity, and security cooperation.[34] The strategy's emphasis on preserving national sovereignty and territorial integrity, as well as on maritime and air defense, likely reflects leadership's priorities in deciding whether to grant the United States conflict-phase access. This could indicate that, in response to threats that affect its territorial or maritime integrity, for example, when territorial disputes are involved over the Scarborough Shoal and the Spratly Islands in the SCS, the Philippines might react more strongly than to other national security concerns, particularly given domestic pressure to respond to Chinese aggression in these areas (as discussed in Question 1). As one interviewee noted, the likelihood of the Philippines granting the United States access depends on whether the conflict directly involves Philippine interests.[35] If the conflict involved a border dispute in India, for example, the Philippines likely would not involve itself by granting access. If the conflict involved the Spratly Islands, the country might grant access in return for U.S. help defending its territory.[36] The apparent Philippine emphasis on direct threats to territory as a reason to grant access could mean that Manila would hesitate to grant access in a conflict involving Japan or Taiwan, unless, in the leadership's assessment, a Chinese victory over the United States in these scenarios would presage a threat to Philippine territory through a new regional order that would lend itself to Chinese expansion in the SCS.

Second, limited domestic military capability would likely factor into the Philippine leadership's assessment of whether granting the United States access would improve the country's security position. Until relatively recently, the Philippines had focused its military resources on internal security given domestic terrorism issues.[37] However, over the past decade, an increasingly aggressive China with modern military capabilities that has engaged in coercive

---

[33] Mico A. Galang, "The Philippines' National Defense Strategy—Analysis," *Eurasia Review*, December 20, 2019; see also Mazarr et al., 2023, pp. 61–68.

[34] Galang, 2019; Department of National Defense, Republic of the Philippines, *National Defense Strategy 2018–2022*, 2018.

[35] Interview with U.S. government official, May 19, 2022.

[36] Interview with U.S. government official, May 19, 2022.

[37] For example, the secessionist movement in Mindanao and the terrorist threat from the Abu Sayyaf Group remain today. See Charmaine G. Misalucha, Julio S. Amador III, "U.S.-Philippines Security Ties: Building New Foundations?" *Asian Politics & Policy*, Vol. 8, No. 1, January 2016.

efforts in the SCS has changed this calculus, directly affecting the types of defense capabilities the country has sought to procure, including naval frigates, maritime patrol aircraft, and fighter jets to secure the Philippines' coastline and maritime territory in the SCS.[38]

Despite this, the Philippine military still lacks the capacity and capability to defend the country's territory and ensure maritime and airspace security in any potential conflict with China.[39] The Philippines Armed Forces rely mostly on secondhand equipment from other countries, loans, and grants.[40] According to interviewees and secondary-source analysis, the military's primary shortcomings are air combat; sea and air logistics and transport; maritime surveillance and patrol; and command, control, communications, computers, intelligence, surveillance, and reconnaissance.[41] In particular, the country's navy has suffered from a lack of modernization; as a result, the navy does not have the capacity to defend the Philippine coastline or disputed maritime territory.[42] These gaps are difficult to fill given the current lack of funding—requiring the Philippines to rely on the United States and other partners, such as Australia and Japan, for improvements to its military capabilities.[43]

This lack of domestic defense capacity has likely been a factor in the Philippine leadership's calibration of how far to go in confronting China on the SCS territorial claims and would likely make the country more reluctant to support U.S. access in a conflict unless the United States was clear that it would defend the Philippines if China escalated the conflict to include attacks on Philippine territory.[44] For example, the Duterte administration dampened the contentious rhetoric on the SCS and sought closer bilateral ties with China.[45] While pursuing closer ties with China could be viewed as particular to Duterte's personal goals, his administration's approach over the past six years of his administration was also consistent with a logical caution, given the Philippines' military weakness—caution that President

---

[38] Janes, "Southeast Asia, Armed Forces of the Philippines Assessment 2021," Sentinel Security Assessment, February 10, 2021.

[39] The National Defense Strategy is stark in assessing the Philippine military's limitations, stating that it is "one of the weakest in Asia," which raises "doubt [about Manila's] ability to protect and defend the [country's] sovereignty and territorial integrity." See Mico Galang, "PacNet #61—The South China Sea and the Philippines' National Security Strategy," Pacific Forum, August 28, 2018.

[40] Harold et al., 2019, pp. 298–299.

[41] Lukasz Stach, "The Philippines Maritime Forces and Its Maritime Military Power Projection Capabilities: Unfulfilled Ambitions?" *Defense & Security Analysis*, Vol. 37, No. 4, 2021.

[42] For an assessment on the Philippine Navy and defense expenditures, see Stach, 2021.

[43] Janes, 2021.

[44] The United States and the Philippines have a mutual defense treaty; however, the treaty is ambiguous on what it obligates the U.S. to do. For example, the treaty is unclear on what the United States is willing to protect (e.g., the Philippines' territorial waters, its EEZ, its larger maritime claims in the SCS, etc. This ambiguity has led to uncertainty in the Philippine leadership as to whether and how the U.S. would come to its aid if China attacked Philippine territory or forces in the SCS. See Felix C. Chang, "The U.S.-Philippines Mutual Defense Treaty and Philippine External Defense Forces," Foreign Policy Research Institute, August 3, 2021.

[45] Janes, 2021.

Marcos is also likely to have. On the other hand, the lack of domestic defenses might also make the Philippine leadership more willing to host U.S. capabilities if the United States would clearly be willing to use those capabilities to protect Philippine territory or if not granting access would negatively affect the U.S.-Philippine security alliance to such an extent that it would reduce the likelihood of future U.S. assistance.[46] The United States pulling defense capabilities away from the Philippines or reducing security cooperation could increase the Philippines' vulnerability to Chinese military coercion.

Third, Philippine leaders also appear to consider whether granting access will make the Philippines a direct target in a conflict and how to balance the benefits of the U.S.-Philippine relationship with the retaliatory risk from China. One interviewee stated that the Philippine leadership has considered access decisions in peacetime through the lens of whether the United States can offer the Philippines enough—either through agreements or military capabilities—to ensure the country's defense if it became a target in a conflict.[47] During the Cold War, for example, U.S. security guarantees through the U.S.-led alliance structure in Asia, combined with economic incentives to keep bases in the country, were enough to satisfy the Philippine leadership's security concerns and allow U.S. basing access (the economic benefits of U.S. military presence in the Philippines are discussed in more detail in Question 5).[48]

The type and level of access the United States requests would potentially affect the leadership's assessment of whether granting access would increase the risk of retaliation from China and whether the capabilities and access granted, combined with the U.S. security alliance, would be enough to offset the additional risk for Manila. Several interviewees stated that, in a conflict, the most likely form of access the leadership would support is ISR and overflight, which would still be viewed as supporting the United States and the alliance but would invite less risk of Chinese attack.[49] However, as discussed previously, much would depend on the location and stakes of the conflict in terms of how much risk Manila would be willing to take by allowing more aggressive or kinetic types of access, such as U.S. combat operations and deployment of capabilities to the Philippines that could target Chinese forces in the SCS.

What Factors Specific to the Conflict Might Shape the Decisions?

The primary conflict-specific characteristic, discussed earlier, is whether the conflict involves China directly attacking Philippine territory. Several interviewees noted that the Philippine

---

[46] Interview with U.S. SME on the Philippines, March 25, 2022.

[47] Interview with U.S. SME on the Philippines, March 25, 2022.

[48] Interview with U.S. SME on the Philippines, March 25, 2022. The Philippines was reported to have told the United States that it would grant access if the Ukraine conflict spilled over to Asia. However, because an expansion of the Russia-Ukraine conflict would be unlikely to involve direct attacks on the Philippines, the country would clearly not be a target, so granting access would likely be a symbolic gesture of opposition to Russian aggression or of support for Washington more than anything else. See Sebastian Strangio, "Philippines Pledges to Back US if Ukraine Conflict Spreads to Asia," *The Diplomat*, March 11, 2022a.

[49] Interview with U.S. SME on the Philippines, April 1, 2022; interview with U.S. government official, April 29, 2022.

leadership is not particularly concerned about a widespread Chinese attack of the Philippines home islands, although a localized attack on U.S. and Philippine military facilities or forces is more of a concern in a military conflict.[50] If an attack occurred, the country would likely grant the United States access to defend Philippine territory and counter Chinese military operations. Another consideration that follows from this is whether China has directly attacked other U.S. allies that have granted access in the conflict, which could highlight the risk to Philippine security and territory if Manila granted similar access.[51] For example, China attacking U.S. bases in Japan or broader Japanese military infrastructure that supports U.S. military operations could intensify the Philippine leadership's assessment that the home islands could become a target if the leadership granted the United States access and could reduce the likelihood of access being granted.[52]

Question 3: Would Granting the United States Conflict-Phase Access Affect the Outcome of the Conflict?

Philippine leadership would likely consider three factors in addressing this question:

1. the leadership's assessment of the country's location relative to the location of the conflict
2. the leadership's assessment the importance of access to the U.S. ability to conduct military operations in a regional contingency
3. the leadership's assessment of the type of access that the United States is requesting and the importance (or lack of importance) of the U.S-Philippine alliance to Philippine security.

The first factor is the country's location relative to the location of the conflict and its importance to the U.S. ability to conduct military operations in a regional contingency. According to interviewees, the Philippine leadership is aware that the country is in a desirable geographic location for U.S. conflict-phase operations—particularly air operations—for both SCS and Taiwan contingencies. The leadership is also aware that the U.S. ability to operate from the Philippines could drastically affect the outcome of a regional contingency if the United States did not have to flow as many naval and air forces from locations farther away or outside the region.[53] The Philippines would likely watch Japan and Singapore to see whether they grant or expand access to U.S. forces and how that might affect the operational

---

[50] Interview with U.S. SME on the Philippines, March 25, 2022.

[51] Interview with U.S. SME on the Philippines, April 21, 2022.

[52] Discussion with U.S. SME on the Philippines, March 25, 2022.

[53] Interview with U.S. SME on the Philippines, March 25, 2022; interview with U.S. government official, May 19, 2022.

outcomes. However, the Philippines' unique location would be critical for U.S. operations in a regional conflict, meaning that granting access would always add operational value.

U.S. access to the Philippines is also important for logistics in a regional conflict, including the ability to preposition U.S. defense materials and equipment, which is part of the EDCA agreement.[54] In February 2023, the United States and the Philippines designated four additional sites under the agreement.[55] The new facilities would support U.S. and Philippine responses to humanitarian and climate-related disasters in the Philippines, as well as to other joint security challenges.[56] Some regional analysis also highlights the Philippine perspective that allowing U.S. forces more access through EDCA could enhance Philippine combat preparedness for a regional conflict and extend the Philippines' military power projection further into the SCS, which is a key national security interest.[57]

Second, the type of access that the United States was requesting would also likely be a key consideration. In a regional conflict, the Philippines might want to hedge against retaliation from China if Beijing were the victor in a regional contingency, while also remaining close to the United States. This might lead Manila to take a middle-ground approach, granting certain types of access to U.S. forces if the leadership thinks that the capabilities are enough to support the U.S.-Philippine alliance and help the United States and its allies win the conflict and if Philippine territorial interests are not involved. In this case, Manila might grant access to such capabilities as prepositioning, logistics, and ISR but preclude U.S. combat missions directly from its territory.[58] As discussed earlier, the EDCA allows U.S. forces to preposition military supplies, equipment, and materiel, which U.S. forces could potentially access in wartime.[59] The U.S. military has already been assisting the Philippine armed forces with enhancing ISR capabilities—most recently by delivering Scan Eagle unmanned aircraft systems—so there is a precedent for U.S.-Philippine military cooperation on ISR capabilities that could be maintained in a conflict.[60]

---

[54] See Agreement Between the Government of the United States of America and the Government of the Republic of the Philippines, 2014. For a description of U.S.-Philippine security agreements and cooperation, see Thomas Lunn, Christina L. Arabia, and Ben Dolven, *The Philippines: Background and U.S. Relations*, Congressional Research Service, R47055, March 28, 2022, pp. 12–13.

[55] Rene Acosta, "U.S., Philippines Add Four More Sites to EDCA Military Basing Agreement," *USNI News*, February 2, 2023; DoD, "Philippines, U.S. Announce Four New EDCA Sites," press release, February 1, 2023.

[56] Acosta, 2023; DoD, 2023.

[57] For example, one analysis of EDCA quoted a Philippine official as stating that "Manila seeks to promote its effective control in the West Philippine Sea by maximizing its geopolitical projection," which EDCA would help with (Joseph Hammond, "Philippine, U.S. Forces Improve Defense Cooperation," Indo-Pacific Defense Forum, November 9, 2021).

[58] Interview with U.S. SME on the Philippines, April 21, 2022.

[59] Acosta, 2023; DoD, 2023.

[60] USINDOPACOM, "U.S. Military Delivers Advanced Unmanned Aerial System to Philippine Air Force," press release, October 14, 2021.

Interviewees noted that asking Manila to provide access for combat operations would be difficult unless China attacked Philippine territory directly. Interviewees were uncertain about whether the Philippine leadership would consider an attack on a U.S. base in the Philippines as attacking Philippine territory and whether that would be sufficient to draw the Philippines into the conflict by granting additional access for combat operations.[61] Several interviewees did think that a Chinese attack on Philippine territorial interests in the SCS might be enough for Manila to support granting the access as long as it was clear that the United States would use some of its operations to defend Philippine interests in the SCS.[62]

Third, the Philippine leadership's assessment of the importance (or lack of importance) of the U.S-Philippine alliance to its country's security could factor into the decisionmaking process for this question. If the Philippine leadership assesses the alliance to be vital to Philippine interests, particularly over the long term after a conflict has ended, it might be more willing to grant access to assist the United States in winning the conflict, knowing the risks to the relationship that could occur if the United States were to lose after Manila had refused access. The Philippines presents a complex challenge in this regard, given current and past leadership views of the U.S. alliance and Philippine security interests. President Duterte's ambitions to balance Philippine relations between the United States and China, his pivot away from the United States, and his lack of support for the alliance resulted in challenges for the U.S.-Philippines alliance and the existing security agreements, for example. Past Philippine presidents had been publicly positive toward the alliance with the United States, however. In a joint press conference with President Barack Obama in 2014, for example, President Benigno Aquino III described the United States as a "key ally, a strategic partner, and a reliable friend of the Philippines" and that the alliance between the two countries "has been a cornerstone of peace and stability in the Asia-Pacific region for more than 60 years."[63] How President Marcos balances the U.S.-Philippines alliance with relations with China in an era increasing U.S.-China tensions remains to be seen.

While at times expressing frustration about being considered the junior partner of the alliance, almost all previous Philippine presidents, including Ferdinand Marcos, Sr., have publicly pledged commitment to the mutual defense treaty and the mutual responsibility of coming to each other's defense in the event of military aggression or attack.[64] However, the election of Duterte in 2016 and his anti-American posture, fueled by perceived slights by U.S.

---

[61] Interview with U.S. SME on the Philippines, March 25, 2022; interview with U.S. SME on the Philippines, April 21, 2022.

[62] Interview with U.S. SME on the Philippines, April 21, 2022; interview with U.S. government official, April 29, 2022.

[63] Barack Obama and Benigno Aquino III, "Remarks by President Obama and President Benigno Aquino III of the Philippines in Joint Press Conference," transcript, White House, Office of the Press Secretary, April 28, 2014.

[64] Interview with U.S. SME on the Philippines, March 25, 2022; interview with U.S. SME on the Philippines, April 1, 2022.

politicians and coupled with his strong anticolonialist stance, saw the trust at the leadership level in the U.S.-Philippine alliance dip to one of its lowest points in recent memory.[65] Duterte frequently curried favor with the PRC and, for a brief period in 2020–2021, threatened to abrogate the VFA, which provides the legal justification for U.S. troops to operate and be temporarily stationed in the Philippines.[66] While support for the alliance does not necessarily guarantee that the Philippines will grant access, it could drive a greater Philippine interest in ensuring that the United States prevails in a regional conflict, which could translate into a greater willingness to provide the United States the access it needs to do so.

What Factors Specific to the Conflict Might Shape the Decisions?

Specific characteristics of the conflict that might influence the Philippine decisionmaking process for this question include whether the conflict becomes protracted such that the Philippines might be more willing to grant the U.S. access if it determines that this would bring about a favorable outcome for the United States, if the leadership is supportive of the U.S.-Philippine security alliance, and if the leadership views the access as essential for the Philippines' long-term security. The location of the conflict would also likely factor into Philippine assessments of the U.S. ability to counter Chinese military operations. If the conflict is in the SCS, for example, the Philippines' geographic proximity would greatly help U.S. military operations and contribute to a U.S. victory.

Question 4: Would Granting the United States Conflict-Phase Access Affect, or be Affected by, Regional Decisions Regarding Granting Similar Access?

For this question, the Philippine leadership would likely consider two key factors:

1. whether other U.S. treaty allies in Southeast Asia, such as Thailand, also granted or (in Japan's case) expanded U.S. access in a conflict and whether close partners, such as Singapore, grant access in a conflict
2. the level of ASEAN support for the United States in the conflict.

For the first factor, the Philippine leadership would likely look at how other key U.S. allies and partners assess the risk of granting access in a conflict and assess regional support for granting or expanding U.S. access in the Philippines.[67] Thailand granting the United States

---

[65] Duterte even stated in July 2017 that he would "never" visit the "lousy U.S." during or after his term, after hearing of criticism from a U.S. congressman. See Kristine Phillips, "Philippines's Duterte Vows Not to Come to the U.S.: 'I've Seen America, and It's Lousy," *Washington Post*, July 22, 2017.

[66] Xave Gregorio, "Duterte Threatens to Terminate VFA If US Does Not Reverse Cancellation of Dela Rosa's Visa," CNN Philippines, January 23, 2020.

[67] Interview with U.S. SME on the Philippines, April 1, 2022; interview with U.S. SME on the Philippines, April 21, 2022.

access, for example—even if in the limited form of overflight access—might signal a high enough level of regional support for the Philippines to follow suit, which could also factor into Philippine domestic political support for granting access. The same logic may be applied if Japan, Australia, or a nontreaty ally (but a close U.S. partner, such as Singapore) were to grant expanded U.S. military access.

A second factor that might influence the Philippine leadership's access decision is the level of support for the United States in the conflict from ASEAN, which could help bolster Manila's regional standing with Southeast Asian countries if it decided to support U.S. operations in a conflict. Because of its mutual defense treaty with the United States, the Philippines has historically balanced the opinions of ASEAN members against its obligations to the United States.[68] At times, the Philippines has aligned itself with U.S. interests and objectives when ASEAN is split on a particular issue, such as when the Philippines supported the U.S.-led Operation Desert Storm or Operation Enduring Freedom, despite opposition from some ASEAN members.[69] Signals or statements of support for the United States from ASEAN members during a conflict would presumably exert some degree of influence over the Philippine access decision.

Another aspect of ASEAN that may influence Philippine access decisionmaking is which country is the chair of ASEAN during the time of the conflict.[70] There is evidence, for example, that the chair of ASEAN has been able to influence the type of rhetoric in official ASEAN Chairman Statements on politically sensitive issues, such as Myanmar and the SCS.[71] If the Philippines were the chair during the conflict, Philippine diplomats may be able to persuade fence-sitting members to allow language in ASEAN joint statements condemning China's actions or use of force or increasing support for U.S. operations. As mentioned earlier, such language may signal a level of regional support and would also, in theory, provide a degree of domestic political cover for the Philippines to grant the U.S. military access to Philippine bases. If the chair is a more neutral country, such as Malaysia or Indonesia, the Philippines may have a more difficult time convincing ASEAN members to support U.S. operations against China through joint statements and messaging. If neutral ASEAN members (or the chair), decide to support China or not to support the United States, the Philippines would likely find it more difficult to grant access without regional support. Of course, the stakes are high in a conflict and, given concerns over potential Chinese retaliation, finding a degree of ASEAN consensus to support the United States will be difficult regardless.

---

[68] Donald E. Weatherbee, "The Philippines and ASEAN: Options for Aquino," *Asian Survey*, Vol. 27, No. 12, December 1987.

[69] Nattapat Limsiritong, Apiradee Springall, and Onkanya Rojanawanichkij, "The Difficulty of ASEAN Decision Making Mode on South China Sea Dispute: The ASEAN Charter Perspective," *Asian Political Science Review*, Vol. 3, No. 1, 2019.

[70] The current chair of ASEAN is Cambodia. See Charles Dunst, "What to Expect of Cambodia as ASEAN Chair," Center for Strategic and International Studies, November 4, 2021.

[71] David Hutt, "Has the ASEAN Chair Become Too Powerful?" *The Diplomat*, January 14, 2022.

What Factors Specific to the Conflict Might Shape the Decisions?

The location of the conflict might affect the Philippine leadership's decisionmaking on access for this question. If the conflict is more focused on the SCS and involves China militarily taking over disputed territory, for example, other countries in the region might support the Philippines' decision to grant the United States access or even follow up by granting access as well, if they believe that granting the U.S. military access might help protect their territories or deter China. Another characteristic might be who the other countries perceive to be the primary aggressor in the conflict. If regional states believe China initiated the conflict or was the primary aggressor, for example, it is likely they would speak out against China's actions or support U.S. operations, potentially providing the Philippines with greater regional support for granting access.[72]

Question 5: Would Granting the United States Conflict-Phase Access Affect the Economic Prosperity of the Country?

The Philippine leadership would likely consider two factors for this question when deciding whether to grant conflict-phase access:

1. the country's reliance on China as a trade and investment partner and the scope of potential retaliation during and after the conflict if the Philippines granted the United States access in a conflict
2. the country's economic relationship with the United States and the potential economic benefits of expanding U.S. military access.

For the first factor, the Philippine leadership would likely consider the country's bilateral trade with China and the degree to which Chinese economic retaliation during and after the conflict could affect the Philippine economy. China has been the Philippines' top trading partner since 2012; China-Philippines trade topped $98 billion in 2021.[73] By comparison, the Philippines' trade with the United States, major U.S. allies, and Taiwan combined was only around $80 billion in 2021 (see Table 4.3).[74]

The amount of trade between China and the Philippines is one example of China's economic influence over the country. In addition, Beijing has provided, or pledged to provide, substantial funding for infrastructure projects to the Philippines under China's Belt and Road Initiative (BRI). The Philippines is a member of the Asian Infrastructure Investment Bank

---

[72] For a discussion of how Southeast Asia might react to conflict in the region involving China, see International Crisis Group, *Competing Visions of International Order in the South China Sea*, Asia Report No. 315, November 29, 2021a.

[73] Lin et al., 2020. Also, Ralf Rivas and Sofia Tomacruz, "How Duterte's Love Affair with China Shaped the PH Economy," Rappler, July 21, 2021.

[74] Office of the U.S. Trade Representative, "Philippines," webpage, undated-b.

TABLE 4.3

Philippines Total Bilateral Trade, by Country

Year	China	United States	Japan	Australia	Taiwan	South Korea	Germany	UK	France
2012	47.0	15.0	16.80	1.8	11.0	11.5	4.9	1.0	1.9
2013	47.2	15.8	17.60	1.6	12.0	12.5	5.4	0.9	2.5
2014	54.9	14.7	19.50	1.7	11.6	13.4	6.3	1.0	3.1
2015	56.9	16.4	19.14	1.3	9.3	11.6	5.7	0.9	1.6
2016	59.2	16.4	21.90	1.5	10.9	10.5	5.4	1.1	1.8
2017	66.2	18.0	22.70	2.3	12.3	14.3	6.4	1.3	2.0
2018	70.7	18.9	20.90	2.0	11.4	15.6	7.4	1.3	2.7
2019	75.5	20.1	21.90	1.9	8.3	12.0	7.3	1.5	2.5
2020	75.2	18.8	18.15	1.8	7.8	10.2	6.0	1.0	1.1
2021	98.8	23.3	22.00	3.3	9.1	13.6	6.9	1.1	1.7

SOURCES: OEC, "Philippines/China," webpage, undated-e; U.S. Census Bureau, undated; World Bank, undated-c; JETRO, various years; Australian Government, Department of Foreign Affairs and Trade, undated; Bureau of Foreign Trade, Taiwan, undated; Korea Customs Service, undated, for export/import by country; German Federal Statistics Office, 2022; Office for National Statistics, 2022; UN, undated, trade data for Philippines.

NOTE: China includes Mainland China, Hong Kong, and Macau. Amounts are in billions of U.S. dollars.

(AIIB), which China uses to fund BRI projects. In 2016, AIIB funded several transportation and flood-control projects in Manila, and China signed 27 deals worth $24 billion to invest in Philippine infrastructure and energy projects. However, as of 2022, several of these had yet to begin.[75] China was also the Philippines' second-largest foreign investor in 2019, behind Singapore, with an estimated FDI of $1.7 billion.[76]

In addition to BRI funding, China has provided a small amount of medical assistance to the Philippines during the pandemic. For example, in May 2020, Beijing sent medical support and personal protective equipment worth $292,000 to Manila to assist with the COVID-19 pandemic, and China has provided 2.5 million doses of its vaccine to the Philippines.[77] Beyond funding and security assistance, China also boosts the Philippine economy through tourism. For example, in 2019, China was the second-largest source of tourists arriving in the

---

[75] Jonina A. Fernando, "China's Belt and Road Initiative in the Philippines," East West Center, December 16, 2020; Jason Koutsoukis and Cecilia Yap, "China Hasn't Delivered on Its $24 Billion Philippines Promise," Bloomberg, July 25, 2018.

[76] Department of Trade and Industry, Republic of the Philippines, "Philippines Invites Investments from China During CIFIT 2021," 2021a.

[77] Rommel C. Banlaoi, "Philippines-China Cooperation in South China Sea During Pandemic," *Eurasia Review*, May 12, 2020. See also Cecilia Yap, "Philippines Asks U.S. for Vaccine Help as China Tensions Grow," Bloomberg, April 11, 2021.

Philippines, with the top country for tourism to the Philippines being South Korea. Chinese tourists also spent more than $2.3 billion in the country in 2019.[78]

The Philippines' economic reliance on China would likely play a role in the leadership decisions on access by increasing concern over China's use of these economic levers to inflict retaliation on the Philippines, both during and after a conflict. China has relied on levers of economic power in the past to punish the Philippines for adopting policies antithetical to Chinese interests during peacetime.[79] For example, during the Scarborough Shoal dispute in 2012, China instituted quality control restrictions on mango, pineapple, and banana imports from the Philippines.[80] The restrictions cut off 30 percent of Philippines' total banana exports, resulting in economic hardship for the Filipino workers in that sector.[81] In addition, China curtailed tourist visits to the Philippines.[82] Given that China has used these economic levers to coerce the Philippines in the past and given the ties that Manila now has with Beijing's BRI and ongoing China-funded infrastructure projects, the Philippine leadership would likely worry about the scope of Chinese economic retaliation if the Philippines granted the United States access in a conflict, particularly if China ends up as the victor.

Perhaps the most important single economic factor that plays in favor of the United States is the number of remittances sent to the Philippines from individuals working in the United States. In 2021, overseas workers sent almost $13 billion in remittances to the Philippines from the United States.[83] This number is nearly six times higher than for the next nearest country, which is Singapore. Altogether, the remaining countries in the top five from which overseas workers send remittances back to the Philippines were all close American partners: Saudi Arabia, Japan, and the United Kingdom. In 2021, Mainland China and Hong Kong combined saw roughly $750 million in remittances flow back to the Philippines.[84] While total

---

[78] "Chinese Tourists Spend More Than $2.3b in Philippines in 2019," Xinhua, March 3, 2020. See also Philippines Department of Tourism, "Tourist Arrivals in the Philippines by Country of Residence, January–December 2019," table, February 12, 2020.

[79] Bonny Lin, Cristina L. Garafola, Bruce McClintock, Jonah Blank, Jeffrey W. Hornung, Karen Schwindt, Jennifer D. P. Moroney, Paul Orner, Dennis Borrman, Sarah W. Denton, and Jason Chambers, *Competition in the Gray Zone: Countering China's Coercion Against U.S. Allies and Partners in the Indo-Pacific*, RAND Corporation, RR-A594-1, 2022. See also Peter Harrell, Elizabeth Rosenberg, and Edoardo Saravalle, *China's Use of Coercive Economic Measures*, Center for New American Security, 2018.

[80] "China's New Complaint About Bugs in PHL Fruits Puzzles Agriculture Exec," GMA News Online, May 16, 2012. See Michael J. Green, Kathleen Hicks, Zack Cooper, John Schaus, and Jake Douglas, *Countering Coercion in Maritime Asia: The Theory and Practice of Gray Zone Deterrence*, Center for Strategic and International Studies, Rowman & Littlefield, May 9, 2017, pp. 95–98.

[81] "The China-Philippine Banana War," *Asia Sentinel*, June 6, 2012.

[82] "Philippines Seeks New Markets Amid Sea Dispute with China," Reuters, May 17, 2012.

[83] Department of Trade and Industry, Republic of the Philippines, "Trade and Investment QuickStats," 2021b.

[84] Bangko Sentral NG Pilipinas, "Statistics—External Accounts: Cash Remittances, by Country and by Source," webpage, May 2022.

trade with China still swamps that of the United States, its major allies, and Taiwan, remittances are a significant people-to-people connection and a large flow of money that stands in the United States' favor.[85]

For the second factor, the Philippine leadership would also consider the bilateral trade and investment relationship with the United States, as well as the possible economic benefits to the local economy from expanding U.S. military access and presence in the Philippines, particularly after the conflict ends. The Philippines has a robust economic relationship with the United States, although not as substantial as the one it has with China. In terms of bilateral trade, as Table 4.3 illustrates, U.S.-Philippine bilateral trade was $18 billion in 2020 and $23 billion in 2021. Philippine trade with the United States, its major allies, and Taiwan was $65 billion in 2020 and more than $80 billion in 2021, with almost $48 billion from major regional countries and $9 billion from major European Union allies in 2021. Still, this is significantly less trade than the Philippines conducted with China over the same two years, which amounted to $75 billion and $98 billion, respectively (see Table 4.3).[86] The United States was the Philippines' third-largest country supplier in 2020, with a 7-percent share of the country's imports. However, China holds the top position at 23 percent.[87] That said, the United States ranks among the top investors in the Philippines, with an estimated $6.9 billion in FDI 2019.[88]

The Philippine leadership would also potentially consider the value of hosting U.S. forces or facilities to the local economy. When they were operational, U.S. bases in the Philippines historically provided the local economy with substantial economic benefit, acting as a source of rent to the Philippine government in exchange for U.S. access and to compensate for the additional risk to Philippine security from hosting U.S. forces.[89] For example, in 1983, the United States pledged to compensate the Philippine government $900 million over a five-year period for the five U.S. bases operating there.[90] The current EDCA does not include this type of compensation agreement because it does not allow permanent U.S. military bases on Philippine soil. However, it is possible that the United States could pay rent for nonpermanent bases under an expanded agreement.[91] The Philippine government does benefit economically

[85] Bangko Sentral NG Pilipinas, 2022.

[86] OEC, undated-e.

[87] OEC, undated-e.

[88] International Trade Administration, "Philippines: Country Commercial Guide," webpage, U.S. Department of Commerce, July 25, 2022.

[89] William E. Berry, Jr., "The Effects of the U.S. Military Bases on the Philippine Economy," *Contemporary Southeast Asia*, Vol. 11, No. 4, March 1990.

[90] Daniel Druckman," Negotiating Miliary Base Rights with Spain, the Philippines, and Greece: Lessons Learned," Center for Conflict Analysis and Resolution, Occasional Paper 2, 1990, p. 2.

[91] Reynaldo Rudy Kristian Montolalu, and Anak Agung Banyu Perwita, "Philippine–US Defense Cooperation: The Implementation of 'The Enhanced Defense Cooperation Agreement' to Respond China's Assertiveness in the South China Sea (2010–2016)," *Journal Asia Pacific Studies*, Vol. 3, No. 1, January–June 2019.

from the EDCA through the provision of jobs and construction activities in the five bases, which involves DoD procurement of local goods, supplies, and labor.[92]

Beyond the direct financial implications of U.S. military bases, however, the U.S. government has supported the Philippines economically through foreign military financing and other forms of security assistance and military aid. The United States has allocated more than $4.5 billion in assistance to the Philippines in the past 20 years, some of which has gone toward HA/DR and building civilian infrastructure.[93]

President Duterte also used security assistance as leverage for U.S. military access to the Philippines in peacetime: In February 2021, Duterte stated that the United States would need to give more in security assistance if it wanted to maintain the VFA. He eventually backed away from this request and renewed the VFA.[94] While these are examples of U.S. military economic benefits to the Philippines in peacetime, it is reasonable to assume that aspects of these economic incentives, such as foreign military financing and security assistance funding, would continue in conflict, particularly if the United States were to have a larger military presence in the Philippines.

What Factors Specific to the Conflict Might Shape the Decisions?

The location of the conflict might factor into the Philippines' assessment of this question. If the conflict is in the SCS and directly threatens Philippine interests, Manila might be willing to grant access to protect its interests despite Chinese economic retaliation that would affect the economy. However, if the conflict takes place further afield, over a border dispute in India, for example, the Philippines might not want to face economic retaliation for a conflict that does not directly involve its territorial interests. Additionally, the stakes of the conflict to China might matter in terms of the Philippine leadership's assessment of the likelihood of Chinese economic retaliation postconflict if Manila assisted. If the conflict is over Taiwan—an existential issue for the Chinese Communist Party—the likelihood of postconflict economic retaliation, if China still had the economic influence, would be higher than it would be for a more limited conflict in the SCS—an important interest to China, but less important than Taiwan. The lower likelihood of Chinese economic retaliation in the SCS scenario, in addition to a direct impact on Philippine territorial interests, might increase the likelihood of Manila granting access. Finally, if the conflict is of high intensity and involves substantial regional economic disruption (for example, if China is blockaded), Manila might be more willing to grant access, given that China's ability to retaliate economically, during and, likely, postconflict, would be reduced.

---

[92] Department of Foreign Affairs, Republic of the Philippines, "Frequently Asked Questions on the Enhanced Defense Cooperation Agreement," April 28, 2014.

[93] U.S. Embassy in the Philippines, "U.S. Provides Php269 Million in New COVID-19 Assistance, Total Aid Exceeds Php470 Million," press release, April 22, 2020.

[94] Karen Lema, "Philippines Wants More Than 'Loose Change' for U.S. Troops Deal," Reuters, February 15, 2021.

How Might the Philippines' Decisions Vary Depending on the Types of Access Requested?

In addition to these factors, the Philippine response to U.S. access requests would potentially vary by the type of request. Granting access to U.S. requests for nonkinetic or lower-end capabilities, such as ISR, overflight, and logistics, would be easier for the Philippine leadership because the perception is that this type of access would invite less risk of kinetic retaliatory attack from China and would likely enjoy more support from the Philippine public, given the population's overall positive views toward the U.S.-Philippine security alliance. In addition, some of these capabilities—such as the U.S. ability to preposition wartime materiel and equipment in certain locations in the Philippines—are already part of the EDCA and so would be easier for the Philippine leadership to expand on.

Philippine leadership responses to U.S. access requests for higher-end kinetic capabilities, such as long-range fires, or direct combat operations from Philippine soil would likely depend on whether Philippine interests are directly involved or are under attack—such as an attack on territorial interests in the SCS or on Philippine soil. The Philippine leadership might also be more willing to grant access for higher-end capabilities to target Chinese forces or direct combat operations if the conflict is highly kinetic, resulting in significant U.S. and allied casualties. In this case, the Philippine leadership—particularly one that has supported the alliance with the United States and wants to see a U.S. victory—might be pressured to grant access for these types of capabilities. Granting access for higher-end capabilities would also potentially depend on whether the Philippine leadership thinks that the U.S. is providing enough in economic compensation or security benefits to offset the increased risk of Chinese attack or other retaliatory measures, such as Chinese economic coercion.

Summary

Despite being a U.S. ally, the question of whether the Philippines would grant the United States access in a conflict is complicated by various domestic, political, and regional dynamics. That said, several key insights arose from this analysis that point to several particular factors that the Philippine leadership would most likely consider in its conflict-phase access decisionmaking process.

First, the Philippine leadership's assessment of whether the U.S. military is likely to defend Philippine territory in a conflict would also potentially factor into the access decisionmaking process. Many of the interviewees we spoke with emphasized that Manila is uncertain whether the United States would defend Philippine territory in the SCS, for example, and this could negatively affect the leadership's willingness to grant the United States access in a conflict, absent a clear U.S. security guarantee to defend Philippine territory. Statements by Secretary Antony Blinken reaffirming U.S. commitment to defend Philippine forces in the SCS have likely somewhat mitigated this concern for Philippine leadership, at least in peacetime.[95] However, a question likely remains about how far U.S. forces will go to defend Philippine disputed territory in the SCS in a conflict, for example. Given that the Philippines is in an alliance with the United States, an additional consideration might be whether refusing access might degrade the alliance and reduce likelihood that the U.S. military would defend the Philippines in the future.

A second factor that the analysis highlights is the potential for Chinese economic retaliation, particularly postconflict, if the Philippines granted access. As discussed in Question 5, the Philippine economy is significantly dependent on Chinese trade, investment, and tourism and is vulnerable to Chinese economic coercion. This vulnerability has been demonstrated by past Chinese economic retaliatory actions against the Philippines over Scarborough Shoal. While a regional conflict would, of course, involve economic losses on all sides, the loss of China as a top Philippine economic partner would have political consequences for the Philippine leadership and would significantly affect the local economy throughout the Philippines. One potential avenue for increasing the likelihood of access would be if the current EDCA, or a new agreement, specifies compensation for hosting U.S. forces, as was the case for U.S. bases in the Philippines during the Cold War. The current EDCA does not include these parameters.

Third, the leadership has historically shown a strategic preference for balancing between the United States and China, and this is likely to continue in the post-Duterte era. Philippine public sentiment remains largely positive toward the United States, the alliance, and the U.S. military and has trended more negative regarding China, in particular, related to Chinese coercion in the SCS. However, the Philippine leadership also has substantial concerns about the potential for Chinese retaliation if it granted the U.S. military access, particularly in the economic realm, given the reliance of the Philippine economy on Chinese trade and investment. Given these concerns, when considering granting access in a conflict, the Philippine leadership will likely assess how to balance relations with the United States and the security benefits of the alliance if it granted access against the potential for Chinese retaliation and China-Philippine relations in a postconflict environment.

In addition to these factors, the conflict characteristics would also matter for the likelihood of the Philippine leadership granting access to U.S. forces. The proximity of the conflict to the Philippines—in the SCS—would potentially increase the likelihood of access because the threat to Philippine territory and interests would be greater. Similarly, conflicts directly involving Philippine territory in the SCS could increase the likelihood of Manila granting access. If the conflict results in substantial diminishment of China's economy and its ability to economically coerce the Philippines, the Philippine leadership might consider granting or expanding access. Characteristics that could decrease the likelihood of access being granted include if the conflict occurs farther from the Philippines (such as a Taiwan conflict) and does not directly involve threats to Philippine territory. Philippine leaders' uncertainty over U.S. commitment to defend Philippine interests in a particular scenario could also decrease

---

[95] "U.S. Will Defend Philippines If Attacked in the South China Sea," Reuters via CNN, August 6, 2022.

the likelihood of access being granted. Finally, China attacking other U.S. allies and partners that have granted access could heighten the Philippine leadership's fear of retaliation and lead, making U.S. access less likely.

Aside from these characteristics, the type and level of access requested by the United States would potentially affect the decision to grant access. It is more likely, for example, that the leadership would support granting U.S. ISR and overflight in a conflict because this would signal support for the United States and the security alliance but could invite less risk of Chinese attack than U.S. kinetic or offensive operations from Philippine soil. Requests for capabilities that are already part of the current EDCA, such as logistics and prepositioning of equipment and materiel, could potentially be expanded more easily than requests for new types of access.

Table 4.4 summarizes the key factors that appear to affect Philippine leadership calculations for each question when determining whether to grant access to the U.S. military in a conflict, as well as the conflict characteristics that their assessment might depend on.

TABLE 4.4

Summary of Adaptation of Conflict-Phase Access Decisionmaking Framework for the Philippines

Framework Question	Key Factors That Affect Leaders' Calculations	Conflict Characteristics on Which Assessment Depends
Would granting the United States conflict-phase access affect the leader or the regime's political survival?	• Philippine domestic public opinion on the U.S.-Philippines security alliance; the public's views of China • The leadership's preference for a balance between the United States and China	• Whether the conflict is a direct security threat to Philippine territory or interests might increase public support for U.S. access • The scale of Chinese attacks against the United States and allies and partners might increase political pressure to grant access if U.S. casualty numbers are high
Would granting the United States conflict-phase access affect the country's direct security position?	• Philippine assessment of national interests and whether U.S. access will help defend them • Philippine domestic military weakness • Balance between U.S. alliance and Chinese retaliation	• A direct attack on Philippine territory might increase willingness to grant access • Whether China has attacked other U.S. allies that have granted access might decrease willingness to grant access
Would granting the United States conflict-phase access affect the outcome of the conflict?	• The Philippines' location and its importance to U.S. operations • The type of access the United States is requesting • Philippine leadership's assessment of the importance of the U.S.-Philippine security alliance to Philippine security	• A direct threat to Philippine interests such that China winning the conflict would degrade Philippine security interests could increase willingness to grant access • In a protracted conflict, the Philippines might be more willing to grant access if it will bring about a victory for the United States and if the Philippine leadership views the alliance as essential for long-term security
Would granting the United States conflict-phase access affect, or be affected by, regional decisions regarding granting similar access?	• Whether other U.S. treaty allies in Southeast Asia, such as Thailand and Singapore, also granted or expanded U.S. access in a conflict • The level of support for the United States in the conflict from ASEAN, which could bolster Philippine regional standing if it supports U.S. operations	• If the location of the conflict is in the SCS and involves China taking over disputed territory, states in the region might support a Philippine decision to grant the United States access or follow suit • States in the region perceiving China as the primary aggressor might bolster regional support for U.S. operations and make the Philippines more likely to grant access

Table 4.4—Continued

Framework Question	Key Factors That Affect Leaders' Calculations	Conflict Characteristics on Which Assessment Depends
Would granting the United States conflict-phase access affect the economic prosperity of the country?	• Reliance on China as a trade partner and the scope of potential retaliation during and after the conflict if the Philippines granted access • Philippine economic relations with the United States and economic benefits of expanding U.S. military access	• If the conflict is in the SCS or affects Philippine territory, the Philippines might be more willing to grant access and face Chinese economic retaliation • If the stakes are high for China (e.g., Taiwan), any economic retaliation from it might be stronger and might reduce the likelihood of the Philippines granting access • If the conflict is of high intensity and results in severe economic disruption to China, the Philippine leadership might assess that China has limited ability to retaliate and be more likely to grant access

CHAPTER 5

Adapting the Conflict-Phase Access Framework to Singapore

Singapore is the closest and most capable U.S. security partner in Southeast Asia and is one of a quintet (together with Japan, South Korea, Australia, and New Zealand) of highest-tier Indo-Pacific partners in terms of capability, compatibility, and reliability of access. As with each of these partners, however, there may be a significant difference between conflict-phase and non–conflict-phase access. In Singapore's case, a decision on whether to grant the USAF or other branches of the U.S. military access during conflict might be more difficult than it would be for the other four, given that they (unlike Singapore) are all American treaty allies. During the Vietnam war, Singapore's dockyards served as maintenance hubs for U.S. naval vessels, which were integral to U.S. operations. Since that time, the United States had never sought, and Singapore had never offered, conflict-phase access. The level of peacetime access given to the USAF and U.S. Navy for routine operations is considerable: Today, Singapore provides logistics access and infrastructure for U.S. maritime and air forces and basing for regional operations and is the foremost Southeast Asian location for in-region support facilities.

Singapore is not treaty-bound to grant access to U.S. forces during a conflict and would very much prefer not to be forced to make such a decision. From Singapore's standpoint, any access would be easier to permit if it could be portrayed as merely falling within the framework of the existing 1990 memorandum of understanding (MOU) (and the follow-on agreements negotiated in subsequent years) rather than representing a substantive break from past practice.[1] Current peacetime agreements permit a wide variety of logistics, resupply, and other facilities short of combat engagement. If the types of requests U.S. planners make fall within the orbit of activities currently permitted by existing agreements, the likelihood that these requests will be granted would increase. Singapore would likely be more resistant to expanding these permissions.

The central motivation for Singaporean policymakers in considering granting U.S. conflict-phase access requests will be Singapore's desire to maintain its position as an open

---

[1] Ministry of Defence, Singapore, "Fact Sheet: 2019 Protocol of Amendment to the 1990 Memorandum of Understanding," September 24, 2019a; Memorandum of Understanding (MOU) Regarding United States Use of Facilities in Singapore, 1990.

regional hub in any postconflict environment, with no territorial ambitions and no security aims beyond upholding the regional status quo. This means Singapore will look with disfavor on any PRC attempt to settle territorial disputes in the SCS, ECS, or elsewhere by force. Singapore is not itself party to any such disputes and is under no treaty obligation to assist any of the regional states that are, but its strong attachment to the rule of law, current regional order, and principles of sovereignty will provide policymakers with a motivation and a rationale for backstopping the United States and other nations that may take a more kinetic response. Depending on the circumstances, Singapore might or might not participate directly in such a multilateral response as well.

This commitment to uphold the status quo, however, could also greatly complicate granting access to the United States if U.S. actions that would be enabled by this access were seen as overreaching, or upsetting the regional modus operandi. For example, Singapore is acutely aware of its role as guardian (along with Malaysia and Indonesia) of universal safe passage through the Strait of Malacca.[2] That all nations are free to use the Strait of Malacca is a matter of national identity among Singapore's policymakers. If the U.S. request for access were seen as an attempt to close the strait to air or maritime transit by PLA Air Force (PLAAF), PLA Navy (PLAN), or other PRC military forces or civilian assets, Singapore is almost certain to decline U.S. access requests. The other main potential impediment to granting conflict-phase access would be a scenario in which Singaporean troops (let alone the nation's civilian population) were placed directly in harm's way. Alignment with the United States is not particularly politically dangerous for Singapore's leadership—but the prospect of substantial Singaporean casualties is. All Singaporean male citizens and permanent residents are conscripted for a brief stint of national service, so any substantial casualties are more likely to be suffered by a broad cross-section of the entire population.[3] In the past, Singaporean political leaders have been extremely risk-averse in placing their troops in combat situations.[4]

As noted earlier, in deciding whether to grant conflict-phase access, Singapore's policymakers will be guided primarily by one question: After the conflict is over, will the decision have permanently degraded Singapore's position as an open, trusted, reliable regional hub for finance, trade, and goods—for the United States, China, and all other players alike? If the answer is "no," Singapore will likely privilege its interest in ensuring U.S. presence in the region and Singapore's status as the most important regional partner for the United States above its concerns about alienating China. But if the answer is "yes"—that is, if Singapore believes it will suffer permanent degradation of its status as regional hub—there are likely no inducements that Washington could provide that would persuade Singapore to shift

---

[2] The concern that Singapore might shut the Strait of Malacca is highlighted in Chinese security literature; see, for example, Wei Hong [韦红] and Yin Nannan [尹楠楠], "The Choice of Strategic Pivotal States in Southeast Asia for '21st Century Maritime Silk Road'" ["'21 世纪海上丝绸之路' 东南亚战略支点国家 的选择"], *Socialism Studies* [社会主义研究], No. 6, 2017. See also Lin et al., 2020, p. 24, footnote 71.

[3] Ministry of Foreign Affairs, Singapore, "National Service Obligation," webpage, undated-b.

[4] Ministry of Defence, Singapore, "Overseas Operations," webpage, undated.

its stance. Singapore sees its hub status as nearly existential for its political and economic survival and is unlikely to sacrifice this. If Singapore were to decline more ambitious U.S. conflict-phase access requests, the more successful U.S. strategy would likely be to rescope its request to the point at which Singapore is more comfortable that its status as a regional hub (including for goods and services to and from China) would not suffer significant long-term degradation.

Singapore's conflict-phase access decisions will also depend on the characteristics of the conflict in question. Singapore's desire to maintain a position as an open regional hub—and the nation's strong commitment to and reliance on the rule of law and regional order—means that policymakers will look with disfavor on any PRC attempt to settle territorial disputes in the SCS, ECS, or elsewhere by force. If China were very clearly the aggressor in this situation and if another local state were very clearly aggrieved, Singapore is likely to support conflict-phase access short of kinetic action. The level of intensity of the fighting and the amount of risk Singapore perceives to its population would likely also have a strong influence on the decision to grant access. The geographic context of the conflict is also important. Singapore may be more likely to grant access during a conflict over Taiwan simply because it is more likely to be a scenario in which China is clearly the aggressor. A conflict in the SCS would likely be inherently muddier, and Singapore may be less enthusiastic about providing access in this case.

History of U.S. Access in Singapore

In the words of former USINDOPACOM commander ADM Philip Davidson, "[N]o other Southeast Asian country has done more to facilitate U.S. presence than our partners in Singapore."[5] Singapore is the foremost Southeast Asian location for in-region logistics access and infrastructure for U.S. maritime and air forces and for basing for regional operations. U.S. access in Singapore dates to the Vietnam war. In the late 1960s, the Naval Regional Contracting Center served as the coordinator for ship maintenance within Southeast Asia, and Singapore's dockyards were used as repair stations for U.S. naval vessels, which were integral to America's Vietnam operations.[6] At the end of the end of the Vietnam war, Singapore's first prime minister, Lee Kuan Yew, came to believe in the need for the United States to maintain a

---

[5] Philip S. Davidson, "Statement of Admiral Philip S. Davidson, U.S. Navy Commander, U.S. Indo-Pacific Command," before the Senate Armed Services Committee on U.S. Indo-Pacific Command Posture, March 9, 2021.

[6] Christopher Rahman, "Singapore: Forward Operating Site," in Carnes Lord and Andrew Erickson, eds., *Rebalancing U.S. Forces: Basing and Forward Presence in the Asia-Pacific*, Naval Institute Press, 2014, p. 118; Ankush Wagle, "Analyzing U.S. Singapore Maritime Security Cooperation through the Indo-Pacific Lens," in Jeffrey Ordaniel and Ariel Stenek, eds., *The United States and Singapore: Indo-Pacific Partners*, Pacific Forum, December 2021, p. 37.

naval presence in the region to balance against both the Soviet Union and China.[7] Economic ties between the United States and Singapore expanded and were bolstered by a growing strategic relationship. As early as 1978, U.S. Navy aircraft conducted long-range Indian Ocean patrols from Tengah Air Base, while the USAF supported transport flights from Paya Lebar Air Base in the 1980s.[8] Figure 5.1 provides an overview of Singapore's geography.

The possibility of U.S. forces being denied access to Subic Naval Base and Clark Air Base in the Philippines led the United States and Singapore to sign the Memorandum of Understanding (MOU) Regarding United States Use of Facilities in Singapore in 1990.[9] The 1990 MOU is the foundational agreement that facilitates U.S. forces' access to Singapore's military facilities for transit and logistics support. Specifically, the MOU provided for expanded American access to the Singaporean facilities of Sembawang wharves and Paya Lebar Air

FIGURE 5.1

Map of U.S. Military Facilities in Singapore

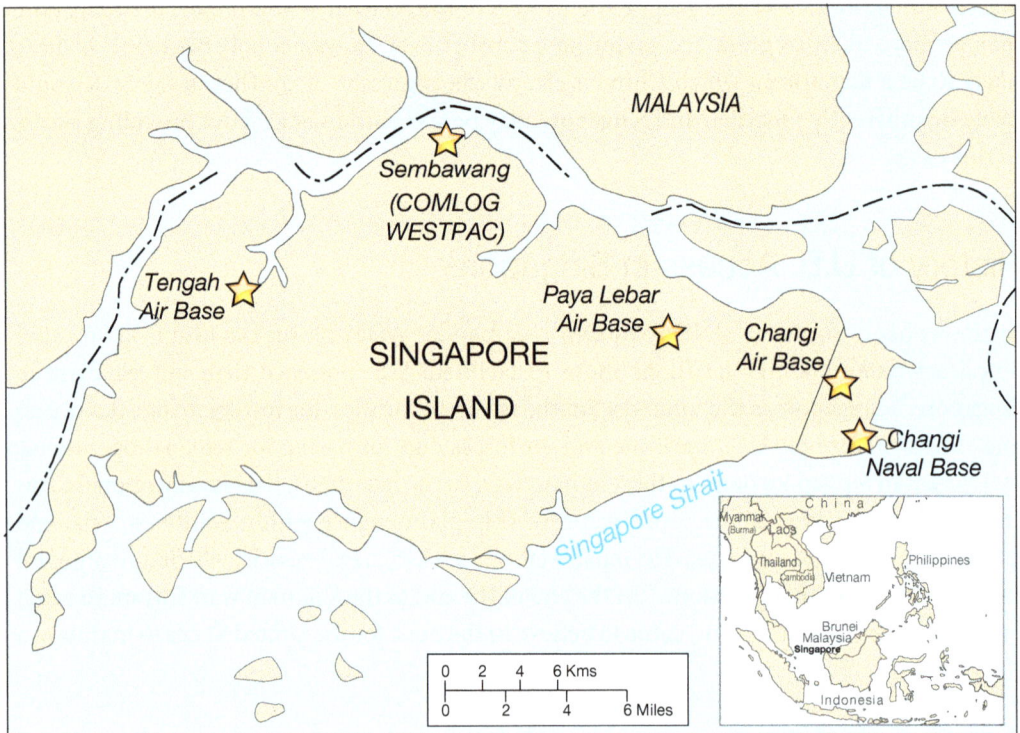

SOURCE: Adapted from Rahman, 2014.

NOTE: Paya Lebar Air Base is slated for closure in the next 10–15 years or so; operations will move to Changi Air Base.

---

[7] See Seng Tan, "Facilitating the US Rebalance: Challenges and Prospects for Singapore as America's Security Partner," *Security Challenges*, Vol. 12, No. 3, 2016, p. 23.

[8] Rahman, 2014, p. 119.

[9] Rahman, 2014, p. 119.

Base, increasing U.S. air and naval forces' use of Singaporean facilitates, with the 497th Tactical Fighter Training Squadron established at Paya Lebar to support USAF detachments.[10] Singapore played a proactive role in bringing about the 1990 MOU, with Prime Minister Lee Kuan Yew publicly inviting the United States to use Singaporean facilities in 1989.[11] Manila's ultimate rejection of a new treaty with the United States in 1991 led the United States to negotiate an addendum to the 1990 MOU, which moved COMLOG WESTPAC to Sembawang Wharves in Singapore.[12] In 1998, a second addendum to the 1990 MOU allowed U.S. naval vessels access to Changi Naval Base. Notably, the base was purpose-built to dock aircraft carriers, entirely at Singapore's cost, even though it does not own any.[13] When the facility opened, one senior Singaporean minister noted that Singapore built "the Changi naval base at our own expense to facilitate the deployment of the U.S. 7th Fleet in Southeast Asian waters . . . . [A]t a time when the region is going through a dramatic political change, the presence of these ships has a stabilizing effect."[14] In addition, reciprocal logistics support between U.S. and Singaporean forces was enabled by a 2000 ACSA.[15]

In 2005, reflecting a mutual desire to "expand the scope of defense and security cooperation reflected in their 1990 MOU," Washington and Singapore signed the Strategic Framework Agreement.[16] The agreement elevated bilateral relations to designate Singapore as a Major Security Cooperation Partner. Moreover, under the umbrella of the agreement, the two countries also concluded the 2005 Protocol of Amendment to the 1990 MOU, which extended the 1990 MOU for 15 years, and the 2005 Defence Cooperation Agreement.[17] The Strategic Framework Agreement and Defence Cooperation Agreement "consolidated existing defense cooperation activities and provided for new areas of mutually beneficial coopera-

---

[10] Rahman, 2014, p. 119.

[11] Rahman, 2014, p. 119.

[12] Jeffrey Ordaniel and Collin Koh, "Pragmatic and Principled—U.S.-Singapore Relations as a Model Partnership in the Indo-Pacific," in Jeffrey Ordaniel and Ariel Stenek, eds., *The United States and Singapore: Indo-Pacific Partners*, Pacific Forum, 2021, p. 3; See Seng Tan, "(Still) Supporting the Indispensable Power: Singapore's Relations with the United States from Trump to Biden," *Asia Policy*, Vol. 16, No. 4, October 2021, p. 80. Among other tasks, COMLOG WESTPAC provides combat-ready logistics to the U.S. Seventh Fleet.

[13] Tan, 2016, p. 24; Rahman, 2014, p. 120; Ordaniel and Koh, 2021, p. 3.

[14] Rahman, 2014, p. 120.

[15] Acquisition and Cross-Servicing Agreement Between the Department of Defense of the United States of America and the Ministry of Defence of Singapore, April 2000.

[16] Strategic Framework Agreement Between the United States of America and the Republic of Singapore for a Closer Cooperation Partnership in Defense and Security, July 12, 2005.

[17] Ministry of Defence, Singapore, "Factsheet—The Strategic Framework Agreement," press release, July 12, 2005.

tion, in the military-to-military, policy and technology areas."[18] Among other things, the two countries agreed to increase

> defense cooperation through the provision of facilities in Singapore for U.S. military vessels, aircraft, personnel, equipment and materiel; supporting deployments of the Parties' respective forces, conducting bilateral and multilateral exercises in the region and in the United States and exchanging military training.[19]

In 2011, the United States announced it would begin rotational deployments of littoral combat ships (LCSs) to Singapore to support the Navy's forward posture.[20] In 2015, the two countries enhanced the 2005 Defense Cooperation Agreement to, among other things, allow the United States to position Navy P-8A Poseidon maritime surveillance aircraft in Singapore to support the LCS deployments.[21] Both deployments are ongoing as of this writing.[22] Several sources noted that U.S. P-8s are reported to be flying one mission per day out of Singapore, on routine surveillance and monitoring tasks. Most recently, in 2019, the United States and Singapore renewed the 1990 MOU until 2035, an indication of Singapore's continued support for access for U.S. forces in the country and U.S. presence throughout the region.[23] As of this writing, U.S. policymakers are preparing for the closure of Paya Lebar, and plans are underway to move the air base to a more modern facility, called Changi East, near Changi Naval Base.[24]

Evaluating the Framework for Conflict-Phase Access Decisions in Singapore

Question 1: Would Granting the United States Conflict-Phase Access Affect the Leader or the Regime's Political Survival?

Two key factors would likely play a role in Singapore's conflict-phase access decisions related to this question:

---

[18] Ministry of Defence, Singapore, 2019a.

[19] Strategic Framework Agreement . . . , July 1, 2005.

[20] Rahman, 2014, p. 120.

[21] Tan, 2021, p. 80.

[22] White House, "Fact Sheet: Strengthening the U.S.-Singapore Strategic Partnership," August 23, 2021. LCS deployments stopped in summer 2020 because of COVID-19 and returned in early May 2022. See Mohammad Issa, "LCS Returns to Singapore," press release, Command Destroyer Squadron 7 Public Affairs, May 3, 2022.

[23] Ministry of Defence, Singapore, 2019a.

[24] Interview with U.S. military official, April 29, 2022; interview with former U.S. military official, May 26, 2022.

1. elite preferences for a greater U.S. role in region
2. mass cultural affinity with China, which is restrained by Singapore's top-down political system.

The first political factor that is likely to play a role in Singapore's conflict-phase access decisions is elite preference for a greater U.S. role in the region. While Singapore seeks to maintain autonomy in its foreign policy, the country's hedging is informed by a general preference for the United States as the strategic guarantor of regional order and security in Southeast Asia. The leadership's overall view of the region aligns largely with that of the United States, and the leadership supports the U.S. vision for the region over the long term.[25] This vision includes stability and prosperity for all states in a region that is not dominated by an assertive China. Surveys from the ISEAS–Yusof Ishak Institute make clear that Singapore's leadership values the security relationship with the United States. The polling, which surveyed a cross section of Singapore's governmental and nongovernmental elite, showed that nearly 85 percent of respondents welcomed America's "growing regional and strategic influence."[26] Similarly, almost 70 percent of Singaporean respondents expressed confidence in the United States as a "strategic partner and provider of regional security."[27] Most notably, when asked the question, "if ASEAN were forced to align itself with one of the two strategic rivals, which should it choose," 66 percent of Singaporean elites chose the United States over China.[28] In contrast, nearly one-half of Singapore's elites view China as a revisionist power that intends to turn Southeast Asia into its sphere of influence, and only about 23 percent of respondents are confident or very confident that China will "do the right thing" to contribute to global peace, security, and prosperity.[29] According to a Singaporean analyst, if the United States appeared to be in danger of losing a conflict with China and subsequently downgraded its presence in the Indo-Pacific, this would leave Singapore to fend for itself because it sees U.S. military presence in the region as guarding against a belligerent PRC that would otherwise dominate and destabilize the region. Moreover, in the view of Singapore's leadership, withdrawal of the United States from the region would have a domino effect: Other Singaporean partners, such as Japan, South Korea, and Australia, would likewise become far more reluctant to challenge the PRC, resulting in Chinese hegemony throughout the Indo-Pacific.[30]

---

[25] Mazarr et al., 2023, p. 87.

[26] Sharon Seah, Hong Thi Ha, Melinda Martinus, and Pham Thi Phuong Thao, *The State of Southeast Asia: 2021 Survey Report*, ISEAS–Yusof Ishak Institute, February 10, 2021, p. 23. The survey polled a total of 1,032 respondents from ten ASEAN member states in "five categories of affiliation: (1) academia/research, (2) business/finance, (3) government, (4) civil-society/non-governmental/media, and (5) regional/international organizations" (p. 1).

[27] Seah et al., 2021, p. 40.

[28] Seah et al., 2021, p. 33.

[29] Seah et al., 2021, pp. 35, 42.

[30] Interview with Singaporean defense analyst, March 25, 2022.

Elite preferences matter for conflict-phase access decisions because, in Singapore, foreign policy is largely elite-driven. Singapore has been governed by the People's Action Party (PAP) for the entirety of its existence as a nation, and this tenure does not appear to be in danger of ending soon.[31] Singapore's political system allows for some political pluralism but generally constrains the growth of credible opposition parties and limits freedoms, such as expression, assembly, and association.[32] The PAP currently holds 83 of the 93 seats in Parliament and has won each of Singapore's 12 postindependence general elections with at least 60 percent of the popular vote.[33] The current prime minister, Lee Hsien Loon, is the son and political heir to Lee Kwan Yew—the nation's founding father and prime minister for the first quarter-century of its history. Foreign policy issues have never been a key determinant of politics in Singapore. The PAP owes its longevity to its successful management of domestic issues, particularly the delivery of economic prosperity and effective government administration.[34] The PAP is currently sorting out a transition to its next generation of leadership, but there is little prospect of a drastic change of outlook or of the party losing control of the government in the near term.[35] As one analyst notes, "[n]o alternation of political parties in power and weak opposition parties in parliament mean that the PAP's leadership of the city-state's foreign policy is unchallenged at home."[36]

The second political factor that is likely to play a role in the leadership's conflict-phase access decisions is a mass cultural affinity for China, which is restrained by Singapore's top-town political system. China is popular among ordinary citizens in Singapore. Polling from the Pew Research Center—which surveys representative foreign publics—provides some insight into these trends. Pew's 2021 survey of publics in 17 advanced economies found that, overall, only 27 percent of respondents had a favorable view of China. Singapore, however, bucked this trend, with about 64 percent having a favorable view of China. That compares to 10 percent of Japanese, 21 percent of Australians, and 22 percent of South Koreans. For the United States, 51 percent of Singaporeans surveyed had a favorable view (which was below the survey's overall median of 61 percent). The Singaporean public's perception of Chinese Presi-

---

[31] Shashi Jayakumar, *A History of the People's Action Party, 1985–2021*, National University of Singapore Press, 2022.

[32] Freedom House, "Freedom in the World 2022: Singapore," webpage, undated.

[33] Steven Oliver and Kai Ostwald, "Explaining Elections in Singapore: Dominant Party Resilience and Valence Politics," *Journal of East Asian Studies*, Vol. 18, No. 2, 2018; Hannah Beech, "In Singapore, an Orderly Election and a (Somewhat) Surprising Result," *New York Times*, July 10, 2020.

[34] Kenneth Paul Tan, "The Ideology of Pragmatism: Neo-Liberal Globalisation and Political Authoritarianism in Singapore," *Journal of Contemporary Asia*, Vol. 42, No. 1, 2012.

[35] Michael D. Barr, "Singapore's Succession Headache," *The Diplomat*, March 1, 2022; Sebastian Reyes, "Singapore's Stubborn Authoritarianism," *Harvard Political Review*, September 29, 2015.

[36] Lam Peng Er, "Singapore-China Relations in Geopolitics, Economics, Domestic Politics and Public Opinion: An Awkward 'Special Relationship'?" *Journal of Contemporary East Asia Studies*, Vol. 10, No. 2, 2021, p. 208.

dent Xi Jinping also ran contrary to that of other publics surveyed: 70 percent expressed confidence in the Chinese leader, compared with other nations, whose confidence in Xi ranged from a low of 10 percent to a high of 36 percent.[37]

The government is keenly aware of the threat China's soft power and pervasive cultural influence pose. Three-quarters of Singapore's population is ethnic Chinese, and much of the nation's cultural outlook is influenced by sources in China. With a population of less than one-half of 1 percent that of the PRC, Singapore naturally draws much of its entertainment and news from its far-larger neighbor.[38] Local media published or broadcast in Mandarin or various southern Chinese dialects tend to take a position on international affairs strongly supportive of PRC narratives.[39] Relatively little music or other popular entertainment is created in Singapore itself. Most forms of popular culture in Chinese languages or dialects originate in the PRC (including Hong Kong), with a far smaller amount of content originating in Taiwan, and the ubiquity of broadband internet service has drastically increased the availability of PRC origin content in Singapore. This inevitably has affected popular attitudes: "When the heroes of every [historical] soap opera are Chinese," said a Singapore-based analyst, "and the bad guys are Japanese or Western, that can't help but influence people's mindset."[40] Indeed, in 2018, veteran Singaporean diplomat Bilhari Kausikan accused Beijing of using Chinese-language social media to try to shape narratives among the Singaporean public.[41] These narratives varied from the idea that "America is the past and China is the future" to more-specific messages that, as a nonclaimant of the SCS, Singapore should support China.[42] However, younger generations are at least as likely to take their entertainment and media cues from Western, South Korean, Japanese, and Taiwanese sources as from those in the PRC, and the older citizens most likely to favor PRC media are precisely the segment of the population the constituting the governing party's base and is most likely to trust its direction. The same Singaporean security analyst summarized rhetorically: "Would there be a risk of political backlash to conflict-phase access? Yes, there would. But it would be a low to medium risk."[43]

Moreover, Singapore's top-down political system restrains the influence of China's relative popularity on Singapore's foreign policy decisions. As noted earlier, the PAP derives

---

[37] Laura Silver, "China's International Image Remains Broadly Negative as Views of the U.S. Rebound," Pew Research Center, June 30, 2021.

[38] Department of Statistics, Singapore, "Census of Population 2020, Statistical Release 1: Demographic Characteristics, Education, Language and Religion," Ministry of Trade and Industry, June 2021.

[39] Interview with Singapore-based defense analyst, March 17, 2022.

[40] Interview with Singapore-based defense analyst, March 17, 2022.

[41] Charissa Yong, "Singaporeans Should Be Aware of China's 'Influence Operations' to Manipulate Them, Says Retired Diplomat Bilhari," *Straits Times*, June 27, 2018.

[42] Yong, 2018.

[43] Interview with Singaporean defense analyst, March 25, 2022.

its legitimacy and has maintained its hold on power by delivering economic prosperity and effective government administration to its citizens. As one author has noted,

> Singapore's considerable economic success is justification enough for its authoritarian means. The people's overall trust in these principles creates the conditions for political obedience, acceptance of unpopular policies and political apathy, in general.[44]

Similarly, one Singaporean security analyst has noted that "[m]ost of the population is politically apathetic about foreign affairs. China versus the U.S.—so what? People are more concerned with food, sports and investments."[45] To the extent that foreign affairs or external security issues become topics of domestic political debate, the PAP is extremely effective at marshalling all credible voices to present a united front in support of government policy. Public protest is difficult in Singapore, but laws preventing such movements are seldom invoked: The PAP is able to gain widespread consensus for its positions through less-coercive methods, so it does not need to make use of the legal tools (mostly inherited from British colonial legislation) at its disposal.[46] Moreover, in addition to the nature of Singapore's political system, the country's political leaders have worked hard throughout their history as a nation to prevent demographics from creating political rifts by reinforcing the unique nature of Singaporean identity and rejecting ethnic nativism among its citizens.[47]

This does not mean that Singaporean leaders are unaffected by popular sentiment or unconcerned about the prospect of dissent. While the PAP's hold on power seems firm, the party is extremely sensitive to the possibility that the Workers' Party, the main opposition party, could eventually challenge its dominance. The steps taken have been primarily in the domestic realm, such as limiting the work permits granted to expatriates in an effort to address complaints that too many desirable jobs are given to foreigners instead of Singaporeans.[48] However, security topics, such as Singapore's approach to defense spending and its acquisition of fighter jets, were mentioned by opposition figures during Singapore's last election to a degree not seen before.[49]

---

[44] Tan, 2012, p. 71.

[45] Interview with Singaporean defense analyst, March 25, 2022.

[46] Interview with Singapore-based defense analyst, March 17, 2022.

[47] Cortez A. Cooper III and Michael S. Chase, *Regional Responses to U.S.-China Competition in the Indo-Pacific: Singapore*, RAND Corporation, RR-4412/5-AF, 2020, p. 21.

[48] Seventy percent of Singapore's residents called for strict limits on the number of foreigners coming into the country, according to a 2021 survey from the Institute of Policy Studies (Mathew Mathews, Teo Kay Key, Meelvin Tay, Alicia Wang, *Attitudes Towards Institutions, Politics, and Policies: Key Findings from the World Values Survey*, Institute of Policy Studies, Lee Kuan Yew School of Public Policy, 2021, p. 114). See also Kwan Wei Kevin Tan, "Singapore's Expat Angst Forces Simmering Political Debate," Bloomberg, July 29, 2021.

[49] Cooper and Chase, 2020, p. 35.

What Factors Specific to the Conflict Might Shape the Decisions?

The degree of political risk Singaporean policymakers would incur in granting the United States conflict-phase access would likely depend on popular perceptions about which nation was the "good guy" in the conflict. If China was widely perceived to have initiated the conflict unnecessarily or to be inflicting needless harm on a peaceful neighbor, the decision to grant access would be politically easier. Likewise, the target of perceived aggression being a nation that enjoyed considerable goodwill among the Singaporean population would incline leadership to grant access. Such goodwill could be the result of cultural soft power (South Korea, Japan, or Taiwan) or ties of ethnicity among a significant portion of the population.[50] Conversely, there might be less pressure for Singaporean involvement if the target were a nation with less domestic support (Vietnam, Brunei, or the Philippines).

Regardless of which party was perceived to hold the moral high ground, the severity of the fighting and amount of risk would likely have a strong influence on the decision to grant access. "Getting into a conflict that directly endangers Singaporean troops would be a tricky problem politically," said a Singaporean analyst, who was otherwise quite bullish on the possibility of conflict-phase access. "Singaporean deployments always try to avoid putting troops in harm's way."[51] Since 1989, for example, Singapore has participated in only 17 UN peacekeeping missions, typically in relatively low-risk operations, such as medical support, advising national reconciliation efforts, and supervision of elections.[52] It has been more forward-leaning in HA/DR missions, both in the region and further afield:[53] These missions use the considerable effectiveness and capability of the Singaporean military without exposing troops to as much danger as potential combat would. Another former U.S. military official also noted that Singapore's leadership's extreme risk aversion for troop casualties was an important factor in conflict-phase access decisionmaking.[54]

As noted earlier, all male citizens and permanent residents of Singapore are required to perform national service, either in the military or the domestic security agencies. This service is not seen as particularly onerous: In a nation as small as Singapore, where one can drive from one end of the nation to the other in 40 minutes (or even make the trip by rapid transit), conscripts are easily able to spend their days off at home and socialize freely with civilian friends.[55] But this universal sharing of military risk results in a lowered public tolerance for

---

[50] That would primarily be Malaysia, but it is possible that Indonesia would engender a similar response among at least some ethnic-Malay Singaporeans.

[51] Interview with Singaporean defense analyst, March 25, 2022.

[52] Ministry of Foreign Affairs, Singapore, "International Peacekeeping," webpage, undated-a.

[53] Ministry of Defence, Singapore, "Overseas Operations," webpage, March 8, 2022.

[54] Interview with former U.S. military official, May 26, 2022. This former official recounted an incident in 2018 in which a Singaporean navy ship was at Guam when North Korea threatened to hit Guam. The official's interactions with Singaporean officials at the time made clear that Singapore "is always trying to get the risk to zero."

[55] Interview with Singaporean defense analyst, March 25, 2022.

potential casualties: As the United States learned during the Vietnam War, universal conscription requires far more popular support for risky deployments than might be the case in nations with an all-volunteer force.[56]

Question 2: Would Granting the United States Conflict-Phase Access Affect the Country's Direct Security Position?

Three key factors would likely play a role in Singapore's conflict-phase access decisions related to this question:

1. Singapore's national identity centering around autonomy
2. limited concern over potential for PRC kinetic retaliation
3. a strong commitment to and reliance on rule of law and regional order.

Singapore's national identity is deeply rooted in the principles of autonomy and impartiality. Throughout its history, Singapore's leaders have perceived the city-state as intensely vulnerable to external aggression because of its small size, critical geostrategic location, lack of natural resources, and trade dependence. Before its independence, Singapore was a supposedly impenetrable British colony that nonetheless fell to Japan in World War II, demonstrating to its leaders that security guarantees from great powers cannot secure survival.[57] As Singapore's first prime minister, Lee Kuan Yew, noted in the preface to his first memoir, "I thought our people should understand how vulnerable Singapore was and is, the dangers that beset us, and how we nearly did not make it."[58] Stemming from this vulnerability is a deep-rooted preference for autonomy among Singapore's leaders. As veteran Singaporean diplomat Bilahari Kausikan has noted, Singapore's foremost challenge is to "position ourselves so as to preserve maximum autonomy and avoid being forced into invidious choices."[59] Singapore therefore aims to cultivate positive relations with all great powers, while preventing itself from becoming too close to (or dependent on) any single power. This strategy allows Singapore to preserve its autonomy and adapt its security policies to changing dynamics.[60] Given that Singapore's leaders see impartiality and neutrality as concepts fundamental to the nation's survival, they would likely be reluctant to take actions that upset the balance they have created through the cultivation of a dense network of partnerships. For example, about

---

[56] Michael C. Horowitz and Matthew S. Levendusky, "Drafting Support for War: Conscription and Mass Support for Warfare," *Journal of Politics*, Vol. 73, No. 2, April 2011.

[57] Darren J. Lim and Zack Cooper, "Reassessing Hedging: The Logic of Alignment in East Asia," *Security Studies*, Vol. 24, No. 4, 2015, p. 722.

[58] Lee Kuan Yew, *The Singapore Story: Memoirs of Lee Kuan Yew*, Straits Times Press, 1998.

[59] Bilahari Kausikan, *Singapore Is Not an Island: Views on Singapore Foreign Policy*, Straits Times Press, 2021, p. 206.

[60] Lim and Cooper, 2015, p. 722.

one month after Singapore and the United States most recently extended the 1990 MOU in 2019, Singapore also signed an updated defense agreement with Beijing, although, from a U.S. perspective, this agreement with China is largely seen as necessary political posturing from Singapore rather than one that provides the PLA with any real advantages.[61] Regardless of the operational implications, the political signal Singapore intended to send was clear. Owing to its history and geostrategic outlook, Singapore's leaders believe that it would be risky in many realistic scenarios for Singapore to provide the U.S. military conflict-phase access—although the exact level of risk would depend on the characteristics of the conflict. However, as noted in Question 1, Singapore's preference for foreign policy independence is informed by a recognition that a strong partnership with the U.S. military guarantees Singapore's autonomy. Singapore supports the U.S. vision for the region over the long term, and believes that the U.S. presence is critical to guard against an unstable region dominated by an assertive China.

On the second factor, there is very little fear in Singapore that China might invade and occupy the nation during a potential conflict. There is considerable concern, however, that China would retaliate against Singapore in the gray zone, most notably by using economic weapons. If China's enormous economic engagement with Southeast Asia, and much of the Indo-Pacific region, were to bypass Singapore, the city-state (its leaders fear) would lose the most powerful guarantor of its independence. This issue will be analyzed in greater detail in the discussion for Question 5. However, in conventional military terms, the primary threat Singapore perceives to its security is Malaysia and secondarily Indonesia.[62] Singapore has no publicly released military doctrine, but analysts assess that Singapore's armed forces are primarily configured for deterrence or defense against the neighboring state of Malaysia.[63] Singapore began its postcolonial history as part of a unitary state with Malaysia, and its independence in 1965 was characterized by racial tension, political contestation, and the real prospect of military conflict.[64] Singapore has conducted wargames with scenarios involving lightly

---

[61] In October 2019, Singapore and China signed the enhanced Agreement on Defence Exchanges and Security Cooperation (ADSEC), which is built on a January 2008 agreement that provided for PLA-Singapore armed training and has been broadened to include the establishment of a regular ministerial dialogue, a VFA for troops participating in bilateral exercises, mutual logistics support, and a bilateral hotline. See William Choong, "China-US Relations: Singapore's Elusive Sweet Spot," ISEAS–Yusof Ishak Institute, July 23, 2020, pp. 4–5.

[62] Tim Huxley, *Defending the Lion City: The Armed Forces of Singapore*, Allen & Unwin, 2001; Tim Huxley, "Singapore and Malaysia: A Precarious Balance?" *Pacific Review*, Vol. 4, No. 3, 1991, p. 204; Jonah Blank, *Regional Responses to U.S.-China Competition in the Indo-Pacific: Indonesia*, RAND Corporation, RR-4412/3-AF, 2021b, p. 37.

[63] Huxley, 2001; Huxley, 1991, p. 204.

[64] Political tensions between the United Malays National Organization, Malaysia's oldest political party, and the PAP became so significant that Singapore was separated from the Malaysian Federation to forestall racial conflict in 1965. Following independence, one of the principal fears in Singapore was that Kuala Lumpur might close the causeway between the two countries and cut off the water supply. An added anxiety was that some of Singapore's key installations were guarded by Malaysian troops. Finally, race relations were contentious, with anti-Chinese sentiment bubbling to the surface in the form of riots in Malaysia and

disguised Malaysia and Indonesia as adversaries. Malaysia is the nation of particular concern: "[Singapore] is acutely tuned to signals from [Malaysia's capital of] Kuala Lumpur," said a Singapore-based analyst. "When Malaysia conducts exercises, Singapore always monitors—and often mirrors. Their posture, intelligence, and plans are all geared towards Malaysia."[65] Moreover, U.S. military officials in Singapore note that the city-state wants F-35 fighter aircraft in part to deter potential aggression from Indonesia and Malaysia.[66]

According to defense analyst Tim Huxley (who, until 2021, served as the Singapore-based executive director of the International Institute for Strategic Studies–Asia), Singapore's primary strategic plan to repel any foreign invasion is essentially an update of Britain's pre–World War II Operation Matador.[67] According to Huxley, contemporary Singapore Armed Forces officers confirmed that this plan still formed the basis for modern planning. Although the book is 21 years old, informed sources believe it to express a plan that is still current.[68]

In terms of conventional conflict, Singapore is concerned about China only as a black-swan potential adversary. No source interviewed in Singapore believed that the Singapore Armed Forces had exercised a scenario against the PLA, but there was some disagreement over the degree to which the PRC constituted a conventional threat. "I don't think Singapore envisions a military clash with China," said one analyst.[69] "China doesn't pose a kinetic threat to Singapore—they have so many agreements and a working relationship," said another.[70] "The army is not postured for combat against the PLA," noted another, "but the air force and navy see the PLAAF and PLAN as at least potential adversaries."[71] He noted that the navy, in particular, is focused more on maritime gray zone activities than on conventional combat against its Chinese counterparts and foresees any conflict with China as unfolding largely in the sphere of cyber and information operations.[72]

Indonesia in 1964, 1969, and 1989. See Albert Lau, *A Moment of Anguish: Singapore in Malaysia and the Politics of Disengagement*, Times Academic Press, 1998, pp. 451–453; Ron Matthews and Nellie Zhang Yan, "Small Country 'Total Defence': A Case Study of Singapore," *Defence Studies*, Vol. 7, No. 3, September 2007, p. 376.

[65] Interview with Singapore-based defense analyst, March 17, 2022.

[66] Blank, 2021b, p. 37.

[67] This plan involves a preemptive strike through Malaysia, up to the border of Thailand; Britain never got a chance to use it against Imperial Japan, but the topography of Peninsular Malaysia forces any would-be combatant into a rather limited set of prospective strategies. See Huxley, 2001.

[68] Interview with Singapore-based defense analyst, March 17, 2022; interview with Singaporean defense analyst, March 25, 2022.

[69] Interview with Singapore-based defense analyst, March 17, 2022

[70] Interview with U.S. military official, April 29, 2022.

[71] Interview with Singaporean defense analyst, March 25, 2022.

[72] In 2017, Singapore established the Defence Cyber Organisation to lead the nation's cybersecurity efforts across all branches of the military. See Ministry of Defence, Singapore, "Cyber Defence," webpage, May 10, 2021.

The third factor that would likely play a role in Singapore's conflict-phase access decisions related to this question is Singapore's strong commitment to and reliance on rule of law and principles of regional order. As a small state in a rough neighborhood, Singapore relies on the principles of international law, sovereignty, and independence to ensure its security. An international or regional order driven more by the whims of larger, more powerful states would leave Singapore at greater risk of attack or absorption, as occurred during World War II. For this reason, as one of our interviewees noted, "Singapore is considered a world leader and voice for other small nations. It punches above its weight in terms of speaking out strongly on the principles of territorial integrity."[73]

A recent example of this commitment is Singapore's actions in response to Russia's invasion of Ukraine. Singapore's response as of this writing has been more robust than might have previously been assumed: It is the only nation in ASEAN to have condemned the invasion at the time of the initial attack and the only ASEAN nation to have strongly supported the U.S.-led sanctions regime.[74] In his August 2022 remarks at Singapore's National Day Rally, Prime Minister Lee argued that Russia's invasion

> violates the UN Charter and fundamental principles of sovereignty and territorial integrity.... Our security, even our existence, relies on countries upholding these principles. We cannot legitimise Russia's wrongful actions. Russia claims that what it calls a "special military operation" in Ukraine is justified by "historical errors and crazy decisions." If we accept this logic, what happens if one day others use this same argument against us?[75]

Singapore's national survival and prosperity are not possible without international and regional order. "That's why Singapore responded so vigorously to Russia's invasion of Ukraine," one Singaporean analyst noted.[76] Singapore's joint statement with the United States in late March also included a reference to how Russia's violation of the rules-based international order has negatively affected security in the Indo-Pacific region.[77] "The lesson to draw here," according to one analyst, is that "Singapore will stand up for the rights of small states."[78]

---

[73] Interview with U.S. Department of State official, April 29, 2022

[74] Prime Minister Lee Hsien Loong warned that, if international relations were based on "might is right," the "world would be a dangerous place for small countries like Singapore." See Ian Storey and William Choong, "Russia's Invasion of Ukraine: Southeast Asian Responses and Why the Conflict Matters to the Region," Singapore: ISEAS–Yusof Ishak Institute, March 9, 2022.

[75] Lee Hsien Loong, "NDR 2022: Prime Minister Lee Hsien Loong's English Speech in Full," August 21, 2022.

[76] Interview with Singaporean defense analyst, March 25, 2022.

[77] Joseph R. Biden, Jr., and Lee Hsien Loong, "U.S.-Singapore Joint Leaders' Statement," March 29, 2022.

[78] Interview with U.S. Department of State official, April 29, 2022.

What Factors Specific to the Conflict Might Shape the Decisions?

Given the perceived centrality of these principles to its security, Singapore is concerned about the way China has pursued its territorial claims in the SCS, the ECS, and Taiwan. As a vulnerable city-state, Singapore relies on the principle of the protection of the rule of law for small states and would look with disfavor on PRC actions that attempted to change the status quo by force.

By far the greatest concern to Singapore is Chinese behavior in the SCS.[79] While Singapore is not a claimant, it does depend on trade and has a vital interest in freedom of navigation and respect for international law.[80] Singapore has expressed concern about China's actions in the SCS. Following the 2016 ruling of an arbitral tribunal that found China's expansive maritime claims contrary to the UN Convention on the Law of the Sea, Singapore urged "all parties to fully respect legal and diplomatic processes, exercise self-restraint and avoid conducting any activities that may raise tensions in the region."[81] Singaporean diplomats accused China of attempting to divide ASEAN after China's foreign minister announced that China had reached consensus on SCS with Brunei, Laos, and Cambodia.[82] In 2015, Singapore also decided to allow U.S. P-8 reconnaissance flights from its territory (as described in this chapter's first section) at a particularly sensitive time of Chinese activity in the SCS, reflecting Singapore's willingness to send strong signals of its commitment to its security relationship with the United States.[83] Singapore's role as a regional air hub also caused it to express concern over the precedent that could be set by China's 2013 unilateral declaration of an air defense identification zone over the ECS.[84]

Taiwan is another area of discord between the PRC and Singapore. Singapore and Taiwan have deep historical ties on defense and security. Lacking land for large-scale exercises and maneuvers, Singapore has long relied on Taiwan's support for annual joint training exercises. For more than 40 years, beginning in 1975, Singapore trained troops in Taiwan under the

---

[79] David Capie, "The Power of Partnerships: US Defence Ties with Indonesia, Singapore, and Vietnam," *International Politics*, Vol. 57, February 19, 2020, p. 246.

[80] Wagle, 2021, p. 40.

[81] Ministry of Foreign Affairs, Singapore, "MFA Spokesman's Comments on the Ruling of the Arbitral Tribunal in the Philippines v China Case Under Annex VII to the 1982 United Nations Convention on the Law of the Sea (UNCLOS)," July 12, 2016.

[82] Cooper and Chase, 2020, p. 11. Singapore's foreign policy elites have also put forward blunt statements. For example, on the SCS, Ambassador Bilahari Kausikan stressed the importance of pursuing claims of sovereignty within "common frameworks of norms," not "unilateral actions based on superior force," noting that, in the SCS, the record is mixed and that "China has not behaved consistently . . . . [P]articularly unsettling is [Beijing's] increased reliance on history" (Kausikan, 2021, pp. 103, 135). However, other foreign-policy luminaries in Singapore have argued that Singapore should have been more circumspect on the judgement of the arbitral tribunal and be "restrained in commenting on matters involving great powers" (Kishore Mahbubani, "Qatar: Big Lessons from a Small Country," *Straits Times*, July 1, 2017).

[83] Cooper and Chase, 2020, p. 19.

[84] Capie, 2020, p. 246.

Project Starlight military training program.[85] Singapore's support for Taiwan has angered China and provoked retaliatory actions from Beijing.[86] As with the SCS, Singapore's leaders have expressed concern about China's invocation of history on the Taiwan issue: "By casting reconciliation with Taiwan as an instance of the rectification of historical injustice done to a weak China, it suggested and left open a broader settling of accounts."[87]

However, it is not clear how, exactly, these strategic dynamics would affect Singapore's decisions regarding granting the United States military access during a conflict involving these locations. The context, however, is key. If China were very clearly the aggressor and if another local state is very clearly aggrieved, Singapore is likely to support conflict-phase access short of kinetic action.[88] Russia's invasion of Ukraine provides a good model (although, for Singapore, crossing Moscow is considerably less risky than crossing Beijing): Singapore sided squarely against Russia—and thereby China). However, if the context had been muddier, Singapore probably would not have done so. Thus, most interviewees saw Singapore as less enthusiastic about providing access during a SCS scenario. "Singapore believes they should remain neutral on the SCS issue because they are not a claimant. [Singapore] got slapped down when they came out in support of the Philippines after the 2016 SCS arbitration," one former U.S. military official noted; "the stakes are just lower for the SCS. The reluctance is tied into the ASEAN noninterference principle. They don't want to get involved in a multilateral fight over the islands. They won't gain politically—it is too fraught and close to home."[89] Similarly, a current U.S. military official noted that the conflict dynamics in the SCS are inherently muddier: Nobody lives there, and all nations' claims are conflicting, so even if China took over islands by force, it would not look like an invasion.[90] One U.S. government official had a slightly different perspective, noting that Singapore may be more willing to grant access because the SCS is their neighborhood, because other ASEAN members have claims, and because Singapore values ASEAN centrality.[91]

A Taiwan scenario may, in some ways, be an easier choice for Singapore, simply because it is more likely to be a scenario in which China is clearly the aggressor against Taiwan. A

---

[85] Ernest Bower and Charles Freeman, "Singapore's Tightrope Walk on Taiwan," *Southeast Asia from the Corner of 18th & K Streets*, Vol. 1, No. 26, August 17, 2010; Ralph Jennings, "Taiwan's Beleaguered Foreign Relations Find Stable Support in Singapore," Voice of America, October 6, 2017.

[86] For example, in November 2016, Hong Kong Customs seized nine Singaporean Terrex infantry transport vehicles transiting a Hong Kong container terminal while returning from a training exercise in Taiwan. This illustrated concerns about how China could use various forms of leverage to pressure Singapore. See Cooper and Chase, 2020, pp. 11–12.

[87] Kausikan, 2021, p. 104.

[88] Interview with former U.S. military official, May 26, 2022; interview with U.S. military official, June 1, 2022.

[89] Interview with former U.S. military official, May 26, 2022.

[90] Interview with U.S. military official, June 1, 2022.

[91] Interview with U.S. Department of State official, April 29, 2022.

possible exception to this would be if Taiwan declared independence or engaged in what Singapore considered to be an unwise provocation.[92] Singapore may also have more space politically to be supportive in a Taiwan scenario because a Chinese invasion of Taiwan would be on a much larger scale, and Singapore knows that the United States would have far more at stake. Moreover, Taiwan is far enough away geographically that there is a lower chance of the conflict's consequences directly affecting Singapore.[93] One U.S. government official had a slightly more nuanced perspective, warning that Singapore is "not likely to risk jeopardizing their relationship with China to support U.S. efforts in Taiwan."[94] Singapore's ultimate decision will, of course, not be based on conflict location alone and will depend on the specific conflict scenarios and all five of the questions surveyed in this chapter.

Question 3: Would Granting Conflict-Phase Access Affect the Outcome of the Conflict?

Two key factors would likely play a role in Singapore's conflict-phase access decisions related to this question:

1. a perception that U.S. access is good for Singapore and the region
2. an assessment that the access Singapore provides is relatively unique in certain conflict scenarios.

On the first factor, U.S. military access in Singapore is unlikely to be the deciding factor in any U.S.-China conflict, but Singapore's policymakers are intent on maintaining their friendly relationship with the world's foremost superpower. "We have an alliance in all but name," one Singaporean analyst noted; "it is very much in Singapore's own national interest to make sure that the U.S. does *not* suffer a military defeat."[95] While it refrains from over-emphasizing it in public, Singapore sees Washington's power and presence as being vital to its own regional security.[96] Singapore would also likely be more willing to grant access if it thought that refusing to do so would affect the U.S.-Singapore partnership. For example, "Singapore understands that if they took away the logistical access provided under the 1990 MOU and follow-on agreements on short notice, it would affect the bilateral relationship irreparably," according to one former U.S. military officer, "but unless Singapore believed the PRC would retaliate, I think Singapore would hold the line [in terms of continuing to provide

[92] Interview with U.S. military official, June 1, 2022.

[93] Interview with former U.S. military official, May 26, 2022.

[94] Interview with U.S. Department of State official, April 29, 2022.

[95] Interview with Singaporean defense analyst, March 25, 2022.

[96] Choong, 2020, p. 3; Lim and Cooper, 2015, p. 723.

the type of logistical access in the 1990 MOU]."[97] Additionally, the risk of attack would be more likely be weighed against the prospect of a U.S. defeat, which would harm Singapore's own security.

On the second factor, Singapore believes that the type of access it provides is relatively unique in certain circumstances and would cause a disruption if the U.S. military had to rely on states elsewhere in the region. According to one former U.S. military official, the primary advantage of Singapore's access is a permanent, reliable logistics hub, in particular for the U.S. oilers and replenishment ships coming in and out of Sembawang Wharves: "Singapore is a reliable hub. Access is easy and established with a friendly political government. The access we receive is not impossible to replace, but it would be extremely disruptive to attempt to gain that access somewhere else, especially in a crisis."[98] In addition to logistics, the United States also deploys P-8 aircraft to Singapore, which can assist with antisubmarine and antisurface warfare. As one Singaporean analyst noted, "Malaysia, Indonesia, Vietnam, and even Thailand haven't provided the United States with as much access as we have. . . . In the Philippines, it all depends on who is in power at any moment. So, the obligation falls to Singapore to come through as America's primary security partner in the region."[99] However, this type of access is not uniquely valuable in all plausible scenarios, which Singapore's leaders recognize.

Other types of access, beyond the resupply, logistics, and other services already granted under the 1990 MOU, would have limited operational value for the U.S. military. For example, a request to use Singapore's bases to fly combat aircraft missions would not be operationally useful to the United States. According to one U.S. military officer, Singapore's size and geography mean that "the U.S. military wouldn't ask them for access for combat aircraft because they don't have enough airspace to do offensive counterair (OCA) and defensive counterair (DCA). It is just not a realistic request."[100] Moreover, in a Taiwan scenario, given Singapore's location, it simply would not be efficient to run bomber sorties out of Singapore to Taiwan.[101] These access requests—U.S. aircraft taking off from Singapore and conducting kinetic operations—are also clear redlines for Singapore, as multiple people we spoke with noted. One U.S. military official suggested that another type of access that might be useful for the U.S. military would be prepositioned stock, fuel, ammunition, or missiles. However, this would be unrealistic in Singapore due to space constraints.

A final type of request to Singapore during a conflict with China might be a U.S. Navy request for expanded access to help run a blockade in the Strait of Malacca. The U.S. government could feel that such economic pressure would be essential for winning an extended fight with China. Operating a blockade in Malacca would be very difficult without access

---

[97] Interview with former U.S. military official, May 26, 2022.

[98] Interview with former U.S. military official, June 9, 2020.

[99] Interview with Singaporean defense analyst, March 25, 2022.

[100] Interview with U.S. military officer, April 29, 2022.

[101] Interview with former U.S. military official, May 26, 2022.

to Singapore. This question will also be discussed in more detail under Question 5—given the strait's importance to trade, Singapore's lifeblood—but in this section we discuss Singapore's perception of whether helping the U.S. military with a blockade in Malacca would affect the outcome of the conflict. A blockade of the Strait of Malacca to, for example, cut off oil exports to China, would not, by itself, accomplish this goal. The U.S. military would also have to block off another regional chokepoint: the Sunda Strait.[102] According to one former U.S. official, "a U.S. request to shut the Strait of Malacca off to traffic would be futile. China would just ask Indonesia for passage via the Sunda Strait."[103] Thus, Singapore is unlikely to see a request to close the Strait of Malacca, on its own, because this would not have sufficient operational value to affect the outcome of the conflict.

What Factors Specific to the Conflict Might Shape the Decisions?

Specific characteristics of the conflict will influence the relevance of this question for Singaporean decisionmakers. A protracted conflict between the United States and China in which a U.S. defeat looked likely would increase Singapore's willingness to provide access because it sees the power and presence of the United States in the Asia Pacific as being vital to its own security and the security of the region.

The operational utility of Singapore's access very much depends on the scenario in question. Singapore's access will be most valuable in an SCS scenario. Singapore extends the operational reach of the U.S. Navy well up into the southern Pacific and SCS.[104] For logistical access, for example, Singapore's location on the Strait of Malacca would allow oilers and replenishment ships to deploy from ports in Singapore and sail directly to the SCS. According to one former U.S. military officer, port access in Singapore would rapidly enable routing for U.S. ships passing from the Middle East or Indian Ocean to the SCS or into the Pacific: "These ships will have to get people and parts, and Singapore's access makes this a lot easier."[105] If the conflict was in the ECS or Taiwan, instead of the SCS, Singapore would be less relevant, although, if the conflict spread from these locations into the SCS, Singapore's access would again be relevant.

Question 4: Would Granting the United States Conflict-Phase Access Affect—or Be Affected by—Regional Decisions Regarding Granting Similar Access?

For this question, Singapore's decision would hinge on at least three key factors:

1. the practical limits of ASEAN in the security realm

---

[102] Interview with former U.S. military official, June 9, 2022.

[103] Interview with Singaporean defense analyst, March 25, 2022.

[104] Interview with former U.S. military official, June 9, 2022.

[105] Interview with former U.S. military official, June 9, 2022.

2. regional expectations of Singaporean support for the United States
3. the limited importance of the access decisions of key regional states outside ASEAN.

On the first factor, in Southeast Asia, every nation in Southeast Asia typically discusses important foreign policy decisions in the framework of ASEAN centrality.[106] To try to insulate itself from great power politics to some degree, Singapore often seeks to act through ASEAN, both to amplify its own power when working with larger powers from outside Southeast Asia and to insulate itself from more direct consequences if a larger neighbor opposes an action.[107]

While Singapore prefers to act in concert with ASEAN nations, ASEAN's mandate for consensus ensures that the group can very seldom take meaningful action in the security arena. Thus, in practice, Singapore does not envision regional multilateralism through ASEAN as an alternative or replacement for a stable regional balance of power.[108] Indeed, Singapore knows that ASEAN struggles to play a significant role in the direction of events in Southeast Asia and that, in practice, great powers will have "the decisive influence."[109] Politically, however, Singapore cannot openly admit that the organization is weak.[110] In the case of a conflict between the United States and China, Singapore recognizes that acting through ASEAN would almost certainly be impossible. Thus, Singapore is unlikely to take its cues on conflict-phase access decisions from any collective decision by ASEAN or even the individual decisions of its members. In particular, the decisions of other ASEAN nations to refuse access are unlikely to have a large effect on Singapore's decision to grant access, given that Singapore has other interests that could still motivate it to do so (including, importantly, its desire for a strong U.S. presence in the region).

However, on the second factor, both Singaporean leaders and others in the region likely expect Singapore to be the most supportive of U.S. requests for conflict-phase access. For most conflict scenarios, this likely means that, if any other ASEAN member were to decide to grant access (other than if that country was responding to a direct attack on its territory), it is likely that Singapore would have already granted access because of its status as the closest U.S. partner in Southeast Asia. But Singapore had not already done so, for whatever reason, it could increase pressure on Singapore to act. As one former U.S. military official observed: "Singapore recognizes the access they provide the U.S. military is unique and are happy to be out ahead of ASEAN. If, for example, Malaysia decided to provide access before Singapore, that would make policymakers uncomfortable."[111] But regional expectations of a close U.S.-Singapore partnership mean this pressure would likely not apply in reverse: If Singapore *did*

---

[106] Kausikan, 2021.

[107] Mazarr et al., 2023, p. 86.

[108] Tan, 2016, p. 25.

[109] Bilahari Kausikan, "Threading the Needle in Southeast Asia," *Foreign Affairs*, May 11, 2022, p. 116.

[110] Cooper and Chase, 2020, p. 13.

[111] Interview with former U.S. military official, May 26, 2022.

provide access, that would not necessarily persuade any other ASEAN member to provide access as well because doing so would be unlikely to generate substantial political or diplomatic pressure on these countries.

Finally, Singapore's decisions are unlikely to be affected by the calculus of Indo-Pacific states outside ASEAN. Singapore knows that the U.S. military already has high levels of access with treaty allies in the region, such as Australia, New Zealand, Japan, and South Korea.[112] Because these are all treaty allies of the United States, their decisions are not likely to be viewed in Singapore as evidence that Singapore, which is not a treaty ally, should or is expected to make the same decision. That said, these nations' granting access might still influence Singapore's calculations more indirectly. Singapore has closer soft power ties with South Korea, Taiwan, and Japan, particularly among the younger generations, which could help increase political or diplomatic solidarity with those countries in a conflict. In general, however, as discussed earlier, Singapore's cultural relationships with other states have not historically translated to the security arena.[113] To sum up: Singapore may be more likely to grant access if all (or most) of these close U.S. partners are doing so—and far less likely to grant access if all (or most) were withholding access. But absent a clear pattern or unanimity in either direction, Singapore's decision is more likely to be driven by other factors.

What Factors Specific to the Conflict Might Shape the Decisions?

Two conflict characteristics may shape Singapore's conflict-phase access decision related to this factor. The first is the degree of clear Chinese aggression and the regional perception of Chinese aggression. Inherently, an SCS scenario is likely muddier, with a greater number of regional states perhaps unwilling to stand up against a PRC land-grab of uninhabited atolls. In this sense, a conflict access decision in the event of a lack of clear regional consensus over the aggressor would be more difficult for Singapore—which indeed is not an SCS claimant (although it strongly supports adherence to the rule of law). A Taiwan scenario involving an unprovoked PRC invasion of the island would be an easier decision (although the access Singapore could provide in such a scenario is not of great utility to the U.S. military, as discussed in Question 3).

The states directly involved in the conflict are also relevant. For example, at least three ASEAN members have much closer relations with China than they do with the United States (Myanmar, Cambodia, and Laos; since its 2014 military coup, Thailand arguably falls into this camp as well). Five of the other ASEAN members have territorial or maritime disputes with China: Vietnam, Malaysia, the Philippines, and Brunei in overlapping claims in the SCS and Indonesia over fishing rights in the EEZ surrounding the Natuna Islands. None of these five members, however, has any real appetite for a military confrontation with China, even in the case of its own individual territorial claims (let alone those of other ASEAN members). Given these geopolitical realities, a PRC attack on one of these states is unlikely to

---

[112] White House, *Indo-Pacific Strategy of the United States*, February 2022.

[113] Interview with Singaporean defense analyst, March 25, 2022.

significantly affect Singapore's perception of its own calculus, which it views as separate and distinct from possible parties involved in SCS conflict. In a Taiwan scenario, as mentioned earlier, Taiwan's decision to grant access is so unique to its own circumstances that it, on its own, would also be unlikely to influence Singapore's decision.

Question 5: Would Granting the United States Conflict-Phase Access Affect the Economic Prosperity of the Country?

Three key factors would likely play a role in Singapore's conflict-phase access decisions related to this question:

1. Singapore's reliance on PRC trade and investment, including both formal and informal networks
2. Singapore's concern over losing its status as regional economic hub
3. Singapore's trade and investment with the United States and its regional allies.

For the policymakers of Singapore, economic prosperity is inextricably linked both to the survival of the regime and to the national security of the nation. Economic prosperity is the foundation on which the PAP's claim to continued governance rests and, indeed, the foundation on which Singapore's entire rationale as an independent nation rests.[114] The economic weapon China could burnish in response to a Singaporean decision to grant access is far more dangerous to Singapore than any likely PLA conventional military threat because it could do at least as much damage to the nation's existence as any likely military attack—and is far more likely to be used.

On the first factor—Singapore's reliance on PRC trade and investment—Singapore is a tiny island nation, which produces virtually none of the food or tangible goods that it needs simply to keep its citizens alive. For all of these items, the country relies entirely on trade. Indeed, Singapore has the fourth-highest trade–to–gross domestic product ratio in the world.[115] Since 2013, Singapore's largest trading partner has been China. China is also the leading destination for Singapore's exports. The two countries signed a free-trade agreement, which entered into force in 2009 and was upgraded in November 2018.[116] Singapore and China also collaborate on three state-level projects in the Chinese Mainland: Suzhou Industrial Project, Tianjin Eco-city, and Chongqing Connectivity. According to one analyst, "[t]his mode of economic cooperation, with Singapore taking the lead, is unrivaled by any

---

[114] Christopher Tremewan, *The Political Economy of Social Control in Singapore*, Palgrave Macmillan, 1994, p. 105.

[115] Singapore's ratio is 326 percent (Ankit Panda, "Singapore: A Small Asian Heavyweight," Council on Foreign Relations, April 16, 2020).

[116] Cooper and Chase, 2020, p. 23.

other country doing business in China."[117] Singapore is a firm supporter of the AIIB and an early and active backer of Beijing's BRI, for which it provides financial and other support services in managing projects, despite U.S. concerns about China extending political influence through the scheme.[118] Unsurprisingly, then, the overwhelming majority of Singapore's elites (85.3 percent) view China as the most influential economic power in Southeast Asia. Of those who see China as the most influential economic power, 66.7 percent are worried about its growing regional economic influence.[119]

Thus, the most significant factor for this question in Singapore's calculus to grant the United States conflict-phase access is the significant power China has to greatly reduce the demand for Singapore's goods and services overnight. Singapore could cope, but it would likely suffer immense economic hardship. "Such moves would hurt China as well," notes the chief financial officer (CFO) of a Singaporean company, "but China is big enough to absorb the blow far better than Singapore could."[120]

But Beijing's economic impact reaches considerably further than companies overtly based in China. A huge amount of "Singaporean" investment and financial resources comprises pass-through accounts funded by ethnic-Chinese families and institutions, both in the PRC and in the Chinese diaspora throughout the Indo-Pacific region.[121] So-called family offices often establish themselves in Singapore due to the nation's efficient, noncorrupt enforcement of contracts and scrupulous adherence to the rule of law.[122] Such an environment is vital for aboveboard business transactions, and a variety of interests are willing to pay a premium for it. Whether these funds ultimately have their origin in ethnic-Chinese communities in Indonesia, Thailand, or the PRC itself is ultimately irrelevant: When they are channeled through Singaporean institutions, they feed and maintain the entire financial ecosystem of the nation. At the top are bankers, financiers, lawyers, and accountants; on par, or perhaps a rung down, are the doctors, teachers, and realtors necessary to keep middle-class life humming; and further down the chain are all the service-sector workers and manual laborers. Were the PRC to decide to disrupt these financial relationships, the damage to Singapore's economy and society could therefore be profound.

The second economic factor that would affect Singapore's decision to grant access is leaders' overriding, existential concern for the potential future loss of Singapore's status as a regional economic hub. Singapore's status is not primarily due to its strategic location along the Strait of Malacca—this still matters for the transportation of goods, but it was more

---

[117] Lam, 2021, p. 208; interview with Singaporean defense analyst, March 25, 2022.

[118] Lye Liang Fook, "Singapore-China Relations: Building Substantive Ties Amidst Challenges," *Southeast Asian Affairs*, 2018, p. 326; Cooper and Chase, 2020, p. 23; Lam, 2021, p. 208.

[119] Seah et al., 2021, p. 21.

[120] Interview with CFO of Singapore-based high-tech company, March 17, 2022.

[121] Blank, 2021b, pp. 19–20.

[122] Andy Mukherjee, "Singapore's Tougher Stay-at-Home Rules for the Superrich," Bloomberg, May 5, 2022.

important in the 19th and 20th centuries than it is in the 21st.[123] Instead, Singapore's status as a regional economic hub is based on its identity as an island of safety, efficiency, reliability, and rule of law in a part of the world where such things are often in short supply.[124] War, or even the realistic prospect of war, could prevent Singapore from offering such a safe, reliable haven.

Like other financial hubs (Dubai, Hong Kong—or, for that matter, the City of London and Wall Street), Singapore is utterly dependent on relationships. It produces very little, and the money that makes it rich originates elsewhere. It is the transit point between buyers and sellers. "If Singapore lost the ability to offer buyers and sellers a safe, secure, trustworthy place in which to make their exchanges," said the CFO, "the business would quickly move elsewhere."[125] If a decision to offer the United States conflict-phase access risked China's enmity in a way that Singapore feared might be permanent, motivating China to take more enduring steps to isolate Singapore or discourage firms and countries from doing business there, it could fundamentally threaten Singapore's approach to the region and the world. Business interests might therefore try to influence PAP leaders against granting conflict-phase access: Indeed, sentiments of some members of the Singapore Business Federation and Singaporean investors in China were critical of the government's position on international law in the disputed SCS.[126] This is the economic threat that China holds over Singapore's head. And this threat strongly influences all security decisions that could have an adverse impact on its relationship with China.

Singapore is well aware of what a degraded economic hub looks like—not far away, in Hong Kong. Beijing's crackdown on political activity in Hong Kong in 2019 and 2020 had a powerful impact on the city's status as an economic entrepôt: Many global firms have drastically cut back their Hong Kong presence and relocated much of their business to rival locations (including Singapore).[127] "Hong Kong may never recover," said the CFO of a Singapore-

[123] Michael G. Vann, "When the World Came to Southeast Asia: Malacca and the Global Economy," *Maritime Asia*, Vol. 19, No. 2, Fall 2014.

[124] As Lee Kuan Yew noted,

> [Singapore] sought to provide an environment that our neighbors did not provide—first-world standards of reliability and predictability. Important for investors and economic growth, is the rule of law, implemented through an independent judiciary, an honest and efficient police force, and effective law enforcement agencies. Had we not differentiated Singapore in this way, it would have languished and perished as a shrinking trading centre and never become the thriving business, banking, shipping, and civil aviation hub it is today. (Lee Kuan Yew, "Why Singapore Is What It Is Now," *Estudios Internacionales*, No. 159, 2008, p. 171)

[125] Interview with CFO of Singapore-based high-tech company, March 17, 2022.

[126] Lam, 2021, p. 210.

[127] Martin Farrer, "Hong Kong: International Companies Reconsider Future in Wake of Security Law," *The Guardian*, September 6, 2021; John Lyons and Frances Yoon, "'Do We Need to Be in Hong Kong?' Global Companies Are Eyeing the Exits," *Wall Street Journal*, June 7, 2021.

based company in the high-tech sector. "It may become just another southern Chinese city."[128] While Hong Kong could survive as another Shanghai or Guangzhou (wealthy and successful within the context of China but with drastically reduced regional impact), Singapore does not have this option. As a city-state, it has no vast hinterland linked to its trading center. Even if it could structure some sort of symbiotic relationship with Malaysia or Indonesia, this would inevitably place Singapore in a subordinate position and force it to sacrifice a considerable measure of its independence. For Singapore, loss of its status as a regional economic hub could, over time, become tantamount to loss of its ability to exist as an independent political entity.

China could devastate Singapore's position as a regional economic hub in two main ways. The first way would involve the PRC cutting off all Chinese money that flows through Singapore. It has direct and indirect levers to do so. Directly, the Chinese government controls all Chinese trade and FDI and, increasingly, that of Hong Kong as well. China could cut off or threaten to cut off these flows to Singapore as it was considering a U.S. conflict-phase access request. Indirectly, the PRC could decide to disrupt the financial relationships mentioned earlier—the family offices. These communities are not agents of the Chinese government, but there are connections, and China would have significant leverage over whether or not their money continues to pass through Singapore. The second way would involve China interfering with shipping by announcing that any ship from any country stopping in Singapore would not be permitted to pass through China's nine-dash line. The United States would not accept such a move by Beijing, but it may be more difficult to find ways to encourage or support third parties ignoring China's edict.

Finally, the third economic factor related to Singapore's conflict-phase access decisions would be the level of trade and investment with the United States and its allies in the region. In general, there are few good outside options for Singapore for trade and capital, if China decided to retaliate in the ways described earlier in response to a decision in Singapore to grant the U.S. military conflict-phase access. As the first factor outlined, Singapore is a nation entirely reliant on trade for its existence, and China is Singapore's largest trading partner. But in contrast to China's importance as Singapore's trade partner, the United States is the largest investor in Singapore, with the United States accounting for 21 percent of foreign investment in Singapore; China accounts for only 3.5 percent.[129] Cooper and Chase have noted that, while China might be Singapore's most important bilateral trading partner, "China's economic influence decreases when you combine the percentage of total Singaporean trade that the U.S. and its allies (U.S., Australia, and Japan) could wield."[130] In 2021, for example, combined bilateral trade with the United States, Australia, Japan, Taiwan, and South Korea amounted to more $181 billion, compared with $158 billion from China. Table 5.1

---

[128] Interview with CFO of Singapore-based high-tech company, March 17, 2022.

[129] Cooper and Chase, 2020, p. 24.

[130] Cooper and Chase, 2020, p. 24. This point is also highlighted by the data in Table 5.1.

TABLE 5.1

Singapore's Total Bilateral Trade by Country

Year	China	United States	Japan	Australia	Taiwan	Republic of Korea	Germany	UK	France
2012	112.2	59.1	42.1	22.5	28.2	32.6	15.0	11.5	13.5
2013	117.2	62.2	38.3	20.9	28.1	32.7	14.8	9.6	11.3
2014	123.0	61.4	37.1	23.3	28.9	35.0	15.0	8.3	10.4
2015	123.9	56.7	34.5	16.7	24.4	23.0	13.8	6.9	8.7
2016	115.5	53.8	35.9	13.1	23.7	19.3	13.4	7.9	9.2
2017	128.2	58.8	37.5	14.1	26.3	20.6	15.2	8.6	10.1
2018	136.4	74.0	42.1	18.1	25.7	19.8	17.2	8.4	12.5
2019	138.8	78.3	37.0	17.6	26.1	19.4	14.6	9.8	13.7
2020	141.4	57.7	26.2	13.0	28.1	18.3	12.5	7.8	10.1
2021	158.8	64.8	29.0	29.1	37.8	21.0	13.5	8.6	10.4

SOURCES: OEC, "Singapore/China" webpage, undated-f; U.S. Census Bureau, undated; World Bank, undated-c; JETRO, various years; Australian Government, Department of Foreign Affairs and Trade, undated; Bureau of Foreign Trade, Taiwan, undated; Korea Customs Service, undated, for export/import by country; German Federal Statistics Office, 2022; Office for National Statistics, 2022; UN, undated, trade data for Singapore.

NOTE: Amounts are in billions of U.S. dollars. China includes Mainland China, Hong Kong, and Macau.

compares U.S. and allied trade with Singapore against Chinese trade with Singapore. Despite this, interviewees did not believe that the United States and its allies were likely to be able to make up for the economic loss Singapore would experience if China decided to cut off trade in a conflict.

To conclude, any challenge to Singapore's status as a regional economic hub has the potential to become an existential security threat. For Singapore, the maintenance of its status as the fulcrum of the region is more than a matter of economic success—it is a matter of national survival. If China's enormous economic engagement with Southeast Asia and much of the Indo-Pacific region were to bypass Singapore, the city-state, its leaders fear, would lose the most powerful guarantor of its independence. Such a move would be difficult for China to accomplish and would result in considerable economic pain for the PRC—but Singaporean planners are quite aware that China could bear such pain far more easily than Singapore could.

What Factors Specific to the Conflict Might Shape the Decisions?

Singaporean planners see the economic impact of a conflict as a potential existential national security threat, given that regime survival is dependent on economic success. In Singapore's case, economic prosperity and national security are essentially one and the same. In particular, Singapore is acutely aware of its role as guardian (along with Malaysia and Indonesia) of universal safe passage through the Strait of Malacca. It considers itself the guardian of free passage through the strait for all nations (as, under international law, it is). Thus, one analyst noted that it would be much for Singapore to grant access if the conflict involved an "existential threat" to Singapore—which this analyst defined broadly enough to include shutting down international trade, internal subversion, and closing the sea lines of communication.[131]

However, if the United States wanted to use bases in Singapore to block passage through the strait to air or maritime transit by PLAAF, PLAN, or other PRC military or civilian forces, Singapore would see this not just as an attack on China but as an attack on its own status. Any U.S. access request to Singapore to enforce a blockade of the Strait of Malacca is going to be off the table.

How Might Singapore's Decisions Vary Depending on the Types of Access Requested?

The easiest requests for Singapore to grant in a conflict would be those that it is already granting in peacetime—under the terms of the 1990 MOU and follow-on agreements—on a daily basis. For Singapore, the specifics of the conflict would influence a decision on conflict-phase access, but in most reasonable scenarios, conflict specifics would not be as determinative as the imperative to maintain the overall U.S.-Singapore relationship. That is, unless the U.S. request was particularly onerous, or the United States was perceived in Singapore as clearly being in the wrong, the presumption would favor granting most forms of access currently provided in the 1990 MOU and follow-on agreements. "What type of access can the U.S. request?" asked a former DoD official with close knowledge of Singaporean security decision-making. "What we're already getting. There are already massive depots for spare parts and munitions, as well as smoothly flowing logistical support."[132]

The types of access that Singapore is most likely to deny or that would, at a minimum, result in serious political blowback for the Singaporean government are those Singapore would perceive that China sees as going well beyond the existing MOU and successor agreements. These can be summarized as *actions that might prompt China to seek retribution against Singapore after the conflict by applying economic and political pressures to bring about the long-term loss of Singapore's status as the regional hub linking trade and finance throughout Southeast Asia.* Specifically, observers flag two types of access as being particularly problematic.

The first would be access that China would interpret as making Singapore a direct combatant in the conflict. This might be more of a deep-pink line than a red one, since the distinction between direct and indirect combatants can be difficult to draw clearly. "There can be no sinking of Chinese ships by U.S. planes flying out of Singapore," said a Singapore-based defense analyst.[133] While it would technically be possible to put missiles on the P-8s currently

---

[131] Interview with Singaporean defense analyst, March 25, 2022.

[132] Interview with former U.S. military official, May 26, 2022.

[133] Interview with Singapore-based defense analyst, March 17, 2022.

flying out of Singapore, for example, it would be problematic for Singapore if they were fired at a PLAN vessel. And transitioning from surveillance to direct-combat aircraft would be presumptively dangerous: "A B-52 is not a P-8," noted the same analyst.[134] One former U.S. military official similarly noted that a U.S. request to fly aircraft from Singapore to conduct kinetic operations would be a redline for Singapore's leadership. Alluding to Singapore's deeply rooted preference for autonomy, this former military official further noted, "Singapore doesn't want to be viewed as supporting military operations. They view themselves as kind of the Switzerland of Asia, they want to be everyone's friend."[135]

Second, any request to facilitate U.S. efforts to shut down the Strait of Malacca to PLAAF or PLAN transit would be a hard redline. "Singapore must keep all choke points open," said one Singapore-based defense analyst; "Singapore is the guardian of free transit to all."[136] Singapore would likely reject closure of the strait in most scenarios. "Under international law, the strait can never be shut to traffic—whether civilian or military, no matter what. Singapore, Malaysia and Indonesia all have the legal obligation to keep it open. And we take that very seriously," said a Singaporean defense analyst.[137] Another analyst also noted that a request to station weapon systems, such as Harpoon Ashore missile batteries, in Singapore, directed at the strait, would likely cross this line as well.[138] A U.S. military official concurred with this assessment: "Asking them to close the Strait of Malacca would be a nonstarter."[139] If the Strait of Malacca were shut, PLAAF could ask for overflight rights from Indonesia, and PLAN may be granted passage through the Sunda Strait. If this were to happen, Singapore would sacrifice its existential claim to be the regional upholder of the rule of law—and would not have materially affected the course of the conflict.[140] At a minimum, if the United States were engaged in a blockade of the strait, Singapore would stick to as restrictive an interpretation of the MOU as it could—and even then, China's provocation would have to have been extreme. The only condition under which some experts could envision Singapore providing access for a blockade of the strait would be if Singapore decided to become a de facto combatant against China.[141] In that case, the conflict would be large and widespread—or the politics within China would have changed enough that the PRC was no longer a major economic partner of Singapore.

---

[134] Interview with Singapore-based defense analyst, March 17, 2022.

[135] Interview with former U.S. military official, May 26, 2022.

[136] Interview with Singapore-based defense analyst, March 17, 2022.

[137] Interview with Singaporean defense analyst, March 25, 2022.

[138] Interview with Singapore-based defense analyst, March 17, 2022.

[139] Interview with U.S. military official, April 29, 2022.

[140] Interview with Singapore-based defense analyst, March 17, 2022.

[141] Interview with U.S. military official, June 1, 2022.

Summary

Today, Singapore is the foremost location in Southeast Asia for logistics access and infrastructure for U.S. maritime and air forces. While Singapore's leaders would very much prefer not to have to make a decision on granting conflict-phase access during a potential U.S-China clash, several key factors would be central to their decisionmaking. The principal motivation would likely be their desire to protect Singapore's position as an open and stable regional hub in a postconflict environment, which could be threatened by PRC economic retaliation. The survival of Singapore's current political regime—as well as the security and independence of the nation—are inextricably linked with the endurance of this hub.

A second critical motivation will be elite preferences for a greater U.S. role in the region and elite convictions that the United States is the strategic guarantor of regional order and security in Southeast Asia. While there is a cultural affinity for China among much of Singapore's population, it is constrained by a top-down political system in which elites make most decisions regarding the nation's security policy—and these policy decisions are generally supported so long as the government continues to deliver economic prosperity and effective government administration.

But Singapore's conflict-phase access decisions will also depend heavily on the nature of the conflict in question. Singapore's desire to maintain a position as an open regional hub and the nation's strong commitment to and reliance on the rule of law and regional order for small-state security mean that policymakers will look with disfavor on any PRC attempt to settle territorial disputes in the SCS, ECS, or elsewhere by force. If China were very clearly the aggressor and if another local state were clearly aggrieved, Singapore would be likely to support conflict-phase access short of kinetic action. The level of intensity of the fighting and the amount of risk Singapore perceives to its population would likely also have a strong influence on the decision to grant access: Anything that directly endangers Singaporean troops would likely be off the table. The geographic context of the conflict is also important. Singapore may be more likely to grant access during a conflict over Taiwan simply because it is more likely that China would clearly be the aggressor against Taiwan. A conflict in the SCS will likely be inherently muddier, and Singapore may be less enthusiastic about providing access in this case.

Finally, Singapore's decision will depend on the types of requests for access that U.S. planners make. If these requests fell within the orbit of activities currently permitted by the existing MOU and follow-on agreements, the likelihood that Singapore would grant these requests would increase. Singapore would likely be more resistant to providing access that goes beyond the terms in the MOU, such as kinetic action against China by U.S. forces departing from Singapore. Moreover, Singapore's role as the guardian of the Strait of Malacca and its obligations under international law to keep the strait open for free passage from all nations mean that leaders would find a U.S. request to close the strait to PRC transit as part of a blockade very difficult to grant. At a minimum, if the United States initiated a blockade of the strait, Singapore would stick to as restrictive an interpretation of the MOU as it could—and even then, the PRC provocation that resulted in the U.S. blockade would have to have been extreme. Moreover, U.S. requests to Singapore should be scoped to a point where Singapore is most comfortable that it can retain its status as a regional hub without long-term degradation. The type of conflict-phase access most likely to fall within these parameters is what the United States is already getting under existing agreements. Table 5.2 summarizes both the key factors and conflict characteristics highlighted by our analysis of each of the five framework questions.

TABLE 5.2

Summary of Adaptation of Conflict-Phase Access Decisionmaking Framework for Singapore

Framework Question	Key Factors That Affect Leaders' Calculation	Conflict Characteristics on Which Assessment Depends
Would granting the United States conflict-phase access affect the leader or the regime's political survival?	• Elite preferences for a greater U.S. role in region • Mass cultural affinity for China restrained by a top-down political system	• Whether China is widely seen as the aggressor • If the target of PRC aggression enjoys goodwill among the population • Potential for casualties
Would granting the United States conflict-phase access affect the country's direct security position?	• Singapore's national identity centered around autonomy • Limited concern over potential for PRC kinetic retaliation • A strong commitment to and reliance on rule of law and regional order for small-state security	• Whether China is widely seen as the aggressor and whether the other state(s) was widely seen as the victim • Conflict dynamics in SCS inherently less clear-cut; Singapore may be less likely to grant access • Conflict dynamics over Taiwan may be more clear-cut (with the exception of Taiwan declaring independence); Singapore may be more likely to grant access
Would granting conflict-phase access affect the outcome of the conflict?	• Perception that U.S. access is good for Singapore and the region • Assessment that access provided is relatively unique in certain scenarios	• In a protracted conflict, the genuine prospect of a U.S. defeat would increase Singapore's willingness to provide access because Singapore sees the U.S. power and presence in the Asia Pacific as being vital to its own security and the security of the region • Singapore is more likely to perceive its access as more valuable in a SCS scenario • Singapore is less likely to see its access as necessary in a Taiwan scenario • In a Malacca Strait blockade scenario, Singapore would not see the access it provides alone as critical; the PRC could try to circumvent a blockade via the Sunda Strait

Table 5.1—Continued

Framework Question	Key Factors That Affect Leaders' Calculation	Conflict Characteristics on Which Assessment Depends
Would granting the United States conflict-phase access affect—or be affected by—regional decisions regarding granting similar access?	• Practical limits of ASEAN in the security realm • Regional expectations of Singaporean support for the United States • Limited importance of the access decisions of key regional states outside ASEAN.	• Degree of clear Chinese aggression and the regional perception of Chinese aggression • Which states are directly involved in the conflict
Would granting the United States conflict-phase access affect the economic prosperity of the country?	• Singapore's reliance on PRC trade and investment, including both formal and informal networks • Singapore's concern over losing status as a regional economic hub • Singapore's trade and investment with the United States and regional allies	• If a conflict involved an existential threat to Singapore's existence, which would include shutting down international trade or closing sea lines of communication, Singapore would be more likely to grant access • A Malacca Strait blockade scenario would be the most difficult scenario for Singapore because it sees itself as the guardian of free passage through the strait and depends on the free and open flow of goods and services for its economic prosperity

CHAPTER 6

Adapting the Conflict-Phase Access Framework to Indonesia

Indonesia has presented a particular challenge to the United States when it comes to access because the country has followed a nonalignment policy aimed at preventing entanglements with great powers by avoiding alliances or security agreements with any nation. The U.S.-Indonesia military-to-military relationship has also been fraught over the past several decades because of human rights abuses under the Suharto regime. This led to the severing of security cooperation and continued to affect ties between Indonesian and U.S. military officials, although most of those ties have since been restored.[1] Against this complicated backdrop, U.S. forces have had almost no access to Indonesia beyond security cooperation activities and bilateral military exercises with Indonesian forces.

Overall, we found that Indonesia is unlikely to grant access for U.S. forces unless Indonesian territory or that of other key ASEAN states is directly threatened because of the fear of military and economic retaliation from China. Our research indicated that there is very little appetite among the Indonesian public and leadership to shift away from the nonalignment policy, even in a conflict, and that Indonesian leaders are far more likely to want to work through ASEAN to express support for U.S. forces or grant access. However, the lack of unity within ASEAN would make it challenging for Jakarta to have the level of regional support it might be looking for when considering whether to grant access and still be able to maintain its nonalignment policy. If Indonesia granted access, it would likely be very low-level access involving such capabilities as ISR and overflight, with nothing kinetic or combat-oriented likely to be approved. However, interviewees noted that Indonesian leaders would view even that level of access as changing the status quo and as stepping away from the nonalignment policy.

---

[1] In 1999, the United States suspended all military aid to Indonesia in response to its widespread human rights violations in East Timor. See Larry Niksch, *Indonesia: U.S. Relations with the Indonesian Military*, Congressional Research Service, August 10, 1998; Joshua Kurlantzick, *Keeping the U.S.-Indonesia Relationship Moving Forward*, Council on Foreign Relations, Center for Preventative Action, 2018, p. 5.

History of U.S. Access in Indonesia

U.S. forces have historically had very little access to Indonesia, largely because Indonesia's foreign policy strategy throughout its postcolonial history has been avoidance of de facto (let alone de jure) alliances with any nation.[2] The Non-Aligned Movement was literally created in Indonesia—at the Asian-African Conference of 1955, held in the West Java city of Bandung. The nation's founding President Sukarno (like many Indonesians, he used only one name) was, along with India's Prime Minister Jawaharlal Nehru, the key initiator of this movement.[3] Even when the U.S. drew other regional states into the Southeast Asia Treaty Organization, Indonesia remained steadfastly outside.

In the post–Cold War era, Indonesia has pursued the same policy with regard to both U.S.-China and U.S.-Russia competition. Currently, Indonesia perceives that it derives its status on the world stage from its nonalignment policy. According to one interviewee, "Indonesia doesn't see non-alignment as neutrality, but it's the key to Indonesia's legitimacy and participation in global dialogue . . . in the minds of Indonesians, they have credibility to mediate *because* they're non-aligned."[4] Indeed, when Indonesia hosted a meeting of the G-20 in July 2022, President Joko Widodo (more commonly referred to as Jokowi) used this rationale to try to serve as a mediator between the United States and Russia in the wake of Moscow's invasion of Ukraine.[5]

Indonesia pursues this nonalignment via an "obsession with maintaining balance among its security partners," meaning that it has not granted significant access to U.S. forces or to those of any other country.[6] As one RAND report on the topic noted,

> From the standpoint of U.S.-China competition, the most noteworthy result of this non-aligned attitude is Indonesia's policy of balancing its security partnerships among as wide a field as possible. This means the United States is competing not only against China (as well as rival Russia) but also against its allies and partners, such as Australia, South Korea, Japan, Singapore, India, and several European nations.[7]

In recent years,[8] U.S. military cooperation with Indonesia has primarily been through the recurring bilateral naval, air, and ground force exercises and security assistance through

---

[2] Blank, 2021b.

[3] Blank, 2021b.

[4] Interview with U.S. Department of State Official, July 21, 2022.

[5] Katie Lamb, "Not 'Business as Usual' for G20 Foreign Ministers Meeting in Bali," Reuters, July 6, 2022.

[6] Blank, 2021b, p. 29.

[7] Blank, 2021b, p. 17.

[8] Following the passage of the Leahy Amendment in 1997 and its expansion from counternarcotics to all military operations in 1999, U.S. security cooperation with the National Military of Indonesia (Tentara Nasional Indonesia [TNI]) was essentially shut off for the period spanning the end of the Suharto regime

sales of equipment and upgrading air and naval capabilities. Cope West is an example of one of the largest bilateral exercises, which originated as a joint training mission for the C-130 Hercules airframe and has evolved into a joint fighter-aircraft training exercise.[9] Cope West 2021 included 100 U.S. airmen flying six F-16 Fighting Falcons alongside Indonesian Air Force service members for a total of 52 flying missions. Cope West 2022 was oriented toward "developing and expanding [combined] airlift capabilities with the Indonesian Air Force."[10] A recently approved $14 billion U.S. arms sale package to Indonesia included F-15 fighter jets, and training is ongoing between the U.S. and Indonesian navies and coast guards.[11]

The challenge that Indonesia's nonalignment policy presents to U.S. forces seeking access was illustrated by Indonesia's rejection of a 2020 U.S. proposal to allow U.S. Navy P-8 Poseidon maritime surveillance planes to land and refuel at Indonesian military bases.[12] Following (successful) U.S. pressure on Indonesia to reject Chinese and Russian arms sale offers in April 2020, the United States made "multiple 'high-level' approaches in July and August" to propose access for the P-8 Poseidon maritime surveillance planes.[13] Indonesia was surprised by this proposal, according to Indonesian officials, because Indonesia "has never allowed foreign militaries to operate in the archipelago."[14] In a September 2020 interview, Indonesia's Foreign Minister Retno Marsudi said, "[w]e don't want to get trapped by this rivalry [between the U.S. and China]; Indonesia wants to show all that we are ready to be your partner."[15] Given the centrality of Indonesia's nonalignment policy to its approach to its national identity and to its military and security affairs, the challenges to U.S. forces in gaining access to Indonesian bases and facilities in a conflict remain high.

---

and the beginning of post-Suharto reformation. Remediation actions in accordance with Leahy procedures enabled nearly full cooperation to be restored by 2010. For more information on application of Leahy vetting for Indonesia and other nations, see Michael J. McNerney, Jonah Blank, Becca Wasser, Jeremy Boback, and Alexander Stephenson, *Improving Implementation of the Department of Defense Leahy Law*, RAND Corporation, RR 1737 OSD, 2017.

[9] For example, Cope West 2017 involved USMC F/A-18D Hornets and Indonesian F-16 Fighting Falcons and was "the first fighter-focused exercise in Indonesia in 19 years involving the U.S. Military and the Indonesian Air Force." See Aaron Henson, "Pacific Air Forces, US Marine Corps Conclude Exercise Cope West 17," press release, U.S. Marine Corps, November 16, 2016; George W. Maddon, Jr., "PACAF, U.S. Marines Conclude Fighter Ops in Cope West 17," press release, U.S. Indo-Pacific Command, November 10, 2016; Benjamin Felton, "Indonesia and the United States Kick Off Nine Day Military Exercise Cope West 2021," Overt Defense, June 16, 2021.

[10] Pacific Air Forces Public Affairs, "US, Indonesian Air Forces to Conduct Cope West 22 Exercise," June 6, 2022.

[11] Matthew Lee, "US Approves Major $14 Billion Arms Sale to Indonesia," ABC News, February 10, 2022.

[12] Tom Allard, "Exclusive: Indonesia Rejects U.S. Request to Host Spy Planes," Reuters, October 20, 2020.

[13] Allard, 2020.

[14] Allard, 2020.

[15] Allard, 2020.

Evaluating the Framework for Conflict-Phase Access Decisions in Indonesia

Question 1: Would Granting the United States Conflict-Phase Access Affect the Leader or the Regime's Political Survival?

Two key factors would likely play a role in Indonesian conflict-phase access decisions related to this question:

1. the potential for backlash from the Indonesian public against the leadership if the public perceived that Indonesian leaders are endangering the nation's security for the sake of an outside power
2. the Indonesian public's views at the time of the conflict on China and the United States.

On the first factor, public opinion polling in Indonesia shows that there is overwhelming Indonesian public preference for the leadership to avoid entanglement in any regional conflict seen as being outside the nation's own direct interests. A 2022 poll conducted by the Lowy Institute showed that 84 percent of Indonesians responded that, in the event of a potential conflict between the United States and China, Indonesia should remain neutral.[16] Only 4 percent said that Indonesia should support the United States, and 1 percent said Indonesia should support China.[17] Some of the public's opinion on not choosing sides may reflect uncertainty about which country is most likely to be the primary regional power in the future. When asked about whether China or the United States will be the leading military power in Asia in 20 years, 36 percent of respondents said it would be the United States, 22 percent responded that it would be China, and 36 percent responded that they did not know.[18]

Several responses to questions from *the State of Southeast Asia* 2021 survey report also indicate that Indonesians would prefer to avoid siding with either the United States or China, regardless of the specifics of the conflict, and would want ASEAN to remain neutral. According to the survey, most respondents emphasized the importance of ASEAN remaining an independent bloc and enhancing its ability to resist pressure to side with China or the United States.[19] These responses highlight the Indonesian public's strong preference for avoiding alignment even in peacetime competition, which would likely be a significant consideration

---

[16] Ben Bland, Evan Laksmana, and Natasha Kassam, *Charting Their Own Course: How Indonesians See the World*, Lowy Institute, 2022, p. 33.

[17] Bland, Laksmana, and Kassam, 2022, p. 33.

[18] Bland, Laksmana, and Kassam, 2022, p. 33.

[19] Seah et al., 2021, p. 32. In the survey, respondents were asked: "ASEAN is caught in the crossfire as Beijing and Washington compete for influence and leadership in Southeast Asia. How should ASEAN best respond?" A clear majority, 60.5 percent, chose "ASEAN should enhance its resilience and unity to fend off pressure from the two major powers," while only 3.1 percent chose "ASEAN has to choose between one of the two major powers as remaining impartial is impractical."

for the Indonesian leadership when making the potentially far more difficult decision to grant conflict-phase access.

For the second factor, the Indonesian public's views on China and the United States at the time of the conflict would likely shape any decision on conflict-phase access. Historically, the Indonesian public has displayed varying levels of antipathy for both nations, with each viewed highly negatively (and occasionally positively), depending on both global and domestic events. The low point for public opinion toward the United States may have come during the Iraq War, while the nadir of popular sentiment toward China came during and in the years following the eradication of the Communist Party of Indonesia in 1965–1966.[20]

In general, current polls indicate that the public views China more negatively now than a decade ago, and that Indonesians are more concerned about China's regional ambitions than they were in the recent past. For example, according to the 2021 Lowy Institute poll, only 43 percent of Indonesians now say that "China's growth has been good for Indonesia," a view previously held by the majority (54 percent in 2011), and 48 percent agree that China's aim is to dominate Asia.[21] Even fewer Indonesians (42 percent) trust China to act responsibly, a decline of 18 points over the past decade.[22] In addition, 60 percent responded that they either strongly agree or agree that "Indonesia should join with other countries to limit China's influence," an increase of ten points since 2011.[23]

However, a more negative view on China has not necessarily translated into a more positive view of the United States. The Lowy poll indicates that, while China ranks less favorably than the United States across a range of indicators, including military, economic, influence, and security matters, trust in both China and the United States has clearly declined among Indonesians in the past decade.[24] For example, the poll showed that while 56 percent responded that they trust the United States, this is 16 percent less than in 2011.[25] While 49 percent of respondents viewed China as the country that posed the most threat to Indonesian security in the next ten years, 43 percent stated that the United States posed the most

---

[20] The Communist Party of Indonesia [Partai Komunis Indonesia, or PKI] was a legal political party with about 2 million members heavily based in the nation's ethnic-Chinese communities. It maintained connections to Beijing but had a decade-long history of overt operation within Indonesia's established political system. In 1965, it represented the most robust threat to the TNI's political and social power. On September 30–October 1, 1965, a small group of conspirators launched an abortive coup, the details of which (including the potential complicity of Sukarno himself) remain in dispute. TNI, led by then–Major General Suharto, captured the plotters and instituted military rule, which would last for the next 34 years. While no convincing evidence was put forward linking the coup attempt to either the Communist Party of Indonesia or China, the following months saw a bloodbath of ethnic-Chinese and others belonging to (or merely suspected of sympathizing with) the communist party.

[21] Bland, Laksmana, and Kassam, 2022.

[22] Bland, Laksmana, and Kassam, 2022, p. 7.

[23] Bland, Laksmana, and Kassam, 2022, p. 32.

[24] Bland, Laksmana, and Kassam, 2022, p. 32.

[25] Bland, Laksmana, and Kassam, 2022, p. 32.

threat.[26] In all, these numbers suggest that, while Indonesians might increasingly view China negatively, their opinion of the United States, while more positive than that of China, has not improved over the past decade. These perspectives, combined with the Indonesian public's clear preference for its leadership to hew to the nonalignment policy, would make it difficult for Indonesian leaders to grant the United States conflict-phase access without experiencing some level of domestic backlash that could affect a leader's political standing.

What Factors Specific to the Conflict Might Shape the Decisions?

Public reactions would differ depending on where the conflict was based and which other nations were involved. An SCS conflict might permit Indonesian leaders more space to side with the United States than a Taiwan invasion scenario would, given public concern for Indonesian territory in the SCS. While Indonesia is not itself a direct claimant to any of the disputed SCS territories, it has its own territorial dispute with China over use of maritime territory surrounding the Natuna Islands.[27] Beyond geographical concerns, if China is the clear aggressor in any conflict (for example, an unprovoked invasion of Taiwan), this might help sway public opinion to be more favorable to supporting the United States. A further consideration would be the degree of anti-Chinese sentiment prevalent among the public at the time. While 1965–1966 was the most violent instance of anti-Chinese fervor, it was not the only such episode in recent Indonesian history; in January 1998, for example, the downfall of Suharto was preceded by anti-Chinese pogroms in Jakarta and elsewhere.[28] In the absence of any such overwhelming factors, however, the Indonesian public is likely to favor a position of neutrality in a U.S.-China conflict.

Question 2: Would Granting the United States Conflict-Phase Access Affect the Country's Direct Security Position?

Three factors might affect Indonesian leaders' decision to grant the U.S. military access in a conflict:

1. concern over possible Chinese military responses to Indonesia's sovereign territory (particularly the Natuna Islands)

---

[26] While causality is difficult to determine, those viewing the United States as a threat might be considering U.S. support for Israel; the vast majority of Indonesians support the creation of an independent Palestinian state. See Sebastian Strangio, "Indonesian Public Opinion Ambivalent About Rising Geopolitical Tensions: Report," *The Diplomat*, April 5, 2022b.

[27] The Natuna Islands lie slightly outside the area disputed (in whole or in part) by China, Taiwan, the Philippines, Vietnam, Malaysia, and Brunei. China does not recognize Indonesia's right to the waters in the Natuna's EEZ, and this has created a persistent flash-point between the two nations.

[28] Neither the 1965–1966 nor the 1998 programs arose from the grassroots level against the wishes of the governing regimes: They were fueled from above, then took on life at the grassroots level. This dynamic is important to keep in mind when evaluating the degree to which anti-Chinese sentiment will shape—rather than merely reflect—the decisionmaking of Indonesian leadership.

2. the Indonesian leadership's focus on internal security threats
3. Indonesia's assessment of the reliability of the United States as a long-term security partner.

For the first factor, Indonesian leaders are concerned over potential Chinese military responses, particularly involving the Natuna Islands, if they were to grant U.S. forces access, This concern could make the leadership quite reluctant to even consider access in conflict. The most recent Indonesian defense white paper discusses the SCS disputes and maritime sovereignty as areas of security concern but emphasizes Indonesia's position as a nonaligned country with a foreign policy aimed at "realizing a peaceful region," where countries involved in the disputes should refrain from aggressive action to resolve them.[29] The white paper also states that security challenges should be worked out multilaterally—reflecting Jakarta's preference to work through ASEAN to reduce regional tensions and to not do anything that would particularly anger Beijing.[30]

However, there are some signs that Indonesia might be more willing to push back on China along with the United States, at least under the right circumstances. Policymakers have been increasingly willing to engage in bilateral and multilateral exercises, suggesting an increased openness to security partnership. The Indonesian and U.S. militaries are expanding their annual bilateral Garuda Shield exercise to include 14 countries (including Australia, Canada, Japan, Malaysia, Singapore, and the United Kingdom), making the exercise the largest ever.[31] Indonesia also released a statement in 2020 rejecting China's claims in the SCS as having "no legal basis."[32] In March 2022, the office of the Indonesian president issued a regulation on sea zoning specifically in Natuna and the Natuna Sea.[33] This stance is broadly supported by the Indonesian public; the 2021 Lowy Institute Poll found that 61 percent of Indonesian respondents consider "protecting Indonesia's sovereign/archipelagic waters" to be "very important" and 30 percent consider it "fairly important," compared with 9 percent of respondents who rated it "not very important," "not important at all," or "don't know."[34]

That said, Indonesia's limited military capability and concerns over potential Chinese retaliation mean that the Indonesian leadership will likely continue to build diplomatic and economic relations with China despite the PRC's coercive actions in the SCS and in Indonesian

---

[29] Defence Ministry of the Republic of Indonesia, *Defence White Paper 2015* (English version), 2015, pp. 122–124.

[30] Indonesia is not a party to the SCS territorial disputes and has historically preferred to be viewed as a neutral broker rather than aligned with one country or another (Defence Ministry of the Republic of Indonesia, 2015, pp. 122–124).

[31] Ralph Jennings, "Indonesia Leans Further Toward US Amid Growing Maritime Dispute with China," Voice of America, April 16, 2022b.

[32] "Indonesia Rejects China's Claims Over South China Sea," Reuters, January 1, 2020.

[33] Kornelius Purba, "Will Jokowi's Decree on Natuna Change the Equation?" *Jakarta Post*, April 18, 2022.

[34] Bland, Laksmana, and Kassam, 2022, p. 10.

waters and will likely work through ASEAN to address regional security issues rather than confront China directly.[35] In addition, whatever the degree of concern they might have about the potential for Chinese invasion or kinetic retaliation, Indonesian leaders are likely even more worried about the risk of Chinese economic retaliation (discussed later).[36] Jakarta's concerns over the potential risk of Chinese military actions combined with economic retaliation would likely mean that the leadership would not view granting the United States access and hosting U.S. capabilities as improving its security position. In fact, the Indonesian leadership could fear that China would interpret Indonesia's granting the United States access as a move away from the nonalignment policy, angering Beijing and raising the risk of retaliation.[37]

On the second factor, Indonesia's most recent national defense white paper illustrates that the government's assessment of its security threats is largely focused on internal challenges.[38] The top security threats include terrorism, cybercrime, epidemics, natural disasters, and human trafficking.[39] The domestic focus of the Indonesian leadership on security was also emphasized in a 2019 rollout of Indonesia's diplomatic priorities for 2019–2024, which include bolstering Indonesia's economy through economic diplomacy and strengthening sovereignty and nationality through the settlement of national borders.[40] On maritime security issues, Indonesia views itself as a critical transit point for global trade; however, TNI has largely focused its efforts on addressing the internal security threats discussed earlier—terrorism, insurgency, and internal stability.

Furthermore, TNI has not significantly invested in the air and maritime capabilities needed to secure the country's territory and littoral waters against a peer adversary (let alone one as militarily superior as the PRC). The Indonesian Navy lacks adequate maritime domain awareness to track potential maritime threats, such as Chinese incursions in Indonesia's territorial waters.[41] TNI is working on building these capabilities, including through U.S. security assistance focused on increasing maritime patrol capacity, ISR integration, and sup-

---

[35] The 2015 defense white paper states that "Indonesia has 92 outermost islets, 12 of which require priority management so the sovereignty and territorial integrity of the Republic of Indonesia can be secured optimally" (Defence Ministry of the Republic of Indonesia, 2015, p. 9). Indonesian fishermen have repeatedly claimed that Chinese fishing fleets illegally fish in Indonesian waters. The Indonesian government has so far played down these incursions to avoid conflict with Beijing. See Hannah Beech, "China Chases Indonesian Fishing Fleets, Staking Claim to Sea's Riches," *New York Times*, March 31, 2020.

[36] Interview with U.S. government SME, July 21, 2022.

[37] Interview with U.S. government SME, July 21, 2022.

[38] Defence Ministry of the Republic of Indonesia, 2015.

[39] Blank, 2021b, p. 46.

[40] Ministry of Foreign Affairs of the Republic of Indonesia, "Indonesian FM Presents the Diplomacy Priorities 2019–2024 to the House of Representatives," November 14, 2019.

[41] For a discussion of Indonesia's maritime security threats and capabilities, see Lyle J. Morris and Giacomo Persi Paoli, *A Preliminary Assessment of Indonesia's Maritime Security Threats and Capabilities*, RAND Corporation, RR-2469-RC, 2018.

porting the Indonesian Coast Guard's development, but the country still remains vulnerable to maritime threats.[42] However, the military's and government's focus on internal security threats makes it unlikely that they would view granting the United States access in a conflict as improving their security position, particularly if the action would increase the threat by China to Indonesian waters and territory.

For the third factor, Indonesian leaders would likely consider whether the United States would be a reliable security partner if Indonesia granted access. This includes assessing whether U.S. forces would help defend Indonesian territory if Indonesia were targeted by China for granting access, as well as whether the United States would be a beneficial long-term security partner. On the first point, Indonesian leadership does not generally believe that the United States would defend Indonesian territory in a conflict, even if Indonesia grants access.[43] Unlike with the Philippines, the United States has no formal alliance with Indonesia and is not obligated to defend Indonesian territory; the disparity between obligations toward a treaty ally and a mere security partner were shown starkly to Indonesian security planners in the different U.S. response toward its NATO allies (whose defense the United States is legally bound to support militarily) and Ukraine (toward which the United States has no such binding obligation). The lack of a clear imperative for U.S. forces to defend Indonesian territory in a conflict would likely present challenges for Indonesian leaders to justify granting access without a U.S. security guarantee.

The Indonesian leadership appears to have mixed views on whether the United States would be a reliable long-term security partner, which might factor into the leadership's assessment of Indonesia's security in a postconflict environment. Security cooperation between the U.S. and Indonesian militaries includes the Indonesia-U.S. Security Dialogue, U.S.-Indonesia Bilateral Defense Dialogue, security assistance programs, International Military Education and Training, foreign military sales, and the Foreign Military Financing Program.[44] However, despite these efforts, Indonesia has expressed concern about the United States' reliability as a security partner.[45] Some of these concerns are based in historical issues, such as the United States cutting military ties to the TNI in the last decade of the Suharto regime because of human rights abuses. This severing of security cooperation, which was required by U.S. law, continued to affect ties between TNI officials and their U.S. counterparts even after most

---

[42] U.S. Embassy & Consulates in Indonesia, "U.S. Building Maritime Capacity in Southeast Asia," fact sheet, undated.

[43] Interview with SME, June 23, 2022.

[44] Many of these security-cooperation activities are codified in the Framework Arrangement on Cooperative Activities in the Field of Defense Between the Ministry of Defense of the Republic of Indonesia and Department of Defense of the United States of America, signed 2010 and enhanced with a joint statement dated October 26, 2015. See also Blank, 2021b, pp. 40–41.

[45] Interview with U.S. government SME, June 24, 2022.

forms of cooperation had resumed during the first decade of the 21st century.[46] Currently, when U.S. naval forces make port calls in Indonesia, they do not provide crew rosters—a policy based on U.S. interpretation of international law but that is an "additional irritant [fueling] anti-U.S. attitudes among TNI leaders" and a "relatively arcane legal dispute but [one that causes] considerable tension."[47]

Jakarta might also be concerned about possible impacts of U.S. sanctions and tariffs if it purchased goods or equipment from such countries as Russia and China.[48] For example, U.S. programs, such as the 2017 Countering America's Adversaries Through Sanctions Act, which introduced restrictive rules governing the purchase and transfer of sensitive technology, might also give Indonesia pause when considering the United States as a security partner, given China's investment in developing Indonesia's technology infrastructure.[49] These concerns illustrate some of the issues the Indonesian leadership might have when considering the reliability of the United States as a security partner if Indonesia granted the U.S. military access.

In sum, Indonesia's concern over potential Chinese military action; preference for maintaining good bilateral relations with China, in keeping with Jakarta's nonalignment policy and to lower the risk of PRC retaliation; national security focus on domestic threats; and hesitation regarding the United States as a reliable long-term security partner make it unlikely that the Indonesian leadership would assess that granting access would bolster its security position. Even peacetime access that would bolster Indonesia's maritime domain awareness capabilities along its littoral waters and enhance maritime security is not unproblematic. In 2020, Indonesia rejected a U.S. proposal to allow U.S. P-8 Poseidon aircraft to land and refuel in the country, so it remains unclear whether the leadership would allow deployment of such capabilities in a conflict.[50]

What Factors Specific to the Conflict Might Shape the Decisions?

Although unlikely, a conflict in which China directly threatens Indonesian territory or access to Indonesian littoral waters could potentially increase the likelihood of the Indonesian leadership granting access. However, even in this situation, Indonesia is more likely to be cautious about the type of access it grants, likely focusing only on lower-level, nonkinetic capabilities, such as ISR, maritime domain awareness, and overflight.

---

[46] In 1999, the United States suspended all military aid to Indonesia in response to its widespread human rights violations in East Timor (Niksch, 1998; Kurlantzick, 2018, p. 5).

[47] Blank, 2021b, pp. 43–44.

[48] Interview with SME, April 26, 2022.

[49] Gayatri Suroyo, "China Agrees to Invest $3 Bln in Indonesia Sovereign Wealth Fund," Reuters, July 4, 2022; Blank, 2021b, pp. 41–42.

[50] Allard, 2020.

Question 3: Would Granting Conflict-Phase Access Affect the Outcome of the Conflict?

There is one key factor that the Indonesian leadership would potentially consider for this question: whether U.S. forces already have access to nearby countries, such as Singapore, the Philippines, and Australia, which would make access to Indonesia less critical to U.S. operations, particularly in a Taiwan conflict in which Indonesian territory is not directly threatened.[51] For example, if U.S. forces have access to the Philippines, Indonesia might be less likely to grant access, given that the Philippines is a treaty ally of the United States, unlike Indonesia, and is in a critical location to support U.S. operations in a conflict. Similarly, if Singapore grants access to U.S. forces, Indonesia might perceive that the U.S. has the operational access it needs in Southeast Asia and would be less likely to grant access in this circumstance. A similar calculus might concern access granted by Australia, Japan, or other Indo-Pacific nations, depending on the scenario and distance from Indonesian territory and waters.

Even if Indonesia grants access to the United States, the type and level of access that it is likely to grant would be minimal and would seek to reduce the risk of Chinese retaliation as much as possible while keeping Indonesia's reputation as an independent and nonaligned country. As one interviewee noted, operational access is likely a redline for Indonesia.[52] Access, if granted, would therefore likely not involve allowing U.S. combat operations or offensive capabilities to be used from Indonesian soil. Rather, Indonesia would potentially offer low-level nonkinetic access, such as overflight, ISR, and potentially refueling and maintenance facilities.

What Factors Specific to the Conflict Might Shape the Decisions?

For this question, the location of the conflict might bear on whether Indonesia grants access. Conflicts in the SCS that could threaten Indonesian territory or interests (particularly the Natuna Islands) or those of ASEAN nations might make the Indonesian leadership more willing to grant access if Indonesia's proximity to the conflict would help the United States win and would deter further Chinese aggression in Southeast Asia or would help protect Indonesian territory from attack. For a conflict involving Taiwan, however, Indonesia might perceive that access from its territory is less crucial, particularly if the United States already has access in other nearby countries, such as Japan.

Question 4: Would Granting the United States Conflict-Phase Access Affect—or be Affected by—Regional Decisions Regarding Granting Similar Access?

Indonesian leaders would likely focus on two factors when considering this question:

---

[51] Interview with U.S. government SME, June 24, 2022.

[52] Interview with U.S. government SME, June 24, 2022.

1. whether ASEAN supports U.S. operations against China
2. whether access has been granted by other ASEAN members.

For the first factor, even though the leadership is reluctant to enter into military alliances, it does believe that working multilaterally through ASEAN is the best way to solve regional security challenges and preserve Indonesia's nonaligned status.[53] The preference to be as in sync with ASEAN as possible on supporting the United States would likely remain for Indonesia in a conflict. As one interviewee noted, Jakarta would initially look to ASEAN to gauge the level of regional support for U.S. operations when considering whether to grant access.[54] In a conflict, support for the United States from most ASEAN members, for example, might make it easier for the Indonesian leadership to grant access to U.S. forces and say that the decision was multilaterally supported by ASEAN rather than due to U.S. influence over Indonesia.[55]

A data point for this is Indonesia's stance toward Russia following the invasion of Ukraine. Russia is one of the nation's major security partners, and China has supported the invasion (with barely any diplomatic cover to the contrary). Given Indonesia's strong preference for nonalignment, these facts might well have led to a decision to abstain from condemnation of the invasion at the UN and other international forums. This position, indeed, is the one that the other historical bastion of nonalignment, India, has taken. New Delhi joined its rival China in abstaining from the two crucial votes against Russia's invasion in the UN General Assembly. Indonesia, however, joined with six of the other ASEAN nations (and over 140 other nations, led by the United States) in both the March 2 and March 24, 2022, votes.[56] The only ASEAN nations abstaining were Vietnam (heavily reliant on Russian military hardware), Laos (which largely subordinates its security decisions to those of China), and Brunei (the smallest nation in ASEAN). Even Cambodia and Myanmar, led by nondemocratic regimes closely tied to Beijing, voted with the United States rather than China.[57] Without the company of two-thirds of ASEAN nations, Indonesia might well have made a different decision.

That said, there are real limitations to ASEAN agreement on security issues closer to home. Cambodia, Myanmar, and Laos all have closer relations with China than with the United States and might be more apt to support Beijing's objectives in a conflict.[58] No ASEAN member—even close U.S. security partner Singapore—has any appetite for a conflict, and all

---

[53] Evan Laksmana, "An Indo-Pacific Construct with Indonesian Characteristics," *The Strategist*, February 6, 2018a.

[54] Interview with U.S. government SME, July 21, 2022.

[55] Interview with U.S. government SME, July 21, 2022.

[56] Storey and Choong, 2022.

[57] Storey and Choong, 2022.

[58] Shaun Turton, "Beijing-Friendly Cambodia and Laos Pushed Out to ASEAN's Fringe," Nikkei Asia, November 13, 2020.

would prefer to remain in the background of any potential clash that did not involve their own territory. Indonesia might also be concerned that China could interfere with Indonesia's relations with other ASEAN members through retaliatory political or economic actions. Therefore, while the level of ASEAN support for U.S. operations in a conflict might increase the likelihood that Indonesia would grant access, the barriers to widespread ASEAN cooperation on military and security issues make it unlikely that members would provide Indonesia the level of multilateral consensus it might be looking for.

For the second factor, Indonesian leaders would potentially consider *which* other ASEAN member states have granted access in the conflict. Several other members granting access—such as Singapore, the Philippines, and Malaysia—might induce the Indonesian leadership to also grant some level of access (for example, allowing U.S. overflight or hosting of ISR capabilities), to show solidarity with ASEAN member states. Indonesia might also perceive that *not* granting access when other key ASEAN states have done so might diminish its regional position or its influence in ASEAN. Such concerns, however, would be balanced against the prospect of abandoning its nonaligned status and degrading its ability to bargain with both powers postconflict.[59]

While Indonesia might consider the decisions of neighboring states when determining whether to grant access, Indonesia's own decision to grant access might have less influence on the decisions of other key states in Southeast Asia, such as the Philippines and Singapore. This is partly because of Indonesia's limited defense ties with these regional countries but is primarily due to the Philippines and Singapore's individual relationships with the United States as an ally and security partner, respectively.[60] Indonesia's nonaligned posture has prevented it from forging extensive bilateral defense cooperation, not merely with the United States but also with any other country. Its defense cooperation activities include 2+2 ministerial dialogues with the United States, Australia, Japan, and South Korea, and it participates in some military training and exercises with neighboring countries, including the Philippines.[61] As discussed in Question 2, Indonesia's kinetic defense activities have been more focused on internal than on external security, and its policy has been focused on bolstering regional economic and political cooperation to reduce security tensions; as a result, its military-to-military activities with regional countries are not as robust as those of other states in South-

[59] Yohanes Sulaiman, "Whither Indonesia's Indo-Pacific Strategy?" French Institute of International Relations, Center for Asian Studies, January 2019.

[60] Interview with SME, June 23, 2022. See also the country deep dives on the Philippines and Singapore for an in-depth discussion of the factors that the national leaders of those countries would consider for conflict-phase access.

[61] Harold et al., 2019, p. 228; U.S. Department of State, "Fourth Annual U.S.-India 2+2 Ministerial Dialogue," press release, April 11, 2022b. Ministry of Foreign Affairs, Republic of Korea, "First Korea-Indonesia Foreign and Defense (2+2) Senior Officials' Meeting," webpage, August 27, 2021.

east Asia, such as Singapore and the Philippines.[62] Given these limitations, other states are unlikely to ground their own access decisions on Indonesia's course of action.

What Factors Specific to the Conflict Might Shape the Decisions?

The location of the conflict in the SCS, and particularly if it involves ASEAN member nations, could increase the Indonesian leadership's willingness to grant access, given Jakarta's leading position in that organization. Conversely, conflicts in which ASEAN members are not directly involved or threatened could decrease the likelihood of Indonesia granting access.

Question 5: Would Granting the United States Conflict-Phase Access Affect the Economic Prosperity of the Country?

The leadership would potentially consider two key factors:

1. Indonesia's reliance on China's trade and investment and preference to maintain economic relations with China in a postconflict environment
2. the potential for substantial damage to Indonesia's economy, were China to retaliate.

For the first factor, Indonesia's economy is substantially dependent on Chinese trade and investment, and this would likely factor into any Indonesian conflict-phase access decision, particularly if the Indonesian leadership considered postconflict economic relations. China has been Indonesia's largest trading partner since 2013, and the total value of Indonesia's trade with China in 2021 reached $131 billion.[63] By contrast, trade with the United States, Taiwan, and several large U.S. allies put together came to $122.6 billion in 2021, as shown in Table 6.1. Whether China or the United States and its allies and partners has a larger share of Indonesian trade is not the essential question; what the data show is the large scale of Indonesian economic dependence on trade with China, a dependence that China has repeatedly threatened to use to punish states that take stances with which it disagrees. In 2020, China was the top Indonesian export destination, accounting for 18.3 percent of total exports ($32.6 billion).[64] China was also the top source of imports in the same year, accounting for 29 percent of total Indonesian imports ($40.8 billion).

In addition to trade, Chinese investment in Indonesia is also substantial. The annual flow of FDI from China to Indonesia has been increasing since 2010 ($0.2 billion) to 2020

---

[62] Frega Wenas Inkiriwang, "Recalibrating Indonesia's Defense Diplomacy for the New Normal," National Bureau of Asian Research, May 8, 2021; Evan A. Laksmana, "Buck Passing from Behind: Indonesia's Foreign Policy and the Indo-Pacific," Brookings Institution, November 27, 2018b.

[63] Unless otherwise noted, all dollar amounts are in U.S. dollars. William Yuen Yee, "Explaining China's Relationship with Indonesia, Its Gateway to Southeast Asia," China Project, December 2, 2021. UN Comtrade database of $39.6 billion imported from China to Indonesia and $31.8 exported in 2020: UN, undated.

[64] OEC, "Indonesia," webpage, undated-b.

TABLE 6.1

Indonesia's Total Bilateral Trade by Country

Year	China	United States	Japan	Australia	Taiwan	Republic of Korea	Germany	UK	France
2012	71.7	26.5	52.9	10.2	12.5	29.6	9.2	2.1	4.0
2013	74.0	24.8	46.4	9.4	12.3	24.8	8.9	2.1	4.2
2014	69.4	24.8	40.1	10.6	11.2	23.6	8.7	1.9	4.2
2015	59.8	23.9	31.3	8.5	9.0	16.7	7.3	1.9	4.3
2016	59.1	23.5	29.1	8.5	7.1	14.9	6.9	2.1	4.9
2017	69.6	26.0	31.9	9.6	8.1	18.0	7.5	2.3	4.0
2018	83.5	28.7	37.5	8.6	8.8	20.0	7.9	2.2	3.7
2019	86.4	27.2	31.7	7.8	7.6	16.5	7.1	2.2	3.9
2020	84.0	27.6	24.6	7.1	6.8	13.9	6.4	1.9	2.3
2021	131.1	36.4	33.0	10.6	11.0	19.3	7.7	2.2	2.4

SOURCES: OEC, "Indonesia/China," webpage, undated-c; U.S. Census Bureau, undated; World Bank, undated-c; JETRO, various years; Australian Government, Department of Foreign Affairs and Trade, undated; Bureau of Foreign Trade, Taiwan, undated; Korea Customs Service, undated, for export/import by country; German Federal Statistics Office, 2022; Office for National Statistics, 2022; UN, undated, trade data for Indonesia.

NOTE: Amounts in billions of U.S. dollars. China includes Mainland China, Hong Kong, and Macao.

($2.2 billion),[65] accounting for 11.5 percent of total net inflows in 2020.[66] Much of this financing comes through BRI, which has invested $12.7 billion into Indonesian steel and nickel projects alone since 2013.[67] Additional recent examples of BRI investments include a 2021 $2.8 million copper smelting project in Weda Bay[68] and a 2021 $350 million lithium project for electric vehicle batteries.[69] Chinese private investment also plays a role in the Indonesian economy: China ranks second for foreign private capital in Indonesia, totaling approximately $4.8 billion in 2020, and Chinese private investment in Indonesia has increased annually since 2016.[70]

---

[65] Statista, "Annual Flow of Foreign Direct Investments from China to Indonesia Between 2010 and 2020," Statista, January 4, 2022.

[66] World Bank, "Foreign Direct Investment, Net Inflows (BoP, current US$)—Indonesia," webpage, undated-a.

[67] Liza Lin, Yifan Wang, and Jon Emont, "Chinese Workers Say They Are Lured Abroad and Exploited for Belt and Road Jobs," *Wall Street Journal*, October 27, 2021.

[68] Fathin Ungku, Bernadete Christina Munthe, and Tom Daly, "Freeport, Tsingshan Finalising $2.8 Billion Copper Smelter Next Week—Minister," Reuters, March 24, 2021.

[69] Tom Daily and Min Zhang, "China's Chengxin, Tsingshan Team Up for $350 Million Indonesia Lithium Project," Reuters, September 23, 2021.

[70] Embassy of the Republic of Indonesia—Beijing, People's Republic of China, "Indonesia's Exports to China and Chinese Investment to Indonesia in 2020 Are Increasing," February 28, 2021.

By comparison, the United States was Indonesia's third-largest trading partner in 2020, with two-way trade equal to $27.6 billion, although this falls far below China's $71.4 billion in trade with Indonesia for the same year.[71] The United States was also the second-largest destination for Indonesia's exports in 2020, at 11.0 percent ($19.6 billion), and fifth, or 5.41 percent, of total imports ($7.59 billion).[72] Although complete data for 2022 were not available as this writing, official data from the Indonesia Ministry of Investment rank FDI investor countries of origin in Q1 2022 as follows: "Singapore (US$ 3.6 billion, 34.8 percent); Hong Kong (US$ 1.5 billion, 15.0 percent); China (US$ 1.4 billion, 13.2 percent), Japan (US$ 0.8 billion, 8.0 percent); and United States (US$ 0.6 billion, 6.1 percent)."[73] Notably, the ministry publication highlights that the United States has entered the top-five countries of FDI origin for the first time—although U.S. FDI still comprises less than one-quarter of combined investment from China and Hong Kong.[74]

Indonesians clearly perceive that China is more influential economically than the United States. In *The State of Southeast Asia: 2021 Survey Report*, 70.5 percent of Indonesian respondents chose China as "the most influential economic power in Southeast Asia," and 52.4 percent "welcome its growing regional economic influence"—an increase from 43.5 percent in 2020.[75] Given how tied Indonesia's economy is to Chinese trade and investment and the leadership's and public's preference to remain nonaligned, it is likely that Indonesian leaders would prefer to keep the option of maintaining economic relations with China in a post-conflict environment. Jakarta's access decisionmaking calculus in a regional conflict would therefore likely include an assessment of the potential risk of losing China as a trade and investment partner postconflict, even if the United States wins and China's economic power diminishes. The United States could potentially increase trade and investment to fill some of the gap, if China withdrew from trade with Indonesia, but the increase would have to be significantly more than the current amount to make up for the loss of China as a trade partner.

The second factor the Indonesian leadership would likely consider is the risk of Chinese economic retaliation—both during and after the conflict. As discussed earlier, the reliance of Indonesia's economy on Chinese trade and investment makes it particularly vulnerable to economic coercion and retaliation from China. As an interviewee noted, the threat of Chinese economic retaliation would be one of the top concerns of Indonesian leaders if the country were to move away from its nonalignment policy and be viewed as siding with the United States.[76]

---

[71] Office of the U.S. Trade Representative, "Indonesia," webpage, undated-a.

[72] OEC, undated-b.

[73] Indonesia Ministry of Investment, "Indonesian Investment Moves to Rise After Pandemic, First Quarter 2022 Investment Realization: IDR 282.4 Trillion," April 2022.

[74] Indonesia Ministry of Investment, 2022.

[75] Seah et al., 2021, p. 21.

[76] Interview with U.S. government SME, July 21, 2022.

China has threatened Indonesia with economic reprisals in the past, stemming from a territorial conflict just outside the disputed areas of the SCS. While China does not dispute the sovereignty of Indonesia's Natuna Islands, it does not accept Indonesia's claim to an EEZ in all the waters around them. In late 2019, dozens of Chinese fishing boats entered those waters, and Indonesia responded not only by summoning the PRC ambassador but also by sending warships and fighter jets to patrol the area.[77] Beijing appears to have defused the situation in the short term by instructing fishing boats to withdraw to the edge of Indonesia's claimed EEZ but simultaneously issued a diplomatic warning that Indonesia could put its BRI funding for several Indonesian infrastructure projects in jeopardy if it escalated the situation over the Natuna Islands.[78]

If China is willing to threaten such punishment over Indonesia defending its own territorial claims, it is reasonable to assume that China would certainly threaten comparable—or even more severe—punishment if Jakarta supported the United States by granting the military access in a conflict. The high risk of Chinese economic retaliation would likely further dampen Indonesia's willingness to grant access to the United States.

What Factors Specific to the Conflict Might Shape the Decisions?

If the conflict is of high intensity and involves substantial regional economic disruption such that China had significantly less economic power and Indonesia perceived that China might emerge from the conflict with diminished economic influence, Indonesia might be more willing to grant access, given that China's ability to retaliate economically would be reduced. Indonesia might be less likely to grant access in a Taiwan conflict because the stakes in such a scenario are high for China, and Beijing would be more likely to impose severe economic hardship on Indonesia.

How Might Indonesia's Decisions Vary Depending on the Types of Access Requested?

As discussed throughout this chapter, it is unlikely that Indonesia would offer U.S. forces significant access for operations from Indonesian bases or host kinetic capabilities that China and others would view as Indonesia altering the status quo and abandoning its nonalignment policy because this would open up the country to increased risk of Chinese retaliation. Several interviewees stated that security cooperation between the United States and Indonesia is increasing but also noted that Jakarta would view granting the United States any type of conflict-phase access as changing the status quo.

---

[77] Derek Grossman, "Why Is China Pressing Indonesia Again Over Its Maritime Claims?" *The RAND Blog*, January 16, 2020.

[78] Grossman, 2020.

That said, if Indonesia is willing to grant access in a conflict—to show regional support for other ASEAN members that have granted access, for example—it is more likely to do so if the United States requests low-level, nonkinetic access, such as overflight and ISR. Even access requests for maintenance or refueling of U.S. ships or aircraft may be refused because Jakarta would potentially fear that allowing U.S. ships or aircraft to stay on Indonesian soil would be perceived as hosting U.S. forces and abandonment of its nonaligned stance. Therefore, substantial challenges remain in terms of turning U.S.-Indonesian security cooperation into access in a conflict.[79]

Summary

This analysis points to several key factors that would likely be more important to the Indonesian leadership when assessing whether to grant the United States conflict-phase access. First, Indonesia's view that the nonalignment policy is the best way to keep the country secure, and the potential for public backlash if the leadership were perceived as compromising that policy by siding with an outside power, would likely be one of the primary considerations for the leadership. The literature we reviewed for this study and our discussions with interviewees emphasized how important maintaining nonalignment is to the Indonesian leadership and public and that the overwhelming public preference is for the leadership to avoid endangering the country's security interests by choosing between the United States and China. In addition, public opinion polling indicates that, while the Indonesian public's views of China have trended more negative, the public's view of the United States has not become more positive—in fact, the Indonesian public's trust in both the U.S. and China has declined over the past decade. This, along with the clear preference for the leadership to maintain the nonalignment policy, would likely be a key factor in the leadership's calculus for whether to grant access in conflict.

Second, the risk of retaliation from China, particularly economic retaliation, is a significant concern for Indonesian leaders. Our research indicates that Indonesian leadership is particularly concerned about the potential for Chinese military retaliation involving the Natuna Islands if Indonesia granted access to U.S. forces, especially because Indonesian military forces cannot fully protect the waterways and airspace around the islands. In addition to potential military retaliation, another concern for Jakarta is the risk of Chinese economic retaliation, given that Indonesia's economy is substantially tied to Chinese trade and investment and that Indonesian leaders view China as the country's primary economic partner.[80] In a conflict, the Indonesian leadership would likely consider both the economic damage to Indonesia's economy during the conflict if China were to retaliate and the potential for post-conflict economic retaliation and the long-term effects on the Indonesian economy if China

---

[79] Interview with U.S. government SME, July 21, 2022; interview with U.S. government SME, June 24, 2022.

[80] Interview with U.S. government SME, July 21, 2022.

chose to withdraw as an economic partner. Rather than courting Beijing's ire by granting access, the Indonesian leadership would be more likely to try to maintain its nonalignment status or show support through ASEAN to preserve the option of keeping economic ties with China postconflict.

Third, whether ASEAN supports U.S. operations against China in a conflict would also likely be a key factor in Indonesia's decision to grant access. Given its nonalignment policy, Indonesia vastly prefers to address security challenges through ASEAN, so that its position can be framed as being supported multilaterally by other countries in the region rather than being due to Indonesia's relationship with the United States. Therefore, a conflict in which more ASEAN states support the United States might make it easier for Indonesian leaders to grant access. This could include a statement from ASEAN supporting U.S. operations or, potentially, other ASEAN states granting access to U.S. forces. The reality is that there are significant barriers to widespread ASEAN cooperation on military and security issues that make it unlikely that members would provide Indonesia the level of multilateral consensus it might be looking for. However, as one interviewee noted, Indonesia would definitely "look first to ASEAN" to determine how to align its support in a conflict.[81]

Finally, in addition to these factors, the conflict characteristics would also matter to Indonesian leaders when assessing whether to grant access to U.S. forces. These characteristics are location, whether China is the perceived as the aggressor in the conflict, and the potential for China to economically retaliate against Indonesia if it should grant the United States access.

The location of the conflict would likely factor into Indonesia's response. The public might be more likely to support a conflict in the SCS more if it involved Indonesian territory or affected access to littoral waterways, which could increase the likelihood of Indonesia granting access. Likewise, an SCS conflict that involved other ASEAN members might induce Jakarta to show support by granting access. Conversely, a Taiwan conflict that does not directly involve Indonesian territory or that of ASEAN members would potentially decrease the likelihood of access.

A conflict in which China is the clear aggressor and/or is perceived to be expanding its ambitions to taking over territory in the SCS, for example, might lead to increased likelihood of Indonesia granting access to protect its security interests.

Finally, if there were a high-intensity conflict that involved significant economic disruption to China, Indonesia might be less fearful of economic retaliation if China's economic status were severely weakened. Conversely, Indonesia might be less willing to grant access in a conflict in which the stakes are high for China—such as over Taiwan—because China would be more apt to use economic retaliation as a lever to prevent Indonesia and other countries in the region from supporting the United States and Taiwan.

Table 6.2 summarizes the key factors and conflict characteristics highlighted by our analysis for each of the five framework questions.

---

[81] Interview with U.S. government SME, July 21, 2022.

TABLE 6.2

Summary of Adaptation of Conflict-Phase Access Decisionmaking Framework for Indonesia

Framework Question	Key Factors That Affect Leaders' Calculations	Conflict Characteristics on Which Assessment Depends
Would granting the United States conflict-phase access affect the leader or the regime's political survival?	• Potential for backlash from the public against the leadership if it is perceived that Indonesian leaders are endangering the nation's security for the sake of an outside power • The Indonesian public's views on China and the United States	• The location of the conflict matters: The public might be more likely to support an SCS than a Taiwan conflict • China becoming the aggressor in the conflict could shape public opinion to be more favorable to supporting the United States and increase the likelihood of access
Would granting the United States conflict-phase access affect the country's direct security position?	• Leadership concern over possible Chinese military response affecting Indonesia's sovereign territory • Indonesian leaders' focus on internal security threats • Indonesia's assessment of the reliability of the United States as a security partner	• If China were threatening Indonesian territory or access to littoral waters, the likelihood of Indonesia granting access could increase
Would granting the United States conflict-phase access affect the outcome of the conflict?	• Whether U.S. forces already have access to other nearby countries, making access to Indonesia less critical to U.S. operations	• A conflict location being in the SCS could threaten Indonesian or ASEAN territory or interests, which could increase the likelihood of Indonesia granting access • Conversely, a Taiwan scenario where Indonesian interests are not directly threatened could reduce the likelihood of access being granted, especially if the U.S. already has access in other countries
Would granting the United States conflict-phase access affect, or be affected by, regional decisions regarding granting similar access?	• Whether ASEAN supports U.S. operations against China • Whether other ASEAN members have granted access	• The location of the conflict in the SCS, particularly if it involves ASEAN members, could increase the likelihood of access given Indonesia's position in ASEAN • A conflict that does not affect ASEAN members could decrease the likelihood of Jakarta granting access

Table 6.2—Continued

Framework Question	Key Factors That Affect Leaders' Calculations	Conflict Characteristics on Which Assessment Depends
Would granting the United States conflict-phase access affect the economic prosperity of the country?	• Reliance on China's trade and investment and preference to maintain economic relations with China postconflict • The risk of Chinese economic retaliation during and after the conflict	• If the conflict is of high intensity and involves economic disruption or significantly weakens China's ability to economically retaliate, the likelihood of access could increase • If the stakes of the conflict are high for China (e.g., Taiwan), China might be more apt to economically retaliate, which could decrease Indonesia's willingness to grant access

CHAPTER 7

Adapting the Conflict-Phase Access Framework to India

India is the most capable and significant U.S. security partner in South Asia. Its size and geopolitical interests make it one of the most important U.S. partners in the Indo-Pacific region. Like the United States, India sees China as its greatest long-term strategic challenge and is, therefore, in basic harmony with America's broad security goals. Cooperation on security issues between the United States and India has increased steadily under each of the past five U.S. presidents and three Indian prime ministers, spanning both major political parties in each nation.[1] These factors provide a firm foundation for many aspects of future cooperation, but U.S. strategists should not underestimate the depth and endurance of India's traditional reluctance to join any sort of military alliance: Whether India regards binding alliances, whether de jure or de facto, as infringements on its sovereignty and national identity. Any expectation of conflict-phase access in India should be filtered through this lens, regardless of the overall trendline of cooperation on security, which is most likely to remain positive.

If India were itself a party to a future conflict with China, it might not only grant but request the presence of USAF assets; this has occurred once, in 1962, although that conflict ended before USAF aircraft arrived in country. In any scenario not involving an encroachment on India's own territory, however, New Delhi would be highly reluctant to take any action that could draw it into direct conflict with China. This deep reluctance should be taken as the baseline for any Department of the Air Force planning. But any decision by New Delhi would be based on the specific conditions at the time of the conflict.[2] For example, if India and China were already at a position of strong hostility, positive responses to U.S. access requests might be more likely than if the overall state of relations between India and China were relatively cordial, although it may still not be likely.

---

[1] U.S. Department of State, "U.S. Security Cooperation with India," January 20, 2021b.

[2] One New Delhi–based analyst noted the significance of circumstances *before* a conflict: "A lot will depend on China's behavior. If present [hostile] trendlines continue, redlines might shift more quickly than many realize" (interview with Indian security analyst, July 4, 2022).

India perceives the stakes of any conflict with China to be greater for itself than for the United States: As Indian strategists like to say, one cannot choose one's neighbors.[3] China will always be India's neighbor, and, for the foreseeable future, Beijing will be a militarily superior rival. China has invaded India once (in 1962), and has engaged in numerous border skirmishes throughout the decades.[4] The most recent fatal encounter came in June 2020 at Galwan, resulting in the deaths of 20 Indian soldiers.[5] From India's point of view, any U.S. military conflict with China is likely to be comparatively a matter of less-than-existential stakes for Washington: New Delhi perceives the PLA as unlikely to launch an out-of-the-blue attack on any American territory, least of all on any of the 50 U.S. states. For India, however, any large-scale clash with China is likely to be seen as a battle for the nation itself. Historically, all conflicts with Beijing have been (at least in the view of Indian policymakers) merely a matter of defending sovereign territory rather than jockeying over far-away priorities. Therefore, while India sees the United States as a key security partner, an important factor in India's decisionmaking would be the degree to which India perceives the United States as firmly committed to the conflict. From India's perspective, the worst-case scenario would be for New Delhi to provide access to the United States and generate long-term hostility and retaliation risks from China—only to have the United States stop short of a decisive confrontation and reach a separate settlement with the PRC.

When the PLA invaded Indian territory in 1962, Prime Minister Jawaharlal Nehru is said to have asked U.S. President John F. Kennedy for the deployment of 12 squadrons of USAF fighters and two squadrons of bombers.[6] In 1990–1991, two Indian prime ministers granted access to USAF aircraft for refueling en route from the Pacific to the Middle East in support of the first Gulf War.[7] Apart from these two instances, India is not publicly known to have provided access to USAF aircraft during any active interstate conflict.[8]

---

[3] As one interviewee put it, "We cannot change our neighbors—not even [arch-rival] Pakistan" (interview with former senior Indian diplomatic official, July 4, 2022).

[4] Jonah Blank, *Regional Responses to U.S.-China Competition in the Indo-Pacific: India*, RAND Corporation, 2021a, p. 42.

[5] The Galwan Valley is a remote part of the disputed border between the two countries. The June 2020 incident in the valley was the first fatal clash between India and China since 1975 and the most deadly since 1967. The deaths were particularly shocking because all patrols of the Line of Actual Control (which separates Himalayan territories administered by India from those administered by China)—Indian and Chinese alike—have been unarmed since 1996. The 20 Indian fatalities, and an unknown number of Chinese ones, were all the result of hand-to-hand combat without the use of firearms. This incident heightened tensions between India and China.

[6] Bruce Riedel, *JFK's Forgotten Crisis: Tibet, the CIA, and the Sino-Indian War*, Brookings Institution, 2017.

[7] J. K. Baral and T. N. Mahanty, "India and the Gulf Crisis: The Response of a Minority Government," *Pacific Affairs*, Vol. 65, No. 3, 1992, p. 374.

[8] This discussion is limited to information in the unclassified arena. *Conflict* refers to active combat operations against a nation-state. This distinction is useful because it excludes (for example) limited instances of access granted to USAF aircraft during the 2001–2022 operations against the Taliban in Afghanistan. Nei-

Even in times of peace, the access that India has given to the USAF and other branches of the U.S. military has historically been extremely limited. Throughout the Cold War, India explicitly followed a policy of nonalignment—equidistant (at least in theory) between the two competing geopolitical blocs. From the late 1960s until the dissolution of the Soviet Union, such theoretical equidistance was, in reality, closer to an alignment with the Soviet Union than with the United States, which resulted in American military personnel and assets having virtually no significant access for several decades. Even after the breakup of the Soviet Union, nonalignment remained at the core of India's foreign policy ideology throughout the 1990s.[9]

In the early 21st century, nonalignment was rebranded as *strategic autonomy*, but the basic idea—that is, that India should refrain from aligning or making a binding alliance with any nation or bloc of nations—remains a point of near-consensus among Indian policymakers.[10] The original idea of nonalignment is closely associated with Nehru and his Indian National Congress Party, which governed the nation (apart from a brief 1977–1980 interregnum) from its founding until the 1990s. The rise of the Bharatiya Janata Party (BJP) and its supplanting of the Indian National Congress as the nation's dominant political force, however, have not resulted in a corresponding rejection of Nehruvian nonalignment and strategic autonomy. The BJP has governed from 1998–2004 and 2014 to the present and appears secure in its political dominance for the foreseeable future; it has not, however, significantly moved away from the idea of strategic autonomy.

In August 2016, the administrations of U.S. President Obama and Indian Prime Minister Narendra Modi signed the Logistics and Exchange Memorandum of Understanding (LEMOA). This agreement formalized a previously ad hoc arrangement under which either nation could request access to the other's military facilities for fueling and other logistical support, then reimburse the host nation for any services provided.[11] This was followed by two other Foundational Agreements: the Communications Compatibility and Security Agreement (COMCASA) in 2018 and the Basic Exchange and Cooperation Agreement (BECA) in 2020.[12] These agreements, LEMOA in particular, form the basis for U.S. access to Indian military facilities outside a conflict and would be the foundation for any Indian decision on whether to grant such access during a conflict. The simplest way to address the question of conflict-phase access in India (according to Indian analysts interviewed for this report) is to

---

ther the United States nor India recognized the Taliban regime and successor insurgency as the legitimate government of Afghanistan; from New Delhi's perspective, this puts any access granted during the long conflict against these entities in a category completely different from any potential conflict with China.

[9] Blank, 2021a, p. 18.

[10] Blank, 2021, p. 18.

[11] Rajeswari Pillai Rajagopalan, "Logistics Pact with U.S.: Why LEMOA Is Significant for India," Observer Research Foundation, August 31, 2016.

[12] Sanjeev Miglani and Nigam Prusty, "India Says to Sign Military Agreement with U.S. on Sharing of Satellite Data," Reuters, October 26, 2020; Sanjeev Miglani, "India Set to Approve Military Communications Deal with U.S.—Indian Defence Sources," Reuters, September 5, 2018.

take the types of access currently available under LEMOA and examine the circumstances under which such access might be continued during a conflict.[13] Anything not already granted by LEMOA is unlikely to be added during a conflict unless India were itself the direct target of foreign invasion.

According to all these sources, New Delhi's starting point would be to reflexively deny any access that could potentially inflame China's sensibilities and draw India into an unwanted conflict. As one analyst put it, "If India isn't directly involved in the conflict, New Delhi will be ultra-cautious."[14] This does not mean, however, that a "no" could not be turned into a "maybe" or, under the right circumstances, a "yes." Such decisions, however, would depend entirely on the specifics of the conflict and the overall geopolitical circumstances. If important Indian partners, such as Japan, Australia, and Singapore,[15] were involved in the conflict, New Delhi might be more inclined to provide access than if it were simply a bilateral contest between the United States and China. Likewise, if the only other parties were nations less important to India (for example, an SCS dispute involving the Philippines but no nation other than the United States entering the fray), India might be less inclined to participate. But India has never formulated a comprehensive security doctrine beyond a very general level of discussion, and its security decisions have always been ad hoc. This is likely to be the case for the foreseeable future.

The characteristics of a notional U.S.-China conflict will have an impact on India's decision. The key conflict characteristic is whether India's own territory (as defined by Indian policymakers) is directly threatened by the conflict.[16] While certain uninhabited or lightly inhabited areas claimed by India have been occupied by China for decades (most notably, Aksai Chin), any PLA action to seize more territory would be seen as a threat to India's core national interests that could overrule concerns about permitting U.S. access. The arena of the

---

[13] Interview with Indian security analyst, July 2, 2022; interview with former senior Indian diplomatic official, July 4, 2022; interview with Indian security analyst, July 4, 2022; interview with former senior Indian diplomatic official, July 12, 2022.

[14] Interview with Indian security analyst, July 2, 2022.

[15] India's security relationship with Singapore does not typically receive as much attention as its relationship with (for example) members of the Quad, but the city-state enjoys greater access to Indian military facilities than almost any other nation. Because of the geographic limitations at home, Singapore regularly sends its air force and army (particularly armor and artillery) to train on Indian soil. The relationship moves in both directions. As a Singaporean analyst noted, "We could not have developed our submarine capability without India" (interview with Singaporean defense analyst, March 25, 2022).

[16] The distinction between territory recognized by the international community and territory claimed by India itself is not relevant to Indian policymakers: Across the political spectrum in India, policymakers see all territories regarded as "disputed" by rivals (China, Pakistan), partners (including the United States), and the UN as indisputably sovereign parts of the nation. This includes all parts of the Indian states of Jammu and Kashmir (disputed by Pakistan) and Arunachal Pradesh (disputed by China). Certain uninhabited or lightly inhabited Himalayan territories along the Line of Actual Control are also disputed with China (for example, much of the de facto border between the Indian territory of Ladakh and the Chinese territory of Tibet).

conflict would also be somewhat important but much less influential. According to Indian sources interviewed for this study, New Delhi is likely to be slightly more receptive to requests for access in the case of a PRC invasion of Taiwan than in scenarios involving islets in the SCS. From New Delhi's perspective, threats to Taiwan (a long-standing friend and trade partner) could be more likely to justify the risk of conflict with the PRC, while disputes over uninhabited atolls may be less likely to do so.[17]

One Indian interlocutor—a former ambassador who has also served at other top policymaking posts—suggested a pathway for U.S. strategists to improve the likelihood of overcoming New Delhi's instinctive reaction to deny conflict-phase access requests: Raise the potential for such requests and have the issues surrounding them thoroughly hashed out in *advance* of a conflict. He suggested raising these questions at a session of the 2+2 ministerial dialogues, the Quad, or at think-tank sessions and tabletop exercises. "If there were prior consultations, rather than waiting until a conflict was underway, it is more likely that India would say 'yes.'"[18]

History of U.S. Military Access in India

India has provided conflict-phase access to the United States in two publicly known instances. The first was during the Sino-Indian War in 1962. During China's invasion of the strategically important Ladakh region, India was being badly defeated by the PRC. The U.S. ambassador to India at the time, John Kenneth Galbraith, characterized the situation for India as "unbelievably dismal" because the Chinese had "taken over most of the political division known as the North-East Frontier Agency, over 30,000 square miles of northeastern India, and with incredible speed."[19] At the height of the crisis—which occurred during the Cuban Missile Crisis—Prime Minister Nehru wrote two letters to President Kennedy, in which he requested that U.S. air assets be deployed to India to stem the tide of the Chinese advance. Specifically, Nehru stated that a

> minimum of 12 squadrons of supersonic all-weather fighters are essential. We have no modern radar cover in the country. The United States Air Force personnel will have to man these fighters and radar installations while our personnel are being trained. . . . U.S. fighters and transport planes manned by U.S. personnel will be used for the present to protect our cities and installations . . . [and] assist the Indian Air Force in air battles with the Chinese air force over Indian areas.[20]

---

[17] Interview with former senior Indian diplomatic official, July 12, 2022; interview with Indian security analyst, July 4, 2022; Joe Thomas Karackattu, "The Case for a Pragmatic India-Taiwan Partnership," Carnegie India, April 2019.

[18] Interview with former senior Indian diplomatic official, July 12, 2022.

[19] Riedel, 2017.

[20] This request was in addition to the United States and the United Kingdom providing India with substantial military aid and weapons (Riedel, 2017).

Nehru was the founder of the nonalignment movement, but China's aggression had jolted him out of his view of equidistance when the Soviet Union did nothing to help him. This was the first time that India had accepted and actively sought large-scale military assistance from a superpower.[21] China issued a unilateral cease-fire and withdrawal before Kennedy could respond to Nehru's appeal.[22] However, scholars assess that Kennedy "almost certainly would have responded positively. His track record on India in general and the 1962 crisis in particular shows he believed that the rivalry between India and China was an existential issue for the United States."[23] Moreover, after receiving Nehru's letter, Kennedy proposed to send a high-level mission to assess India's needs, increase the airlift of supplies, and to deploy the U.S. Navy to the Bay of Bengal. An aircraft carrier was dispatched to sail to Madras but was later recalled when China declared a cease-fire and withdrew.[24] Scholars note that the immediate dispatch of the mission of experts and advisors to assess India's needs "was the action of a president preparing for war."[25]

The second notable instance of conflict-phase access occurred in 1990–1991, when India decided to allow U.S. military aircraft to refuel in Bombay during the First Gulf War.[26] In September 1990, the V. P. Singh government granted overflight permission for U.S. warplanes, and the Chandra Shekhar government permitted the aircraft to refuel at Bombay's Sahar airport as they transited between the Philippines and Dubai.[27] The Indian Foreign Ministry said publicly at the time that the planes carried only nonlethal supplies.[28] The access ended when photos of refueling planes were published in the press in January 1991, and the

---

[21] Nehru saw that accepting military assistance from the United States was an imperative to defend India but was still concerned about how this would be perceived by the Soviet Union. According to Ambassador Galbraith: "Prime Minister [Nehru] said India did indeed have to have aid and it would have to come from the United States. He went on to say they wanted to avoid irritating the Soviets as much as possible. The Soviets indicated that they realized that assistance from us was inevitable, but hoped that this would not mean a military alliance between the United States and India. I told him of course we insisted on no such thing." Michael Brecher, "Non-Alignment Under Stress: The West and the India-China Border War," *Pacific Affairs*, Vol. 52, No. 4, Winter 1979–1980, p. 614.

[22] Riedel, 2017.

[23] Bruce Riedel, "Kennedy's Almost Quagmire Was Far from Cuba," *Politico Magazine*, November 29, 2015.

[24] Riedel, 2017.

[25] Riedel, 2015.

[26] At the time, the city was still officially known as *Bombay*. Its name was formally changed to the Marathi spelling and pronunciation of *Mumbai* in 1995.

[27] Baral and Mahanty, 1992, p. 374.

[28] "War in Brief: India: U.S. Planes Refuel for Gulf Missions," *Los Angeles Times*, January 29, 1991; Barbara Crossette, "India in an Uproar Over Refueling of U.S. Aircraft," *New York Times*, January 30, 1991; J. Mohan Malik, "India's Response to the Gulf Crisis: Implications for Indian Foreign Policy," *Asian Survey*, Vol. 31, No. 9, September 1991, p. 853.

Congress Party strongly objected.[29] The Shekhar government was criticized by the Congress Party of "pandering to American imperialism" and "violating India's traditional posture of nonalignment."[30]

Finally, it should be noted that India provided the U.S. military access during the early stages of Operation Enduring Freedom in Afghanistan. At this time, India "facilitated coalition ship repairs at its navy yards and naval port calls" and also "provided an escort for coalition ships through the Strait of Malacca and reportedly offered the United States use of its airbases and airspace in conducting operations (the U.S. alliance with Pakistan made this unnecessary)."[31] From New Delhi's perspective, however, this was considered a counterterrorism operation and, therefore, not subject to the same level of sensitivity as a conflict against a state actor. This puts any access granted during the long U.S. conflict in Afghanistan, from India's perspective, in a category completely different from any potential conflict with China.

State of Current Access

The three foundational agreements noted earlier establish the parameters for peacetime cooperation between the United States and India and would be the basis for any Indian decision on whether to grant access during a conflict. While these agreements were being negotiated, they were controversial and hotly debated among Indian policymakers and analysts because of concerns about compromising Indian military autonomy and independence. Today, however, they are broadly accepted, and India has signed similar agreements with a range of other countries.[32]

---

[29] V. P. Singh and Chandra Shekhar were both prime ministers leading fragile coalitions of parties not associated with either the Congress Party or the BJP. Between 1989 and 1999, India's politics were much more disorderly than at any time before or since. The Congress Party dominated politics from 1947 to 1989; from 1999 to the present, all governments have been led by one of these two parties. Since 2014, the BJP has supplanted the Congress Party as the dominant political force in the country; as of this writing, its most likely challenger could be a Third Front of smaller regional parties reminiscent of the coalitions of the 1990s.

[30] Crossette, 1991.

[31] K. Alan Kronstadt and Sonia Pinto, *India-U.S. Security Relations: Current Engagement*, Congressional Research Service, R42823, November 13, 2012.

[32] Mark Rosen and Douglas Jackson noted that Indian concerns revolved around three main strategic concerns and three main operational concerns. On the strategic side, the agreements pave the way for a military alliance and force India to compromise its strategic autonomy and, particularly the LEMOA, primarily benefit the United States because Indian ships are less likely to refuel and resupply at U.S. ports. Also, the agreements are intended to boost U.S. arms sales to India to the benefit of the U.S. economy and American workers. On the operational side, the implementation of the COMCASA could reveal locations of Indian military assets to Pakistan or other countries and would be too burdensome for the Indian military, given U.S. procedures. Also, there is no clear need for the agreements, given the recent ascendancy of bilateral defense cooperation and the use of workaround agreements (Mark Rosen and Douglas Jackson, *The U.S. India Defense Relationship: Putting the Foundational Agreements in Perspective*, CNA, February 2017, p. 10).

In 2016, the United States and India signed the LEMOA. Of the three agreements, the LEMOA is most relevant to considerations of conflict-phase access because it allows the U.S. and Indian militaries to share logistics support—for example, replenish from each other's bases, or access supplies, spare parts, and services from each other's land facilities, air bases, and ports (in return for cash reimbursement or the reciprocal provision of support). The full text of the LEMOA is not publicly available, but it is based on an ACSA, a routine agreement that Washington has signed with more than 100 other countries.[33] The LEMOA is a framework agreement, which means that there are "likely no specific promises to supply particular items or types of logistical support. Rather, these types of agreements create the framework for the exchange and establish boundary conditions for the types of supplies and services that can be exchanged."[34] According to U.S. defense officials, the LEMOA is a unique, bespoke agreement that was more restrictively scoped than a typical ACSA because of concerns from New Delhi about imperiling India's long-held foreign policy of strategic autonomy.[35] At the time of its signing, the LEMOA required national-level approval in India and was signed by the defense minister (in the United States, such logistics agreements are typically approved at the one-star level).[36] The LEMOA is currently scoped only for exercises, and using it outside that context would require approval from India's Ministry of Defence (MoD).[37] The first use of the LEMOA was the replenishment of an Indian Navy vessel in the Sea of Japan in 2017.[38] India has also signed logistics agreements with Australia, Japan, France, Singapore, and South Korea and is in the process of negotiating similar agreements with the UK and Russia.[39]

The other two foundational agreements are the COMCASA and the BECA for Geospatial Intelligence, which the United States and India concluded in 2018 and 2020, respectively. The texts of these agreements are also not publicly available, but they are based on generic agreements that outline the basic terms that are likely present in the India-specific agreements. The COMCASA provides the legal framework to exchange command, control, communications, computers, intelligence, surveillance, and reconnaissance data; establish secure communication channels; and exchange communication systems and services.[40] Secure communications between militaries are essential to arrange and implement any conflict-phase access. The

---

[33] U.S. Government Accountability Office, *DoD Should Improve Oversight and Seek Payment from Foreign Partners for Thousands of Orders It Identifies as Overdue*, GAO-20-309, March 2020.

[34] Rosen and Jackson, 2017, p. 10.

[35] Interview with four U.S. defense and military officials, June 22, 2022.

[36] Cara Abercrombie, "Realizing the Potential: Mature Defense Cooperation and the U.S.-India Strategic Partnership," *Asia Policy*, Vol. 14, No. 1, January 2019, p. 140.

[37] Interview with four U.S. defense and military officials, June 22, 2022.

[38] Abercrombie, 2019, p. 133.

[39] Rajeswari Pillai Rajagopalan, "India's Military Outreach: Military Logistics Agreements," *The Diplomat*, September 9, 2021.

[40] Rosen and Jackson, 2017, p. 7.

absence of the COMCASA prior to 2018 forced India to supply mostly its own communications equipment in certain platforms it had purchased from the United States, such as the P-8I and the C-130J aircraft.[41] The BECA established procedures for the real-time sharing of a range of geospatial intelligence products, including Indian access to U.S. information that will enhance the accuracy of automated systems and weapons and improve navigation and reconnaissance.[42] Like the COMCASA, this agreement helps enable types of classified communication without which conflict-phase access would be difficult or impossible.

U.S. peacetime access in India is limited and often difficult to obtain. According to U.S. defense officials, the United States and India need to continue to develop procedures to build out the full potential of the agreement. For example, thus far, the agreement has been used only for refueling, but it could be applied in many other areas, such as spare parts and repairs.[43] In 2020, a U.S. P-8 aircraft refueled at India's base in the strategic Andaman and Nicobar Islands. The refueling was carried out under the auspices of the LEMOA.[44] The timing was notable: It occurred in late September 2020, mere months after Chinese and Indian soldiers clashed in the disputed Galwan Valley (discussed earlier). According to one U.S. official, the timing was, in part, a signal to the PRC that the United States and India were cooperating.[45]

However, events like these are not regularized, and future occurrences would need to be agreed to on a case-by-case basis.[46] For example, despite the strategic utility of the Andaman and Nicobar Islands, they have been off-limits to U.S. aircraft and naval vessels (with only limited exceptions, including the September 2020 refueling mentioned earlier). Broadly, U.S. officials note that access (such as landing permission, overflight, and fuel stops) in peacetime is difficult because of the need to tie this access to a specific event and because coordination with Indian counterparts takes a long time.[47] Often, U.S. officials note, it is easier to obtain the needed access in neighboring countries, such as the Maldives and Sri Lanka.[48] For example, during the 2015 earthquake in Nepal, India delayed U.S. overflight requests into Nepal

---

[41] Rosen and Jackson, 2017, p. 14.

[42] Ben Schwartz, "New Delhi Is Getting Serious About Its Defense Partnership with Washington," *In-Depth* blog, October 30, 2020.

[43] Interview with four U.S. defense and military officials, June 22, 2022.

[44] Connie Braesch, "U.S. Aircraft Inaugural Refueling in India," press release, Defense Logistics Agency, October 29, 2020.

[45] Interview with three U.S. Department of State officials, May 25, 2022.

[46] Interview with four U.S. defense and military officials, June 22, 2022.

[47] Interview with four U.S. defense and military officials, June 22, 2022.

[48] Interview with four U.S. defense and military officials, June 22, 2022. However, that observation was made before the political and economic turmoil in Sri Lanka in June 2022. Since August 2022, Sri Lanka has been in political and economic turmoil, which was not the case at the time of this interview, so this may no longer hold.

for a relief mission.[49] Another expert noted that India is often reluctant to grant access even to partners less strategically important than the United States and even for missions geared toward HA/DR rather than combat.[50] This shows the depth of reflexive caution in top New Delhi policymaking circles about granting access.

Evaluating the Framework for Conflict-Phase Access Decisions in India

Question 1: Would Granting the United States Conflict-Phase Access Affect the Leader or the Regime's Political Survival?

Four key factors would likely play a role in India's conflict-phase access decisions related to this question:

1. the risk to an Indian leader of any potential military defeat in a conflict with China
2. nonalignment as a matter of elite national identity in India
3. public perceptions of the United States and the U.S.-India relationship
4. a risk-averse and inexperienced civilian national security bureaucracy.

On the first factor, if India were to grant the United States military access to Indian territory in a conflict with China—therefore involving themselves in the conflict—and suffer a military setback, it would be enormously politically challenging for India's leadership. Few political leaders, in any nation, are eager to engage in military ventures that they fear they may lose. Given Beijing's overall military superiority, India has been highly reluctant to become involved in a conflict outside the areas in which it has a localized tactical advantage. (for example, when India deployed troops in 2017 and 2019 to prevent PLA incursions on the Doklam Plateau, a disputed area claimed by China and Bhutan, a de facto protectorate of India), or circumstances in which it believes itself to be defending its own territory against PLA incursion (for example, the major clash between Indian and Chinese troops in the Galwan Valley discussed earlier).[51]

As of this writing, Indian Prime Narendra Modi remains the dominant domestic political figure in India. Modi assumed office in 2014 with an absolute majority sufficient to adopt

---

[49] Interview with four U.S. defense and military officials, June 22, 2022. The access might have been delayed partly because of India's desire to be seen as the lead relief provider in the region.

[50] A recent example of this reluctance was the denial of access rights to Japan for a HA/DR flight bound for Afghanistan (interview with Indian security analyst, July 2, 2022).

[51] Šumit Ganguly and Andrew Scobell, "The Himalayan Impasse: Sino-Indian Rivalry in the Wake of Doklam," *Washington Quarterly*, Vol. 41, No. 3, 2018; Manoj Joshi, *Doklam: To Start at the Very Beginning*, Observer Research Foundation, August 9, 2017; Jonah Blank, "What Were China's Objectives in the Doklam Dispute?" *Foreign Affairs*, September 7, 2017; M. Taylor Fravel, "China's Sovereignty Obsession: Beijing's Need to Project Strength Explains the Border Clash with India," *Foreign Affairs*, June 26, 2020.

large-scale policy changes and was returned to office in May 2019 with an even larger majority.[52] A mistake in dealings with China, however, could still spell Modi's political downfall. "The one thing that could topple him would be a misstep on China," one Indian analyst noted.[53] This analyst explained that even during the height of the 2020 Galwan Valley clash—the deadliest Sino-Indian conflict in more than half a century—Modi was very cautious in his description of Chinese actions. For example, Modi denied that the PRC had ever captured any territory—i.e., territory claimed by India—when, in fact, it did.[54] Modi's rhetoric was similarly muted in the aftermath of the 2017 Doklam standoff.[55] The political ramifications of losing a conflict with China will likely make India extremely cautious of any conflict-phase access decision. It should be noted, however, that, at times of high tension (including the run-up to, and immediate aftermath of, Galwan), an aggressive stance toward China could still have short-term political benefits to go along with the longer-term risks.

Regarding the second factor, India's national ideology remains firmly rooted in a deep-seated belief in strategic autonomy—an ideological disposition that grew out of and is closely tied to the concept of nonalignment. India's fierce attachment to its geopolitical independence goes beyond security considerations (which will be examined in more detail in the discussion of Question 2). Rather, India's attachment to strategic autonomy crosses into the realm of national identity. India's desire to maintain equidistance between and independence from great powers was put into practice almost from the start of its history as an independent nation. The concept of nonalignment had roots in both of India's main postindependence political ideologies—Nehruvian secularism and Hindu nationalism—and represents a national political consensus that spans the entire political spectrum.[56] Today, the positions espoused in India's unofficial security doctrine, Non-Alignment 2.0,[57] have been largely followed by both the Congress Party administration of Prime Minister Manmohan Singh (who was in office when the document was released) and by the BJP Administration of Prime Minister Modi.[58] This elite preference for autonomy is borne out in the survey data. A 2019 survey of India's strategic community (e.g., elites consisting of serving and retired officers of the military and civil services, as well as university professors, think tank academics, journal-

---

[52] Blank, 2021a, p. 3.

[53] Interview with Indian security analyst, July 2, 2022.

[54] C. G. Manoj and Harikishan Sharma, "No One Has Entered Indian Territory or Captured Any Military Post, PM Tells Leaders of All Parties," *Indian Express*, June 20, 2020.

[55] Joshua T. White, *After the Foundational Agreements: An Agenda for U.S. India Defense and Security Cooperation*, Brookings Institution, January 2021, p. 21.

[56] For a detailed explanation of the Nehruvian and the Hindu Nationalist original conception of Non-Alignment, see Blank, 2021a, pp. 15–18.

[57] Sunil Khilnani, Rajiv Kumar, Pratap Bhanu Mehta, Prakash Menon, Nandan Nilekani, Srinath Raghavan, Shyam Saran, and Siddharth Varadarajan, *Non-Alignment 2.0: A Foreign and Strategic Policy for India in the Twenty-First Century*, National Defence College and Centre for Policy Research, 2012.

[58] Blank, 2021a, p. 3.

ists, and a handful of business executives) showed that a majority (75 percent) of Indian elites identified the United States as India's most important global partner (in contrast, 2 percent identified China as India's most important partner). However, when asked what India should do in the event of greater U.S.-China competition, 54 percent of respondents believed that India should remain equidistant between the United States and China (in contrast with the 43 percent who believed India should collaborate more with the United States).[59]

Because strategic autonomy is a matter of long-standing national identify in India, granting the U.S. military conflict-phase access—especially in situations that do not directly involve India or its national interests—would likely be detrimental to the regime's political position. For example, as noted in the introduction to this chapter, the last time the issue of conflict-phase came up (in 1990–1991, during the first Gulf War), U.S. access was abruptly shut down when it became public and sparked a political backlash.[60] Today, with advances in information technology and changes in the information environment, keeping such access out of the public view is considerably more difficult. It is possible that regional or international organizations or groupings could provide political cover for the regime. For example, India might be more inclined to grant access in the context of an operation with UN support. Given China's veto, this would not, of course, come from the Security Council, but it could come from the General Assembly. Moreover, Indian support could be more likely in the context of Quad action than if it were a bilateral U.S. request only. As one Indian analyst remarked, "there is now a greater openness [in New Delhi] to working with partners like the Quad on potential conflicts."[61] Another Indian analyst went further, noting that the "unstated rationale of the Quad is to confront China. So, if there were a Quad action that required access—i.e., rather than a bilateral request by the United States—that might be easier to India to grant. If done collectively, it might work."[62]

A third factor that might affect India's leaders' perceptions of their political survival is India's perception of U.S. action in the conflict. Public opinion in India is generally pro-American and generally more favorable to the United States than to China, although not to an overwhelming degree. For example, according to a 2019 Pew Research Center survey, 50 percent of the Indian public has favorable view of the United States, while 23 percent have an unfavorable view).[63] A slightly different question gauges Indian publics views of U.S. global leadership: 39 percent of Indians have confidence that the United States will do the

---

[59] Dhruva Jaishankar, *Survey of India's Strategic Community*, Brookings India, March 2019. Of note, 54 percent of respondents believed that India's biggest external challenge is China's assertiveness. A minority of respondents (43 percent) believes that India must improve its collaboration with the United States in the event of greater U.S.-China competition. By contrast, only 2 percent believe that India should collaborate more with China.

[60] Baral and Mahanty, 1992, p. 374.

[61] Interview with Indian security analyst, July 4, 2022.

[62] Interview with former senior Indian diplomatic official, July 12, 2022.

[63] Kat Devlin, "A Sampling of Public Opinion in India," Pew Research Center, March 25, 2019.

right thing regarding world affairs, while 32 percent do not have confidence in the United States.[64] In contrast, 46 percent of the Indian public have an unfavorable view of China, while 23 percent have a favorable view of China.[65] On Chinese global leadership, 36 percent of Indians have no confidence that Xi Jinping will do the right thing in world affairs, while 21 percent have confidence that Xi will do the right thing.[66] Another Pew survey question gauged the Indian public's views on China's hard power: 73 percent of Indians said China's growing military is a bad thing for the country, while only 12 percent said it was a good thing.[67] India's younger generation has a slightly more positive view of the United States than of China. For example, a survey of India's urban youth (18 to 35) found that 77 percent of respondents trusted the United States, while only 11 percent trusted China.[68] Similarly, 74 percent of India's youth believed that the United States is likely to become India's leading partner in the next ten years; in contrast, only 15 percent believed that China would become India's leading partner.[69] Finally, 62 percent of India's youth believe that, if U.S.-China tensions continue to rise, India should cooperate with the United States (versus 1 percent who say India should cooperate with China and 32 percent who say India should remain neutral).[70]

However, while public opinion in India tilts toward the United States, this is not the case at all times or on all issues. On the topic of Russia's invasion of Ukraine, for example, the Indian public and policymakers alike have generally taken the position that the United States has unfairly tried to force India to turn against a longtime friend, while China has properly supported (and joined with) India's stance of neutrality.[71] Thus, while Indian policymakers would likely be influenced by the public's general, but not overwhelming, support of the United States, the qualified nature of this support means that it will likely not be a strong factor in any future deliberation about granting conflict-phase access.

Finally, on the fourth factor, the structural characteristics of India's national security bureaucracy will have an impact on any decision to grant conflict-phase access. India's security policymaking structures were not designed for speedy decisions and tend to make them on an ad hoc rather than doctrinal basis.[72] Civilian bureaucrats maintain control over nearly all military decisions—in contrast to the United States, where U.S. commanders have significant latitude over decisions within their areas of responsibility. Despite this arrangement,

---

[64] Devlin, 2019.

[65] Pew Research Center, "Spring 2019 Global Attitudes Survey: Topline Questionnaire," December 5, 2019.

[66] Pew Research Center, 2019.

[67] Pew Research Center, 2019.

[68] Harsh V. Pant, Prithvi Iyer, Nivedita Kapoor, Aarshi Tirkey, and Kartik Bommakanti, *The ORF Foreign Policy Survey 2021: Young India and the World*, Observer Research Foundation, 2021, p. 25.

[69] Pant et al., 2021, p. 27.

[70] Pant et al., 2021, p. 28.

[71] All Indian sources interviewed for this study expressed this view.

[72] Blank, 2021a, p. ix.

most career civil servants in India have very little experience in or around the military. They frequently rotate through positions and, thus, are often reluctant to make decisions that may be politically fraught but that could facilitate greater military cooperation with the United States.[73] Moreover, each decision is subjected to a cumbersome approval process.[74] As Jonah Blank has explained, when seeking a decision from India's security policymaking bureaucracy, there

> are institutional roadblocks at several points in the decision tree. The first is at the Ministry of Defence (MoD), which is staffed largely by career bureaucrats from the Indian Administrative Service (IAS), rather than by officials with specific military skill sets. If a request successfully passes through the barriers at MoD, it must be vetted for potential diplomatic impact by IAS officials at the Ministry of External Affairs (MEA). A U.S. official in New Delhi reported that the MEA, rather than MoD, presented a greater obstacle for increased engagement. If a proposal manages to make its way through MoD and the MEA, it still may fall prey to the competing priorities in the Prime Minister's Office—the ultimate locus of decisions on truly important matters.[75]

With a decisionmaking matrix that is so complex and involves so many actors, it is often easier for Indian officials to deny requests than to approve them. Former Deputy Assistant Secretary of Defense for South and Southeast Asia Cara Abercrombie has similarly noted that India's MEA and MoD are "not staffed to take on the full spectrum of cooperation required in a robust security relationship with the United States."[76] This process is often slow and fails to approve desired security interactions between the United States and India on a relevant timeline. One U.S. official concurred: The MEA "has to approve the most basic things. They are understaffed, have no military experience, don't understand why the military needs certain things, and are very suspicious of foreigners." The official continued, "[t]hese structural factors will make conflict-phase access very challenging."[77]

What Factors Specific to the Conflict Might Shape the Decisions?

Whether a conflict directly threatens India's security is likely to be a crucial factor in determining the Indian government's political calculations in granting U.S. military access requests. Elite identity in India is firmly rooted in a policy of nonalignment—Indian policymakers' attachment to this concept goes beyond security considerations into the realm of national identity. This means that, politically, Indian policymakers are very unlikely to pro-

---

[73] Daniel S. Markey, "Developing India's Foreign Policy 'Software,'" *Asia Policy*, No. 8, July 2009; Abercrombie, 2019, p. 140.

[74] Blank, 2021a, p. 13.

[75] Blank, 2021a, p. 13.

[76] Abercrombie, 2019, p. 141.

[77] Interview with four U.S. defense and military officials, June 22, 2022.

vide access for a U.S.-China contingency that does not directly threaten India's own territory. Most of the Indian analysts we interviewed shared a similar perspective: "If a conflict does not directly involve India, Delhi will be extra cautious," said one analyst.[78] Thus, while India is keen to defend its core interests from Chinese encroachment, it is not at all eager to provide access for U.S. military or coalition operations against China in service of goals beyond territorial defense and the Indian Ocean region. This will be discussed further in the context of India's national security interests in Question 2.

But whether global public opinion is tilted against the United State or China (or both) in a conflict will also matter for India. For example, if China were clearly and unambiguously perceived as being a rogue, unprovoked aggressor in a conflict, it would be politically easier for India to grant U.S. access requests in that doing so would not change its adherence to nonalignment if the rest of the world agreed that China was the aggressor (although, given the growing alignment between China and Russia, Russia would be unlikely to go against China, which in turn would make the decision more difficult for India). Similarly, however, if Washington were perceived as being the aggressor in a conflict situation and if global public opinion were tilted against U.S. actions, it would be easy for India not to provide the United States conflict-phase access.

Finally, the locus of the conflict—beyond whether India's territory is directly affected—would influence India's decision. For example, India has staked out a position on Taiwan and supports the One China policy. India supports a peaceful resolution to the conflict and urges "the exercise of restraint, avoidance of unilateral actions to change to status quo, de-escalation of tensions and efforts to maintain peace and stability in the region."[79] India's position on aggression in the SCS is less established. While India believes that any code of conduct in the SCS should be fully consistent with the UN Convention on the Law of the Sea, unlike the Taiwan Scenario, a PRC land grab in the SCS would not violate the One China Policy).[80] Thus, politically, a Taiwan scenario might make a decision for Indian policymakers easier than an SCS scenario would, simply because India has staked a clear position on Taiwan, and its credibility would be on the line.

Question 2: Would Granting the United States Conflict-Phase Access Affect the Country's Direct Security Position?

Three key factors would likely play a role in India's conflict-phase access decisions related to this question:

1. a national security policy and orientation deeply rooted in nonalignment

---

[78] Interview Indian security analyst, July 2, 2022.

[79] Krishna N. Das, "India Sticks to 'One-China' Policy Stance but Seeks Restraint on Taiwan," Reuters, August 12, 2022.

[80] Interview with Former senior Indian diplomatic official, July 12, 2022; Karackattu, 2019.

2. perceptions of the United States (as a partner and friend, albeit an unreliable one) and China (as India's most powerful direct threat and most significant long-term security challenge)

3. risk aversion to conflict with China—e.g., the likelihood of granting access leading to large-scale conflict or short of large-scale conflict—stemming from India's inability to compete militarily with the PRC in a protracted conflict.

On the first factor, and as discussed earlier, India's security policy is rooted in nonalignment. Indian policymakers hold a genuine, powerful view that the nation's core interests are best served by a foreign policy that balances competing nations against each other. India regards formal alliances, informal security cooperation blocs, or even any partnership that might be characterized as "alignment" as detrimental to its sovereignty and national interests. Any expectation of conflict-phase access must be filtered through this lens, even if the overall trendline on U.S.-India defense cooperation remains positive.

India's traditional attachment to strategic autonomy is reflected in its semiofficial security doctrine (India has never formally written its security doctrine), a document entitled NonAlignment 2.0.[81] According to the document, India believes that its future security will be shaped by the competition between the two largest powers, the United States and China, but that other groupings of powerful states will also be relevant, particularly in regional contexts.[82] India perceives that the transition to an international system that is more multipolar provides New Delhi with greater opportunities (while recognizing that such a system is inherently volatile). Sameer Lawani has outlined the logic of this outlook: "As long as India expects to rise while other major powers reach the plateau of the growth curve or decline, India can expect its bargaining position vis-à-vis both partners and rivals to increase every year into the future."[83] Thus, a multipolar system is seen as providing India the opportunity to develop a wide set of partners, with whom it can balance its engagement and from whom it can extract the best deal for its interests. As one U.S. official noted, "India wants to be another pole in a multipolar world."[84] India can see the benefits of this strategy playing out in the con-

---

[81] Khilnani et al., 2012. According to Jonah Blank:

> *Non-Alignment 2.0* was authored in 2012 by eight of the country's most respected theorists and practitioners in the fields of military science, political science, international relations, and economics. Both the authors and the much wider group of experts with whom the named authors consulted including retired military, diplomatic, and political leaders sympathetic to both of the country's major national parties (the Indian National Congress Party and the Bharatiya Janata Party [BJP]). The goal was to lay out a broad strategic consensus stretching across the political spectrum. (Blank, 2021a, p. 3)

Prior RAND research has used Non-Alignment 2.0 as a stand-in for a formal government-articulated doctrine for this reason.

[82] Khilnani et al., 2012, p. 9.

[83] Sameer Lawani and Heather Byrne, "Great Expectations: Asking Too Much of the US- India Strategic Partnership," *Washington Quarterly*, Vol. 42, No. 3, October 2019, p. 54.

[84] Interview with four U.S. defense and military officials, June 22, 2022.

text of Ukraine: "Russia's war in Ukraine has undoubtedly benefited India as great powers are competing more vigorously for New Delhi's affection, particularly the United States and China."[85]

Unsurprisingly, then, India prioritizes breadth of partnerships over depth of integration in its security relationships, and its instinct is to form many partnerships that require no obligations.[86] Indeed, India even sees its relationship with the United States as a way to expand its network of partners: "Being friends with Uncle Sam has opened other doors for us: Japan, UAE, Israel," said one Indian analyst.[87] India sees the transition to a structure featuring numerous centers of power as an opportunity to recommit to and redefine nonalignment for a new era rather than shift away from it. As Shivshankar Menon (BJP Prime Minister Vajpayee's ambassador to China and Congress Prime Minister Singh's National Security Advisor) noted in 2018:

> We are now in a far more dangerous world, where the Westphalian state has collapsed or vanished to our immediate West, but where traditional great power rivalry between strong and rising states is the norm to our East. Alliance seems to me to be exactly the wrong answer. We should retain the initiative with ourselves and not get entangled in other's quarrels, keep our powder dry and ourselves free to pursue India's national interest.[88]

This desire to maintain freedom of actions regarding security partners means that Indian strategists often see interoperability with the United States as a slippery slope. Said one long-time Indian former diplomat: "There's a lot of skittishness in Delhi not only on prepositioning of military supplies, but even on interoperability."[89] The issue of interoperability comes up often in discussions with Indian interlocutors, and is frequently seen as an American stratagem designed to trap India into a de facto relationship of reliance. India's diverse range of partners includes nations that are both partners and opponents of the United States. India likes to maintain balance and parity between, for example, the United States and Russia. Said one U.S. defense official, "India is very cognizant of not appearing close to the United States . . . if they've signed an agreement with the United Sates, they would have to offer Russia the same thing."[90] Indeed, after India signed the LEMOA with the United States, it began discussions to conclude a bilateral military logistics agreement with Russia called the Reciprocal Exchange of Logistics Agreement.[91] Moreover, India relies on Russia for a significant portion

---

[85] Derek Grossman, "Modi's Multipolar Moment Has Arrived," *Foreign Policy*, June 6, 2022.

[86] Lawani and Byrne, 2019, p. 46.

[87] Interview with Indian security analyst, July 2, 2022.

[88] Shivshankar Menon, "Security Strategies for India as an Emerging Regional Power with Global Ambitions," lecture, United Service Institution of India, December 5, 2018.

[89] Interview with former senior Indian diplomatic official, July 4, 2022.

[90] Interview with four U.S. defense and military officials, June 22, 2022.

[91] Interview with four U.S. defense and military officials, June 22, 2022.

of its military equipment, reflecting New Delhi's desire to achieve balance in military hardware and in part reflecting frustration with the United States' refusal to transfer certain military technologies.[92] As one Indian analyst remarked, "Russia is willing to give us something that we can't get from any other nation [i.e., no-strings military supplies, including technology transfer]. They permitted joint construction of a nuclear submarine."[93]

But the Indian relationship with Russia goes beyond the military domain. One U.S. official argued that partnering with Russia enables India to gain a de facto veto in the UN Security Council: "Russia's help is not just military. [The United States] tends to overlook the importance of Russia's veto at UN: That's very important to India."[94] As Derek Grossman has noted, India has always appreciated Russian support in the U.N. Security Council, where the territorial status of Jammu and Kashmir has routinely come up.[95] In this sense, India's measured response to Russia's invasion of Ukraine should not come as a surprise.[96] As one Indian analyst put it, the "U.S. *assumed* that India would say 'yes' to its demands on Ukraine and was surprised by the refusal; India was surprised that the United States was even asking." A former Indian diplomat stated, "Ukraine doesn't affect us at all—why should we side against Russia?"[97] Some U.S. policymakers interviewed for this study indeed perceived that the India's response to Russia's invasion of Ukraine merely revealed India's position. As one U.S. official noted, "India was *never* going to go against Russia. Nobody in the U.S. government who worked on an India desk was surprised by India's stance. Ukraine just revealed the limits of what India will do."[98] As this commitment to nonalignment shows, U.S. requests for conflict-phase access will likely be viewed through the lens of an imperative to maintain strategic autonomy and keep a balance among many security partners.

On the second factor, while India's commitment to strategic autonomy means that New Delhi will often limit the types of access or cooperation it is willing to provide the United States, India does look favorably on the United States as a friend and one of India's most important security partners as a means of reinforcing India's position in the Indo-Pacific region. U.S.-India defense ties have steadily strengthened over the past two decades, starting with the George W. Bush administration and continuing into the Biden administration. The two countries share a similar basic assessment of "China as a nation that seeks dominance

[92] Cara Abercrombie, "Removing Barriers to U.S.-India Defense Trade," Carnegie Endowment for International Peace, January 10, 2018.

[93] Interview with former senior Indian diplomatic official, July 4, 2022.

[94] Interview with three U.S. Department of State officials, May 25, 2022.

[95] Grossman, 2022.

[96] Ashley J. Tellis, "'What Is in Our Interest': India and the Ukraine War," Carnegie Endowment for International Peace, April 25, 2022.

[97] Interview with former senior Indian diplomatic official, July 12, 2022; interview with Indian security analyst, July 2, 2022.

[98] Interview with three U.S. Department of State officials, May 25, 2022.

over the [Indo-Pacific] region and is often willing to violate international norms in pursuit of such dominance," while India sees the United States as a stabilizing factor in a fragile region.[99] The Indian government recognizes, for example, the U.S. base in Diego Garcia "as an important and permanent hub for U.S. power projections into the Indian Ocean littoral. . . . India has largely lost its aversion to what it previously considered a 'neocolonial' Anglo-American facility."[100] Indeed, New Delhi and Washington's deeper cooperation in recent years—including expanded military exercises and a dialogue with Australia and Japan (the Quad)—has been aided in part by shared concerns over China's assertiveness in the Indian Ocean and along the contested China-India border.[101] In this sense, it is not impossible that U.S. and Indian interests might converge in certain conflict-phase access scenarios.[102]

Conversely, India sees China as its most significant long-term competitor. Unlike in the Southeast Asian nations covered in this report, and in contrast with India's relationship with Russia, there is no desire on India's part to "balance" engagement with China with engagement with the United States. As Non-Alignment 2.0 states, "China will, for the foreseeable future, remain a significant foreign policy and security challenge for India. . . . It is the one major power which impinges directly on India's geopolitical space."[103] China and India have engaged in border skirmishes and standoffs throughout the decades since China's invasion in 1962 and have territorial disputes along the Line of Actual Control in the high Himalayas.[104] India is also increasingly concerned about China's expanding naval push into the Indian Ocean because it perceives that Beijing is "seeking to establish a network of ports and partnerships with countries in the littoral region—including in several nations that have been hostile to India," which "challenges India's perceptions of its preeminent regional status and feeds fears of strategic encirclement."[105] Particularly concerning to India is China's strong and deepening strategic partnership with Pakistan, with some Indian analysts convinced that Pakistan is a Chinese proxy in South Asia.[106] Indeed, Non-Alignment 2.0 notes: "A China which is raising its regional and global profile will provide a more effective shield to

---

[99] Blank, 2021a, p. viii.

[100] Walter C. Ladwig, Andrew S. Erickson, and Justin D. Mikolay, "Diego Garcia and American Security in the Indian Ocean," in Carnes Lord and Andrew Erickson, eds., *Rebalancing U.S. Forces: Basing and Forward Presence in the Asia-Pacific*, Naval Institute Press, 2014, p. 156.

[101] White, 2021, p. 2.

[102] Interview with three U.S. Department of State officials, May 25, 2022.

[103] Khilnani et al., 2012, p. 13.

[104] Manoj Joshi, *Understanding the India-China Border: The Enduring Threat of War in High Himalaya*, Oxford University Press, 2022.

[105] Ladwig, Erickson, and Mikolay, 2014, p. 154; Abhijit Singh, "China's Military Base in Djibouti: Strategic Implications for India," War on the Rocks, August 21, 2017.

[106] Singh, 2017.

Pakistan. In consequence we may need to think of Pakistan as a subset of the larger strategic challenges posed by China."[107]

However, India certainly does not see a shared threat perception of China alone as providing the basis for granting the United States conflict-phase access, particularly in conflicts with China that do not directly involve India. Indeed, both Indian and U.S analysts and officials noted that, in most scenarios, India would be most likely to provide other forms of support. For example, one Indian analyst noted that India "need not be a formal ally or even play a formal role through granting access" to play a role in countering China; rather, "India will do its part simply by presenting a tacit threat to PRC interests in the region."[108] One U.S. official echoed this sentiment: India would perceive that it could be most helpful in a U.S.-China contingency by "covering the Western Theater Command and keeping the Chinese forces having to think about the border, which is something they would do anyways."[109]

Moreover, India remains deeply distrustful of the United States and perceives it to be an unreliable security partner. This distrust is primarily based on three factors: India perceives the United States to have a long track record of not coming to India's aid in prior conflicts (e.g., India's conflict with Pakistan); India perceives that Washington's capability to defend India's interests is deteriorating over time as its global influence wanes; and, finally, India is particularly irritated by what it perceives as an unwillingness to freely transfer certain military hardware or dual-use technology.[110] This perception of the United States as an unreliable security partner is likely to directly affect conflict-phase access deliberations. From India's perspective, the worst-case scenario would be for New Delhi to provide access to the United States only to have Washington stop short of a decisive confrontation and reach a separate settlement with China. As one Indian analyst noted, India would be less likely to grant access if it feels that the United States will ultimately back down. That would expose India to all the risks of angering China but without the benefit of a great-power showdown that could ultimately reduce PRC capabilities or influence.[111]

Finally, on the third and final factor, while New Delhi does not seek to balance engagement with the United States against engagement with China, India does not actively seek confrontation with Beijing. India is concerned that granting access would lead to conflict of China—whether large scale or short of large scale —and that risk aversion will act as a brake in any decisionmaking. At the root of this risk aversion is a recognition on the part of policymakers in New Delhi that they cannot currently compete with China militarily or economically in any sustained confrontation—China is simply too powerful. Non-Alignment 2.0 is careful to highlight the need to avoid provoking China into a conflict: "If China perceives

---

[107] Khilnani et al., 2012, p. 18.

[108] Interview with Indian security analyst, July 2, 2022.

[109] Interview with four U.S. defense and military officials, June 22, 2022.

[110] Blank, 2021a, pp. 52–52.

[111] Interview with former senior Indian diplomatic official, July 12, 2022.

India as irrevocably committed to an anti-China containment ring, it may end up adopting overtly hostile and negative policies towards India, rather than making an effort to keep India on a more independent path."[112] Scholars have noted that India's reactions to the 2019 Doklam standoff and the 2020 Sino-Indian border crisis show that India is extremely hesitant to antagonize China, hoping to maintain stability and quietly diminish Chinese inroads in the region.[113] As Joshua T. White has noted,

> the Modi government's muted rhetoric tells [an] ambiguous story, and should suggest to U.S. observers that India's posture toward China will likely continue to be marked by caution, concession, and contradiction. A more subtle Chinese approach . . . might conceivably prompt a new bout of Indian reticence about overt defense cooperation with the United States.[114]

Said one Indian analyst interviewed for this report, "India very gingerly describes 'friction points' with PRC. There is no fiery rhetoric."[115] This same analyst later noted, "In a defensive mode, as we're now in, the aim is just to stay out of trouble."[116] Moreover, U.S. officials noted that India does not perceive the border skirmishes with China in Galwan as "real aggression": "They have a high tolerance for low levels of violence, but they are very cautious about attracting China's ire."[117] Another U.S. official similarly noted, "They are very concerned that the PRC could take a lot of Indian territory in response to any U.S. access."[118]

India is most concerned about whether providing conflict-phase access to the United States would provoke a full-scale conflict with China but is also concerned about a PRC reaction less than full-scale war but sufficiently dangerous to warrant caution. This could include limited combat along the Line of Actual Control, stepped up Chinese support to Pakistan's military capabilities, or Pakistani support for anti-Indian terrorism.[119] As one Indian analyst noted, such provocations are the justification for an overly hostile relationship with the PRC: "China works in concert with Pakistan. This means that we *must*, for our long-term interests, stay engaged with PRC. We can't alienate them, out of concern for the Beijing-Islamabad connection"[120] Another U.S. official echoed this sentiment: "India feels China owns Pakistan,

---

[112] Khilnani et al., 2012, p. 14.

[113] Lawani and Byrne, 2019, p. 48.

[114] White, 2021, p. 21.

[115] Interview with Indian security analyst, July 2, 2022.

[116] Interview with Indian security analyst, July 2, 2022.

[117] Interview with four U.S. defense and military officials, June 22, 2022.

[118] Interview with three U.S. Department of State officials, May 25, 2022.

[119] Interview with former senior Indian diplomatic official, July 12, 2022; interview with former senior Indian diplomatic official, July 4, 2022.

[120] Interview with former senior Indian diplomatic official, July 4, 2022.

and worries the Chinese might retaliate in the form of inciting Pakistan to act against India, so that will be a factor in whether they decide to grant conflict-phase access."[121] In sum, India's extreme concern for actions that its leaders would consider provocative to China would likely be a significant limiting factor in their willingness to provide the U.S. military access in a conflict with China. However, one Indian analyst noted that India's decision on access might not necessarily only depend on what the PRC does during a conflict but on the trendlines of Sino-Indian relations before such a conflict: "A lot will depend on China's behavior. If present trendlines continue, redlines might shift more quickly than many realize."[122]

What Factors Specific to the Conflict Might Shape the Decisions?

One of the most important factors that might shape India's security-related decisions to grant conflict-phase access is if India's own territory—as defined by Indian policymakers—has been attacked or is directly threatened by the conflict. India is first and foremost interested in its own neighborhood: The Indian Ocean and the country's land borders are first-order concerns in India's national security paradigm.[123] The imperative to secure its sovereignty against encroachment of any would-be regional power in a future conflict will be of paramount concern in a conflict-phase access decision. Certain U.S. officials perceive that India is likely to grant access only if its own interests are threatened or at stake.[124] Most of the Indian analysts we interviewed had a similar perspective: "In the absence of a direct threat to India's territorial integrity, it would be a difficult sell in Delhi."[125] If India is not a party to the conflict, it does not want to irk China and will likely not provide conflict-phase access. But India being a party to the conflict would change the equation.[126] Thus, while India is keen to defend its core interests from Chinese encroachment, it is not at all eager to join a coalition against China for broader goals.

Another conflict characteristic likely to be highly relevant in India's decisionmaking on granting U.S. access requests is the degree to which India sees the United States as firmly committed to the conflict in question. New Delhi does not want to provide access in what it sees as a pointless confrontation—but would be more willing to provide access in a situation that serves India's interests. India's nightmare scenario is that it provides access—and then is left to confront China on its own after the United States reaches a separate accommodation. In this situation, India would bear all the costs of confronting China (generating long-term

---

[121] Interview with four U.S. defense and military officials, June 22, 2022.

[122] Interview with Indian security analyst, July 4, 2022.

[123] Sujan R. Chinoy, "India and the Changing Dynamics of the Indo-Pacific," *Asia Policy*, Vol. 15, No. 4, October 2020, p. 35.

[124] Interview with three U.S. Department of State officials, May 25, 2022

[125] Interview with Indian security analyst, July 2, 2022; interview with former senior Indian diplomatic official, July 4, 2022.

[126] Interview with former senior Indian diplomatic official, July 12, 2022.

hostility and risking retaliation from China) but none of the benefits. If the United States is seen as less than fully committed to the conflict, that—rather than India's role in assuring success or failure—is more likely to be determinative in India's decisionmaking. This is a subtle distinction in Indian policymaking that is often lost on U.S. officials: India does not want to be involved in what it perceived to be merely U.S. attempts to posture and advance its own agenda vis-à-vis China (and Russia). However, if China poses what India perceives to be a real threat to the region, including to India and if the United States intends to embark on an existential fight for the future of the region, it is a different calculation for Indian policymakers.

India is committed to the defense of a global rules-based order. Indeed, Non-Alignment 2.0 notes that New Delhi's interlinked development and national security goals depend on such an order, and that "India therefore has to strive to maintain an open global order at many different levels."[127] India would thus look more favorably on any U.S. access request in a conflict where China was clearly the aggressor attempting to subvert the rules-based order through force. In this sense, the locus of combat for the conflict might play a role in India's conflict-phase access decision. As is the case for Singapore, a Taiwan scenario may in some ways be an easier choice for India than one that occurs in the SCS because it is more likely to be a scenario in which China is clearly the aggressor (in this case against Taiwan). "The realization is gradually dawning on India," said one Indian analyst based in New Delhi, "that potential conflict between the People's Republic and Taiwan is not far off."[128] While it is of course possible for the PRC to be clearly the aggressor in an SCS scenario, Chinese aggression in the SCS would not necessarily be a clear transgression—it would be more like salami slicing over disputed territory, sometimes with multiple claimants. The lack of a clear aggressor and victim and the fact that India has no real policy on SCS disputes mean that it is extremely unlikely that India would provide access in this scenario.

Access is perhaps slightly more likely in a Taiwan scenario than in an SCS scenario. India would regard a PRC invasion of Taiwan as dangerous adventurism. However, a former Indian official assesses that, if an invasion occurred and despite India's relationship with Taiwan, the answer to a request for access "would probably still be a no."[129] U.S. officials similarly assess India's willingness to grant conflict-phase access in a Taiwan scenario as extremely low, given that its own interests are not threatened.[130] Moreover, while New Delhi is increasingly conscious about the need to step up relations with Taiwan, one Indian analyst noted that New Delhi is simultaneously aware of the fact that Beijing could use India's involvement or grant-

---

[127] Khilnani et al., 2012, p. 8.

[128] Interview with Indian security analyst, July 4, 2022.

[129] Interview with former senior Indian diplomatic official, July 12, 2022.

[130] Interview with three U.S. Department of State officials, May 25, 2022.

ing of conflict-phase access as an excuse to step up pressure over Kashmir.[131] This is because Beijing sees Taiwan as an internal matter rather than a cause for international action, which is the same way that New Delhi views Kashmir.[132]

Question 3: Would Granting Conflict-Phase Access Affect the Outcome of the Conflict?

Two key factors would likely play a role in India's conflict-phase access decisions related to this question:

1. whether India perceives that providing access is in India's own long-term interests, independent of U.S. interests in the immediate conflict
2. whether India assesses that the access it provides would be relatively unique and valuable in the specific conflict scenario and not merely giving the United States a pawn to be sacrificed that is not essential for U.S. victory.

On the first factor, India will weigh the potential for long-term security risks from China extending beyond the immediate conflict. Indian policymakers do perceive that they need the United States to continue to play an active role in the region to balance China and that there is simply no one else who can do this.[133] Of greatest importance to India is American's help maintaining awareness and control over Chinese actions in the Indian Ocean, which India views as its traditional sphere of influence and regional dominance.[134] "The U.S. Navy is the most powerful navy in the Western Pacific *and* in the Indian Ocean," one Indian analyst acknowledged.[135] Indeed, Non-Alignment 2.0 highlights the desirability for India of the "retention of strong U.S. maritime deployments in the Asia-Pacific theater."[136] If the United States went to war with China, this would "confirm [India's] fears about Chinese desires to

---

[131] China has increased its support for Pakistan's position on Kashmir, particularly since 2019, when India abolished the region's semiautonomy. China could step up efforts against India in the UN General Assembly by continuing to issue pro-Pakistan statements and/or by moving forces along the Ladakh border in Kashmir to keep the pressure up on India. See Interview with Indian security analyst, July 2, 2022; Aijaz Hussain, "At 75, India's Kashmir Challenge Shifts Foreign Policy Focus," Associated Press, August 10, 2022; Parajanya Bhatt, ""Revisiting China's Kashmir Policy," issue brief, Observer Research Foundation, November 2019.

[132] Tara Kartha and Jalil Jilani, "The Latest Kashmir Conflict Explained," United States Institute of Peace, August 28, 2019.

[133] Blank, 2021a, p. 51.

[134] Sameer Lawani, "Reluctant Link? India, the Quad and the Free and Open Indo-Pacific," in Sharon Stirling, ed., *Mind the Gap: National Views of the Fee and Open Indo-Pacific*, The German Marshall Fund of the United States, 2019, p. 31.

[135] Interview with Indian security analyst, July 2, 2022.

[136] Khilnani et al., 2012, p. 13.

dominate the region," a U.S. defense official noted.[137] India is thus very concerned with the long-term implications of the outcome of a U.S.-China conflict and the threats to India's security that may come after Washington leaves. India is therefore greatly invested in the United States at a minimum not losing a large-scale conflict with China. This should not, however, lead planners to overestimate the degree to which India will provide assistance to the United States when its interests are not directly threatened. Said the same Indian analyst bluntly: "The United States can't expect India to play any role in the Western Pacific."[138]

On the second factor, India knows that U.S. military access in India is unlikely to be the deciding factor for the outcome of a U.S.-China fight. It is hard to see a realistic scenario in which the United States wins or loses based on whether or not India provides access. The U.S. military has numerous other options for access in the region—facilities in other nations, including Diego Garcia, U-Tapao (Thailand), and Singapore. The leadership would not want to provide the United States access that is not critical to the outcome of a U.S.-China conflict, thereby exposing India to the risk of PRC retaliation for no substantial gain in an increased likelihood of U.S. victory. India will not provide access just to help the United States score political points or provide access that would merely serve to complicate China's decision-making in a notional conflict by dispersing basing. Providing access for such reasons would be good for the United States, but Indian policymakers would likely not perceive it as being good for India. The leadership is extremely cautious in confronting China, but that does not mean India will never do so. New Delhi simply does not want to provide access in what they see as a pointless confrontation—but would be more willing to provide access in a situation that serves their interests.

What Factors Specific to the Conflict Might Shape the Decisions?

The operational utility of India's access very much depends on the scenario in question. According to U.S. defense officials, the most important access India could likely provide for scenarios in the Western Pacific would be access to the Andaman and Nicobar Islands bases, shown in Figure 7.1.

These bases would likely be of the most utility to the U.S. military because of their proximity to most likely theaters of combat. These bases are much closer than any other Indian facilities to the Pacific and closer to mainland Southeast Asia than to the Indian mainland.[139] The Andaman and Nicobar Island bases could reduce response time to a PRC attack: "Port Blair is about the same distance from New Delhi as is it is from the Chinese city of Chongqing (1,528 miles) and is about 500 miles closer to vital Chinese targets than are most existing Indian launching sites."[140] U.S. access to the island could spread logistics out to mul-

---

[137] Interview with four U.S. defense and military officials, June 22, 2022.

[138] Interview with Indian security analyst, July 2, 2022.

[139] Blank et al., 2015, p. 14.

[140] Blank et. al., 2015, p. 168.

FIGURE 7.1

India's Andaman and Nicobar Bases

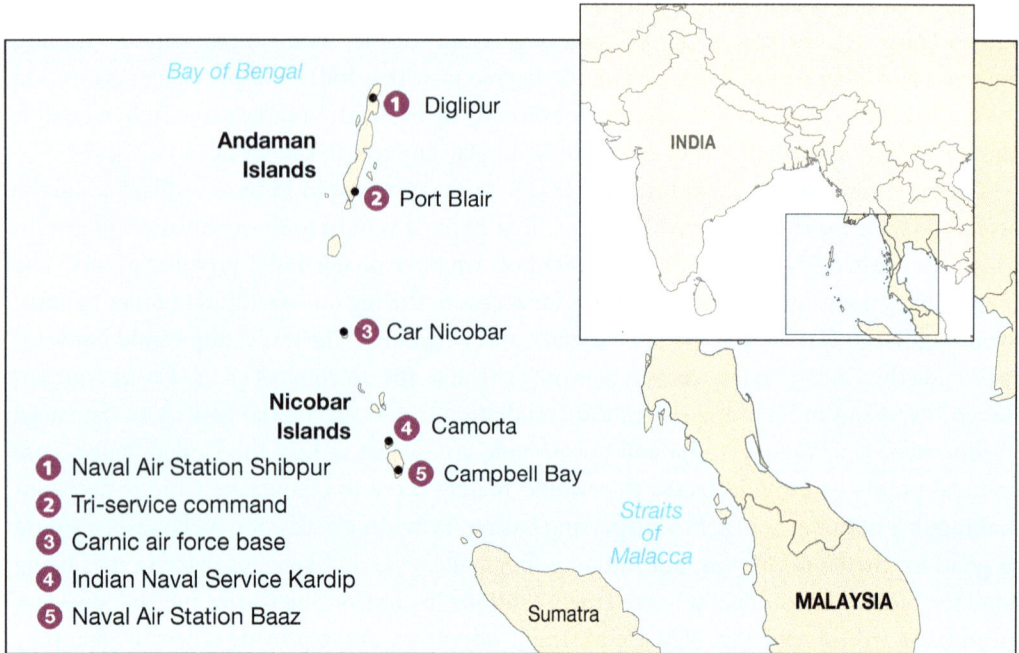

SOURCE: Reproduced from Jonah Blank, Jennifer D. P. Moroney, Angel Rabasa, and Bonny Lin, *Look East, Cross Black Waters: India's Interest in Southeast Asia*, RAND Corporation, RR-1021-AF, 2015, p. 60.

tiple locations, thus requiring PRC attention in multiple theaters and potentially making Beijing think twice about certain courses of action.[141]

While U.S. access to the Andaman and Nicobar Island bases would certainly cause concern to PLA, PLAAF, and PLAN planners, it is unclear how much actual logistical benefit they would provide to the USAF and Department of the Air Force in a conflict. Geographically, these bases would obviously be most useful for a scenario in the Indian Ocean—although a crisis involving China in that area is not commonly assessed as a U.S. defense planning scenario. For an SCS scenario, the access these bases provide may overlap with alternative facilities in other nations, including Diego Garcia, U-Tapao (Thailand), and Singapore. One U.S. defense official noted that the "things that India could provide that would be a game changer, they would never do, and anything else could be replicated elsewhere."[142] Moreover, in any future conflict scenario, if the United States had failed to secure alternative access from nations closer to the locus of an SCS or ECS conflict than the Andaman and Nicobar Islands, this would likely reflect a very limited level of regional support for U.S. operations.

---

[141] Interview with four U.S. defense and military officials, June 22, 2022; Blank et al., 2015, p. 168.

[142] Interview with four U.S. defense and military officials, June 22, 2022.

As discussed elsewhere, this low level of regional support for the U.S. campaign would itself likely reduce India's willingness to grant access.

Question 4: Would Granting the United States Conflict-Phase Access Affect—or Be Affected by—Regional Decisions Regarding Granting Similar Access?

India's decision would hinge on two key factors:

1. the involvement of key Indian partners
2. a preference for consensus and true multilateralism (rather than simply a U.S.-dictated effort), which can be overridden when core interests are at stake.

On the first factor, India's stance will be influenced by the actions taken by other U.S. partners—but to a lesser degree than such states as Singapore or the Philippines or other U.S. treaty allies. India will look at the position that other Quad members (Japan and Australia) have taken. India is rapidly drawing closer to Australia, and likewise with Japan.[143] Experts with whom we spoke had differing views on how salient the decisions of other Quad members would be for India. One Indian analyst said that it would not matter much, noting that "the Quad is unlikely to become any sort of military alliance. Hence, AUKUS [the Australia–United Kingdom–United States Partnership]."[144] Another Indian analyst differed, noting that "there is now a greater openness to working with partners like the Quad on potential conflicts."[145] One analyst went further, noting that the unstated rationale of the Quad is to confront China, so if there were Quad action that required access—i.e., rather than a bilateral request from the United States—access for that might be easier to grant in India.[146] The positions of other key security partners of India—such as Singapore, Israel, France, and the UK—may also affect India's decision.

On the second factor, India is much less likely to provide access for an effort that is perceived as being an American operation than one perceived as representing a far broader international consensus. An example here is the difference between the first and second Gulf wars. In 1990–1991, for an operation seen as reflecting broad international consensus (with corresponding UN mandate), India granted refueling access to U.S. planes transiting between the Philippines and Dubai.[147] More than a decade later, in 2003, for an operation seen as advanc-

---

[143] Harsh V. Pant, "India, Australia, and the Indo-Pacific," Australia India Institute, April 14, 2022; Harsh V. Pant and Shashank Mattoo, "The Rising Sun in India-Japan Relations," *The Hindu*, May 1, 2021.

[144] Interview with Indian security analyst, July 2, 2022.

[145] Indian security analyst, July 4, 2022.

[146] Interview with former senior Indian diplomatic official, July 12, 2022.

[147] The military actions of the Persian Gulf War were authorized under UN Security Council Resolution 678, on Iraq and Kuwait, November 29, 1990. This resolution demanded that Iraq withdraw from Kuwait and authorized member states to use "all necessary means" to enforce the resolution.

ing the agenda of the U.S. administration rather than a global one, India declined.[148] India publicly stated that the refueling option for U.S. aircraft would not be repeated, reportedly preempting an official request by U.S. officials.[149] To illustrate the point further: India was initially committed to sending troops to Iraq under the aegis of a UN mission. However, when the United States failed to reach consensus in the UN Security Council, Indian policymakers retracted their original commitments.[150] Thus, a key consideration for India may be whether there is a general global consensus for action. A UN Security Council resolution is likely impossible because of PRC veto power—but India would consider a General Assembly vote and how overwhelming the international consensus it reflects is. To do so, India would look at the position of other regional states. Pakistan can be assumed to side with China, but New Delhi would look closely at the position of less immediately predictable nations, including Bangladesh, Sri Lanka, Malaysia, and Indonesia.[151]

However, while India would far prefer to be in the majority than in the minority, New Delhi is more willing than many other U.S. partners to dance to its own drum when core interests are involved. A data point here is Russia's 2022 invasion of Ukraine: India was the only significant U.S. security partner to abstain from UN votes condemning Russia's invasion.[152] The positions of neighbors was a major influence on the decisionmaking of many other nations (for example, Singapore, Indonesia, and other Southeast Asian states).[153] It is possible to imagine scenarios in which many individual Western nations—even U.S. treaty allies—might have sat the Ukraine vote out if not for the combined pressure of a united pro-Western front. India proved immune to such pressure. In a key vote of the UN General Assembly on March 2, 2022, 141 nations (including the United States and all U.S. treaty allies) condemned the invasion of Ukraine and demanded Russia's withdrawal; India, along with China and 32 smaller nations (all but a few of them firmly nondemocratic), abstained.[154] As the vote on the Ukraine conflict shows, India is willing to act in opposition to a near con-

---

[148] By contrast, the 2003 invasion of Iraq was seen in India as reflecting U.S. ambitions rather than global consensus, with corresponding UN Security Council Resolution 1441 on the situation between Iraq and Kuwait, November 8, 2002, containing no language explicitly authorizing member state action. The participation of nations in the "coalition of the willing" was seen by many in India as bowing to U.S. pressure rather than acting in genuinely national interests.

[149] Kronstadt and Pinto, 2012.

[150] Kurt M. Campbell, Nirav Patel, and Richard Weitz, "The Ripple Effect: India's Responses to the Iraq War," Center for a New American Security, October 2008.

[151] Shannon Tiezzi, "How Did Asian Countries Vote on the UN's Ukraine Resolution?" *The Diplomat*, March 3, 2022.

[152] Gareth Price, "Ukraine War: Why India Abstained on UN Vote Against Russia," Chatham House, March 25, 2022.

[153] Tiezzi, 2022.

[154] Price, 2022.

sensus in the UN General Assembly when core interests (in this case, its relationship with Russia) are involved.

What Factors Specific to the Conflict Might Shape the Decisions?

If a future conflict between the United States and China occurs in the Asia-Pacific, as most U.S. defense planning scenarios indicate, it is highly likely that Russia will side with China.[155] As discussed in Question 2, from India's perspective, Russia "has been a long-time friend of India, it not only provided the Indian arms to maintain a formidable military profile, but also provided invaluable political support to India on a variety of regional issues."[156] For these reasons, Russia's likely support for China in a conflict in the Asia-Pacific is likely to dampen India's enthusiasm for providing access across most high-intensity conflict scenarios.

Question 5: Would Granting the United States Conflict-Phase Access Affect the Economic Prosperity of the Country?

Two key factors would likely play a role in India's conflict-phase access decisions related to this question:

1. the degree to which Indian leadership perceives India's economy as being able to withstand the economic blowback of a conflict between the United States and China
2. the state of India's economy at the time of the conflict.

On the first factor, India is much less reliant on PRC trade than many other Indo-Pacific nations, particularly those of Southeast Asia. India does not face the same prospect of economic dominance by China: India's economic ties with the PRC are significant but not nearly as strong in percentage terms as ASEAN nations. Its economy is large enough and sufficiently self-contained to weather considerable international economic headwinds, if it so chooses. "India's response won't be determined by commercial factors," said a former Indian diplomat. "Chinese investment isn't as big a factor as it is for ASEAN economies."[157] Tables 7.1 and 7.2 provide a snapshot of U.S. and allied trade and investment in India compared with that of China. As shown, both the United States and Japan have somewhat smaller levels of trade with India than does China, but, together, the United States and its allies have a far larger share. India is not part of China's BRI. New Delhi is not opposed to infrastructure development in the region but is wary of the strategic implications of certain initiatives that

---

[155] Andrew Radin, Andrew Scobell, Elina Treyger, J. D. Williams, Logan Ma, Howard J. Shatz, Sean M. Zeigler, Eugeniu Han, and Clint Reach, *China-Russia Cooperation: Determining Factors, Future Trajectories, Implications for the United States*, RAND Corporation, RR-3067-A, 2021.

[156] Manoj Joshi, "India's Strategy in the China-Russia-USA Triangle," Observer Research Foundation, December 20, 2019.

[157] Interview with former senior Indian diplomatic official, July 4, 2022.

TABLE 7.1

India's Total Bilateral Trade by Country

Year	China	United States	Japan	Australia	Taiwan	South Korea	Germany	UK
2012	88.1	61.3	19.0	15.6	6.0	18.8	22.4	13.4
2013	87.8	64.6	17.8	13.3	6.2	17.6	21.4	12.7
2014	96.0	69.0	69.0	12.5	5.9	18.1	21.2	11.9
2015	95.9	60.8	60.8	12.7	4.8	16.3	19.2	11.3
2016	97.6	62.4	62.4	11.7	5.0	15.8	19.3	11.1
2017	119.3	70.1	70.1	18.2	6.3	20.0	21.7	13.4
2018	125.5	90.5	90.5	21.2	7.0	21.5	25.3	14.7
2019	118.5	89.2	89.2	13.5	5.8	20.7	23.9	14.8
2020	108.4	78.3	78.3	10.3	4.8	16.8	22.4	10.6
2021	153.7	113.2	113.2	18.6	7.7	23.7	27.6	15.1

SOURCES: OEC, "India/China," webpage, undated-a; U.S. Census Bureau, undated; World Bank, undated-c; JETRO, various years; Australian Government, Department of Foreign Affairs and Trade, undated; Bureau of Foreign Trade, Taiwan, undated; Korea Customs Service, undated, for export/import by country; German Federal Statistics Office, 2022; Office for National Statistics, 2022; UN, undated, trade data for India.

NOTE: Amounts are in billions of U.S. dollars. China includes Mainland China, Hong Kong, and Macao.

TABLE 7.2

U.S. and Allied Trade and Investment in India Compared with China

Country	Percentage of Total Indian Trade (2019)	Percentage of Total FDI Stock in India (2020)
China	10.68	0.00
United States	11.12	8.73
United States, Australia, Japan	15.00	15.14

SOURCE: World Bank, undated-c; World Bank, "GDP (current US$)—India," webpage, undated-b; American Enterprise Institute, "China Global Investment Tracker," webpage, undated; International Monetary Fund, "Coordinated Direct Investment Survey (CDIS)," webpage, December 18, 2021; UN Conference on Trade and Development, *World Investment Report*, 2022a; Bureau of Economic Analysis, U.S. Department of Commerce, "Direct Investment & Multinational Enterprises (MNEs)," webpage, November 18, 2022; Government of India, Ministry of Tourism, "India Tourism Statistics 2021," December 2021; JETRO, various years; Australian Bureau of Statistics, "International Investment Position, Australia: Supplementary Statistics," 2021; Government of India, Ministry of Commerce and Industry, "FDI Statistics Archive," webpage, undated; Organisation for Economic Co-operation and Development, "Data: Outward FDI flows by partner country," webpage, 2021.

it sees as PRC attempts to establish a foothold in what India sees as its neighborhood.[158] Non-Alignment 2.0 specifically calls out the "potential for [PRC] espionage and intelligence" through Chinese infrastructure.[159]

Nevertheless, China is one of India's largest trade partners, and any loss of this relationship would result in substantial costs to India's own economy. China's position as a key market means that India would be cautious about risking alienating China.[160] As Sameer Lawani noted,

> India lacks the hard and soft power tools to blunt counter-reactions: As a developing country with significant limitations, India has generally shied away from decisions or actions that risk jeopardizing the flow of Chinese investment and trade, Russian arms, and Iranian oil that could also impede its economic growth.[161]

On the second factor, India would suffer economic hardship from any conflict with China. But the degree to which this would shape Indian decisions will vary, depending (in part) on the condition of India's economy at the time. India faces significant poverty, underemployment, and skills deficits, as well as infrastructure investment and technology transfers. As a result, one of India's core strategic priorities is "economic growth and development that leverages advanced industrialization and manufacturing to generate exports as well as employment."[162] If India is already experiencing economic setbacks or fragility at the time of a U.S.-China conflict, leadership might be less inclined to take actions that could cause suffering for massive numbers of citizens. If the conflict were to come at a time of economic strength, however, leadership might be more inclined to accept the hardship as a necessary price for security.

What Factors Specific to the Conflict Might Shape the Decisions?

India is economically dependent on the Western Indian Ocean for trade, maritime transit of exports, critical energy resources, and migrant workers and remittances. Maritime commerce is the basis of India's trade relations and a central part of its economy; about 90 percent of which by volume is seaborne.[163] Therefore, a key conflict consideration would be the locus of the conflict and the potential it has to disrupt India's maritime commerce. The characteristics of the conflict would affect how it would affect India's trade with China. For example, would India's trade with China be affected simply by Beijing cutting it off—or as an inevitable

---

[158] Darshana M. Baruah, "India's Answer to the Belt and Road: A Road Map for South Asia," Carnegie Endowment for International Peace, August 21, 2018.

[159] Khilnani et al., 2012, p. 15.

[160] Blank, 2021a, p. 24.

[161] Lawani and Byrne, 2019, p. 52.

[162] Lawani, 2019, p. 30.

[163] Lawani, 2019, p. 30.

consequence of the conflict? That is, if the United States shut down PRC shipping, might that in of itself—even without any decision on Beijing's part—cripple India's economy, rendering concerns about Chinese economic retaliation moot? Further, to what extent is India's trade with other parts of Asia likely to be disrupted regardless of its decision on granting the United States military access?

How Might India's Decisions Vary Depending on the Types of Access Requested?

India's decision to grant the U.S. military access may to some degree depend on the type of access Washington is requesting. According to those with whom we spoke, U.S. and Indian officials have not discussed in any detail what such access could look like in practice under different scenarios. One senior Indian former policymaker noted that the type of access the United States requests would not matter: "There is no real difference in access between, for example, the Andaman and Nicobar bases and those on the mainland. Even though Andaman and Nicobar would likely be more useful for US."[164] Nevertheless, our analysis points to several types of access that would be more or less difficult for India to provide.

India may look more favorably on conflict-phase access requests that are invisible to the public—for example, not the type of easily photographed refueling at sites that are accessible to journalists, as was seen in Bombay during the first Gulf War. The more remote and controlled the site in question is, the easier it may be to keep quiet, and the fewer domestic political challenges it might cause for India. Another type of access that would be somewhat easier to grant is access that does not cause great alarm to Beijing. For example, if the United States wanted access at bases far from PRC territory (a gas-and-go in Kerala, a state on India's Malabar Coast, for example), that would be less threatening than access at bases much closer to the PRC (such as the Andaman and Nicobar Island bases and bases in Northern Indian plains). Finally, in terms of the types of platforms that the United States might ask to position in India, lower-profile and nonlethal assets, such as ISR drones, would be likely be easier. The decision could still be decision but would be less so than permission for fighters or bombers, which would be extremely unlikely.

There are also certain types of access that would be extremely difficult for India to grant the U.S. military. For example, any access in sensitive Himalayan areas near territory directly claimed by the PRC would likely be especially difficult to provide. As one U.S. official noted, "[India] would be reluctant to provide support around the border with China because they'd be worried about retaliation from the PRC."[165] As alluded to earlier, providing access for U.S. lethal assets, such as fighters and bombers, would be more difficult than providing access

---

[164] Interview with former senior Indian diplomatic official, July 12, 2022.

[165] Interview with four U.S. defense and military officials, June 22, 2022.

for C-130s, again because of fear of retaliation from the PRC and India's desire to remain nonaligned. Access that the PRC could consider to be direct support for U.S. combat operations would also be difficult. For example, if U.S. fighters or bombers were loading munitions in the bases in the Andaman and Nicobar islands, dropping them on Chinese targets, then returning to refuel and rearm, the PRC would see that as equivalent to a declaration of war. India is unlikely to grant such access unless it is willing to go to war itself.

Summary

U.S. policymakers will face deep, instinctive reluctance from India to grant any type of conflict-phase access. Several key factors would be central to New Delhi's decisionmaking. India is concerned that granting the United State conflict-phase access would lead to conflict with China—whether large-scale conflict or short of it—and that risk aversion will act as a brake in any decisionmaking. India knows it cannot currently compete with China militarily or economically in any sustained confrontation—China is simply too powerful. Thus, India's starting point would be to reflexively deny any access that could potentially inflame China's sensibilities and draw India into an unwanted conflict. However, any decision New Delhi made would be based on the relationship with China at the specific time of conflict rather than on a generic framework. For example, If India and China were already at a position of strong hostility, access might be more likely than if the overall state of relations was relatively friendly.

Another factor is the depth and endurance of India's traditional reluctance to join any sort of military alliance. This commitment to nonalignment not only reflects a genuine belief on the part of Indian policymakers that such a security policy is in India's best interest but is also a matter of national identity and represents a national consensus that spans the entire political spectrum. Any expectation of conflict-phase access in India will first be filtered through this lens. Related to and following from this factor is India's preference for consensus and multilateralism. India is much less likely to provide access for an effort that is perceived to be an American operation than to one perceived as representing a far broader international consensus. However, while India would far prefer to be in the majority than the minority, New Delhi is more willing than many other U.S. partners to dance to its own drum when core interests (such as its relationship with Russia) are involved.

Several key characteristics specific to the conflict would also bear on India's decision. Any PLA action that directly involved India's territory would be seen as a threat to India's core national interests that could overrule concerns about permitting U.S. conflict-phase access. Another characteristic would be the degree to which India perceives the United States as firmly committed to the conflict. From India's perspective, the worst-case scenario would be for New Delhi to provide access to the United States and generate retaliation risk and long-term hostility from China—only to have the United States stop short of a decisive confrontation and reach a separate settlement with the PRC. Which nation is perceived as the aggressor would also be important to India's calculus: A conflict in which China was clearly the aggressor attempting to subvert the rules-based order through force would make the choice easier for India. Finally, if a future conflict between the United States and China occurred in the Asia-Pacific, it is highly likely that Russia would side with China. India sees Russia as a long-time friend and source of important military and political support. Russia's likely support for China in most high-intensity conflict scenarios in the Asia-Pacific is likely to dampen India's enthusiasm for providing access.

Finally, India's decision may, to some degree, depend on the type of access Washington is requesting. Conflict-phase access requests that are invisible to the public would likely cause fewer domestic political challenges for India and, therefore, be easier to grant. Access that China perceived as less threatening (such as refueling access at bases far from PRC territory) would be more palatable. Finally, access that the PRC could consider direct support for U.S. combat operations would also be difficult. India would be reticent to provide this unless it was willing to go to war itself. Table 7.3 summarizes the key factors and conflict characteristics that our research highlighted for each of the five framework questions.

TABLE 7.3

Summary of Adaptation of Conflict-Phase Access Decisionmaking Framework for India

Framework Question	Key Factors That Affect Leaders' Calculation	Conflict Characteristics on Which Assessment Depends
Would granting the United States conflict-phase access affect the leader or the regime's political survival?	• The risk to an Indian leader of potential military defeat in a conflict with China • Nonalignment as a matter of elite national identity • Public perception of the United States and the U.S.-India relationship • A risk-averse and inexperienced civilian national security bureaucracy	• Whether a conflict directly threatens India's own territory • Whether global public opinion is tilted against China (e.g., if the PRC is clearly the aggressor) • The locus of the conflict—unlike a Taiwan conflict, a PRC land grab would not violate India's official One China policy
Would granting the United States conflict-phase access affect the country's direct security position?	• National security policy and orientation deeply rooted in nonalignment • Perception of the United States as a partner (albeit an unreliable one) and China as India's most significant long-term security challenge • Risk aversion to conflict with China (e.g., the likelihood of granting access leading to conflict)	• Whether a conflict directly threatens India's own territory • The degree to which India sees the United States as firmly committed to the conflict in question • A conflict in which China was clearly the aggressor attempting to subvert the rules-based order through force • A Taiwan scenario may be an easier choice for India than an SCS one (because it is more likely a scenario in which China is clearly the aggressor)

Table 7.3—Continued

Framework Question	Key Factors That Affect Leaders' Calculation	Conflict Characteristics on Which Assessment Depends
Would granting conflict-phase access affect the outcome of the conflict?	• The potential long-term security risks stemming from the United States losing • Whether India assesses that the access it provides would be unique and valuable in the specific conflict scenario, not merely giving the United States a pawn to be sacrificed that is not essential for U.S. victory	• The most important access India could likely provide for scenarios in the Western Pacific would be access to the Andaman and Nicobar Islands bases • But this access may overlap with alternative facilities of other nations closer to the locus of likely conflicts
Would granting the United States conflict-phase access affect—or be affected by— regional decisions regarding granting similar access?	• The involvement of key Indian partners • A preference for consensus and true multilateralism (rather than simply a U.S.-dictated effort), which can be overridden when core interests are at stake	• In high-intensity conflict scenarios, Russia's likely support for China in a conflict in the Asia-Pacific is likely to dampen India's enthusiasm for providing access
Would granting the United States conflict-phase access affect the economic prosperity of the country?	• The degree to which Indian leadership perceives India's economy as being able to withstand the economic blowback of a conflict between the United States and China • The state of India's economy at the time of the conflict	• The locus of the conflict and the potential it has to disrupt India's maritime commerce

U.S. Peacetime Policy Levers to Increase the Likelihood of Conflict-Phase Access

Having established what factors U.S. allies and partners are likely to consider when deciding whether to grant U.S. conflict-phase access requests, we next proceed to the question of what the United States, and the USAF in particular, may be able to do to affect these decisions. Are there particular policies that could be pursued during peacetime that would increase the likelihood of conflict-phase access being granted? Or are host-nation decisions likely to be driven almost entirely by broader structural or strategic considerations that U.S. policy may struggle to shift?

Perhaps the most commonly considered policy lever thought to improve conflict-phase access is seeking to expand peacetime access. It is often assumed that "obtaining and maintaining peacetime access is necessary for securing access to bases during a contingency."[1] However, as discussed in Chapter 2, the link between peacetime and conflict-phase access decisions may be quite tenuous. There are numerous historical examples of this linkage failing to materialize. Despite existing basing-rights agreements and hosting American forces for three decades, Spain denied the United States access to Spanish airspace in 1986 for Operation El Dorado Canyon, a set of airstrikes on targets in Libya as punishment for Muammar Qaddafi's support of terrorism.[2] Conversely, despite the absence of basing-rights agreements, Hungary granted NATO access to Hungarian airfields for Operation Allied Force in 1999, an air offensive against Serbia for its human rights abuses of ethnic Albanians in Kosovo.[3]

In this chapter, we assess whether and to what extent peacetime policies may be able to influence conflict-phase access decisions. To do so, we first present a descriptive overview of potential U.S. peacetime policy levers. Drawing on case-specific examples and a survey of the academic and policy literature, we identify which actions the United States can take in peacetime that might help secure access to and use of foreign territory, military facilities, and airspace during conflict. We draw from a broader literature on influence in interna-

---

[1] Pettyjohn and Kavanagh, 2016, p. 6.

[2] Pettyjohn and Kavanagh, 2016, pp. 65–67.

[3] Pettyjohn and Kavanagh, 2016, p. 8; Stephen T. Hosmer, *The Conflict Over Kosovo: Why Milosevic Decided to Settle When He Did*, RAND Corporation, MR-1351-AF, 2001.

tional relations to identify actions that have been shown to influence states' foreign policies and decisionmaking, and discuss the potential applicability of these levers to conflict-phase access decisions. Our review of these various policy levers categorizes them by the instruments of national power—the diplomatic, informational, military, and economic (DIME) framework.[4]

Following our description of potential U.S. policy levers, we investigate which levers might most plausibly be used to increase levels of access during a hypothetical conflict in the five specific countries that have been the subject of close analyses in the preceding chapters: Japan, the Philippines, Singapore, India, and Indonesia. We identify potential policy levers with the greatest potential to influence these decisions through the specific key factors we have shown to be most important for host-nation decisionmaking. The findings are suggestive rather than definitive; they identify U.S. policy levers that have the most plausible argument for shifting host-nation decisionmaking and, therefore, the levers that appear most deserving of further consideration for implementation. But, as discussed in the deep-dive analyses earlier, host-nation decisionmaking on these issues is highly complex and context dependent, so U.S. policymakers should have limited confidence in the ability of any peacetime policy lever to reliably shift host-nation conflict-phase access calculations.

U.S. Basing and Access Policy Levers

The second half of the 20th century witnessed a profound shift in U.S. foreign basing policy:

> Before World War II, the United States had a limited military presence abroad, and most of its overseas bases were located on U.S. territories and dependencies. . . . This dramatically changed with the outbreak of World War II in Europe as the United States began to seek rights to air bases within the Western Hemisphere to defend against a possible Nazi invasion. Later, as U.S. military officials planned for the postwar era, they concluded that the United States needed a large network of air and naval bases to head off future threats far from the U.S. homeland.[5]

---

[4] Joint Doctrine Note (JDN) 1-18, *Strategy*, April 25, 2018.

[5] Pettyjohn and Kavanagh, 2016, p. 3. On the strategic shift toward a global defense posture and the purpose of forward deployed troops, see Mira Rapp-Hooper, *Shields of the Republic: The Triumph and Peril of America's Alliances*, Harvard University Press, 2020; Stephen Wertheim, *Tomorrow, the World: The Birth of U.S. Global Supremacy*, Harvard University Press, 2020; Dan Reiter and Paul Poast, "The Truth About Tripwires: Why Small Force Deployments Do Not Deter Aggression," *Texas National Security Review*, Vol. 4, No. 3, Summer 2021; and Mark David Nieman, Carla Martinez Machain, Olga V. Chyzh, and Sam R. Bell, "An International Game of Risk: Troop Placement and Major Power Competition," *Journal of Politics*, Vol. 83, No. 4, 2021.

Such a shift in strategic thinking about foreign bases required an accompanying shift in practice. What actions, then, has the United States taken to secure access to military bases and facilities abroad, both in peacetime and in preparation for their use in conflict?[6]

In this section, we review policy actions that the United States has either previously undertaken to influence the decisions of host nations or that the literature suggests could be used for this purpose. We then discuss the potential utility of these actions for shifting host-nation conflict-phase access decisions specifically. Rather than present a long list of particular actions, we aggregate individual policy levers into general subcategories and sort these lower-level groupings into higher-level categories using the DIME categories. Table 8.1 summarizes these policy lever categories and subcategories.

TABLE 8.1

U.S. Peacetime Basing and Access Policy Levers

Category	Description	Subcategory
Diplomatic	"The essence of the diplomatic instrument is engagement—how a nation interacts with state or non-state actors"	• Support host-nation policies and priorities toward other states • Arrange or encourage third-party–provided benefits for the host nation • Build consensus against PRC aggression within international or regional organizations • Address local concerns about peacetime U.S. troop presence • Conduct high-level consultations to clarify potential conflict-phase access requests in advance
Informational	"The informational instrument is about creating, exploiting, and disrupting knowledge"	• Conduct information campaigns targeting public and elite attitudes in the host nation toward the United States • Conduct information campaigns targeting public and elite attitudes in the host nation toward China • Support host-nation messaging toward any domestic challenges
Military	"The use of force . . . . This use can entail applying force, threatening the application of force, or enabling other parties to apply force"	• Provide equipment • Provide military training and education • Provide security guarantees against external threats • Clarify that security guarantees against external threats may not remain feasible in the event of a U.S. defeat • Provide security guarantees against internal threats • Reassure host nations of U.S. commitment (e.g., through troop presence, visits, public statements) • Regularize peacetime access requests
Economic	"[F]urthering or constraining others' prosperity"	• Provide economic benefits (e.g., aid, trade agreements, investment) • Withdraw economic benefits • Help secure alternative sources for critical resources

NOTE: Descriptions are quoted from JDN 1-18, 2018.

---

[6] On *influence* in international relations, see Michael J. Mazarr, Bryan Frederick, John J. Drennan, Emily Ellinger, Kelly Eusebi, Bryan Rooney, Andrew Stravers, and Emily Yoder, *Understanding Influence in the Strategic Competition with China*, RAND Corporation, RR-A290-1, 2021, pp. 12–14; Lin et al., 2020, p. 8.

DIME is a common method for organizing the instruments of national power—the resources and capabilities the United States can wield in pursuit of its strategic ends.[7] Each element aligns with "the major executive branches applying the power: the Departments of State, Defense, and Commerce, as well as the intelligence community."[8] It should also be noted that, while the lower-level subcategories may not be exhaustive, they are extensive. Furthermore, policy actions that do not fit neatly into one of the subcategories can be organized under one of the broader DIME elements.

Diplomatic Levers

Through diplomacy, the United States seeks to promote its interests and build support for its policies abroad. Diplomacy is also the means whereby Washington can resolve disagreements with partners and allies or cooperate to reach mutually beneficial agreements. However, the effectiveness of any diplomatic policy lever often faces several obstacles. First, as international-relations scholars have long recognized, domestic politics can constrain or shape international diplomacy.[9] Perhaps one of the most influential articulations of this argument comes from Robert Putnam, who likened diplomacy to a two-level game played simultaneously at the national and international level:

> The politics of many international negotiations can usefully be conceived as a two-level game. At the national level, domestic groups pursue their interests by pressuring government to adopt favorable policies, and politicians seek power constructing coalitions among those groups. At the international level, national governments seek to maximize their own ability to satisfy domestic pressures, while minimizing the adverse consequences of foreign developments. Neither of the two games can be ignored by central decision-makers.[10]

According to this view, and in the context of conflict-phase military access, foreign leaders may or may not be able to grant the United States access depending on the constraints to their political survival at home.

The two-level game obstacle to diplomacy is in agreement with our first heuristic question that guides leaders' decisionmaking, discussed in Chapter 2, which asks about the domestic political feasibility of granting the United States basing and access rights. Because domestic politics can shape and constrain international diplomacy, these policy levers ought to have "an individualized approach to ensure that . . . collective needs are aligned and in the best

---

[7] JDN 1-18, 2018, p. II-5. See also Matthew L. Higgins, "DIME: Not just an acronym," *Marine Corps Gazette*, July 2021.

[8] JDN 1-18, 2018.

[9] Robert D. Putnam, "Diplomacy and Domestic Politics: The Logic of Two-Level Games," *International Organization*, Vol. 42, No. 3, Summer 1988, p. 434.

[10] Putnam, 1988, p. 434.

interest of both countries."[11] That is, that they should be politically palatable at home, at least among the constituents who keep the central decisionmaker in power.

Second, the regular turnover of ambassadors, key diplomats, and presidents may undermine the credibility of American commitments if U.S. policies are perceived to vary widely across officeholders.[12] Consider, for example, the American withdrawal from the Joint Comprehensive Plan of Action and the Intermediate-Range Nuclear Forces Treaty during the Trump administration or the withdrawal from the Anti-Ballistic Missile Treaty during the Bush administration. Such repeated unilateral withdrawals stoke concerns that, with turnover in personnel and leadership, the United States may not live up to its commitments, given the potential for future American leaders to change their minds, back out, and pursue other policies. While the stakes of something like the Joint Comprehensive Plan of Action are much lower than those for the potential situations considered here, lack of consistency in international agreements over time has been shown to be a problem in political science literature by undermining the credibility of commitments.[13] The inability to make credible commitments that outlast a single presidency inhibits the degree to which security guarantees can be made and believed by regional partners. Whether or not turnover undermines the credibility of commitments, the potential for dramatic policy change at least creates the need for the United States to routinely reassure allies and partners.

Third, while inconsistencies in national policy may create uncertainties about future American policy, there is always the enduring concern, independent of personnel changes, that the United States simply might not follow through on its commitments. For example, in 1983, the United States renegotiated its basing rights with the Philippines. As part of the renewed deal, American officials pledged $900 million in compensation but were ultimately unwilling to commit the funds and instead assured the Philippine government that it would "make a 'best effort' to secure the agreed level of funding."[14] American unwillingness to fully commit to the agreed-on compensation and the doubt this raised in the Philippines that the United States would live up to its agreement "remained a source of irritation in future discussions."[15] It is plausible that concerns over the United States' willingness or ability to follow through on its commitments might affect the outcome of diplomatic engagements.

Fourth, diplomatic policy levers face the potential for linking the United States to unpopular leaders. With respect to U.S. basing and access rights in Spain, for example, American officials worried throughout the 1950s and 1960s that negotiating with Francisco Franco's regime would

---

[11] Higgins, 2021, p. 64.

[12] Higgins, 2021, p. 64.

[13] Kenneth A. Schultz, "Perils of Polarization for U.S. Foreign Policy," *Washington Quarterly*, Vol. 40, No. 4, 2017; Dan Reiter, "Security Commitments and Nuclear Proliferation," *Foreign Policy Analysis*, Vol. 10, No. 1, January 2014; Matthew A. Baum and Philip B. K. Potter, "Media, Public Opinion, and Foreign Policy in the Age of Social Media," *Journal of Politics*, Vol. 81, No. 2, April 2019.

[14] Druckman, 1990, p. 3.

[15] Druckman, 1990, p. 3.

legitimize his rule and be interpreted as support for his policies.[16] In turn, U.S. officials feared this would alienate the more liberal and democratic elements of Spanish society, placing them in opposition to the United States and its interests because of its association with Franco and creating backlash to the American military presence.[17] Thus, among the United States' primary objectives in renegotiating its basing-rights agreement with Spain in 1963 was to have close enough relations to ensure cooperation yet avoid being tied too closely to the Franco regime.[18]

These obstacles notwithstanding, several diplomatic policy levers have historically been associated with successful U.S. basing and access agreements. While it is ultimately through international negotiations that the United States has secured peacetime and conflict-phase access to foreign territory, these negotiations often included other diplomatic and political efforts. We next review five subcategories of diplomatic policy levers that emerged from our review of the literature and relevant historical episodes.

Reassure Host Nations of U.S. Commitment

Host nations fear that the United States may abandon them in the event of conflict and worry that granting the United States basing and access rights risks military retaliation from adversaries.[19] These concerns necessitate American efforts to reassure allies and partners that the United States is committed to supporting their defense. Indeed, "reassuring allies has been central to U.S. foreign policy since the Cold War, with U.S. officials making countless foreign visits and public statements to demonstrate support for American partners."[20] Reassurance may also be an end in itself. As Blankenship observed,

> President Richard Nixon, for example, made a great effort to reassure U.S. allies both publicly and privately when he came into office in the late 1960s and early 1970s, with the Assistant Secretary of State noting that "Statements by both the President and [the Secre-

---

[16] Daniel Druckman, "Stages, Turning Points, and Crises: Negotiating Military Base Rights, Spain and the United States," *Journal of Conflict Resolution*, Vol. 30, No. 2, 1986; Angel Viñas, "Negotiating the U.S.-Spanish Agreements, 1953–1988: A Spanish Perspective," *Jean Monnet/Robert Schuman Paper Series*, Vol. 3, No. 7, September 2003; Tongfi Kim, "Why Alliances Entangle But Seldom Entrap States," *Security Studies*, Vol. 20, No. 3, 2011.

[17] Druckman, 1986; Viñas, 2003; Kim, 2011.

[18] U.S. Department of State, "Report on U.S. Policy Toward Spain," undated, in Charles S. Sampson and James E. Miller, eds., *Foreign Relations of the United States, 1961–1963*: Vol. 13, *Western Europe and Canada*, 1994.

[19] Glenn H. Snyder, "The Security Dilemma in Alliance Politics," *World Politics*, Vol. 36, No. 4, July 1984; Glenn H. Snyder, *Alliance Politics*, Cornell University Press, 2007; Leeds, 2003; Pettyjohn and Kavanagh, 2016.

[20] Brian Blankenship, "Promises Under Pressure: Statements of Reassurance in US Alliances," *International Studies Quarterly*, Vol. 64, No. 4, December 2020, p. 1017. See also James H. Lebovic and Elizabeth N. Saunders, "The Diplomatic Core: The Determinants of High-Level US Diplomatic Visits, 1946–2010," *International Studies Quarterly*, Vol. 60, No. 1, March 2016.

tary of State] can still do much to influence European attitudes toward this country, given their continuing psychological need for assurances from us."[21]

A more recent example of attempts at reassurance followed President Biden's inauguration. Once in office, the new administration engaged in a flurry of diplomatic activity that consisted of high-level official visits and public statements with the express intent to repair relationships that had been strained during Donald Trump's presidency and to reassure allies and partners about the credibility of America's commitments.[22]

Such statements are not simply cheap talk. As stated earlier, they put the reputation of the United States on the line for its allies and partners. Reputation is, in many situations, the currency of international relations that determines which states others are willing to work with in military, economic, or diplomatic ways.[23] Reputation must be constantly maintained and can be gained in a variety of ways. One is simply living up to a country's promises by providing support when the country said it would. Another is through the demonstration of expertise, skill, capacity, and competence in such things as military exercises and military exchanges and through the provision of advanced weapon systems to partner states.[24] This kind of demonstration establishes a high-reputation state as perhaps likely the most capable within the international system and promotes the idea that partners should bandwagon with this technologically and militarily dominant state that defines the status quo.[25] These demonstrations create expectations about future performance in conflict and the future international balance of power that are favorable to the United States.

All these different expectations enhance the impact of U.S. efforts to assure allies.[26] For example, when the United States conducts exercises with a regional partner, American forces portray a model of professionalism and competence to its partners. U.S. personnel are highly trained and capable and invariably demonstrate capabilities that no other country on earth possesses. Something as relatively simple as rotating an Air National Guard wing through the Western Pacific demonstrates the logistical capability of the U.S. military that far outstrips any other. Another such example is a Bomber Task Force mission from the continental United

---

[21] Blankenship, 2020, p. 1017.

[22] See, for example, Antony J. Blinken, "Reaffirming and Reimagining America's Alliances," speech, Brussels, March 24, 2021.

[23] Michael Tomz, *Reputation and International Cooperation: Sovereign Debt Across Three Centuries*, Princeton University Press, 2008.

[24] Aimée M. Plourde, "The Origins of Prestige Goods as Honest Signals of Skill and Knowledge," *Human Nature*, Vol. 19, No. 4, December 2008; Xiaoyu Pu, *Rebranding China: Contested Status Signaling in the Changing Global Order*, Stanford University Press, 2019.

[25] T. V. Paul, Deborah Welch Larson, and William C. Wohlforth, *Status in World Politics*, Cambridge University Press, 2014.

[26] Zeev Maoz, *Networks of Nations: The Evolution, Structure, and Impact of International Networks, 1816–2001*, Cambridge University Press, 2010.

States through nearly any country on earth. The simple possession of strategic bombers puts the United States in a club with only two other states, but the ability to project the power of the bombers anywhere on earth establishes the United States as the preeminently capable state in this area. Such capabilities assure allies and partners that they are likely choosing the side that would prevail in any conflict due to these advantages in capabilities.

Support Host-Nation Policies and Priorities Toward Other States

In exchange for granting the United States basing and access rights, historical evidence suggests that host nations will sometimes seek American support for their polices and priorities toward other states. For example, following World War II, American officials increasingly recognized the strategic value of establishing and maintaining a military presence on Spanish territory.[27] In addition to economic compensation for granting the United States access in 1953, the Franco regime also sought broader political goals. By breaking with its relative "neutrality in international affairs" and aligning more closely with the United States, Franco intended to enhance his perceived legitimacy at home and abroad.[28] In the years following the 1953 Pact of Madrid, the Spanish government continued to seek greater international recognition, pushing the United States to aid its efforts to join NATO and the European Community.[29] The United States had very little say in the European Community and was initially unable to convince all NATO members of the desirability of Spanish entry into the alliance.[30] Nonetheless, "with U.S. prodding and support Spain gradually inserted itself in the international cooperation schemes of the post–World War II era: the UN and its specialized agencies and the OECE [Organization for European Economic Co-operation]."[31]

Further, as part of the basing and access negotiations and renegotiations, the Spanish government sought American security guarantees, which the United States flatly rejected for years.[32] As scholars have noted, behind the repeated Spanish requests for a security commitment was "the wish to apply U.S. political support to the Spanish security scenarios in North Africa."[33] The United States refused to assist Spain with its problems in North Africa, but the experience shows a tendency for host nations to link other foreign policy priorities with basing and access agreements.

As another example, consider U.S. naval and air bases in Greece. The United States and Greece had reached a basing agreement in the early 1950s, but this was due for renegotiation in the 1970s. A primary obstacle during these renegotiations "was the Greek perception of a

---

[27] Viñas, 2003; Kim, 2011.

[28] Viñas, 2003.

[29] Viñas, 2003, pp. 3–4; U.S. Department of State, 1994.

[30] Viñas, 2003, pp. 3–4.

[31] Viñas, 2003, p. 3.

[32] Viñas, 2003, pp. 3–4.

[33] Viñas, 2003, pp. 14–15.

disparity between the deal with Turkey and the deal that the U.S. proposed for them."[34] Greek leadership felt that the deals unfairly advantaged Turkey, and they sought an American commitment to oppose "any attempt by either Turkey or Greece to settle Aegean issues by other than peaceful means."[35] The example illustrates, again, how host nations may try to condition basing and access agreements on other foreign policy objectives. U.S. willingness to support these other objectives may therefore be an important lever for increasing the likelihood that the host nation will grant conflict-phase access.

Arrange or Encourage Third-Party–Provided Benefits for the Host Nation

Similar to supporting host-nation policies and priorities toward other states, the historical record also reveals U.S. attempts to arrange or encourage third-party–provided benefits. The specific benefits the United States seeks to arrange for host nations vary across cases and time, and third parties may be states, international organizations, or specific agencies within organizations. By encouraging third-party support, the United States can help host nations further their interests, enhance their political and economic cooperation with others, and augment the compensation provided in exchange for basing and access rights.

Here, the U.S.-Spain case is again illustrative. The 1953 Pact of Madrid granted the United States relatively unfettered access to Spanish territory.[36] During the ensuing decade, however, the Spanish government became increasingly aware of the disadvantageous position the deal created for them. Recognizing the U.S. strategic interest in maintaining access to facilities in Spain, the Franco regime took a harder stance when U.S. basing rights were renegotiated in 1963.[37] Spanish officials felt they could push for greater concessions. For their part, American officials wanted an extension of the original agreement but suspected that the terms of the access agreement would have to change to accommodate some Spanish demands. A 1963 report on U.S. policy toward Spain revealed as much:

> We have generally taken the line with Spanish officials that we want a simple extension of the 1953 Defense Agreement for five more years, as provided for in the agreement. We have asked them what changes Spain might want in the agreement and have said that we would study any Spanish suggestions. The Embassy at Madrid has not yet confirmed from any other source the allegation by Ambassador Garrigues that Franco himself holds the view that some new quid pro quo is required if Spain is to agree to an extension. We believe it would be realistic to assume that some quid pro quo will be required.[38]

---

[34] Druckman, 1986, p. 3.

[35] Druckman, 1986, p. 3.

[36] U.S. Department of State, 1994.

[37] U.S. Department of State, 1994.

[38] U.S. Department of State, 1994.

As part of its efforts to renew the 1953 access agreement, the United States encouraged greater third-party economic assistance to Spain through the Export-Import Bank, the International Bank for Reconstruction and Development, and private markets. Additionally, the United States encouraged improved relations between Spain and the rest of Europe, doing so with the recognition that U.S. interests would be better served "by closer relations between Spain and her European neighbors as well as European organizations."[39] Stemming from Spanish demands and U.S. self-interest, this episode suggests that arranging or encouraging third-party support and benefits for a host nation may be an effective lever for securing military access rights abroad.

Build Consensus Against PRC Aggression Within International or Regional Organizations

The United States can influence others and further its interests by working through international and regional organizations.[40] Such institutions facilitate coordination, cooperation, and collaboration in response to global and regional challenges and create expectations about future state behavior.[41] With respect to Chinese oppression at home and aggression abroad, institutions enable the United States to support or form a collective response that pressures China diplomatically, economically, and militarily.

To illustrate how such efforts may help increase U.S. influence and improve the likelihood of military access being granted, consider U.S. support for the 2016 SCS arbitration between the Philippines and China. Arbitral proceedings began in 2013 when the Philippines alleged that Chinese actions in the SCS violated the United Nations Convention for the Law of the Sea (UNCLOS).[42] In 2016, the arbitration concluded that China's claims to the area and its resources were invalid and that it actually belonged to the Philippines.[43] Beijing rejected this outcome and sought to undermine international support for the ruling by dismissing it as "nothing more than a piece of waste paper, and one that will not be enforced by anyone."[44]

---

[39] U.S. Department of State, 1994.

[40] Kenneth W. Abbot and Duncan Snidal, "Why States Act Through Formal International Organizations," *Journal of Conflict Resolution*, Vol. 42, No. 1, 1998; Robert Jervis, "Realism, Neoliberalism, and Cooperation," *International Security*, Vol. 24, No. 1, 1999; Robert O. Keohane, *After Hegemony: Cooperation and Discord in the World Political Economy*, Princeton University Press, 1984; and John J. Mearsheimer, "The False Promise of International Institutions," *International Security*, Vol. 19, No. 3, 1994–1995.

[41] Susan Park, *International Organisations and Global Problems: Theories and Explanations*, Cambridge University Press, 2018.

[42] Mark Valencia, "Trying to Solve the Philippines' South China Sea Conundrum," *The Diplomat*, June 5, 2018.

[43] Office of the Secretary of Defense, *Annual Report to Congress: Military and Security Developments Involving the People's Republic of China 2018*, May 16, 2018, p. 13. See also "South China Sea Arbitration Case," Xinhua via *Global Times*, March 31, 2018.

[44] "Arbitration Creates Little More Than Noise," editorial, *Global Times*, July 20, 2016. See also Catherine Wong, "'Nothing More Than a Piece of Paper': Former Chinese Envoy Dismisses Upcoming Ruling on South China Sea Claims," *South China Morning Post*, July 6, 2016.

The U.S. response, however, was supportive. American officials urged ASEAN to reaffirm the ruling and, together with regional partners and allies, push back against China's narrative and propaganda regarding the UNCLOS outcome.

More recently, U.S. Secretary of State Antony Blinken highlighted the important role of organizations in American policy in the Indo-Pacific and toward the PRC. "From day one," Secretary Blinken said,

> the Biden administration has worked to reenergize America's unmatched network of alliances and partnerships and to reengage in international institutions. We're encouraging partners to work with each other, and through regional and global organizations. And we're standing up new coalitions.[45]

Through established organizations, such as ASEAN, and a diverse set of new economic and security initiatives, such as the Indo-Pacific Economic Framework for Prosperity, the Quad, and the Australia–United Kingdom–United States Partnership, the United States may align allies and partners behind a common vision for the Indo-Pacific and cooperate with them to shape the strategic environment around China.[46]

How might U.S. efforts to build a consensus against Chinese aggression through international and regional organizations affect a host nation's access decisions? When countries see wider regional and international bodies taking a clear stance, it helps form expectations about the level of support they will have from others. For states in the region, these expectations may make them more likely to act in ways that resist or respond to Chinese aggression, for example, by granting the United States access to their territory, airspace, or military facilities. If the country sees retaliation (either economic or military) from China for doing so, the signal coming from the organization is that it will support the country granting access by providing resources that may help it resist Chinese attempts at coercion. In addition, it signals that fewer additional states would bandwagon with China in its economic or military retaliation.[47] Such signals can be particularly meaningful states contemplating granting access to the United States, demonstrating to domestic audiences that such a decision is unlikely to isolate them from the international community and seeing the most severe consequences as a result.[48]

Working through organizations may also establish expectations for U.S. behavior. For example, regional allies and partners may expect the United States to be committed to the

---

[45] Antony J. Blinken, "The Administration's Approach to the People's Republic of China," speech, George Washington University, May 26, 2022.

[46] Blinken, 2022.

[47] Terrence L. Chapman and Scott Wolford, "International Organizations, Strategy, and Crisis Bargaining," *Journal of Politics*, Vol. 72, No. 1, 2010.

[48] Chapman, 2007.

region and to act in the defense of those who are threatened by China's actions.[49] In this sense, the behavioral expectations the United States created by working through organizations offer regional actors some assurance of U.S. support. Additionally, consensus-building aligns the United States and its allies and partners behind a common understanding that China's aggressive actions violate established norms, risk destabilizing the region, and pose a threat to the rules-based international order. Such a shared vision, together with the expectation of certain behaviors, may incentivize states to grant the United States access to push back against Chinese aggression to uphold regional and international order and stability.

Address Local Concerns About Peacetime U.S. Troop Presence

In communities that host American troops, opposition may arise to the U.S. military presence, which could in turn affect the willingness of the host nation to continue or expand access during a conflict.[50] This opposition may be driven by ideology or pragmatic local grievances.[51] For example, many residents on the Japanese island of Okinawa "want U.S. military bases closed because the horrific memory of the Battle of Okinawa transformed them into 'absolute pacifists.'"[52] In 2019, 72 percent of Okinawans voted against U.S. base relocation plans; in 2022, the island once again reelected antibase governor Denny Tamaki by a sizable margin.[53] Host nations may also object to the American military presence because they perceive it as a sign of subordination, as was the case with Saudi Arabia after the first Gulf War.[54] There are also numerous instances of host nations opposing the U.S. military presence due to pragmatic grievances, such as criminal jurisdiction, pollution, noise, and environmental degradation, known collectively as "not in my backyard" concerns.[55]

Whatever its source, local concerns about the American military presence may inhibit or restrict access agreements in peacetime or conflict. In 1979, for example, the United States was renegotiating its access to a set of naval and air bases throughout the Philippines. The two sides managed to resolve an array of disagreements on issues as varied as a formal secu-

---

[49] Jeffrey W. Knopf, "Varieties of Assurance," *Journal of Strategic Studies*, Vol. 35, No. 3, 2012.

[50] Yeo, 2011; Andrew Yeo, "The Politics of Overseas Military Bases," *Perspectives on Politics*, Vol. 15, No. 1, 2017; Geoffrey F. Gresh, *Gulf Security and the U.S. Military: Regime Survival and the Politics of Basing*, Stanford University Press, 2015; Amy Austin Holmes, *Social Unrest and American Military Bases in Turkey and Germany Since 1945*, Cambridge University Press, 2014; and Yuko Kawato, *Protests Against U.S. Military Base Policy in Asia: Persuasion and Its Limits*, Stanford University Press, 2015.

[51] Pettyjohn and Kavanagh, 2016, pp. 11–20.

[52] Pettyjohn and Kavanagh, 2016, p. 12.

[53] Justin McCurry, "Okinawa Rejects New US Military Base but Abe Vows to Push On," *The Guardian*, February 24, 2019; Elaine Lies and Yoshifumi Takemoto, "Okinawa Voters Re-Elect Opposition-Backed Governor, Media Report," Reuters, September 11, 2022.

[54] McCurry, 2019, pp. 14–15.

[55] McCurry, 2019, pp. 15–20.

rity commitment, compensation, and command and control of the bases.[56] However, one of the major sticking points to a full agreement was the issue of criminal jurisdiction, which was only settled with high-level visits and discussions between U.S. Senator Daniel Inouye and the then-president of the Philippines, Ferdinand Marcos, Sr.

These examples illustrate the potential for local grievances to inhibit or restrict U.S access and basing rights. Addressing these concerns, whether through high-level diplomacy or various forms of targeted compensation, does not guarantee the United States access or basing rights during conflict, but failure to do so may stoke greater opposition to the American military presence or toward the government that agreed to host U.S. troops, which may make granting conflict-phase access less likely. In the event of a crisis, local political officials will at least partially look to how receptive the domestic audience is to hosting American forces. By addressing local concerns, then, the United States may improve its public image and dampen objections to its presence during a conflict.

High-Level Consultations to Clarify Potential Conflict-Phase Access Requests

Host nations determine the conditions under which they are willing to grant the United States access, overflight, or use of military facilities. Consequently, reliable peacetime access may not translate into access during a contingency.[57] Consider, for example, that "all U.S. North Atlantic Treaty Organization (NATO) allies—with the exception of Portugal—famously refused to allow the United States to use air bases in their countries to resupply Israel during the 1973 Yom Kippur War," although "its peacetime basing rights in Europe remained secure."[58] Turkey also famously denied the United States access to its territory in the 2003 invasion of Iraq.[59]

While host nations will continue to regulate the contingencies in which their territories, airspace, and facilities can be used, it may be possible to clarify some of these conditions in advance. For example, when the United States and Spain negotiated the Pact of Madrid in 1953, one of the major obstacles to agreement was "the conditions under which the United States would be allowed to activate or put in a state of alert the bases and military facilities" for their use during a conflict.[60] The United States initially secured a relatively free hand in Spain. On "the timing and manner of the utilization of the military facilities," the two parties ultimately agreed that "[i]n the event of Communist aggression, or imminence thereof . . . [,] U.S. forces may immediately make such use of agreed areas and facilities," so long as they informed the Spanish government. "Should the United States wish to use the agreed

---

[56] Druckman, 1990, p. 2.

[57] Joyce and Blankenship, 2021. See also Pettyjohn and Kavanagh, 2016.

[58] Pettyjohn and Kavanagh, 2016, pp. 6–7. Portugal was the least reliant on Middle Eastern oil at the time, which freed the country to allow U.S. access when other allies feared a disruption in oil supplies.

[59] Joyce and Blankenship, 2021.

[60] Viñas, 2003, p. 8.

areas and facilities for combat purposes as a result of the emergence of any other situation . . . , such use will be subject to prior consultations between the two Governments."[61] This access was later restricted, and all use of Spanish facilities during conflict became subject to consultation.[62]

The Spanish case is highly unusual, however. While such an automatic agreement providing conflict-phase access is quite unlikely, states can still informally discuss what type of access would be requested and used in the event of a conflict. These discussions may help parties know what to expect and ease the access requests in the event of conflict. For example, while NATO does not automatically grant the United States conflict-phase access to member states' territory, long habits of consultation and cooperation between the United States and its allies during the Cold War clearly gave rise to shared understandings of what access would be requested and granted in the event of conflict with the Soviets. In the absence of a binding legal agreement, states may still achieve high-level understandings that can help ensure a high likelihood of conflict-phase access being granted.

Informational Levers

Through information operations, the United States may influence targeted audiences abroad, as well as other states' decisionmaking.[63] Information-related capabilities facilitate a range of activities designed to "affect knowledge, understanding, beliefs, world views, and, ultimately, actions."[64] Through strategic communication, public diplomacy, and cyberspace operations, the United States can create information and disseminate it to key audiences to strengthen or preserve conditions that are favorable to U.S. policies and objectives.[65] Indeed, in peacetime and during conflict, U.S. information operations can be "one of the most crucial, cost-effective, and practical means of furthering American interests."[66]

Beyond the opportunities they create to influence others, informational policy levers also present the United States with several challenges. Among the instruments of national power (DIME), information is the only one not under the purview of a single agency or department, thus leaving open the question of who within the U.S. government is responsible for plan-

---

[61] John Wesley Jones, "The Chargé in Spain (Jones) to the Spanish Minister of Foreign Affairs (Martin Artajo)," March 16, 1953, in David M. Baehler, Ronald D. Landa, Charles S. Sampson, John A. Bernbaum, Lisle A. Rose, and David H. Stauffer, *Foreign Relations of the United States, 1952–1954*: Vol. VI, *Western Europe and Canada*, Pt. 2, No. 885, 1986.

[62] Viñas, 2003, p. 27.

[63] Joint Publication 3-13, *Information Operations*, November 27, 2012.

[64] Catherine A. Theohary, "Defense Primer: Information Operations," Congressional Research Service, IF10771, December 1, 2021.

[65] JDN 1-18, 2018.

[66] Higgins, 2021, p. 65.

ning and executing information operations.[67] Currently, most information-related capabilities reside within the military, but some question whether DoD possesses "the best tools to successfully lead information efforts across the [U.S. government]," while others fear that DoD leadership may represent "the militarization of cyberspace, or the weaponization of information."[68] Despite the concentration of information operations doctrine and capabilities within DoD, legislation passed in 2018 "tasked the State Department's Global Engagement Center (GEC) to 'direct, lead, synchronize, integrate, and coordinate efforts of the Federal Government to recognize, understand, expose, and counter foreign state and foreign non-state propaganda and disinformation efforts.'"[69] Subsequent legislation then "created a Principal Information Operations Advisor within DoD to coordinate and deconflict its operations with the GEC [Global Engagement Center]" to take the lead.[70]

In addition, the United States must also contend with the reality that other states, such as China, also possess information operations capabilities. U.S. efforts to influence the attitudes, beliefs, and behavior of targeted audiences abroad have to compete with countervailing Chinese efforts. For example, following the 2016 UNCLOS ruling that Chinese claims to territory and resources in the SCS were invalid, Beijing used a barrage of information operations to shape the media narrative in its favor and to undermine support for the ruling abroad, particularly in the Philippines.[71] China's efforts were countered by U.S., ally, and partner messaging about the rule of law and the need to uphold and enforce the UNCLOS decision.

A final challenge concerns whether and under what conditions information operations achieve their intended effect. While they may have some impact, the degree to which the use of information capabilities sways beliefs, perceptions, decisionmaking, and actions is highly dependent on context. However, use of the information lever could enhance the effects of other policy levers by shaping narratives and domestic opinion in host nations about the United States and China.

Information Campaigns Targeting Public and Elite Attitudes in the Host Nation Toward the United States

Negative perceptions of the United States among foreign publics and elites are one source of opposition to the American military presence abroad. Under certain conditions, public grievances and negative sentiment may pressure elites into restricting or denying the United

---

[67] Theohary, 2021.

[68] Theohary, 2021.

[69] Theohary, 2021.

[70] Theohary, 2021.

[71] Janvic Mateo, "68 Gov't Websites Attacked," *Philippine Star*, July 16, 2016. See also Anni Piiparinen, "China's Secret Weapon in the South China Sea: Cyber Attacks," *The Diplomat*, July 22, 2016.

States basing and access rights.[72] As a potential redress, public diplomacy and targeted information campaigns among skeptical or affected audiences may help improve the U.S. public image in host nations and thereby mitigate domestic opposition to the U.S. presence. Even in countries where views of the United States are quite positive, it is still necessary to shape or improve the U.S. image. In Japan, for example, "public opinion toward the United States has long been quite positive, with 67 percent of respondents expressing a 'favorable' view in a 2018 Pew Research Center Survey."[73] Despite these positive views, however, experts note the desirability of "increasing public diplomacy outreach" as one method of resisting Chinese pressure and coercion in Japan and throughout Southeast Asia.[74]

What might such an information campaign look like? Historically, the United States has used public diplomacy, such as international broadcasting or cultural and educational exchanges, to shape civilian attitudes and perceptions. Such efforts were "seen as the key weapon in waging the Cold War against the Soviet Union and Eastern bloc."[75] Following the 1956 Hungarian uprising, for example, the aim of U.S.

> civilian information operations was to advance American interests through the creation of a positive image of the United States by fostering knowledge and understanding about the country. By presenting the truth, including negative stories, the United States would build trust and credibility.[76]

Similar efforts could be used today to cultivate positive perceptions of the United States abroad and to build support for American values and interests. Some have suggested that U.S. information operations in the Indo-Pacific today should emphasize "the economic benefits and value of U.S. military and security cooperation for regional countries."[77] This might include highlighting how U.S. disaster relief

> efforts have saved lives and prevented significant economic loss, how U.S. military presence and counterterrorism efforts contribute to stability conducive to investment and trade, and how cooperation on cyber defense and security has significant spillover economic benefits.[78]

---

[72] Gresh, 2015; Kawato, 2015.

[73] Scott W. Harold, *Regional Responses to U.S.-China Competition in the Indo-Pacific: Japan*, RAND Corporation, RR-4412/4-AF, 2020.

[74] Harold, 2020.

[75] Robin Brown, "Spinning the War: Political Communications, Information Operations and Public Diplomacy in the War on Terrorism," in Daya Kishan Thussu and Des Freedman, eds., *War and the Media: Reporting Conflict 24/7*, SAGE Publications, 2003, p. 91.

[76] Brown, 2003, p. 91.

[77] Lin et al., 2020, p. 87.

[78] Lin et al., 2020, p. 87.

Information Campaigns Targeting Public and Elite Attitudes in the Host Nation Toward China

The United States can use its information-related capabilities to shape perceptions of China and disseminate messaging that Beijing "is an unreliable economic partner and will not hesitate to use its economic coercion to achieve strategic and political goals."[79] Such efforts would help undercut countervailing Chinese messaging that the United States' presence in the region is destabilizing, while also countering disinformation and propaganda or shedding light on Chinese abuses at home and aggression abroad.[80]

As a recent example of U.S. information operations targeting public and elite attitudes, consider their use in another context: the Russian invasion of Ukraine. In the run-up to Moscow's invasion, the Kremlin freely disseminated or supported "ludicrous conspiracy theories about anti-Russia plots involving the West and Ukraine" and had planned "to film a fake attack on Russian territory or on Russian speakers in eastern Ukraine to manufacture a justification for an invasion."[81] In response to Russian disinformation and propaganda efforts, the United States and its allies and partners began releasing detailed intelligence reports about Russia's plots. Such operations helped "neutralize Russian propaganda and [allowed] the United States to try and control the narrative rather than ceding to Putin and his propagandists."[82] These efforts may also have further turned public and elite attitudes against Russia and made states throughout Europe more likely to take steps to oppose Moscow following its invasion of Ukraine.

With respect to potential host nations in the Indo-Pacific, U.S. efforts to shape public and elite attitudes against China could increase antipathy toward Beijing, and, by shifting prevailing attitudes, the United States may make states in the region more likely to oppose China by granting access to U.S. military forces than they otherwise might be.

Support Host Nation Messaging Toward Any Domestic Challenges

States that host the American military or states that are candidates to grant the United States access rights might face any number of domestic challenges—political, economic, or security. By supporting messaging and efforts to address such challenges, the United States may be able to improve its standing in these nations. Alternatively, situations may arise in which Washington must avoid supporting a host government's messaging. For example, a key feature of U.S. policy toward Spain in the 1950s and 1960s focused on currying favor with the Franco regime without alienating the liberal and democratic elements of Spanish society,

---

[79] Lin et al., 2020, p. 87.

[80] Higgins, 2021.

[81] Max Boot, "Why the U.S. Ramped Up Its Information War with Russia," Council on Foreign Relations, February 10, 2022.

[82] Boot, 2022.

which American officials viewed as potential allies in the future.[83] To this end, the United States could not support Franco's efforts to curb democracy proponents in Spain or fully embrace the same advocates for fear of losing or being denied access rights. This balancing act did not entirely reduce Franco's willingness to grant the United States access, but the episode highlights the need to think through whether and how supporting host-nation messaging toward domestic challenges can affect basing and access decisions in the present and future.

Military Levers

Military policy levers are a major source of influence and a prominent feature of past and present U.S. basing and access agreements. Although these agreements vary "significantly in form, substance, and scope," they all reflect "fundamentally the same bargain: The host nation circumscribed its authority by allowing U.S. forces to be stationed on its soil in return for security or compensation."[84] Through enhanced security cooperation, the United States can enable host nations to use or threaten to use force to further their own strategic ends and deter or defend against external and internal threats. In this section, we summarize six potential subcategories of military levers that the United States could employ to increase the likelihood of being granted conflict-phase access.

Provide Equipment

In exchange for granting the United States basing and access rights, host nations may seek to modernize and strengthen their own military capabilities through weapon sales or grants. Alternatively, the United States may offer arms sales to bolster regional security and to strengthen "allies and partners worldwide to meet their sovereign self-defense needs and to improve their capabilities to operate with U.S. forces to address shared security challenges."[85] Whether sought by host nations or offered by the United States, arms sales, equipment, and other military assistance often accompany basing and access agreements. In addition, providing equipment may affect a host nation's access decisions by improving its defense capabilities, supplying a source of rent or resources that leaders benefit from personally, or signaling a U.S. commitment to defending the host nation.

To illustrate the provision of equipment and access, consider the 1983 agreement between the Philippines and the United States, in which the United States offered "$300 million in military sales credits, and $125 million in military grants."[86] Or consider the importance of military aid in the 1963 U.S.-Spain agreement. American officials noted

---

[83] U.S. Department of State, 1994.

[84] Pettyjohn and Kavanagh, 2016, p. 3.

[85] U.S. Department of State, "U.S. Arms Sales and Defense Trade," fact sheet, January 20, 2021a.

[86] Druckman, 1990, p. 3.

that military assistance will continue to be the basic quid pro quo for extension of our base rights. We have already informed the Spanish that we can visualize a modernization program for their armed forces, based on their own statement in 1961 of their equipment requirements, of up to $250 million for the five-year period.[87]

Provide Military Training and Education

The United States offers extensive training and education programs for foreign militaries. As Martinez Machain has observed,

> From the perspective of the recipient countries, it is more straightforward to understand why they would agree to have their militaries trained and educated by the United States military. States want their militaries to be as effective as possible, and emulating the most powerful military is one way to do it.[88]

What has been less understood, however, is why the United States would train and educate foreign militaries. One assumed benefit is that such programs increase U.S. influence in recipient countries.[89]

Although they often occur outside the context of basing and access agreements, military training and education programs do influence foreign leaders' decisionmaking in ways that benefit the United States and its preferred policies. There is disagreement, however, over how this happens. Some analysts suggest that military training and education are forms of foreign aid that the United States provides to influence the recipient's policies over time.[90] In this sense, nations that participate in U.S. training programs are thought to grant basing and access requests or risk being cut off from training and education opportunities. This work also suggests that, by participating in U.S.-led programs, foreign military personnel are socialized into viewing the world in a way that is more favorable to U.S. interests.[91] These individuals then return home and often advise their respective leaders on military matters or rise to political power themselves, putting them in a position to advocate for policies that serve U.S. interests. With respect to basing and access issues, then, training and education

---

[87] U.S. Department of State, 1994.

[88] Carla Martinez Machain, "Exporting Influence: US Military Training as Soft Power," *Journal of Conflict Resolution*, Vol. 65, Nos. 2–3, 2021.

[89] Carol Atkinson, "Does Soft Power Matter? A Comparative Analysis of Student Exchange Programs, 1980–2006," *Foreign Policy Analysis*, Vol. 6, No. 1, January 2010; and Carol Atkinson, *Military Soft Power: Public Diplomacy Through Military Educational Exchanges*, Rowman & Littlefield, 2014.

[90] Tomislav Z. Ruby and Douglas Gibler, "US Professional Military Education and Democratization Abroad," *European Journal of International Relations*, Vol. 16, No. 3, 2010; U.S. Department of Defense and U.S. Department of State, *Foreign Military Training Report: Fiscal Years 2016 and 2017*, Vol. I, Joint Report to Congress, 2017.

[91] Martinez Machain, 2021.

may help foreign military personnel see China as a threat and be more willing to respond in manner that fits with U.S. military planning and policy. One problem, however, is that this influence is often lagged. It takes time, for example, for individuals who participate in training programs to rise in the ranks of government in their home countries, if they rise at all, or to influence decisionmaking in other ways, such as acting as a military adviser to a central decisionmaker.

Provide Security Guarantees Against External Threats

States in the Indo-Pacific may be more likely to grant the United States access if the risk of military retaliation from China is mitigated. One way to do this is to enhance deterrence through security guarantees. Such commitments reflect an explicit U.S. promise to defend the host nation.[92] With such assurances, the host nation may be more likely to grant conflict-phase access requests because the U.S. security guarantee may reduce the risk of retaliation that the host nation perceives it might face. Security guarantees tend to be viewed as credible. States care deeply about their reputations and credibility because they affect the degree to which others seek to work with a state. If the United States shirks its guarantees in one situation, other states may begin to wonder about the credibility of that guarantee when it comes to their particular security concerns. Thus, publicly making a commitment to provide protection is likely to increase the host-nation perception that the United States will defend them against a PRC attack.

With that U.S. commitment in hand, host nations are likely to further assess that their risk of attack by a third state, such as China, would be reduced. Security guarantees tend to be part of a larger military agreement, in which states aggregate their capabilities to defend against a powerful opposition. In the absence of an American presence, the likely power differential between the host nation and China would be massive. Thus, a country that expects to see a military threat from China can combine forces with the United States to remedy this power imbalance.[93] Providing guarantees to combine forces in this manner in the event of a conflict that risks a host nation's territory is a potential means of gaining conflict-phase access and for the host nation to mitigate its military vulnerability.

While a security guarantee can stand as a carrot that the United States can offer other states, the risk of the United States *not* providing security can stand as a potential stick. Thus, the United States can threaten to change American policy in ways that would lead to withdrawal or reduction of U.S. security for a state, if that state does not support U.S. access. However, whether the United States can leverage security guarantees for access also depends on other states' perceptions of the U.S. ability to provide security, particularly if the U.S. position is diminished after a conflict. For example, if U.S. military forces are unable to secure victory

---

[92] James D. Morrow, "Alliances: Why Write Them Down?" *Annual Review of Political Science*, Vol. 3, 2000; Brett Ashley Leeds, "Do Alliances Deter Aggression? The Influence of Military Alliances on the Initiation of Militarized Interstate Disputes," *American Journal of Political Science*, Vol. 47, No. 3, July 2003a.

[93] Lake, 2020.

in a conflict, the U.S. ability to provide security into the future would likely be significantly diminished, leaving the host nation more vulnerable. Such a situation occurred during the Vietnam War with American security guarantees to Thailand, which secured Thai support for U.S. operations during the war to keep communist forces at bay.[94] As the U.S. withdrawal began, the Thai government began to negotiate with the Chinese to begin to provide security guarantees that it feared the United States could no longer give.[95] While this case shows a country that saw the risk and supported the United States, Thai behavior toward the end of the conflict demonstrated an understanding of the consequences for the regional security order. Such a situation would likely occur again in any future conflict scenario with China, and the long-term consequences of failure to achieve a U.S. victory could be made plain to help secure access.

Leaders care a great deal about their country's sovereignty and territorial integrity, and there are thus multiple ways in which the United States can provide assurances against threats of these types in the event of a conflict.[96] The difficulty comes when offering such guarantees in the presence of an uncertain threat. Prospective host nations may perceive their risk of external threat to be small in the absence of U.S. forces but higher if U.S. forces are present. In such a situation, access would be perceived as the catalyst for a threat rather than a protection against it. However, the region is quite aware of the military threat that emanates from China, and that is a fundamental reason that states are hedging against rising Chinese power by inviting more U.S. military partnership.[97] In the presence of a conflict, this trend may accelerate, and more states may seek military protection in the shadow of a more militarily confident China.

Provide Security Guarantees Against Internal Threats

Internal threats to a host nation's government may undermine the country's stability and the reliability of American basing and access rights. In such instances, the United States may cooperate with allies and partners to respond to these domestic threats. To illustrate, consider the threat of terrorist activity in the Philippines, which intensified throughout 2016 and 2017. Militant groups with allegiance to the Islamic State occupied cities and fought local populations in the southern part of the country, killing more than 600 people and displacing around 250,000 civilians.[98] In response, the United States and the Philippines conducted

---

[94] Daniel Mark Fineman, *The United States and Military Government in Thailand, 1947–1958*, dissertation, Yale University, 1993.

[95] Arne Kislenko, "A Not So Silent Partner: Thailand's Role in Covert Operations, Counter-Insurgency, and the Wars in Indochina," *Journal of Conflict Studies*, Vol. 24, No. 1, 2004.

[96] Saunders, 2011.

[97] Cheng-Chwee Kuik, "How Do Weaker States Hedge? Unpacking ASEAN States' Alignment Behavior Towards China," *Journal of Contemporary China*, Vol. 25, No. 100, 2016.

[98] Sheena Chestnut Greitens, "Terrorism in the Philippines and U.S.-Philippine Security Cooperation," Brookings Institution, August 15, 2017.

bilateral counterterrorism operations and helped Philippine security forces reassert control over Marawi.[99]

Assisting potential host nations with internal threats may demonstrate that the United States is committed to their security. A host nation that is reliant on the United States for help with domestic stability may also be unwilling to risk a breach by refusing to grant conflict-phase access requests.

Regularize Peacetime Access Requests

Peacetime agreements and regular access requests can help contextualize conflict-phase access decisionmaking, although this is more likely for lower-level access requests and may not apply to all states. It may potentially be easier for host nations to grant certain types of access during a conflict if the requests are the status quo in peacetime because both domestic publics and potential adversaries may come to expect these requests to be granted and may, therefore, be less likely to react negatively or punish the host nation for doing so. As we discussed in Chapter 2, access requests that diverge greatly from the status quo may be less likely to be granted than are access requests that closely align with the status quo. One instance of the United States seeking to regularize access requests occurred in May 2022 with the announcement that the littoral combat ship USS *Jackson* would complete maintenance using Changi Naval Base in Singapore.[100] With the planned rotational deployment of littoral combat ships to Singapore for logistics and maintenance, the United States and Singapore are strengthening "the core of [their] security relationship" and establishing a peacetime status quo that the United States hopes will also serve as a baseline for Singapore's conflict-phase access decisions.[101]

Economic Levers

Host nations frequently offer the United States peacetime basing and access rights in part in exchange for some form of economic compensation. Indeed, in addition to security-related issues, economic compensation can often be a primary driver of basing and access agreements and, often, a sticking point in access negotiations and requests.

Provide Economic Benefits

The United States has several different economic policy levers that it can use to shape access decisions. First, military access often comes in exchange for rental payments on the use of host-nation territory and facilities, along with general compensation for the intrusions that

---

[99] Lunn, Arabia, and Dolven, 2022.

[100] Issa, 2022.

[101] Issa, 2022.

the presence of U.S. forces can cause in terms of traffic, noise, pollution, and more.[102] In particular, the United States made such arrangements in several Central Asia states that provided basing and logistical access to support the U.S. presence in Afghanistan.[103] Such payments can be used to pay for the disruptions that U.S. forces can cause but are also a mechanism the U.S. government might use to compensate host nations for economic retaliation that comes their way as a result of providing military access to U.S. forces.

Similar payments can come in the form of different types of direct U.S. military, economic, or other types of aid.[104] For example, the U.S. government or the military forces hosted in the country can agree to participate in certain kinds of local economic activity, such as purchasing fuel from certain firms and buying food locally. Such agreements can assist certain sectors of the economy that may struggle if they see economic retaliation from China during a conflict. Similarly, conflict with China may mean that some commodities in the host economy are in short supply. Given the size of the U.S. military, it can often be the supplier of last resort when shortages arise.[105] These are all direct mechanisms that the U.S. government can use to either make an access deal more advantageous to the host economy or compensate for any losses that are seen from Chinese retaliation.

More indirectly, the U.S. government has tools at its disposal to incentivize more private economic activity between U.S. sources and foreign entities. These tools can come in the form of tax breaks, low or no interest loans, subsidization of investment activities, trade preferences, and loan guarantees. Many such benefits, particularly those of larger scale or duration, would occur in advance, during peacetime, and may require congressional action to shift U.S. trade and investment policies. More-limited actions, however, could reassure host nations about the U.S. potential to provide benefits to address conflict-phase economic disruptions the countries might face. For example, because of grain trade disruptions following the Russian invasion of Ukraine, the U.S. Agency for International Development (USAID) purchased and paid for the shipping of Ukrainian grain and provided money to the World Food Program to purchase, ship, and store more Ukrainian wheat.[106] Such mechanisms can be further used to ease the economic blow of conflict to partner states.

---

[102] Jean-Pierre Cabestan, "China's Military Base in Djibouti: A Microcosm of China's Growing Competition with the United States and New Bipolarity," *Journal of Contemporary China*, Vol. 29, No. 125, 2020.

[103] Cooley, 2008.

[104] Cooley and Nexon, 2007.

[105] Christine Hauser, "U.S. Military Airlifts Baby Formula from Europe," *New York Times*, May 23, 2022.

[106] Keith Good, "U.S. to Contribute $68 Million to World Food Program to Buy Ukrainian Wheat," Farm Policy News, August 17, 2022.

Withdraw Economic Benefits

Ahead of the U.S. invasion of Iraq in 2003, "the Turkish parliament vacillated in granting the United States basing access and overpass rights to open a northern front into Iraq."[107] In an effort to influence Turkish officials, Washington offered Ankara a $6 billion aid package. However, facing increasing domestic pressure, the "Turkish Grand National Assembly rejected any use of Turkish air bases to launch attacks into Iraq."[108] In response, the United States threatened to withdraw its aid package or at least scale it back, much to the chagrin and frustration of Turkish parliamentarians.[109] While the move did little to change Turkish policy with respect to U.S. access, the episode suggests that the United States may seek to influence foreign leaders' decisionmaking by threatening to withdraw certain benefits unless access requests are met.

Help Secure Alternative Sources for Critical Resources

As noted, a primary source of China's influence in the Indo-Pacific is its economy, and in granting the United States basing and access rights, regional allies and partners worry about economic retaliation from Beijing.[110] While the United States has limited ability to fully compensate for the range of possible economic loses, it may be able to help allies and partners secure alternative sources for critical resources to blunt some of China's retaliation.

The United States has taken similar actions in Europe, where many states rely on Russia for their supplies of oil and gas. For example, a 2019 crisis between Russia and Ukraine left Poland in the cold when Gazprom, the Russian energy giant, shut down a critical supply pipeline that carries gas from Russia to Europe through Ukraine.[111] The event spurred renewed action in Poland to end its energy dependence on Russia and diversify its energy supply. Within years, Poland had constructed liquefied natural gas terminals to receive shipments of from Qatar; Norway; and, increasingly, the United States.[112]

In another example of responding to pressure on critical resources, consider the following dispute between China and Japan. In 2010, a Chinese fishing trawler rammed a Japanese patrol boat, and Japan detained the captain of the ship.[113] Following the incident, China "suspended the export of rare-earth minerals to Japan in an effort to harm the high-tech Japanese

---

[107] Yeo, 2017, p. 129.

[108] Yeo, 2017, p. 129.

[109] Frank Bruni and David Rhode, "Turkey Open to U.S. Using Air Space but Not Bases," *New York Times*, March 19, 2003.

[110] Mazarr et al., 2023.

[111] Stanley Reed, "Burned by Russia, Poland Turns to U.S. for Natural Gas and Energy Security," *New York Times*, February 26, 2019.

[112] Reed, 2019. See also Robbie Gramer, "First U.S. Natural Gas Shipped to Poland," *Foreign Policy*, June 8, 2017.

[113] Hui, 2021.

industries that rely on them."[114] Rather than succumb to China's economic pressure, Japan relied on its allies to push back by filing a grievance on China's rare-earth export suspension with the World Trade Organization, developing new techniques that used fewer rare-earth materials, and diversifying its sources.[115]

Although these examples occurred outside the context of access requests, they illustrate the potential for states to secure alternative sources of critical resources. By helping in this way, the United States may increase a host nation's willingness to provide access by mitigating the pain caused by possible Chinese economic retaliation.

Summary

The United States possesses a number of policy levers it can use to attempt to influence foreign leaders' basing and access decisions. In this section, we identified the types of policies commonly associated with U.S. access agreements and other policies that may affect access decisions. This set of policies emerged from a historical review and survey of the academic and policy literature. The specific policy levers aside, it is worth noting that, in the past and present, American basing and access rights abroad are founded on negotiated peacetime agreements. Despite their differences, these agreements form the status quo from which conflict-phase access decisions are made. Although host nations will always regulate the conditions under which access is granted or denied, "access arrangements should be in place before crisis erupts."[116]

Conflict-Phase Access Decisions: Country-Specific Key Factors and Policy Levers

The previous section described the range of peacetime policy levers that the United States has used, or could use, to potentially improve the likelihood of access in conflict. In this section, we take advantage of the earlier deep-dive analyses of particular countries to identify which of these peacetime policy levers have the most potential to influence the host country leadership's future conflict-phase access decisions. For each of these five countries, we describe the key factors that the earlier analysis highlighted as most important to the country's leadership when considering conflict-phase access. We then assess which peacetime policy levers, if any, have the greatest potential to affect these key factors and, through them, the likelihood of the country agreeing to U.S. requests for military access in a potential future conflict.

---

[114] Howard Schneider, "A Key Chinese Advantage Erodes," *Washington Post*, October 27, 2012.

[115] Hui, 2021; Schneider, 2012.

[116] Joyce and Blankenship, 2021.

Japan

While some potential U.S. policies could help improve the likelihood of Japan granting access, as we will discuss, it is important to emphasize up front that their effects are likely to be at the margins. There are likely no specific U.S. government or USAF actions that would prove reliable in fundamentally shifting the likelihood of a Japanese access decision during a war that is not directly related to Japan's self-defense. Our analysis suggests that that decision will be highly contingent, governed by time- and context-specific calculations by the prime minister at the time. Highly idiosyncratic aspects of leadership personality and perspective could make the decisive difference. The potential stakes for Japan would be so high that no discrete promises or threats from the United States or accumulation of actions taken beforehand could be relied on to make the decisive difference. But this is not to say that peacetime activities cannot help shift the likelihood of such a decision.

A critical distinction made in our analysis is between scenarios involving an unprovoked attack on the Japanese homeland and those involving conflicts that do not, at least at first, directly touch Japan. In the former case, Japan would almost surely invoke legal standards involving the existential security of the nation and direct the SDF to defend the homeland. In such a situation, most readings of the U.S.-Japan defense agreements suggest that the United States would not *need* further permission to use its facilities in Japan as part of the defense of Japan, but that permission would likely be forthcoming in any event. For example, China deciding to attack Japan preemptively as part of a war over Taiwan would effectively make Japan's decision for it, and access issues would largely be moot. Japan will be at war, and the United States will have access to its bases to prosecute that war.

In more-indirect or perhaps distant cases, where Japan is not directly attacked or its survival threatened, the most significant factor by far weighing on a prime minister and his or her cabinet at that moment—at least among considerations militating in favor of granting access—will be the risks to Japanese security from saying no. Japan declining, either partially or completely, to grant U.S. access, could put the longer-term U.S. commitment to its security at risk. It could also threaten U.S. success in the conflict, and a clear Chinese victory in a regional contingency could produce a security context far more unfavorable to Japan's interests and security.

Another distinction involves the kind of access the United States is seeking. If it is merely for noncombat, rear-area support functions, not combat operations launched directly from Japanese territory, the likelihood of Japan approving the request, across possible contingencies, would be much higher. From a Japanese standpoint, if it is not directly attacked or threatened, leadership will need to balance Japan's security concerns with its alliance responsibilities. Japanese leaders might therefore see noncombat support as such a middle ground in some scenarios, hoping to placate China and avoid direct attack but also to grant the United States the minimum necessary freedom to operate in Japan to support its campaign. Yet given the importance of bases in Japan to any conflict involving Taiwan, the United States will surely seek unfettered access to its facilities, including the ability to conduct combat operations from them. While less-stressing contingencies may therefore provide Japanese policymakers with the option of approving more-limited access requests, the remainder of this analysis assumes that the operational demands of the future scenario require a more comprehensive U.S. request.

Therefore, our analysis suggests that the United States—and the USAF—should conceive of policies toward Japan aimed at gaining access less as levers to achieve a specific result than as actions to set the context that improves the probability of a favorable decision. The best the United States and the USAF can likely do is to take actions that cumulatively create a situation in which Japan will feel more comfortable saying yes—and less willing to say no.

Attempts to shift Japanese decisionmaking in this regard would take advantage of the two most important, interrelated, factors highlighted in the deep-dive analysis of Japan: Japanese reliance on the U.S. security umbrella and the dependence of the United States on Japanese bases for most regional contingencies. By taking steps to reinforce the interdependence of U.S. and Japanese security in the Indo-Pacific, the United States can help increase the likelihood that Japanese leaders understand U.S. conflict-phase access requests as a necessary outgrowth of the broader alliance on which both Japanese and U.S. security depends.

From a USAF perspective, the effort will necessarily have a private component as well, working with the SDF and Japanese government to expand discussions of needed support for various components of wartime operations. Any opportunity to expand, deepen, and extend this process would help strengthen the connections in the alliance, which would then have indirect effects on Japanese access decisions.

In addition, more-specific and -tangible alliance integration efforts, including in the air domain, that have been underway would be continued and, where possible, accelerated. Already in response to both North Korean and Chinese threats over the past several years, the United States and Japan have developed closer military coordination and integration in various avenues:

- The Alliance Coordination Mechanism allows the allies to coordinate policy and the operational activities of the SDF and U.S. forces in all phases, from peacetime to contingencies. This mechanism also fosters better information sharing and the development of common situational awareness.
- The 2+2 coordination mechanism directed that U.S. fighters operate from Japanese bases to gain greater knowledge of their capacity.
- There have been joint patrols and coordination of U.S. and Japanese airborne warning units.

The United States and Japan have pursued joint research, codevelopment, and coproduction of ballistic missile defense systems. The allies also coordinate their separate deployments of sea- and ground-based missile defense systems (Aegis-equipped destroyers with Standard Missile–3 interceptors and Patriot Advanced Capability–3 surface-to-air interceptor batteries) by sharing early warning information and intelligence from forward-deployed assets.

In addition to expanding these activities, DoD and the USAF could also take other actions. Understanding that there may be legal constraints on the Japanese side, they could find ways to increase the participation of Japanese officers at various command sites in Hawaii to deepen planning integration. The United States could commit to bringing Japan to a higher level of intelligence sharing—not necessarily joining the Five Eyes community but gaining greater access on the model of non–Five Eyes NATO members and other close U.S. allies.

The effort to set the context for the access decision should also include outreach to local base communities, given the influence local leaders can have over central government policies. The 5th Air Force already conducts various community engagement and support missions in Japan, and those could be expanded somewhat to increase the visibility of U.S. forces in Japan and reinforce the message of the value they provide to counter the narrative that their presence makes the community a target of such adversaries as China and North Korea. This effort is especially important on Okinawa, where opposition to the U.S. presence still exists.

Through exercises, posture, and other actions, such efforts emphasize how critical the United States is to the defense of Japanese territory and the U.S. capacity to do so. It would entail, as a basic initial effort, repeated U.S. official promises to defend Japan in any regional contingency and constant public discussion of the necessity of a close partnership to deal with regional threats. It would also involve deployments, cooperative capability development, interoperability, and exercises focused on at least three areas: cyber defense and information resilience, air and missile defense, and defense against attacks on distant Japanese islands. The more tangible evidence there is of the U.S. capacity to help defend Japan, the more a prospective access decisions will be influenced. These areas are already a major focus of DoD and USAF operations in Japan but could be highlighted even more. The United States could offer to support, directly or indirectly, Japanese peacetime self-defense operations, such as maritime and air intercepts. In terms of nonmilitary threats, USAF and broader DoD organizations could engage with Japanese communities to highlight capabilities that could be provided in case of natural disasters and pandemics.

The Philippines

Our analysis identified two key factors that would likely be most influential in Philippine leadership decisionmaking regarding U.S. conflict-phase access requests. The first factor is the Philippine leadership's assessment of whether the United States is likely to defend Philippine territory in a conflict. Our research and interviews highlighted that a major concern for Philippine leaders in considering U.S. access requests is whether U.S. forces would defend Philippine territory if China were to retaliate in response.[117] According to interviewees, Philippine leaders' concerns in this regard are mainly about a crisis in the SCS, where China

---

[117] Discussion with U.S. SME on the Philippines, March 25, 2022; discussion with U.S. government official, May 19, 2022.

might attack Philippine-claimed territory in the Spratly Islands, or as retaliation for the Philippines supporting U.S. forces in a Taiwan conflict.[118] The research highlighted that, despite the existing alliance agreement and ongoing verbal assurances from U.S. officials—such as recent statements from Secretary Blinken about the United States standing by the U.S.-Philippine alliance and defending Philippine forces in the event of an attack—Manila is likely still uncertain about whether the United States would defend Philippine territory in the SCS or refuse to reach a separate accommodation with China after hostilities had begun, which might leave the Philippines on its own.[119]

Our review of the policy levers described earlier in this chapter identified two levers that appear to have the greatest potential to affect Philippine decisionmaking for conflict-phase access for this factor. The first, and likely most effective, lever is that the United States could provide an explicit security guarantee to protect territory claimed by the Philippines in the SCS if China were to attack it. A direct security guarantee to protect claimed Philippine territory in a conflict—including the Spratly Islands and Scarborough Shoal, in addition to Philippine forces—would potentially increase the willingness of Manila to grant access because it would reduce the risk perceived in Manila that the Philippines could be left to defend its territory in the SCS by itself. Philippine leaders may also surmise that such a guarantee could help deter China from aggressive actions against the Philippines in the first place because Chinese forces would then risk an additional confrontation with U.S. forces. Secretary Blinken's recent statements that the United States will come to the defense of Philippine forces are an example of high-level assurance that may be helpful in convincing the Philippine leadership of the U.S. commitment to defend the country's territory. An explicit security guarantee applied to claimed Philippine territory in the SCS would appear to have the potential to increase the likelihood of the Philippines granting U.S. military access in a later conflict.

Providing a clear and credible security guarantee of this type would require coordination and consultation with a number of U.S. government agencies and senior officials, including the White House National Security Council; the U.S. Department of State (Secretary of State); DoD (Secretary of Defense); and, potentially, Congress, depending on the level of security guarantee and whether it requires congressional approval. In addition, the U.S. ambassador to Manila might serve in a coordinating role and as a liaison for conversations with the Philippine leadership.

The second most-promising lever that we identified for this factor is that the U.S. military could assure the Philippines about the U.S. defensive commitment through increased high-level official defense engagements, including military visits and port calls; military exercises;

---

[118] Discussion with U.S. government official, May 19, 2022.

[119] U.S. official statements have assured the Philippines that the United States would defend its forces if attacked—but this does not necessarily extend to disputed territory. For example, in August 2022, Secretary Blinken stated: "We also reaffirm that an armed attack on Philippine armed forces, public vessels, or aircraft in the South China Sea would invoke U.S. mutual defense commitments" under the 1951 U.S.-Philippines Mutual Defense Treaty ("U.S. Will Defend Philippines If Attacked in the South China Sea," CNN, August 6, 2022).

rotational troop presence; and other visible signs of support, such as public statements about U.S. commitment to the security alliance. The U.S. military already undertakes many of these activities. For example, in August 2021, the 7th Fleet sent a littoral combat ship to visit the Philippines shortly after U.S. Secretary of Defense Lloyd Austin met with Philippine officials, marking the first time a commissioned U.S. Navy warship had visited the Philippines since 2019.[120] The United States is a frequent participant in military exercises involving the Philippines, including through the U.S. Army Pacific Command's Pacific Pathways initiative.[121] U.S. and Philippine forces conduct the annual Balikatan exercise, which is the largest joint military exercise between the two countries.[122] These activities could be expanded in peacetime to support a consistent U.S. message of commitment to the Philippine leadership, for example, through more-frequent high-level military engagements or sending larger naval and air assets for port visits or joint exercises. The organizations involved in such assurance activities include the Office of the Secretary of Defense, responsible for the Philippines and Southeast Asia; the U.S. Department of State; the Defense Security Cooperation Agency; USINDOPACOM; the military services, including the military public affairs offices; and the Foreign Area Officers stationed at the U.S. Embassy in Manila and various embassy staff to support activities and assist in shaping the messaging to various audiences in the Philippines.[123] While the embassy already helps coordinate activities and messaging, this role could be expanded commensurate with a more cohesive U.S. military reassurance effort.

Assurance activities would likely help demonstrate the U.S. defense commitment to Manila and send a strong signal of support for the Philippines. However, our research indicates that, these types of activities in peacetime, at least at current scale, are unlikely to significantly change Philippine decisionmaking about access in a conflict on their own because the leadership's overarching concerns about defense of Philippine territory and economic retaliation remain. While these activities would support other U.S. actions, such as instituting a security guarantee and expanding economic aid, they are unlikely to raise the probability of the Philippines granting access in a conflict unless the scale of the activities is substantially increased. For example, conducting several more U.S.-Philippine bilateral military exercises per year would probably not change the Philippine leadership's perceptions about the U.S. defense commitment. However, conducting large and visible joint military exercises with the Philippines focused on defending Philippine claims in the SCS that would

---

[120] Lauren Chatmas, "7th Fleet Ship Visits the Philippines," press release, U.S. Indo-Pacific Command, August 18, 2021.

[121] U.S. Government Accountability Office, *Army Pacific Pathways: Comprehensive Assessment and Planning Needed to Capture Benefits Relative to Costs and Enhance Value for Participating Units*, GAO-17-126, November 2016.

[122] Ralph Jennings, "Why US, Philippines Are Staging Large-Scale Military Exercises," Voice of America, March 31, 2022a.

[123] The J-7 oversees the Joint Center for International Security Force Assistance (JCISFA). See Joint Chiefs of Staff, "J-7 Joint Force Development," webpage, undated.

also increase interoperability of U.S. and Philippine military forces would likely go further to assure the Philippines that the United States will defend Philippine forces and territory in a conflict. This type of activity would potentially increase the Philippine leadership's willingness to grant conflict-phase access.

Our research also indicated that a second factor likely to be highly influential in Philippine decisionmaking on granting U.S. access requests is the risk of Chinese retaliation. When considering whether to grant conflict-phase access, Philippine leaders would likely assess the scope of potential Chinese economic and military retaliation both during and postconflict if Manila granted U.S. forces access. We discussed concerns about U.S. commitment to the defense of the Philippines if China attacked Philippine territory earlier; it is possible that greater signals of U.S. commitment could reduce Philippine perceptions about the risk of PRC military retaliation. But not all PRC retaliation would necessarily be military or likely to be deterred by signals of U.S. military commitment. Our research highlighted how tied the Philippine economy is to Chinese trade and investment; the Philippine assessment of the risk of Chinese economic retaliation, including postconflict, would therefore play a significant role in the access decisionmaking process.

Given the scale of PRC economic influence over the Philippines, assuaging Manila's concerns over how this influence could be used in retaliation for granting access to U.S. forces will be immensely challenging for the United States. In principle, a lever that the United States could use to assuage Philippine concerns about Chinese economic retaliation is to provide additional economic incentives to the country. U.S. economic incentives to the Philippines currently consist of military aid and development assistance totaling more than $4.5 billion over the past 20 years.[124] In 2021, security assistance to the Philippines was $47.9 million.[125] Beyond the U.S. military assistance efforts to the Philippines discussed earlier, USAID engages in a number of economic and governance development, education, environmental protection, disaster relief, and health care capacity development efforts in the country.[126] For example, USAID expanded its disaster relief program to the Philippines in 2022 to $20.2 million to assist with the response to Typhoon Odette.[127] As noted in Chapter 4, these figures are orders of magnitude lower than the scale of PRC economic involvement with the Philippines, which China has proven it may be willing to put at risk to punish countries that take actions with which it disagrees.

That said, U.S. economic assistance could be increased to help partially mitigate the impact of Chinese economic retaliation. In addition to these efforts, the United States could also provide compensation to the Philippines for hosting U.S. forces or in return for basing

---

[124] U.S. Embassy in the Philippines, 2020.

[125] Center for International Policy, *Security Sector Assistance Database*, webpage, Security Assistance Monitor, undated.

[126] USAID, "Our Work, Philippines" webpage, August 10, 2022.

[127] U.S. Embassy in the Philippines, "U.S. Assistance for Typhoon Odette Tops PHP 1 Billion with New Major Announcement," press release, January 5, 2022.

access, as it did in the 1980s, although the current EDCA would have to be expanded or renegotiated to allow this type of compensation.[128] Perhaps more promisingly, the United States could take steps to expand its overall trade and investment relationship with the Philippines more dramatically, including by expanding trade and investment agreements, such as rejoining the TPP, to incentivize greater private U.S. economic activity and to help create an alternative regional center of economic gravity that does not rely on Beijing. Such larger-scale U.S. economic efforts would involve a whole-of-government approach that, at a minimum, would include Congress, the U.S. Department of State, DoD, USAID, and the Office of the United States Trade Representative.

While U.S. economic incentives would provide some additional benefit to the Philippines in peacetime, these incentives are unlikely to be substantial enough to offset the scope of the damage to the Philippine economy if China were to stop trading or investing in the Philippines during or after a conflict. Given the sheer amount of trade and investment China has in the Philippines relative to what the United States has, the U.S. government would need to significantly increase its investment in the country and expand existing aid programs to begin to offset the economic damage if China retaliated.[129] For example, in 2020, Philippine trade with China was $47.4 billion, compared to $18.8 billion in trade with the United States. China was also the Philippines' second-largest foreign investor in 2019, with an estimated FDI of $1.7 billion.[130] While some of the gap is offset by the number of remittances sent to the Philippines from individuals working in the United States—$13 billion in 2021—the gap in trade and investment in the Philippines between the United States and China is still quite large.[131] Greater U.S. economic engagement in advance of a conflict would not entirely displace PRC trade and investment, although its scale could potentially be reduced. China would retain some degree of leverage over the Philippine local economy, so this concern would likely remain for the Philippine leadership when considering conflict-phase access.

Singapore

The deep-dive analysis of Singapore identified two key factors that would likely be most influential in national decisionmaking. The first factor identified was Singapore's concern over losing its status as a regional economic hub. For Singapore's policymakers, economic prosperity is inextricably linked both to the survival of the regime and to the national security of the nation. Economic prosperity is the foundation on which the political regime's claim to continued governance rests and, indeed, the foundation on which Singapore's entire

---

[128] Berry, 1990.

[129] For example, China's ban on Philippine banana imports in 2012 resulted in significant hardship for workers in several locales in the country.

[130] Department of Trade and Industry, Republic of the Philippines, 2021a.

[131] Department of Trade and Industry, Republic of the Philippines, 2021b.

rationale as an independent nation relies.[132] As the deep-dive analysis outlined, China has significant power to devastate Singapore's position as a regional economic hub that offers buyers and sellers a safe, efficient, and trustworthy place in which to make their exchanges. Singapore could cope with Chinese attempts to isolate it but would likely suffer immense economic hardship.[133]

Our review of potential policy levers identified one economic lever that could affect Singapore's decisionmaking: Provide economic benefits (e.g., aid, trade agreements, investment). However, this lever would not be potent or particularly realistic for several reasons. While economic agreements negotiated between the United States and Singapore would be useful, Singapore would value a resumption of some form of the TPP (e.g., a multilateral economic program of significant scale and scope) more than any specific bilateral economic agreement.[134] Such a move, however, faces significant U.S. domestic challenges. Thus, as our interviewees noted, the bottom line is that the United States appears to have no near-term option to address Singapore's concerns about this threat.[135]

The second factor identified in the deep-dive analysis is that Singapore's national identity is centered around autonomy and the importance of the U.S. balancing role in region to guarantee security. Singapore seeks to maintain foreign policy autonomy and cultivate positive relations with all nations—an outlook stemming from the nation's perceived vulnerability as a small state and the desire to avoid becoming too close or too dependent on any single power.[136] Nevertheless, the country's hedging is informed by a general preference for the United States as the strategic guarantor of regional order and security in Southeast Asia. The leaders' overall view of the region is largely in alignment with that of the United States, and they support the U.S. vision for the Asia Pacific over the long term.[137] This vision includes stability and prosperity for all states in a region that is not dominated by an assertive China—which Singapore fears would happen if the United States left the region. If the United States appeared to be in danger of losing a conflict with China and subsequently downgraded its presence in the Indo-Pacific, Singapore might be left to fend for itself. The leadership sees U.S. military presence in the region as guarding against a belligerent PRC that would otherwise dominate and destabilize the region.[138]

Our review of the policy levers described earlier in this chapter identified three that could affect Singapore's decisionmaking. All three would affect access decisionmaking by demonstrating the U.S. commitment to the region and clarifying plans to operate from

---

[132] Tremewan, 1994, p. 105; Lee Kuan Yew, 2008, p. 171.

[133] Interview with CFO of Singapore-based high-tech company, Singapore, March 17, 2022.

[134] Kausikan, 2022.

[135] Interview with CFO of Singapore-based high-tech company, Singapore, March 17, 2022.

[136] Kausikan, 2021, p. 206.

[137] Seah et al., 2021.

[138] Interview with Singaporean defense analyst, Singapore, March 25, 2022.

Singapore—and the region—for the foreseeable future. The first military lever would be regularizing peacetime access requests in Singapore. This would involve the U.S. military conducting exactly the kind of logistical operations in peacetime that it would want from Singapore during a conflict phase. As the deep-dive analysis noted, Singapore is more likely to permit the continuation of any nonkinetic activity already underway or routine prior to the conflict.[139] For Singapore specifically, regularization activities could include conducting gas-and-go activities outside exercises and with different platforms, rotating different types of aircraft (bombers, tankers, airlift, ISR) in Singaporean airspaces, expanding channel missions,[140] and increasing the complexity of the annual U.S.-Singapore exercise Commando Sling.[141] But equally important for this factor would be the U.S. military regularizing peacetime access and plans with other partners and allies in Southeast Asia—such actions would also demonstrate a U.S. commitment to the region at large that would reassure Singapore.

Regularizing access could also possibly change Singapore's perception of the way that China views U.S.-Singapore cooperation (e.g., increasing the amount and complexity of peacetime logistical access covered under the 1990 MOU could, over time, shift Singapore's perceptions about what China considers threatening and worthy of retaliation). However, the application of the lever using this logic has limited power. National-level considerations in conflict are likely to be very different from those in peacetime. Singapore's willingness to provide access is ultimately predicated on the assumption of a muted Chinese reaction (e.g., an assumption that China will not destroy Singapore's position as an open economic hub). If Singapore's leaders' perception of this condition changes during conflict, it ultimately will not matter whether the United States has been increasing the scope and complexity of peacetime access: The world is now different, and Singapore's leaders will update their decisionmaking.

Two other levers are related to this factor: high-level consultations to clarify potential conflict-phase access requests in advance (diplomatic) and efforts to reassure host nations of the U.S. commitment through troop presence, visits, or public statements (military). These levers should be paired with the lever described earlier to ensure that the operational-level impact of regularizing access is translated to and reinforced in Singapore's national-level decisionmaking apparatus. High-level consultations can help provide reassurance that the United States has firm plans to remain present in the region and to continue to guarantee the region's security. Interviewees also noted that high-level conversations about what, exactly, U.S. conflict-phase access requests would be in various scenarios would help reinforce the U.S. commitment to the plans and ensure that Singaporean decisionmakers are not surprised if conflict comes.[142] As one U.S. former military official noted: "We need to gain

---

[139] Interview with U.S. military official, June 2022.

[140] *Channel missions* move cargo from the U.S. West Coast to USINDOPACOM. The missions used to be a way of moving cargo to supply troops in Afghanistan and Iraq but also serve to show U.S. presence to host governments. They were shut during the COVID-19 pandemic but resumed in March 2022.

[141] Interview with U.S. military official, June 2022.

[142] Interview with U.S. military official, June 2022; interview with former U.S. military official, May 2022.

clarity on what exactly we want, and we need to communicate it to Singapore at the appropriate levels."[143] Another diplomatic lever that could affect this factor would be reassuring host nations of U.S. commitment. Any type of reassurance visible to the public would have to be done in close consultation with Singapore itself. For Singapore, the commitment sought is less military than economic: Singapore wants to know that the United States has a plan to be a player in the Indo-Pacific for the long haul—and that means competing with China in the economic sphere rather than just the military arena. On the military side, Singapore prefers to have visible port calls by warships of partner nations and visible air displays in concert with Singapore's air force. The key here is making sure that U.S. forces and assets are seen as equal partners with Singapore's troops, not as Big Brothers or protectors.

The third and final factor that would likely be most influential in Singapore's conflict-phase access decisionmaking is Singapore's strong commitment to and reliance on the rule of law and regional order for small-state security. As a small state in a rough neighborhood, Singapore relies on these principles to ensure its security—and, indeed, its existence. An international or regional order driven more by the whims of larger, more powerful states risks leaving Singapore exposed to attack or absorption. Singapore looks with strong disfavor on the actions of larger states that use force to violate fundamental principles of sovereignty and territorial integrity (e.g., Singapore's robust condemnation of Russia's invasion of Ukraine) out of concern that, one day, those states will use the same argument against Singapore.[144]

The lever most likely to affect this factor is a diplomatic one: building consensus against PRC aggression within international or regional organizations. Singapore much prefers to operate as part of a broader, global framework. Routine and habitual multinational pressure on China from such organizations would help make Singaporean opposition to PRC aggression a reflexive instinct rather than a difficult and controversial political choice. For Singapore, the relevant organizations would be the UN and ASEAN. At the UN, Singapore's prime minister noted that, to confront external dangers, Singapore "must stand firm on fundamental principles of international law. Work with other countries to uphold a rules-based order. For example, by speaking up at the United Nations."[145] Regarding ASEAN, Singapore values ASEAN centrality and prefers to insulate itself from great power politics by acting through the group. However, ASEAN's mandate for consensus ensures that the group will likely not take meaningful action in the security arena in the event of a future U.S.-China clash.[146] Singapore may still be willing to take a principled stand outside ASEAN, as it did after Russia's 2022 invasion of Ukraine, where it was the only nation in ASEAN to have condemned the

---

[143] Interview with former U.S. military official, May 2022.

[144] Lee Hsien Loong, 2022.

[145] Lee Hsien Loong, 2022.

[146] At least three members of ASEAN—Myanmar, Cambodia, and Laos and, since its 2014 military coup, arguably Thailand—have much closer relations with China than they do with the United States. Five of the other ASEAN members have territorial or maritime disputes with China but no appetite for military confrontation.

invasion at the time of the initial attack and the only ASEAN nation to have strongly supported the U.S.-led sanctions regime.

Indonesia

Our analysis identified three key factors that would likely be most important to Indonesian leaders in deciding whether to approve U.S. conflict-phase access requests: Indonesia's continued adherence to the nonalignment policy, the risk of retaliation from China, and whether ASEAN supports U.S. operations against China in a conflict.

The first two factors are linked, in that Indonesia's nonaligned stance is closely tied to its fear of conflict with China. It is useful, however, to consider the two factors separately. Even setting aside the issue of China per se, Indonesian policymakers (and, to a lesser extent, the general public) view nonalignment as a core element of national identity and security. It is seen as a foundation for Indonesia's influence in Southeast Asia and the basis on which it can mediate with both the United States and China on behalf of itself and its neighbors.[147] The Indonesian leadership has very little appetite for abandoning the policy and little incentive to choose sides in a conflict (excepting one in which its own territorial sovereignty is directly threatened). While the general public is likely to follow the lead of political authorities on foreign policy matters, the public could perceive a decision from Indonesian leadership to grant even low-level access to U.S. forces during a conflict as an alteration of the status quo that could potentially endanger Indonesia's security.[148] Given this salience of nonalignment as a basic concept, we assess that U.S. policy levers for this factor are insufficient to overcome the deep reluctance of policymakers to grant access in almost any conflict scenario, excluding direct threats against Indonesia's own territory (such as Chinese incursion against the Natuna Islands).

The second factor (fear of retaliation from China) is closely linked to the first and would deepen Indonesian leaders' caution in any conflict scenario. On the military front, China presents a constant threat to Indonesia's sovereignty in the Natuna Islands and their surrounding EEZ. On the economic front, China's threat is perhaps even more concerning to Indonesian policymakers: Indonesia is so reliant on Chinese trade and direct investment, particularly of infrastructure projects, that a decision in Beijing to withhold such engagement could devastate Indonesia's economy. The United States does have several policy levers that it could use to mitigate these risks, although they are unlikely to prove effective.

To allay concerns about Chinese military retaliation, the United States could provide a security guarantee or conduct military reassurance activities, such as security cooperation, exercises, training, and provision of military aid and equipment to bolster Indonesian military capabilities. However, none of these measures is likely to provide sufficient assurance to Indonesian policymakers of America's long-term commitment. Any security guarantee short

---

[147] Bland, Laksmana, and Kassam, 2022, p. 33.

[148] Interview with SME, June 23, 2022.

of a formal treaty alliance would be seen as hollow, and a treaty alliance is unlikely to be accepted either by Jakarta or Washington. From Indonesia's position, China will always be a powerful neighbor, and the United States will always be a distant (and frequently distracted) external player. Jakarta's strong preference will likely be to maintain its nonalignment policy and work through ASEAN to reduce the risk of retaliation.[149]

American levers on the economic side are even more anemic. The United States could offer increased economic aid, trade, and other incentives to Indonesia to offset the potential damage that Chinese economic retaliation could inflict on Indonesia's economy. But given the gap between current Chinese and American economic engagement, the scale of such aid and investment would have to be substantially greater than currently plausible levels. In 2021 China's trade with Indonesia was $131 billion, while U.S. and its major allies' trade was $115 billion; China was both the top import and export destination for Indonesia, while the United States was fifth and second, respectively.[150] Given this disparity between current economic engagement, the United States would have to triple its engagement just to reach near parity with China—and find a way of persuading Indonesian policymakers that such a ramped-up economic engagement would be maintained over the long term. With China's investment and trade perceived to be not merely high but growing fast, such an argument would be difficult to make.

The third factor identified from this deep-dive analysis as important to Indonesian leaders in conflict-phase access decisions is whether ASEAN supports U.S. operations against China in a conflict. This factor is likely to be less important to Indonesian policymakers than the other two but is perhaps more susceptible to U.S. leverage. As the U.S. leadership of the global response to Russia's 2022 invasion of Ukraine demonstrated, America retains potent tools in the diplomatic arena. In the two key votes in the UN General Assembly, seven out of ten ASEAN nations openly condemned Russia. No member of ASEAN is eager to alienate a great power, particularly on an issue that is not regarded as directly relevant to regional security, and corralling 70 percent of the nations involved significant American diplomatic effort. Indonesia was part of this supermajority, despite its nonaligned stance and significant reliance on Russian military hardware. The decision to side with the U.S.-led majority rather than join China in abstaining from the vote would not have been likely if other ASEAN nations were not making the same choice.

Indonesia's leadership prefers to address security challenges through ASEAN so that it can frame its responses as multilateral rather than as a preference for one country or another.[151] As ASEAN's largest member state and host of the group's secretariat (which is located in Jakarta), Indonesia is deeply vested in the organization. Therefore, the greater the consensus for support for U.S. operations from ASEAN states, the easier it would potentially

---

[149] Sulaiman, 2019.

[150] OEC, undated-b.

[151] Laksmana, 2018a.

be for Indonesia's leaders to grant access to U.S. forces without appearing to stray from the nonalignment policy. Interviewees also emphasized this point, noting that Indonesia would likely first look to ASEAN to gauge regional views on the conflict and level of support for the United States versus China in a conflict.[152]

Our review of the policy levers from the list described in the previous chapter identified the diplomatic lever as one that could affect Indonesia's decisionmaking for conflict-phase access for this factor. U.S. diplomatic efforts could be used to support the Indonesian policies and priorities toward ASEAN members that would assist in building support for U.S. objectives and operations in peacetime, which could increase the likelihood of ASEAN support in conflict and Indonesian willingness to grant access. The United States already conducts a variety of diplomatic activities with ASEAN, including efforts to bolster maritime security, advance science and technology development, address climate change, support energy development, and support transportation initiatives.[153] In November 2022, the U.S. Department of State announced the establishment of the U.S.-ASEAN Comprehensive Strategic Partnership, which was rolled out at the U.S.-ASEAN summit in November 2022. The partnership is intended to expand engagement between the United States and ASEAN member states at the ministerial level on a number of issues.[154]

Additional diplomatic efforts could expand on these initiatives and could include U.S.-led or U.S.-supported multilateral dialogues with Indonesia and key ASEAN members, such as Singapore and the Philippines, to build consensus for addressing security issues related to China's behavior in the SCS; increased high-level diplomatic visits with Indonesia and key ASEAN members to discuss regional priorities; and specific initiatives aimed at enhancing ASEAN security or addressing key Indonesian and ASEAN security concerns—for example diplomatic efforts to bolster information and economic security. These efforts would primarily involve the U.S. Department of State (the Secretary of State and USAID); the U.S. embassy in Jakarta and the ambassador to coordinate activities and liaise with Indonesian officials, and the U.S. ambassador to ASEAN.[155] These diplomatic efforts, combined with other U.S. economic activities with ASEAN, could potentially influence some of the ASEAN member states to support the U.S. in a conflict and create a greater level of consensus that Indonesian leaders might look to when assessing whether to grant U.S. forces access.[156]

---

[152] Interview with SME, June 22, 2022; interview with SME, April 26, 2022.

[153] U.S. Department of State, "The United States–ASEAN Relationship," fact sheet, August 3, 2022.

[154] U.S. Department of State, 2022.

[155] In May 2022, President Biden nominated Yohannes Abraham to be the first U.S. ambassador to ASEAN in five years (Tyler Pager, "Biden Nominates Top National Security Staffer as ASEAN Ambassador," *Washington Post*, May 13, 2022).

[156] The United States has committed $12.1 billion in economic, security, and health assistance to ASEAN member states since 2002, and the United States is ASEAN's largest source of FDI (U.S. Department of State, 2022c).

India

We identified two key factors through our deep-dive analysis of India that would likely be most influential in Indian leadership decisionmaking on granting U.S. conflict-phase access requests.

One factor likely to be highly influential in decisionmaking is Indian policymakers' extreme caution and risk aversion vis-à-vis China. New Delhi's starting point would be to instinctively deny any access that could potentially inflame China's sensibilities and draw India into an unwanted conflict. At the root of this risk aversion is a recognition on the part of policymakers in New Delhi that they cannot currently compete with China militarily or economically in any sustained confrontation—China is simply too powerful.[157] Indian policymakers are concerned that providing conflict-phase access to the United States would lead to full-scale conflict with China or even provoke a PRC reaction that was less than full-scale war but sufficiently dangerous to warrant caution.

We identified two military levers that could affect Indian decisionmaking for conflict-phase access for this factor. The first lever is regularizing peacetime access requests. Regularizing peacetime access would involve U.S. defense policymakers determining what type of access they would want from India during a conflict and trying to normalize that access before a conflict during peacetime. Doing so would enable India to portray conflict-phase access as merely falling within the framework of past practice rather than representing a substantive escalation or change in policy.[158] Steadily and gradually increasing the type of access granted to the U.S. military during peacetime might also help overcome New Delhi's instinct to deny access out of concern about China's reaction. If U.S. policymakers increase peacetime access slowly and over time, policymakers in New Delhi may see that providing access does not lead to PRC retaliation and make them more comfortable with providing access during a conflict.

For India, increasing the type of access granted during peacetime should be deliberate, well planned, and conducted at a pace that does not push India faster than it is comfortable going. India should feel encouraged to move more robustly, but not pressured. Resolving outstanding issues with the LEMOA and continuing to develop the procedures and SOPs required for both sides to use the agreement in peacetime will be critical. Indian experts we interviewed indicated that the U.S.-India foundational agreements will shape U.S. access during the conflict phase, so it is critical that the two militaries leverage and apply the full potential of the agreement during peacetime.[159] American defense officials could also try to regularize U.S. peacetime access to the bases in India's Andaman and Nicobar Islands. U.S. P-8s refueled for the first time at the Islands in September 2020.[160] U.S. officials noted that

---

[157] Blank, 2022a, p. 54.

[158] Interview with U.S. defense officials, June 2022.

[159] Interview with U.S. defense officials, June 2022.

[160] Braesch, 2020.

regularizing access to the islands will be a long-term endeavor, and Washington is unlikely to see strong progress in the short term.[161] Other ideas for regularizing conflict-phase access could include asking U.S. Transportation Command to, for example, route routine cargo missions through India to get Indian officials accustomed to U.S. military aircraft stopping to refuel before transiting to their next destination. U.S. defense officials noted that the U.S. military typically picks routes that include attractive destinations for U.S. personnel (such as the Maldives) but that it should be a USINDOPACOM command priority to stop in India.[162]

One diplomatic lever—holding high-level consultations to clarify potential conflict-phase access requests in advance—may also affect India's decisionmaking. Such consultations would occur with Indian civilian leadership (in India, conflict-phase access can stem only from a top-level decision by civilian leadership—the Indian military is not authorized to make such decisions, and its opinion does not count for much in decisionmaking). The consultations may help the United States better understand India's fear of being left holding the bag in a potential U.S.-China confrontation (e.g., a situation in which the United States was not fully committed to the conflict and reaches a separate accommodation with China, leaving India to bear the brunt of the consequences of providing access but none of the benefits). One Indian interlocutor—a former ambassador who has also served in other top policymaking posts—suggested that U.S. policymakers would do well to raise the potential for such requests and have the issues surrounding them thoroughly hashed out in advance of a conflict.[163] He suggested raising these questions at a session of the 2+2 ministerial dialogues, Quad meetings, and at think-tank sessions and tabletop exercises. If top-level policymakers are acculturated to the decision well ahead of time, they may be more likely to be receptive when the time comes. According to the same former Indian official, "[i]f there were prior consultations rather than waiting until a conflict was underway, it is more likely that India would say 'yes.'"[164]

The second military lever that could affect Indian decisionmaking here is providing equipment. India is hypercautious vis-à-vis China because it is well aware of its inability to compete. U.S. efforts to improve India's defense capabilities could lessen this threat perception by increasing India's qualitative military edge. Technology acquisition is a key Indian bureaucratic and political priority in the U.S-India defense relationship.[165] India seeks the most advanced U.S. military technology—including items available only to treaty allies—and is deeply offended at being denied much of it.[166] India also has a limited defense budget and often does not have the money to afford most of the highest U.S. technology. Moreover, India

---

[161] Interview with U.S. officials, May 2020.

[162] Interview with U.S. defense officials, June 2022.

[163] Interview with former senior Indian diplomatic official, July 12, 2022.

[164] Interview with former senior Indian diplomatic official, July 12, 2022.

[165] White, 2021, p. 14.

[166] Blank, 2022a, pp. 53–54; White, 2021, p. 13.

wants to coproduce technology with the United States (in an effort to indigenize its defense industry) rather than buy U.S. technology off the shelf. Some of these historic obstacles to enhanced defense cooperation have been cleared away with the conclusion of the three foundational defense agreements. But additional barriers to enhanced cooperation remain. Most notably, India faces potential sanctions over its military sales from Russia under the 2017 Countering America's Adversaries Through Sanctions Act. These sanctions are typically waived, but they present a looming challenge.

The other factor identified is the depth and endurance of India's traditional reluctance to join any sort of military alliance. India regards formal alliances, informal security cooperation blocs, or even any partnership that might be characterized as *alignment* as detrimental to its sovereignty and national interests. India's security policy is rooted in the concept of nonalignment. Indian policymakers hold a genuine, powerfully held view that the nation's core interests are best served by a foreign policy that balances competing nations against each other and maintains New Delhi's freedom of action.[167] Granting the U.S. military conflict-phase access in situations that do not directly involve Indian territory or New Delhi's direct national interests is seen as detrimental to the leadership's position and perception of its security interests.[168] India's fierce attachment to its geopolitical independence goes beyond security considerations and into the realm of national identity. This security policy was put into practice almost from the start of India's history as an independent nation and today represents a national consensus that spans the entire political spectrum. India's desire to maintain equidistance between and independence from great powers means New Delhi is far more likely to support a U.S. conflict-phase access request when there is a broad global consensus for action.

Our review of the policy levers identified one diplomatic lever that could affect Indian decisionmaking for conflict-phase access for this factor: Build consensus against PRC aggression within international or regional organizations. India is much less likely to provide access for an effort that is perceived as being an American operation than one perceived as representing a far broader international consensus. Instead, India would feel far more comfortable when operating in a broader global framework than it would be tagging along in a U.S.-led and dominated campaign.

In India's case, the relevant regional and international groups for building consensus against PRC aggression would be the UN and the Quad. For India, an operation for which it would provide conflict-phase access would ideally reflect a broad global consensus and have a corresponding UN mandate. As noted in the deep-dive analysis, India provided conflict-phase access for an operation in 1990 and 1991 (the first Gulf War) that fit these criteria; in 2003, for an operation (the Iraq War) seen as advancing the agenda of the U.S. administration

---

[167] Khilnani et al., 2012.

[168] Interview with U.S. officials, May 2022; interview with Indian security analyst, July 2, 2022; interview with former senior Indian diplomatic official, July 12, 2022.

rather than a global one, India declined.[169] In a future U.S.-China conflict, a UN Security Council resolution is likely impossible because of the PRC veto, but India will look closely at whether is there a General Assembly vote, and how lopsided such a vote is.[170] A U.S. Department of State–led diplomatic campaign that clearly and unambiguously portrayed the PRC as the aggressor attempting to subvert the rules-based order through force—and garnered the support of the largest number of nations—would be more persuasive to India than a smaller group of nations led by the United States. In addition to the UN, U.S. policymakers should also work through the Quad. As our interviewees noted, New Delhi is now more open to working with partners, such as the Quad, on potential conflicts. India might find it easier to grant access if a Quad action required it—rather than a bilateral request from the United States.[171] The more concerted multinational pressure can be applied to PRC, the more muscle memory builds up in India. It should be a U.S. goal to make opposition to PRC aggression (such as opposition to any nation's aggression) a reflexive instinct rather than a gut-wrenching political choice. For example, all U.S. partners typically condemn terrorist actions anywhere in the world, without much controversy—they do not spend a lot of time on internal debates over whether such attacks are the result of terrorists or freedom fighters. This was not always the case.

Summary

Across the countries we assessed, ranging from those with high levels of military cooperation with the United States, such as Japan, to those with very limited current relationships, such as Indonesia, our analysis noted that new or altered U.S. government policies are likely to have only marginal effects on decisions to grant the United States access during a conflict. Such decisions, in many cases likely to be considered tantamount to going to war against the most powerful state in a nation's home region, are ultimately driven by highest-level national strategic calculations. U.S. policymakers should understand up front that changing them will not be easy. That said, our analysis, summarized in Table 8.2, did identify three main areas in which U.S. policies could make a difference at the margins.

The first area relates to the potential value of preplanning and regularizing access requests. Identifying, in advance, the types of access in particular states—of course, short of combat operations from that state's territory—that may be most useful for U.S. contingency operations and then requesting them in peacetime and conducting allowed activities with regularity can have several benefits. Doing so can help shape both host-nation and, potentially, PRC perceptions of what access requests will be considered controversial or aggressive

---

[169] Baral and Mahanty, 1992, p. 374; Kronstadt and Pinto, 2012.

[170] As Ukraine-Russia vote shows, New Delhi is willing to act in opposition to a UN general assembly near consensus when India's core interests are at stake—but it would far prefer to be in the majority than the minority.

[171] Interview with Indian security analyst, July 2, 2022.

TABLE 8.2

Summary of Most Important Key Factors and Most Plausible Policy Levers for Expanding Conflict-Phase Access

Country	Key Factors	Most Plausible Levers
Japan	• Japanese reliance on U.S. security umbrella • U.S. dependence on Japanese bases	• Expand and deepen high-level discussions of joint wartime contingency planning • Increase intelligence-sharing with Japan • Reiterate the U.S. commitment to Japan's defense across all contingencies publicly and privately • Expand preparations for cooperative cyber defense and information resilience, air and missile defense, and defense against attacks on distant Japanese islands
Philippines	• Philippine assessment of the likelihood that the United States will defend Philippine territory • Risk of PRC retaliation	• Provide an explicit security guarantee to protect territory claimed by the Philippines in the SCS • Increase high-visibility commitments to Philippine security • Dramatically expand U.S.-Philippine economic ties
Singapore	• Singapore's concern over losing its status as a regional economic hub • Necessity of the U.S. balancing role in the region to safeguard Singapore's autonomy • Singapore's strong commitment to and reliance on the rule of law and regional order	• Reenter the TPP (U.S.) • Regularize expanded peacetime access requests in Singapore • Regularize expanded peacetime access requests elsewhere in Southeast Asia • Conduct high-level consultations to clarify potential conflict-phase access requests in advance • Build consensus against PRC aggression within international or regional organizations
Indonesia	• Indonesia's nonalignment policy • Risk of retaliation from China • Whether ASEAN supports U.S. operations	• Build consensus against PRC aggression within international or regional organizations • Strengthen U.S. ties with ASEAN
India	• Indian policymakers' extreme caution and risk aversion vis-à-vis China • India's traditional reluctance to join any sort of military alliance	• Build consensus against PRC aggression within the UN General Assembly and the Quad • Gradually regularize peacetime access requests • Conduct high-level consultations in advance of a conflict regarding anticipated access requests • Expand cooperation regarding defense equipment production and related technology transfer

during a conflict and, by contrast, which are normal or expected. In addition, several of the countries we examined already have agreements with the United States for some types of peacetime access, which could be potentially expanded on in peacetime and then applied in conflict. Examples include the MOU with Singapore and the EDCA with the Philippines. While conflict-phase access requests in the former category are likely to be very carefully scrutinized, those in the latter category may be less so. Regularized access and operations can also help enhance host-nation perceptions about the U.S. commitment to their defense, which may in turn increase the host's willingness to face PRC retaliation during a conflict. It is important to note, however, that some types of access, particularly including requests to conduct combat operations from a state's territory, do not have peacetime equivalents and likely cannot be routinized in this manner.

The second category of promising policy levers includes greater direct commitments to and consultations with potential host nations. Several potential host nations remain uncertain about what the United States would do in the event of a conflict with China. Even U.S. treaty allies, such as Japan and the Philippines (although to different degrees in Tokyo and Manila), continue to have concerns about whether, or in what circumstances, the United States would fight to defend them. Both public and private statements and other demonstrations of U.S. commitment could increase the willingness of these states to risk PRC retaliation by providing U.S. access. Similarly, high-level discussions regarding how a conflict with China would be prosecuted and the expectations of the United States for the participation of host nations (whether by providing access or other involvement) can be important signals of the seriousness of U.S. commitment that could help shift host-nation decisions.

The third category of policy levers relates to the important role of regional consensus. Particularly for states that do not have formal security relationships with the United States, such as Indonesia, Singapore, and India, regional attitudes and consensus toward potential Chinese aggression may be highly influential in shaping the states' own decisions. A broad-based regional consensus that a PRC attack constitutes unacceptable aggression that should be resisted, even if not necessarily militarily, may help convince states that they will face either more-diluted PRC retaliation or reduced domestic political costs for supporting the United States more directly by providing access. While primarily involving diplomatic levers and initiatives, U.S. military engagements with a broad range of allies and partners in the region can help build support for and provide emphasis for this viewpoint.

CHAPTER 9

Conclusion

Ensuring access to the territories of allies and partners in the Indo-Pacific in the event of a future conflict with China is a critical concern for U.S. policymakers. Both the physical and the political geography of the region sharply limit U.S. options for access to such an extent that some allied and partner decisions regarding providing access could determine the outcome of a conflict. A clearer understanding of how and why U.S. allies and partners are likely to make conflict-phase access decisions and what U.S. policymakers can do to affect such decisions is therefore essential.

The findings in this report should serve first to limit expectations about the influence that U.S. policies will likely be able to have on allied and partner conflict-phase access decisions. Decisions about whether or not to support U.S. efforts in a conflict by providing access will be among the most important that allies and partners will make, informed by leadership calculations of the state's most vital national interests. Shifting these calculations will be challenging, and U.S. policymakers should not expect large or dramatic changes in host-nation calculations to follow smaller or limited U.S. policy initiatives. U.S. policymakers should also not expect improvements in peacetime access to necessarily carry over to conflict-phase access, although there may be circumstances under which improving peacetime access may still be helpful.

While the challenge of shifting allied and partner calculations about granting conflict-phase access should not be understated, this report shows that there are likely some policies that can help improve the likelihood of such access being granted by focusing on addressing specific allied and partner concerns. With realistic expectations and a clear understanding of the calculations that allies and partners are likely to make during a conflict, some progress is likely possible on this vital national security issue.

This concluding chapter covers three main areas. First, it summarizes the findings of this report regarding how the five U.S. allies and partners in the Indo-Pacific that we investigated are likely to make conflict-phase access decisions, including how their senior leadership is likely to think about this issue and the factors likely to be most influential in their decisions. Second, it summarizes the U.S. policy levers our analysis identified that are most promising because of their potential to shift allied and partner calculations in the direction of approving U.S. conflict-phase access requests. Finally, we identify specific recommendations from our analysis for U.S. policymakers at the USAF, DoD, and broader U.S. government levels.

Findings

How Do U.S. Allies and Partners Make Conflict-Phase Access Decisions?

Our analysis of historical cases and prior research identified five heuristic questions that the leaders of states are likely to confront when deciding whether to approve conflict-phase access requests. These questions incorporate a broad set of strategic, economic, political, and diplomatic considerations and reflect how states in general tend to approach conflict-phase access requests:

1. Would granting access affect the leader or the regime's political survival?
2. Would granting access affect the country's direct security position?
3. Would granting access affect the outcome of the conflict?
4. Would granting access affect—or be affected by—similar regional decisions?
5. Would granting access affect the economic prosperity of the country?

These questions are broadly applicable to all states facing the prospect of deciding whether to approve conflict-phase access requests, but this report is concerned with the calculations and behavior of a more specific set of states: U.S. allies and partners in the Indo-Pacific. To assess how these states are likely to respond to U.S. conflict-phase access requests in a potential future conflict with China more directly, we conducted a deeper analysis of five specific U.S. allies and partners: Japan, the Philippines, Singapore, Indonesia, and India. In these deeper analyses, we explored the specific factors most likely to affect allied and partner decisionmaking through the five heuristic questions. Table 9.1 summarizes the full set of key factors identified in our analysis for each of these five countries. The following highlights the key factors from this set that our analysis suggested are most important for each country:

- Japan
    - *Japanese reliance on the U.S. security umbrella*: Japan's perception that its alliance with the United States is the fundamental guarantee of its security is likely to strongly shape Japanese conflict-phase access decisions. There are substantial fears in Japan that refusing U.S. conflict-phase access requests, including access to existing U.S. bases, could fundamentally undermine the alliance and risk forcing Japan to confront China on its own.
    - *U.S. dependence on Japanese bases*: Relatedly, Japan assesses that, for many scenarios in the Indo-Pacific, particularly for those involving Taiwan, U.S. success in the conflict would require access to U.S. bases in Japan. Japan refusing this access for such scenarios would substantially hamper U.S. efforts, likely worsening long-term Japanese security in the process.

- The Philippines
  - *The risk of PRC retaliation:* Philippine assessment of the potential scope of Chinese retaliation—both military and economic—would weigh heavily into a conflict-phase access decision. Philippine leaders are concerned about the vulnerability of Philippine territory, particularly in the SCS, to Chinese attack. Economic retaliation is even more of a concern because the Philippine economy is substantially tied to Chinese trade and investment and is quite vulnerable to PRC economic coercion.
  - *The Philippine assessment of likelihood United States will defend Philippine territory:* Philippine uncertainty over whether the United States would defend Philippine territory if China attacked, particularly in the SCS, is likely to influence Philippine access decisions. Relatedly, the Philippines would also consider whether refusing access might degrade the U.S.-Philippine alliance and reduce the likelihood that the United States would defend Philippine territory in the future.
- Singapore
  - *Singapore's concern over losing its status as a regional economic hub:* For Singapore's policymakers, economic prosperity is inextricably linked both to the legitimacy and survival of the political regime and the national security of the nation. If Singapore granted access in a potential U.S.-China conflict, China would have significant power to devastate Singapore's position as a regional economic hub that offers a safe, efficient, and trustworthy place in which to make exchanges.
  - *The necessity of the U.S. balancing role in region to safeguard Singapore's autonomy:* Singapore seeks to maintain foreign policy autonomy and avoid becoming too close or too dependent on any single power. But Singapore's hedging is informed by a general preference for the United States as the strategic guarantor of regional order, prosperity, and security in Southeast Asia. Singapore would consider whether refusing access would lead to a U.S. defeat in a potential conflict, which would leave the nation vulnerable to a regional order dominated by an assertive China.
  - *Singapore's strong commitment to and reliance on the rule of law and current regional order:* As a small state in a dangerous neighborhood, Singapore relies on and is committed to the rule of law and the current regional order. An order driven more by the whims of larger, more powerful states risks leaving Singapore exposed to attack or absorption. Singapore may thus be more amenable to access to prevent larger states from using force to violate principles of sovereignty and territorial integrity.
- Indonesia
  - *Indonesia's nonalignment policy:* Indonesia views nonalignment as the best way to keep the country secure by maintaining neutrality and addressing security challenges multilaterally through ASEAN. There is a strong preference among Indonesian elites to maintain the nonalignment policy even in a conflict, which would factor heavily into Indonesia's access decisions.
  - *The risk of retaliation from China:* Indonesian policymakers are concerned about military and economic retaliation from China, and this would factor into conflict-phase

access decisions. Regarding military retaliation, a primary concern is the vulnerability of the Natuna Islands if China were to attack. Indonesia's economy is very vulnerable to Chinese economic retaliation, given the amount of PRC trade and investment, which is significantly greater than that of the United States.

- *Whether ASEAN supports U.S. operations*: Indonesia would also consider the stance of ASEAN member states in its conflict-phase access decisions. While an ASEAN consensus in a U.S.-China conflict is unlikely, Indonesia's position as the head of ASEAN and its preference for working through ASEAN on regional issues would carry weight with Indonesia's policymakers. It is likely that Indonesia would look to ASEAN to assess the level of support for the United States in a conflict before choosing whether to grant access.

- India
  - *Indian policymakers' extreme caution and risk aversion vis-à-vis China*: India will hesitate to take actions it perceives would antagonize China or attract Beijing's ire. India recognizes China is too economically and militarily powerful for India to prevail in any sustained confrontation between the two nations. Indian policymakers fear that providing conflict-phase access to the United States would lead to a full-scale conflict with China or even provoke a PRC reaction less than full-scale war but sufficiently dangerous to warrant caution.
  - *India's traditional reluctance to join any sort of military alliance*: India regards formal alliances, informal security cooperation blocs, or even any partnership that might be characterized as alignment as detrimental to its sovereignty and national interests. Indian policymakers believe the nation's core interests are best served by a foreign policy that balances competing nations against each other and maintains New Delhi's freedom of action. U.S. policymakers should not underestimate the depth and endurance of this worldview.

By developing these more-detailed understandings of how allied and partner decisions are likely to be made, our report is able both to set appropriate expectations regarding how likely, or unlikely, states may be to approve U.S. access requests under different circumstances and to identify the most plausible pathways that U.S. policymakers may try to shift the calculations of allies and partner in favor of approving U.S. requests.

What Policy Levers Are Most Promising for Improving the Likelihood of Conflict-Phase Access?

Having developed our understanding of how U.S. allies and partners are likely to make conflict-phase access decisions, we next analyzed what policy levers, if any, might allow U.S. policymakers to shift these calculations. We began by reviewing the set of potential levers that the United States has or could use to expand its influence on allies and partners in general terms, then identifying those that could be applicable to affecting host-nation conflict-

TABLE 9.1

Summary of Host-Nation Conflict-Phase Access Decisionmaking

Question	Key Factors Informing Each Question for Specific Countries				
	Japan	Philippines	Singapore	Indonesia	India
Would granting the United States conflict-phase access affect the leader or the regime's political survival?	• Degree of economic dependence on PRC • Public opinion • Japanese political situation • Nature of threat to Japan	• Philippine public opinion on the U.S.-Philippines security alliance and the PRC • Leadership's preference to balance between the United States and the PRC	• Elite preferences for a greater U.S. role in region • Mass cultural affinity for China restrained by a top-town political system.	• Potential for backlash from the public • Indonesian public's views on China and the United States	• Risk of military defeat • Nonalignment part of national identity • Public perception of U.S.-India relations • Risk-averse civilian bureaucracy
Would granting the United States conflict-phase access affect the country's direct security position?	• Reliance on U.S. security umbrella • Formal definition of contingency under Japanese constitution • Risk of direct attack on Japan	• Philippine assessment of national interests • Philippine domestic military weakness • Balance between U.S. alliance and Chinese retaliation	• National identity of autonomy • Limited concern for kinetic retaliation • Strong commitment to rule of law and regional order	• Concern over PRC military response • Focus on internal security threats • Indonesia's assessment of the reliability of the U.S.	• Deeply rooted nonalignment • Perception of U.S. unreliability and PRC security challenge • Risk aversion to conflict with China
Would granting conflict-phase access affect the outcome of the conflict?	• Dependence of the United States on Japanese bases for most regional contingencies	• Philippine importance to U.S. operations • Type of access being requested • Leadership view of U.S.-Philippines alliance	• Perception that U.S. access is good for Singapore and the region • Assessment that access provided is unique	• Whether U.S. forces have access to other, comparable locations	• Long-term security risks from U.S. defeat • Whether India assesses that the access it provides would be unique and valuable

Table 9.1—Continued

Question	Key Factors Informing Each Question for Specific Countries				
	Japan	Philippines	Singapore	Indonesia	India
Would granting the U.S. conflict-phase access affect—or be affected by—similar regional decisions?	• Perception of regional and/or global consensus on response to PRC • Weight of Japan's regional relationships	• Whether other U.S. treaty allies also granted access • Level of support from ASEAN	• Limits of ASEAN in security realm • Regional expectation of support to United States • Limited importance of states in the region outside ASEAN	• ASEAN support for U.S. operations • Access granted by other ASEAN members	• Involvement of key Indian partners • Preference for consensus and true multilateralism
Would granting the United States conflict-phase access affect the economic prosperity of the country?	• Perception of threats from economic dependence • Perception of economic risks of conflict	• Potential PRC retaliation • Philippine economic relations with the United States	• PRC economic links • Concern over losing status as regional economic hub • Economic relations with the United States, allies	• Reliance on PRC trade and investment • Risk of PRC economic retaliation	• Indian leadership perceptions of economic vulnerability • The state of India's economy at the time of the conflict

phase decisions. We organized these levers according to the DIME framework, as shown in Table 9.2.

We then assessed which of these levers could most plausibly affect the conflict-phase access decisions of our five focus countries through the most influential key factors summarized earlier. This assessment evaluated both whether we could identify a plausible explanation for how this policy would affect host-nation calculations through the most influential key factors and whether the potential scale of the effect could make a notable difference in these calculations. These criteria were designed to identify the policy levers most likely to affect host-nation conflict-phase access specifically. There may be numerous other policies the United States could adopt toward the host nation that would have other benefits, including improving the overall tenor of the relationship, but our analysis focused specifically on the policy levers likely to improve conflict-phase access decisions. Table 9.3 summarizes the policy levers our analysis highlighted for each country.

These policy levers fell mostly into four main categories:

- *Preplanning and regularizing access requests*: Requesting and regularly using the same types of access the United States is likely to request in a conflict in advance can help shape both host-nation and potentially PRC perceptions about what access requests China may view as routine as opposed to potentially increasing the risk of PRC retali-

TABLE 9.2

Potential U.S. Policy Levers to Influence Conflict-Phase Access Decisions

Category	Subcategory
Diplomatic	• Support host-nation policies and priorities toward other states • Arrange or encourage third-party–provided benefits for the host nation • Build consensus against PRC aggression within international or regional organizations • Address local concerns about peacetime U.S. troop presence • Conduct high-level consultations to clarify potential conflict-phase access requests in advance
Informational	• Conduct information campaigns targeting public and elite attitudes toward the United States in the host nation • Conduct information campaigns targeting public and elite attitudes in the host nation toward China • Support host-nation messaging toward any domestic challenges
Military	• Provide equipment • Provide military training and education • Provide security guarantees against external threats • Clarify that security guarantees against external threats may not remain feasible in the event of a U.S. defeat • Provide security guarantees against internal threats • Reassure host nations of the U.S. commitment (e.g., through troop presence, visits, public statements) • Regularize peacetime access requests
Economic	• Provide economic benefits (e.g., aid, trade agreements, investment) • Withdraw economic benefits • Help secure alternative sources for critical resources

TABLE 9.3

Summary of Most Plausible Policy Levers for Expanding Conflict-Phase Access

Country	Most Plausible Levers
Japan	• Expand and deepen high-level discussions of joint wartime contingency planning • Increase intelligence-sharing with Japan • Reiterate the U.S. commitment to Japan's defense across all contingencies publicly and privately • Expand preparations for cooperative cyber defense and information resilience, air and missile defense, and defense against attacks on distant Japanese islands
Philippines	• Provide an explicit security guarantee to protect territory claimed by the Philippines in the SCS • Increase high-visibility commitments to Philippine security • Dramatically expand U.S.-Philippine economic ties
Singapore	• Reenter the TPP (U.S.) • Regularize expanded peacetime access requests in Singapore • Regularize expanded peacetime access requests elsewhere in Southeast Asia • Conduct high-level consultations to clarify potential conflict-phase access requests in advance • Build consensus against PRC aggression within international or regional organizations
Indonesia	• Build consensus against PRC aggression within international or regional organizations • Strengthen U.S. ties with ASEAN
India	• Build consensus against PRC aggression within the UN General Assembly and the Quad • Gradually regularize peacetime access requests • Conduct high-level consultations in advance of a conflict regarding anticipated access requests • Expand cooperation regarding defense equipment production and related technology transfer

ation in conflict. Regularized access and operations can also help enhance host-nation perceptions of the U.S. commitment to their defense, which may in turn increase their willingness to face PRC retaliation during a conflict. However, this possibility likely applies only to lower-level types of access, such as overflight and logistics and, as Table 9.3 indicates likely applies only to certain states.

- *Greater direct commitments to and consultations with potential host nations*: Several potential host nations remain uncertain about whether, or in what circumstances, the United States would fight to defend them. Public and private statements, high-level discussions of how a conflict with China would be prosecuted and of the goals of the United States for the participation of host nations, and other demonstrations of U.S. commitment could increase the willingness of these states to risk PRC retaliation by providing U.S. access.

- *Building regional consensus*: Regional and international attitudes and consensus toward the importance of opposing potential Chinese aggression may be highly influential in shaping the access decisions of U.S. allies and partners. While primarily involving diplomatic levers and initiatives, U.S. military engagements with a broad range of allies and partners in the region and beyond can help build support and provide emphasis for this viewpoint.

- *Larger U.S. policy changes*: Although most of the policies highlighted were relatively limited in scope and could be undertaken within the contours of the current U.S. approach to the region, others were indicative of broader U.S. policy changes. Rejoining the TPP, for example, was highlighted for multiple countries as the type of shift in U.S. economic engagement in the region that could help provide a more credible economic counterweight to China and reduce concerns about PRC economic retaliation. While such larger-scale policy shifts do not appear to be under consideration in Washington as of this writing, this analysis highlights how the limited expectations in this report for what the United States can do to alter allied and partner decisionmaking are, in part, a function of our assessment of the low probability of such larger shifts in U.S. policy. If senior U.S. policymakers become willing to make larger changes in U.S. policy toward the region, the potential to alter allied and partner calculations around conflict-phase access may expand as well.

Recommendations

Given the preceding analysis, we offer the following recommendations:

- For the U.S. government
  - *Consider clarifying or expanding security guarantees for allies and partners uncertain of U.S. defense commitments:* Several of the countries we analyzed were uncertain of the extent of the U.S. commitment to defend their territory in the event of Chinese retaliation during a conflict. Clarifying or reiterating U.S. security guarantees or, specifically, expanding these guarantees to cover vulnerable territory might increase the willingness of these states to face PRC retaliation if they grant U.S. forces access in a conflict.
  - *Provide a credible regional economic counterweight to China:* This analysis highlighted the vulnerability of allies and partners in the region to Chinese economic retaliation and the lack of confidence that the United States could support allies and partners economically in a manner that would reduce this vulnerability. Altering this dynamic would require large changes in U.S. policy, such as U.S. reentry into the TPP or a similar economic arrangement, and could likely not be meaningfully addressed through modest increases in direct assistance or investment. Committing to a larger economic role in the region, however, could help reduce the risks associated with Chinese threats of economic retaliation and increase the likelihood of conflict-phase access in countries concerned about these risks.
  - *Work to build regional consensus against Chinese aggression:* The level of regional consensus or support for the United States, and against China, in a conflict was highlighted as an important factor for several of the states we examined in this report. The

U.S. government should continue to work with ASEAN member states, in particular, to build consensus on the risks to regional security of PRC aggression and the benefits of a collective opposition to it. Engagements on these issues should extend beyond allies and partners from which the United States might request conflict-phase access because the calculations of these states are likely to be affected by the reactions of the region as a whole.

- For DoD
    - *Expand high-level discussions of likely U.S. access requests in a contingency:* DoD already conducts some discussions on potential conflict-phase access requirements and potential requests with Japan. However, these conversations could be expanded to include other allies and partners from which DoD is likely to request conflict-phase access. While the degree of specificity may vary across states, these conversations would provide the foundation for the potential expansion of existing peacetime access agreements and would set expectations for and help scope U.S. access requests in a conflict in a manner that could help increase the likelihood that they will be approved.
    - *Increase intelligence-sharing, information resilience, and cyber defense coopera-tion with allies and partners:* Expanding the scope of DoD intelligence-sharing and increasing cooperation on cybersecurity and the resilience of information networks with allies and partners could help increase trust between the United States and states in the region, help build consensus against Chinese aggression through increased situational awareness of PRC activities in these domains, and increase information-sharing capabilities that could help reassure allies and partners about U.S. capa-bilities and commitment to the states' defense in a conflict. The level and scope of intelligence-sharing and cyber and information cooperation would differ based on the relationship between the United States and the ally or partner and the ally or partner's capabilities.
    - *Regularize expanded peacetime access requests:* One of the key insights in this report is that regularizing peacetime access requests can help reduce the risks of similar access requests being denied during a conflict for some allies and partners. Which types of access requests are considered to be normal in peacetime can be a powerful anchor for both host nation and, potentially, PRC assessments of what might prompt PRC retaliation in a conflict. While this routinization of access requests likely cannot be extended to include requests to conduct combat operations from an ally's or partner's territory, it could help shift the likelihood of approval of lower-level access requests in a conflict.
    - *Reinforce commitments to allies and partners:* The findings in this report illustrated that visible U.S. actions that reinforce the U.S. defense commitment—such as mili-tary exercises and training, high-level DoD visits, arms sales of requested systems, and public messaging reiterating U.S. defense commitments—can help reassure states that the United States is committed to defend them if they face PRC retaliation from

granting U.S. conflict-phase access requests. These signals of U.S. commitment would need to be tailored to the state in question. For U.S. treaty allies, such as Japan and the Philippines, signals of U.S. commitment can likely be public and definitive. Other states, such as India, may prefer less-public signals of commitment.

- For the USAF

    – *Increase the frequency and regularity of USAF requests for lower-level but operationally essential allied and partner access*: Identifying the types of lower-level access, such as overflight and logistics, that are likely to be valuable in a future contingency and then routinizing USAF requests for them can increase the likelihood of their being granted during a conflict, at least in certain countries. While the benefits of such routinization are unlikely to extend to higher-level access requests, such as requests to conduct combat operations from an ally or partner's territory, increasing the likelihood of lower-level access may still prove important.

    – *Focus USAF activities in the Indo-Pacific on demonstrating U.S. commitment, enhancing capabilities for combined operations with allies and partners rather than building independent allied or partner capabilities.* From combined exercises to rotational deployments, USAF activities in the region can send a clear signal of the broader U.S. commitment and ability to defend allies and partners. This signal can be an important factor in convincing allies and partners to provide conflict-phase access to U.S. forces. While it may be valuable for other purposes, a focus on enhancing allied and partner capabilities to operate independently of the United States risks signaling that Washington expects allies and partners to have to fight on their own if confronted by China.

    – *Prepare to cooperate with allies and partners on their defense against a wider range of contingencies*: USAF operational concerns in the Indo-Pacific appear to increasingly concentrate on a small number of potential contingencies, most notably a conflict over Taiwan. But many allies and partners remain concerned about a broader set of security challenges and may see a sharp U.S. focus on a Taiwan contingency as an indication that the United States is not committed to their security more broadly. Preparing to assist allies and partners with a wider range of challenges and doing so jointly may help underline U.S. commitments to ally and partner security and reduce concerns that the United States may not be prepared to assist them against other types of threats.

Abbreviations

5G	fifth-generation technology
ACSA	acquisition and cross-servicing agreement
ADSEC	Agreement on Defence Exchanges and Security Cooperation
AIIB	Asian Infrastructure Investment Bank
ASEAN	Association of Southeast Asian Nations
BECA	Basic Exchange and Cooperation Agreement
BJP	Bharatiya Janata Party
BRI	Belt and Road Initiative
CFO	chief financial officer
COMCASA	Communications Compatibility and Security Agreement
COMLOG WESTPAC	Commander, Logistics Group Western Pacific
COVID-19	coronavirus disease 2019
DAF	Department of the Air Force
DIME	diplomatic, informational, military, and economic
DoD	U.S. Department of Defense
ECS	East China Sea
EDCA	Enhanced Defense Cooperation Agreement
EEZ	exclusive economic zone
FDI	foreign direct investment
HA/DR	humanitarian assistance and disaster relief
ISR	intelligence, surveillance, and reconnaissance
JETRO	Japan External Trade Organization
JDN	Joint Doctrine Note
LCD	liquid-crystal display
LCS	littoral combat ship
LEMOA	Logistics and Exchange Memorandum of Understanding
MEA	Ministry of External Affairs
MoD	Ministry of Defence
MOU	memorandum of understanding
NATO	North Atlantic Treaty Organization
OEC	Observatory of Economic Complexity
PAP	People's Action Party
PLA	People's Liberation Army
PLAAF	People's Liberation Army Air Force

PLAN	People's Liberation Army Navy
PRC	People's Republic of China
Quad	Quadrilateral Strategic Dialogue
REE	rare-earth element
SAREX	search and rescue exercises
SCS	South China Sea
SDF	Self-Defense Force
SME	subject-matter expert
THAAD	Terminal High-Altitude Area Defense
TNI-AL	Indonesian National Military–Naval Force
TPP	Trans-Pacific Partnership
UK	United Kingdom
UN	United Nations
UNCLOS	United Nations Convention for the Law of the Sea
USAF	U.S. Air Force
USAID	U.S. Agency for International Development
USINDOPACOM	U.S. Indo-Pacific Command
VFA	visiting forces agreement

References

5th Air Force, homepage, undated. As of June 2, 2023:
https://www.5af.pacaf.af.mil/

III Marine Expeditionary Force, homepage, undated. As of June 2, 2023:
https://www.iiimef.marines.mil/

Abbot, Kenneth W., and Duncan Snidal, "Why States Act Through Formal International Organizations," *Journal of Conflict Resolution*, Vol. 42, No. 1, 1998.

Abe, Daishe, "Philippines Radar Deal Marks Japan's First Arms Exports, Nikkei Asia, August 29, 2020.

Abercrombie, Cara, "Removing Barriers to U.S.-India Defense Trade," Carnegie Endowment for International Peace, January 10, 2018.

Abercrombie, Cara, "Realizing the Potential: Mature Defense Cooperation and the U.S.-India Strategic Partnership," *Asia Policy*, Vol. 14, No. 1, January 2019.

Acosta, Rene, "U.S., Philippines Add Four More Sites to EDCA Military Basing Agreement," *USNI News*, February 2, 2023

Acquisition and Cross-Servicing Agreement Between the Department of Defense of the United States of America and the Ministry of Defence of Singapore, April 2000.

Agreement Between Australia and Japan Concerning the Facilitation of Reciprocal Access and Cooperation Between the Self-Defense Forces of Japan and the Australian Defence Force, January 6, 2022.

Agreement Between the Government of the Republic of the Philippines and the Government of the United States of America Regarding the Treatment of United States Armed Forces Visiting the Philippines, February 10, 1998.

Agreement Between the Government of the United States of America and the Government of the Republic of the Philippines on Enhanced Defense Cooperation, April 28, 2014. As of May 19, 2023:
https://www.state.gov/wp-content/uploads/2019/02/
14-625-Philippines-Defense-Cooperation.pdf

Air Force Doctrine Note 1-21, *Agile Combat Employment*, Curtis E. Lemay Center for Doctrine Development and Education, December 1, 2022.

Allard, Tom, "Exclusive: Indonesia Rejected U.S. Request to Host Spy Planes—Officials," Reuters, October 20, 2020.

Allen, Michael Anthony, *Military Basing Abroad: Bargaining, Expectations, and Deployment*, dissertation, Binghamton University, State University of New York, 2011.

Allen, Michael, Michael E. Flynn, Carla Martinez Machain, and Andrew Stravers, "Survey on the Political, Economic, and Social Effects of the United States' Overseas Military Presence, 2018–2020," webpage, Minerva Research Initiative Project, undated. As of July 12, 2023:
https://www.m-flynn.com/minerva.html

Allen, Michael A., Michael E. Flynn, Carla Martinez Machain, and Andrew Stravers, "Outside the Wire: U.S. Military Deployments and Public Opinion in Host States," *American Political Science Review*, Vol. 114, No. 2, 2020.

American Enterprise Institute, "China Global Investment Tracker," webpage, undated. As of June 9, 2022:
https://www.aei.org/china-global-investment-tracker/

"America's Top Brass Responds to the Threat of China in the Pacific," *The Economist*, March 7, 2021.

Andersen, Jørgen Juel, and Silje Aslaksen, "Oil and Political Survival," *Journal of Development Economics*, Vol. 100, No. 1, 2013.

"Arbitration Creates Little More Than Noise," editorial, *Global Times*, July 20, 2016.

Art, Robert J., "To What Ends Military Power?" *International Security*, Vol. 4, No. 4, Spring 1980.

Aspinwall, Nick, "'We Are Filipinos, and We Hate China': China's Influence in the Philippines, and Backlash Against Tsinoys," China Project, June 6, 2019.

"Assassination Attempts Against Pakistan's Musharraf," Reuters, July 6, 2007. As of May 20, 2022:
https://www.reuters.com/article/uk-pakistan-musharraf1/
factbox-assassination-attempts-against-pakistans-musharraf-idUKL0649978720070706

Atkinson, Carol, "Does Soft Power Matter? A Comparative Analysis of Student Exchange Programs, 1980–2006," *Foreign Policy Analysis*, Vol. 6, No. 1, January 2010.

Atkinson, Carol, *Military Soft Power: Public Diplomacy Through Military Educational Exchanges*, Rowman & Littlefield, 2014.

Australian Bureau of Statistics, "International Investment Position, Australia: Supplementary Statistics," 2021.

Australian Embassy, Tokyo, "Strategic Partnership," webpage, undated.

Australian Government, Department of Foreign Affairs and Trade, "Trade Statistical Pivot Tables," undated.

Bangko Sentral NG Pilipinas, "Statistics—External Accounts: Cash Remittances, by Country and by Source," webpage, May 2022.

Banlaoi, Rommel C., "Philippines-China Cooperation in South China Sea During Pandemic," *Eurasia Review*, May 12, 2020.

Baral, J. K., and T. N. Mahanty, "India and the Gulf Crisis: The Response of a Minority Government," *Pacific Affairs*, Vol. 65, No. 13, Autumn 1992.

Barr, Michael D., "Singapore's Succession Headache," *The Diplomat*, March 1, 2022. As of August 29, 2022:
https://thediplomat.com/2022/03/singapores-succession-headache/

Baruah, Darshana M., "India's Answer to the Belt and Road: A Road Map for South Asia," Carnegie Endowment for International Peace, August 21, 2018.

Baum, Matthew A., and Philip B. K. Potter, "Media, Public Opinion, and Foreign Policy in the Age of Social Media," *Journal of Politics*, Vol. 81, No. 2, April 2019.

Beckley, Michael, "The Emerging Military Balance in East Asia: How China's Neighbors Can Check Chinese Naval Expansion," *International Security*, Vol. 42, No. 2, November 2017.

Beech, Hannah, "China Chases Indonesian Fishing Fleets, Staking Claim to Sea's Riches," *New York Times*, March 31, 2020.

Beech, Hannah, "In Singapore, an Orderly Election and a (Somewhat) Surprising Result," *New York Times*, July 10, 2022.

Beiser-McGrath, Janina, and Nils W. Metternich, "Ethnic Coalitions and the Logic of Political Survival in Authoritarian Regimes," *Comparative Political Studies*, Vol. 54, No. 1, 2021.

Berry, William E., Jr., "The Effects of the U.S. Military Bases on the Philippine Economy," *Contemporary Southeast Asia*, Vol. 11, No. 4, March 1990.

Bhatt, Parajanya, "Revisiting China's Kashmir Policy," issue brief, Observer Research Foundation, November 2019.

Biden, Joseph R., Jr., and Lee Hsien Loong, "U.S.-Singapore Joint Leaders' Statement," March 29, 2022.

Biden, Joseph R., Jr., and Suga Yoshihide, "U.S.-Japan Joint Leaders Statement: 'U.S.–Japan Global Partnership for a New Era,'" April 16, 2021.

Blaker, James R., *United States Overseas Basing: An Anatomy of the Dilemma*, Praeger, 1990.

Bland, Ben, Evan Laksmana, and Natasha Kassam, *Charting Their Own Course: How Indonesians See the World*, Lowy Institute, 2022.

Blank, Jonah, "What Were China's Objectives in the Doklam Dispute?" *Foreign Affairs*, September 7, 2017.

Blank, Jonah, *Regional Responses to U.S.-China Competition in the Indo-Pacific: India*, RAND Corporation, RR-4412/2-AF, 2021a. As of August 29, 2022:
https://www.rand.org/pubs/research_reports/RR4412z2.html

Blank, Jonah, *Regional Responses to U.S.-China Competition in the Indo-Pacific: Indonesia*, RAND Corporation, RR-4412/3-AF, 2021b. As of August 16, 2022:
https://www.rand.org/pubs/research_reports/RR4412z3.html

Blank, Jonah, Jennifer D. P. Moroney, Angel Rabasa, and Bonny Lin, *Look East, Cross Black Waters: India's Interest in Southeast Asia*, RAND Corporation, RR-1021-AF, 2015. As of August 29, 2022:
https://www.rand.org/pubs/research_reports/RR1021.html

Blankenship, Brian, "Promises Under Pressure: Statements of Reassurance in US Alliances," *International Studies Quarterly*, Vol. 64, No. 4, December 2020.

Blinken, Antony J., "Reaffirming and Reimagining America's Alliances," speech, Brussels, March 24, 2021.

Blinken, Antony J., "The Administration's Approach to the People's Republic of China," speech, George Washington University, May 26, 2022.

Boot, Max, "Why the U.S. Ramped Up Its Information War with Russia," Council on Foreign Relations, February 10, 2022.

Bormann, Nils-Christian, "Uncertainty, Cleavages, and Ethnic Coalitions," *Journal of Politics*, Vol. 81, No. 2, April 2019.

Bowen, Wayne H., *Spain During World War II*, University of Missouri Press, 2006.

Bower, Ernest, and Charles Freeman, "Singapore's Tightrope Walk on Taiwan," *Southeast Asia from the Corner of 18th & K Streets*, Vol. 1, No. 26, August 17, 2010.

Braesch, Connie, "U.S. Aircraft Inaugural Refueling in India," press release, Defense Logistics Agency, October 29, 2020.

Bragg, Matthew, "31st Iteration of Balikatan Kicks Off," U.S. Indo-Pacific Command, April 20, 2015.

Brasher, Keith, "Amid Tension, China Blocks Vital Exports to Japan," *New York Times*, September 22, 2010.

Brecher, Michael, "Non-Alignment Under Stress: The West and the India-China Border War," *Pacific Affairs*, Vol. 52, No. 4, Winter 1979–1980.

Brown, J. Wellington, and Dean C. Dulay, "Barracks and Barricades: How Internal Security Threats Affect Foreign Basing Access in the Philippines," *Asian Security*, Vol. 17, No. 3, 2021.

Brown, Robin, "Spinning the War: Political Communications, Information Operations and Public Diplomacy in the War on Terrorism," in Daya Kishan Thussu and Des Freedman, eds., *War and the Media: Reporting Conflict 24/7*, SAGE Publications, 2003.

Bruni, Frank, and David Rhode, "Turkey Open to U.S. Using Air Space but Not Bases," *New York Times*, March 19, 2003.

Bureau of Economic Analysis, U.S. Department of Commerce, "Direct Investment & Multinational Enterprises (MNEs)," webpage, November 18, 2022.

Bureau of Foreign Trade, Taiwan, "Bureau of Trade—Trade Statistics: Export/Import Value (by Country)," webpage, undated. As of September 26, 2023:
https://cuswebo.trade.gov.tw/FSCE3000C?table=FSCE3010F

Burke, Paul J., "Economic Growth and Political Survival," *BE Journal of Macroeconomics*, Vol. 12, No. 1, 2012.

Butler, J. R. M., *History of the Second World War: Grand Strategy*: Vol. II, *September 1939–June 1941*, Her Majesty's Stationery Office, 1957.

Cabestan, Jean-Pierre, "China's Military Base in Djibouti: A Microcosm of China's Growing Competition with the United States and New Bipolarity," *Journal of Contemporary China*, Vol. 29, No. 125, 2020.

The Cabinet Office, "Public Opinion Surveys on Self-Defense Forces and Defense Issues ["自衛隊・防衛問題に関する世論調査"], Opinion Polls [世論調査], Government of Japan, 2017.

Calder, Kent E., *Embattled Garrisons: Competitive Base Politics and American Globalism*, Princeton University Press, 2008.

Calonzo, Andreo, "Philippines Isn't Shifting Away from China, Marcos Says," Bloomberg, June 8, 2023.

Camba, Alvin, "China's Bet on Sara Duterte Pays Off," Nikkei Asia, May 15, 2022.

Campbell, Kurt M., Nirav Patel, and Richard Weitz, "The Ripple Effect: India's Responses to the Iraq War," Center for a New American Security, October 2008.

Capie, David, "The Power of Partnerships: US Defence Ties with Indonesia, Singapore, and Vietnam," *International Politics*, Vol. 57, February 19, 2020.

Center for International Policy, *Security Sector Assistance Database*, webpage, Security Assistance Monitor, undated.

Chang, Felix C., "The U.S.-Philippines Mutual Defense Treaty and Philippine External Defense Forces," Foreign Policy Research Institute, August 3, 2021.

Chanlett-Avery, Emma, and Caitlin Campbell, "The U.S.-Japan Alliance," Congressional Research Service, RL33740, June 13, 2019.

Chapman, Terrence L., "International Security Institutions, Domestic Politics, and Institutional Legitimacy," *Journal of Conflict Resolution*, Vol. 51, No. 1, 2007.

Chapman, Terrence L, and Scott Wolford, "International Organizations, Strategy, and Crisis Bargaining," *Journal of Politics*, Vol. 72, No. 1, 2010.

Chatmas, Lauren, "7th Fleet Ship Visits the Philippines," press release, U.S. Indo-Pacific Command, August 18, 2021.

"The China-Philippine Banana War," *Asia Sentinel*, June 6, 2012.

China Power Project, "Does China Pose a Threat to Global Rare-Earth Supply Chains?" Center for Strategic and International Studies, May 12, 2021.

"China's Exports of Rare-Earth Compounds Increased by 90.05% Annually, as of in October 2021" ["中国2021年10月份稀土化合物出口量同比上升90.05%"], Sohu, March 2, 2022.

"China's New Complaint About Bugs in PHL Fruits Puzzles Agriculture Exec," GMA News Online, May 16, 2012.

"Chinese Tourists Spend More Than $2.3b in Philippines in 2019," Xinhua, March 3, 2020.

Chinoy, Sujan R., "India and the Changing Dynamics of the Indo-Pacific," *Asia Policy*, Vol. 15, No. 4, October 2020.

Chiozza, Giacomo, and Hein E. Goemans, "Peace Through Insecurity: Tenure and International Conflict," *Journal of Conflict Resolution*, Vol. 47, No. 4, 2003.

Chiozza, Giacomo, and Hein Erich Goemans, *Leaders and International Conflict*, Cambridge University Press, 2011.

Choong, William, "China-US Relations: Singapore's Elusive Sweet Spot," ISEAS–Yusof Ishak Institute, July 23, 2020.

Christensen, Thomas J., and Jack Snyder, "Chain Gangs and Passed Bucks: Predicting Alliance Patterns in Multipolarity," *International Organization*, Vol. 44, No. 2, Spring 1990.

Commander, U.S. 7th Fleet, homepage, undated. As of June 2, 2023:
https://www.c7f.navy.mil/

Cooley, Alexander, "U.S. Bases and Democratization in Central Asia," *Orbis*, Vol. 52, No. 1, 2008.

Cooley, Alexander, *Base Politics: Democratic Change and the US Military Overseas*, Cornell University Press, 2012.

Cooley, Alexander, and Daniel H. Nexon, "The Bases of Empire: Globalization and the Politics of US Overseas Basing," NUPI, 2007.

Cooper, Cortez A., III, and Michael S. Chase, *Regional Responses to U.S.-China Competition in the Indo-Pacific: Singapore*, RAND Corporation, RR-4412/5-AF, 2020. As of August 29, 2022:
https://www.rand.org/pubs/research_reports/RR4412z5.html

Cooper, Zack, and Sheena Greitens, "What to Expect from Japan and Korea in a Taiwan Contingency," in Henry D. Sokolski, ed., *New Frontiers for Security Cooperation with Seoul and Tokyo, 2021*, Nonproliferation Policy Education Center, 2021.

Crossette, Barbara, "India in an Uproar Over Refueling of U.S. Aircraft," *New York Times*, January 30, 1991.

Cruz De Castro, Renato, "The Duterte Administration's Foreign Policy: Unravelling the Aquino Administration's Balancing Agenda on an Emergent China," *Journal of Current Southeast Asian Affairs*, Vol. 35, No. 3, 2016.

Daily, Tom, and Min Zhang, "China's Chengxin, Tsingshan Team Up for $350 Million Indonesia Lithium Project," Reuters, September 23, 2021.

Das, Krishna N., "India Sticks to 'One-China' Policy Stance but Seeks Restraint on Taiwan," Reuters, August 12, 2022.

Davidson, Philip S., "Statement of Admiral Philip S. Davidson, U.S. Navy Commander, U.S. Indo-Pacific Command," before the Senate Armed Services Committee on U.S. Indo-Pacific Command Posture," March 9, 2021.

Davis, Richard G., ed., *The U.S. Army and Irregular Warfare 1775–2007: Selected Papers from the 2007 Conference of Army Historians: Selected Papers from the 2007 Conference of Army Historians*, Center of Military History, U.S. Army, 2010.

Defence Ministry of the Republic of Indonesia, *Defence White Paper 2015* (English version), 2015

De Mesquita, Bruce Bueno, James D. Morrow, Randolph M. Siverson, and Alastair Smith, "Policy Failure and Political Survival: The Contribution of Political Institutions," *Journal of Conflict Resolution*, Vol. 43, No. 2, 1999.

De Mesquita, Bruce Bueno, and Alastair Smith, "Political Survival and Endogenous Institutional Change," *Comparative Political Studies*, Vol. 42, No. 2, 2009.

De Mesquita, Bruce Bueno, Alastair Smith, Randolph M. Siverson, and James D. Morrow, *The Logic of Political Survival*, MIT Press, 2005.

Department of Foreign Affairs, Republic of the Philippines, "Frequently Asked Questions (FAQs) on the Enhanced Defense Cooperation Agreement," April 28, 2014.

Department of National Defense, Republic of the Philippines, *National Defense Strategy 2018–2022*, 2018.

Department of Statistics, Singapore, "Census of Population 2020, Statistical Release 1; Demographics, Characteristics, Education, Language and Religion," Ministry of Trade and Industry, June 2021. As of May 26, 2023:
https://www.singstat.gov.sg/publications/reference/cop2020/cop2020-sr1/census20_stat_release1

Department of Trade and Industry, Republic of the Philippines, "Philippines Invites Investments from China During CIFIT 2021," 2021a.

Department of Trade and Industry, Republic of the Philippines, "Trade and Investment QuickStats," 2021b.

Devlin, Kat, "A Sampling of Public Opinion in India," Pew Research Center, March 25, 2019.

Diehl, Christopher E., *Small Allies, Big Challenges: The International Politics of Military Access*, thesis, Villanova University, 2009.

Dingman, Roger, "The Dagger and the Gift: The Impact of the Korean War on Japan," *Journal of American-East Asian Relations*, Vol. 2, No. 1, Spring 1993.

Donfried, Karen, *Kosovo: International Reactions to NATO Air Strikes*, Congressional Research Service, RL30114, April 21, 1999.

Druckman, Daniel, "Stages, Turning Points, and Crises: Negotiating Military Base Rights, Spain and the United States," *Journal of Conflict Resolution*, Vol. 30, No. 2, 1986.

Druckman, Daniel, "Negotiating Military Base-Rights with Spain, the Philippines, and Greece: Lessons Learned," Center for Conflict Analysis and Resolution, Occasional Paper 2, 1990.

Dumas, Lloyd J., "Economic Power, Military Power, and National Security," *Journal of Economic Issues*, Vol. 24, No. 2, 1990.

Dumitru, Laurențiu-Cristian, "Preliminaries of Romania's Entering the World War I," *Bulletin of "Carol I" National Defence University*, No. 1, 2012.

Dunst, Charles, "What to Expect of Cambodia as ASEAN Chair," Center for Strategic and International Studies, November 4, 2021.

Eilstrup-Sangiovanni, Mette, "The End of Balance-of-Power Theory? A Comment on Wohlforth et al.'s Testing Balance-of-Power Theory in World History,'" *European Journal of International Relations*, Vol. 15, No. 2, 2009.

Embassy of Japan in the Philippines, "Japan's Development Cooperation in the Philippines: Proactive Support for Inclusive and Sustainable Growth," May 5, 2022.

Embassy of the Republic of Indonesia—Beijing, People's Republic of China, "Indonesia's Exports to China and Chinese Investment to Indonesia in 2020 Are Increasing," February 28, 2021.

Engel, David, "How Far Will Bongbong Marcos Tilt the Philippines Towards China?" ASPI Strategist, May 20, 2022.

Farrer, Martin, "Hong Kong: International Companies Reconsider Future in Wake of Security Law," *The Guardian*, September 6, 2021.

Fearon, James D., "Domestic Political Audiences and the Escalation of International Disputes," *American Political Science Review*, Vol. 88, No. 3, September 1994.

Felton, Benjamin, "Indonesia and the United States Kick Off Nine Day Military Exercise Cope West 2021," Overt Defense, June 16, 2021.

Fernando, Jonina A., "China's Belt and Road Initiative in the Philippines," East West Center, December 16, 2020.

Filson, Darren, and Suzanne Werner, "A Bargaining Model of War and Peace: Anticipating the Onset, Duration, and Outcome of War," *American Journal of Political Science*, Vol. 46, No. 4, October 2002.

Fineman, Daniel Mark, *The United States and Military Government in Thailand, 1947–1958*, dissertation, Yale University, 1993.

Fook, Lye Liang, "Singapore-China Relations: Building Substantive Ties Amidst Challenges," *Southeast Asian Affairs*, 2018.

Foreign Office, "Greece," collected papers, British National Archives, FO 800/63, 1915.

Foreign Office, *Annual Report: Political Survey of Sweden for 1939*, British National Archives, FO 188/351, 1940.

Fravel, M. Taylor, "China's Sovereignty Obsession: Beijing's Need to Project Strength Explains the Border Clash with India," *Foreign Affairs*, June 26, 2020.

Freedom House, "Freedom in the World 2022: Singapore," webpage, undated.

French, David, *British Strategy & War Aims: 1914–1916*, Routledge, 2014.

Frühling, Stephan, "Is ANZUS Really an Alliance? Aligning the US and Australia," *Survival*, Vol. 60, No. 5, 2018.

Galang, Mico A., "PacNet #61—The South China Sea and the Philippines' National Security Strategy," Pacific Forum, August 28, 2018.

Galang, Mico A., "The Philippines' National Defense Strategy—Analysis," *Eurasia Review*, December 20, 2019.

Ganguly, Šumit, and Andrew Scobell, "The Himalayan Impasse: Sino-Indian Rivalry in the Wake of Doklam," *Washington Quarterly*, Vol. 41, No. 3, 2018.

Gartzke, Erik, and Kristian Skrede Gleditsch, "Why Democracies May Actually Be Less Reliable Allies," *American Journal of Political Science*, Vol. 48, No. 4, October 2004.

German Federal Statistics Office, "Exports and Imports (Foreign Trade)," 2022

Golson, Eric B., "Did Swedish Ball Bearings Keep the Second World War Going? Re-Evaluating Neutral Sweden's Role," *Scandinavian Economic History Review*, Vol. 60, No. 2, 2012.

Good, Keith, "U.S. to Contribute $68 Million to World Food Program to Buy Ukrainian Wheat," Farm Policy News, August 17, 2022.

Gould, Joe, "US, Japan Agree to Two Defense Pacts Amid China Worries," *Defense News*, January 7, 2022.

Government of India, Ministry of Commerce and Industry, "FDI Statistics," webpage, undated. As of August 29, 2022:
https://dpiit.gov.in/publications/fdi-statistics/archives

Government of India, Ministry of Tourism, "India Tourism Statistics 2021," December 2021. As of June 9, 2022:
https://tourism.gov.in/sites/default/files/2022-04/India%20Tourism%20Statistics%202021.pdf

Government of Japan, "Relations Between Japan and Other Countries/Regions" ["日本と諸外国・地域との関係"], webpage, undated. As of August 25, 2022:
https://survey.gov-online.go.jp/r03/r03-gaiko/2-1.html

Gözen, Ramazan, "Causes and Consequences of Turkey's Out-of-War Position in the Iraq War of 2003," *Turkish Yearbook of International Relations*, Vol. 36, 2005.

Gramer, Robbie, "First U.S. Natural Gas Shipped to Poland," *Foreign Policy*, June 8, 2017.

Green, Michael J., "Will Japan Fight? Assessing the Scenarios for Conflict on China's Maritime Periphery," testimony before the U.S.-China Economic and Security Review Commission, April 13, 2017.

Green, Michael J., Kathleen Hicks, Zack Cooper, John Schaus, and Jake Douglas, *Countering Coercion in Maritime Asia: The Theory and Practice of Gray Zone Deterrence*, Center for Strategic and International Studies, Rowman & Littlefield, May 9, 2017.

Green, Michael J., and Gregory B. Poling, "The U.S. Alliance with the Philippines," *Hard Choices: Memos to the President, Center for Strategic and International Studies*, December 3, 2020. As of May 22, 2023:
https://www.csis.org/analysis/us-alliance-philippines

Greene, Jay, "Digging for Rare Earths: The Mines Where iPhones Are Born," CNET, September 26, 2012.

Gregorio, Xave, "Duterte Threatens to Terminate VFA If US Does Not Reverse Cancellation of Dela Rosa's Visa," CNN Philippines, January 23, 2020.

Greitens, Sheena Chestnut, "Terrorism in the Philippines and U.S.-Philippine Security Cooperation," Brookings Institution, August 15, 2017.

Gresh, Geoffrey F., *Gulf Security and the U.S. Military: Regime Survival and the Politics of Basing*, Stanford University Press, 2015.

Grossman, Derek, "Why Is China Pressing Indonesia Again Over Its Maritime Claims?" *The RAND Blog*, January 16, 2020.

Grossman, Derek, "Modi's Multipolar Moment Has Arrived," *Foreign Policy*, June 6, 2022.

Grozev, Kostadin, "Bulgaria in the Post-Kosovo Era," *Wilson Center: Insight and Analysis*, January 19, 2000.

Habif, Yola, "The Future of Iraq," *Turkish Policy Quarterly*, Vol. 1, No. 4, 2002.

Hagglof, M. Gunnar, "A Test of Neutrality: Sweden in the Second World War," *International Affairs*, Vol. 36, No. 2, April 1960.

Hale, William, "Turkey and Britain in World War II: Origins and Results of the Tripartite Alliance, 1935–40," *Journal of Balkan and Near Eastern Studies*, Vol. 23, No. 6, 2021.

Hammond, Joseph, "Philippine, U.S. Forces Improve Defense Cooperation," Indo-Pacific Defense Forum, November 9, 2021.

Harkavy, Robert E., *Great Power Competition for Overseas Bases: The Geopolitics of Access Diplomacy*, Elsevier, 1982.

Harkavy, Robert E., *Bases Abroad: The Global Foreign Military Presence*, Oxford University Press, 1989.

Harold, Scott W., *Regional Responses to U.S.-China Competition in the Indo-Pacific: Japan*, RAND Corporation, RR-4412/4-AF, 2020. As of October 3, 2023: https://www.rand.org/pubs/research_reports/RR4412z4.html

Harold, Scott W., Derek Grossman, Brian Harding, Jeffrey W. Hornung, Gregory Poling, Jeffrey Smith, and Meagan L. Smith, *The Thickening Web of Asian Security Cooperation: Deepening Defense Ties Among U.S. Allies and Partners in the Indo-Pacific*, RAND Corporation, RR-3125-MCF, 2019. As of August 2, 2022: https://www.rand.org/pubs/research_reports/RR3125.html

Harrell, Peter, Elizabeth Rosenberg, and Edoardo Saravalle, *China's Use of Coercive Economic Measures*, Center for New American Security, 2018.

Haulman, Daniel Lee, *The United States Air Force and Humanitarian Airlift Operations, 1947–1994*, U.S. Government Printing Office, 1998.

Hauser, Christine, "U.S. Military Airlifts Baby Formula from Europe," *New York Times*, May 23, 2022.

Hayes, Carlton J. H., *Wartime Mission in Spain, 1942–1945*, Hassell Street Press, 2016.

Hedberg, Peter, and Lars Karlsson, "Neutral Trade in Time of War: The Case of Sweden, 1838–1960," *International Journal of Maritime History*, Vol. 27, No. 1, 2015.

Hemmer, Jeff, "The Third Reich and Spain," paper, Cultiv—Gesellschaft für internationale Kulturprojekte, 2004.

Henson, Aaron, "Pacific Air Forces, US Marine Corps Conclude Exercise Cope West 17," press release, U.S. Marine Corps, November 16, 2016.

Herr, W. Eric, "Operation Vigilant Warrior: Conventional Deterrence Theory Doctrine, and Practice," thesis, Air University, School of Advanced Airpower Studies, 1996.

Higgins, Matthew L., "DIME: Not Just an Acronym," *Marine Corps Gazette*, July 2021.

H. M. The King [George V] and Queen Alexandra, collected papers, British National Archives, Folios 621–630, 636–639, 645–647, 649, and 670, 1915.

Holmes, Amy Austin, *Social Unrest and American Military Bases in Turkey and Germany Since 1945*, Cambridge University Press, 2014.

Hornung, Jeffrey, "Japan's Pushback of China," *Washington Quarterly*, Vol. 38, No. 1, 2015.

Hornung, Jeffrey W., "Japan's Growing Hard Hedge Against China," *Asian Security*, Vol. 10, No. 2, 2014.

Hornung, Jeffrey W., "Resolved: Japan-China Rapprochement Will Fail," *Debating Japan*, Vol. 1, No. 2, December 6, 2018. As of June 22, 2022: https://www.csis.org/analysis/resolved-japan-china-rapprochement-will-fail

Hornung, Jeffrey W., *Managing the U.S.-Japan Alliance: An Examination of Structural Linkages in the Security Relationship*, 2nd ed., Sasakawa USA, 2019.

Hornung, Jeffrey W., *Japan's Potential Contributions in an East China Sea Contingency*, RAND Corporation, RR-A314-1, 2020. As of August 02, 2022: https://www.rand.org/pubs/research_reports/RRA314-1.html

Hornung, Jeffrey W., "Abe Shinzō's Lasting Impact: Proactive Contributions to Japan's Security and Foreign Policies," *Asia-Pacific Review*, Vol. 28, No. 1, May 2021a.

Hornung, Jeffrey W., "What the United States Wants from Japan in Taiwan," *Foreign Policy*, May 10, 2021b.

Hornung, Jeffrey W., "Taiwan and Six Potential New Year's Resolutions for the U.S.-Japanese Alliance," War on the Rocks, January 5, 2022.

Hornung, Jeffrey W., and Hayley Channer, "Russia's Invasion of Ukraine May Harden US Indo-Pacific Allies," *The Hill*, May 26, 2022.

Horowitz, Michael C., and Matthew S. Levendusky, "Drafting Support for War: Conscription and Mass Support for Warfare," *Journal of Politics*, Vol. 73, No. 2, April 2011.

Hosmer, Stephen T., *The Conflict Over Kosovo: Why Milosevic Decided to Settle When He Did*, RAND Corporation, MR-1351-AF, 2001. As of May 23, 2023: https://www.rand.org/pubs/monograph_reports/MR1351.html

Hui, Mary, "Japan's Global Rare Earths Quest Holds Lessons for the US and Europe," *Quartz*, April 23, 2021.

Hussain, Aijaz, "At 75, India's Kashmir Challenge Shifts Foreign Policy Focus," Associated Press, August 10, 2022.

Hutt, David," Has the ASEAN Chair Become Too Powerful?" *The Diplomat*, January 14, 2022.

Huxley, Tim, "Singapore and Malaysia: A Precarious Balance?" *Pacific Review*, Vol. 4, No. 3, 1991.

Huxley, Tim, *Defending the Lion City: The Armed Forces of Singapore*, Allen & Unwin, 2001.

Indonesia Ministry of Investment, "Indonesian Investment Moves to Rise After Pandemic, First Quarter 2022 Investment Realization: IDR 282.4 Trillion," April 2022.

"Indonesia Rejects China's Claims Over South China Sea," Reuters, January 1, 2020.

Inkiriwang, Frega Wenas, "Recalibrating Indonesia's Defense Diplomacy for the New Normal," National Bureau of Asian Research, May 8, 2021.

Inoue, Yuko, "China Lifts Rare Earth Export Ban to Japan: Trader," Reuters, September 28, 2010.

International Crisis Group, *Competing Visions of International Order in the South China Sea*, Asia Report No. 315, November 29, 2021a.

International Crisis Group, *The Philippines' Dilemma: How to Manage Tensions in the South China Sea*, Asia Report, No. 316, December 2, 2021b.

International Institute for Strategic Studies, *The Military Balance 2022*, February 2022.

International Monetary Fund, "Coordinated Direct Investment Survey (CDIS)," webpage, December 18, 2021. As of June 9, 2022:
https://data.imf.org/?sk=40313609-F037-48C1-84B1-E1F1CE54D6D5&sId=1482331048410

International Trade Administration, "Philippines: Country Commercial Guide," webpage, U.S. Department of Commerce, July 25, 2022.

Issa, Mohammad, "LCS Returns to Singapore," press release, Command Destroyer Squadron 7 Public Affairs, May 3, 2022.

Jaishankar, Dhruva, *Survey of India's Strategic Community*, Brookings India, March 2019.

Janes, "Southeast Asia, Armed Forces of the Philippines Assessment 2021,"Sentinel Security Assessment, February 10, 2021.

Japan and the United States of America, "The Guidelines for Japan-U.S. Defense Cooperation," April 27, 2015. As of June 2, 2023:
https://www.mofa.go.jp/files/000078188.pdf

"Japan and U.S. Draft Operation Plan for Taiwan Contingency," *Japan Times*, December 23, 2021.

Japanese External Trade Organization, "Japanese Trade and Investment Statistics: Japan's International Trade in Goods (Yearly)," various years. As of August 29, 2022:
https://www.jetro.go.jp/en/reports/statistics.html

Japan-U.S. Security Treaty—*See* Treaty of Mutual Cooperation and Security . . . .

Jayakumar, Shashi, *A History of the People's Action Party, 1985–2021*, National University of Singapore Press, 2022.

JDN—*See* Joint Doctrine Note.

Jennings, Ralph, "Taiwan's Beleaguered Foreign Relations Find Stable Support in Singapore," Voice of America, October 6, 2017.

Jennings, Ralph, "Why US, Philippines Are Staging Large-Scale Military Exercises," Voice of America, March 31, 2022a.

Jennings, Ralph, "Indonesia Leans Further Toward US Amid Growing Maritime Dispute with China," Voice of America, April 16, 2022b.

Jervis, Robert, "Realism, Neoliberalism, and Cooperation," *International Security*, Vol. 24, No. 1, 1999.

JETRO—*See* Japanese External Trade Organization.

Joint Chiefs of Staff, "J-7 Joint Force Development," webpage, undated. As of May 23, 2023:
https://www.jcs.mil/Directorates/J7-Joint-Force-Development/JCISFA/

Joint Doctrine Note 1-18, *Strategy*, April 25, 2018. As of July 12, 2023:
https://irp.fas.org/doddir/dod/jdn1_18.pdf

Joint Publication 3-13, *Information Operations*, November 27, 2012, Change 1, November 20, 2014. As of July 12, 2023:
https://irp.fas.org/doddir/dod/jp3_13.pdf

Jones, John Wesley, "The Chargé in Spain (Jones) to the Spanish Minister of Foreign Affairs (Martin Artajo)," March 16, 1953, in David M. Baehler, Ronald D. Landa, Charles S. Sampson, John A. Bernbaum, Lisle A. Rose, and David H. Stauffer, *Foreign Relations of the United States, 1952–1954*: Vol. VI, *Western Europe and Canada*, Pt. 2, No. 885, 1986. As of July 12, 2023: https://history.state.gov/historicaldocuments/frus1952-54v06p2/d886

Joshi, Manoj, *Doklam: To Start at the Very Beginning*, Observer Research Foundation, August 9, 2017.

Joshi, Manoj, "India's Strategy in the China-Russia-USA Triangle," Observer Research Foundation, December 20, 2019. As of August 29, 2022: https://www.orfonline.org/research/indias-strategy-in-the-china-russia-usa-triangle-59417/

Joshi, Manoj, *Understanding the India-China Border: The Enduring Threat of War in High Himalaya*, Oxford University Press, 2022.

Joyce, Renanah M., and Brian Blankenship, "Access Denied? The Future of U.S. Basing in a Contested World," War on the Rocks, February 1, 2021.

Joyce, Renanah M., and Becca Wasser, "All About Access: Solving America's Force Posture Puzzle," *Washington Quarterly*, Vol. 44, No. 3, September 2021.

Kadercan, Burak, "Military Competition and the Emergence of Nationalism: Putting the Logic of Political Survival Into Historical Context," *International Studies Review*, Vol. 14, No. 3, September 2012.

Kaloudis, George, "Greece and the Road to World War I: To What End?" *International Journal on World Peace*, Vol. 31, No. 4, December 2014.

Kang, David C., "Between Balancing and Bandwagoning: South Korea's Response to China," *Journal of East Asian Studies*, Vol. 9, No. 1, 2009.

Karackattu, Joe Thomas, "The Case for a Pragmatic India-Taiwan Partnership," Carnegie India, April 2019.

Kartha, Tara, and Jalil Jilani, "The Latest Kashmir Conflict Explained," United States Institute of Peace, August 28, 2019.

Kaufman, Robert G., "'To Balance or to Bandwagon?' Alignment Decisions in 1930s Europe," *Security Studies*, Vol. 1, No. 3, Spring 1992.

Kausikan, Bilahari, *Singapore Is Not an Island: Views on Singapore Foreign Policy*, Straits Times Press, 2021.

Kausikan, Bilahari, "Threading the Needle in Southeast Asia," *Foreign Affairs*, May 11, 2022.

Kawato, Yuko, *Protests Against U.S. Military Base Policy in Asia: Persuasion and Its Limits*, Stanford University Press, 2015.

Kelly, Bernard, "Drifting Towards War: The British Chiefs of Staff, the USSR and the Winter War, November 1939–March 1940," *Contemporary British History*, Vol. 23, No. 3, 2009.

Keohane, Robert O., *After Hegemony: Cooperation and Discord in the World Political Economy*, Princeton University Press, 1984.

Khilnani, Sunil, Rajiv Kumar, Pratap Bhanu Mehta, Prakash Menon, Nandan Nilekani, Srinath Raghavan, Shyam Saran, and Siddharth Varadarajan, *NonAlignment 2.0: A Foreign and Strategic Policy for India in the Twenty-First Century*, National Defence College and Centre for Policy Research, 2012.

Kim, Tongfi, "Why Alliances Entangle But Seldom Entrap States," *Security Studies*, Vol. 20, No. 3, 2011.

Kimball, Anessa L., *Alliances from the Inside Out: A Theory of Domestic Politics and Alliance Behavior*, dissertation, Binghamton University, State University of New York, 2006.

Kislenko, Arne, "A Not So Silent Partner: Thailand's Role in Covert Operations, Counter-Insurgency, and the Wars in Indochina," *Journal of Conflict Studies*, Vol. 24, No. 1, 2004.

Knopf, Jeffrey W., "Varieties of Assurance," *Journal of Strategic Studies*, Vol. 35, No. 3, 2012.

Korea Customs Service, "Trade Statistics," webpage, undated. As of September 23, 2022: https://unipass.customs.go.kr/ets/index_eng.do

Koutsoukis, Jason, and Cecilia Yap, "China Hasn't Delivered on Its $24 Billion Philippines Promise," Bloomberg, July 25, 2018.

Kronstadt, K. Alan, and Sonia Pinto, *India-U.S. Security Relations: Current Engagement*, Congressional Research Service, R42823, November 13, 2012.

Kuik, Cheng-Chwee, "How Do Weaker States Hedge? Unpacking ASEAN States' Alignment Behavior Towards China," *Journal of Contemporary China*, Vol. 25, No. 100, 2016.

Kurlantzick, Joshua, *Keeping the U.S.-Indonesia Relationship Moving Forward*, Council on Foreign Relations, Center for Preventative Action, 2018.

Kurlantzick, Joshua, "Duterte's Ingratiating Approach to China Has Been a Bust," Council on Foreign Relations, June 16, 2021.

Labs, Eric J., "Do Weak States Bandwagon?" *Security Studies*, Vol. 1, No. 3, 1992.

Ladwig, Walter C., Andrew S. Erickson, and Justin D. Mikolay, "Diego Garcia and American Security in the Indian Ocean," in Carnes Lord and Andrew Erickson, eds., *Rebalancing U.S. Forces: Basing and Forward Presence in the Asia-Pacific*, Naval Institute Press, 2014.

Lake, David A., "Legitimating Power: The Domestic Politics of US International Hierarchy," *International Security*, Vol. 38, No. 2, Fall 2013.

Lake, David A., *Entangling Relations: American Foreign Policy in Its Century*, Princeton University Press, 2020.

Laksmana, Evan, "An Indo-Pacific Construct with Indonesian Characteristics," *The Strategist*, February 6, 2018a.

Laksmana, Evan A., "Buck Passing from Behind: Indonesia's Foreign Policy and the Indo-Pacific," Brookings Institution, November 27, 2018b.

Lam, Peng Er, "Singapore-China Relations in Geopolitics, Economics, Domestic Politics and Public Opinion: An Awkward 'Special Relationship'?" *Journal of Contemporary East Asia Studies*, Vol. 10, No. 2, 2021.

Lamb, Katie, "Not 'Business as Usual' for G20 Foreign Ministers Meeting in Bali," Reuters, July 6, 2022.

Lamothe, Dan, "Everyone Hates U.S. Bases in Asia—Until Disaster Strikes," *Foreign Policy*, November 12, 2013.

Lau, Albert, *A Moment of Anguish: Singapore in Malaysia and the Politics of Disengagement*, Times Academic Press, 1998.

Lawani, Sameer, "Reluctant Link? India, the Quad and the Free and Open Indo-Pacific," in Sharon Stirling, ed., *Mind the Gap: National Views of the Fee and Open Indo-Pacific*, The German Marshall Fund of the United States, 2019.

Lawani, Sameer, and Heather Byrne, "Great Expectations: Asking Too Much of the US- India Strategic Partnership," *Washington Quarterly*, Vol. 42, No. 3, October 2019.

Lebovic, James H., and Elizabeth N. Saunders, "The Diplomatic Core: The Determinants of High-Level US Diplomatic Visits, 1946–2010," *International Studies Quarterly*, Vol. 60, No. 1, March 2016.

Lee Hsien Loong, "NDR 2022: Prime Minister Lee Hsien Loong's English Speech in Full," August 21, 2022.

Lee Kuan Yew, *The Singapore Story: Memoirs of Lee Kuan Yew*, Straits Times Press, 1998.

Lee Kuan Yew, "Why Singapore Is What It Is Now," *Estudios Internacionales*, No. 159, 2008.

Lee, Matthew, "US Approves Major $14 Billion Arms Sale to Indonesia." ABC News, February 10, 2022.

Leeds, Brett Ashley, "Do Alliances Deter Aggression? The Influence of Military Alliances on the Initiation of Militarized Interstate Disputes," *American Journal of Political Science*, Vol. 47, No. 3, July 2003a.

Leeds, Brett Ashley, "Alliance Reliability in Times of War: Explaining State Decisions to Violate Treaties," *International Organization*, Vol. 57, No. 4, Autumn 2003b.

Lema, Karen, "Philippines Wants More Than 'Loose Change' for U.S. Troops Deal," Reuters, February 15, 2021.

Licht, Amanda A., "Coming into Money: The Impact of Foreign Aid on Leader Survival," *Journal of Conflict Resolution*, Vol. 54, No. 1, February 2010.

Lies, Elaine, and Sam Nussey, "Japan, Philippines Eye Further Defence Cooperation at First 2+2 Meeting," Reuters, April 9, 2022.

Lies, Elaine, and Yoshifumi Takemoto, "Okinawa Voters Re-Elect Opposition-Backed Governor, Media Report," Reuters, September 11, 2022.

Liff, Adam P., "Has Japan's Policy Toward the Taiwan Strait Changed?" Brookings Institution, August 23, 2021.

Lim, Darren J., and Zack Cooper, "Reassessing Hedging: The Logic of Alignment in East Asia," *Security Studies*, Vol. 4, No. 4, 2015.

Limsiritong, Nattapat, Apiradee Springall, and Onkanya Rojanawanichkij, "The Difficulty of ASEAN Decision Making Mode on South China Sea Dispute: The ASEAN Charter Perspective," *Asian Political Science Review*, Vol. 3, No. 1, 2019.

Lin, Bonny, "U.S. Allied and Partner Support for Taiwan: Responses to a Chinese Attack on Taiwan and Potential U.S. Taiwan Policy Changes," testimony presented before the U.S.-China Economic and Security Review Commission on February 18, 2021, RAND Corporation, CT-A1194-1, 2021. As of May 23, 2023: https://www.rand.org/pubs/testimonies/CTA1194-1.html

Lin, Bonny, Michael S. Chase, Jonah Blank, Cortez A. Cooper III, Derek Grossman, Scott W. Harold, Jennifer D. P. Moroney, Lyle J. Morris, Logan Ma, Paul Orner, Alice Shih, and Soo Kim, *Regional Responses to U.S.-China Competition in the Indo-Pacific: Study Overview and Conclusions*, RAND Corporation, RR-4412-AF, 2020. As of August 26, 2022: https://www.rand.org/pubs/research_reports/RR4412.html

Lin, Bonny, Cristina L. Garafola, Bruce McClintock, Jonah Blank, Jeffrey W. Hornung, Karen Schwindt, Jennifer D. P. Moroney, Paul Orner, Dennis Borrman, Sarah W. Denton, and Jason Chambers, *Competition in the Gray Zone: Countering China's Coercion Against U.S. Allies and Partners in the Indo-Pacific*, RAND Corporation, RR-A594-1, 2022. As of September 26, 2022: https://www.rand.org/pubs/research_reports/RRA594-1.html

Lin, Liza, Yifan Wang, and Jon Emont, "Chinese Workers Say They Are Lured Abroad and Exploited for Belt and Road Jobs," *Wall Street Journal*, October 27, 2021.

Lopez, C. Todd, "Building Asymmetric Advantage in Indo-Pacific Part of DOD Approach to Chinese Aggression," press release, U.S. Department of Defense, July 27, 2022.

Lowe, Peter, *The Origins of the Korean War*, Routledge, 1997.

Lunn, Thomas, Christina L. Arabia, and Ben Dolven, *The Philippines: Background and U.S. Relations*, Congressional Research Service, R47055, March 28, 2022. As of August 29, 2022: https://sgp.fas.org/crs/row/R47055.pdf

Lutz, Catherine, and Cynthia Enloe, *The Bases of Empire: The Global Struggle Against US Military Posts*, NYU Press, 2009.

Lyons, John, and Frances Yoon, "'Do We Need to Be in Hong Kong?' Global Companies Are Eying the Exits," *Wall Street Journal*, June 7, 2021.

Maddon, George W., Jr., "PACAF, U.S. Marines Conclude Fighter Ops in Cope West 17," press release, U.S. Indo-Pacific Command, November 10, 2016.

Mahbubani, Kishore, "Qatar: Big Lessons from a Small Country," *Straits Times*, July 1, 2017. As of August 29, 2022: https://www.straitstimes.com/opinion/qatar-big-lessons-from-a-small-country

Malik, J. Mohan, "India's Response to the Gulf Crisis: Implications for Indian Foreign Policy," *Asian Survey*, Vol. 31, No. 9, September 1991.

Mancheri, Nabeel A., and Tomoo Marukawa, "Rare Earth Elements: China and Japan in Industry, Trade and Value Chain," ISS Contemporary Chinese Research Series, No. 17, February 2008.

Manoj, C. G., and Harikishan Sharma, "No One Has Entered Indian Territory or Captured Any Military Post, PM Tells Leaders of All Parties," *Indian Express*, June 20, 2020.

Maoz, Zeev, *Networks of Nations: The Evolution, Structure, and Impact of International Networks, 1816–2001*, Cambridge University Press, 2010.

Markey, Daniel S., "Developing India's Foreign Policy 'Software,'" *Asia Policy*, No. 8, July 2009.

Marquez, Consuelo, "Most Pinoys Do Not Agree Chinese Gov't Has Good Intentions for PH," Inquirer.net, April 5, 2019.

Marquina, Antonio, "The Spanish Neutrality During the Second World War," *American University International Law Review*, Vol. 14, No. 1, 1998.

Martinez Machain, Carla, "Exporting Influence: US Military Training as Soft Power," *Journal of Conflict Resolution*, Vol. 65, Nos. 2–3, 2021.

Mateo, Janvic, "68 Gov't Websites Attacked," *Philippine Star*, July 16, 2016.

Mathews, Mathew, Teo Kay Key, Meelvin Tay, and Alicia Wang, *Attitudes Towards Institutions, Politics, and Policies: Key Findings from the World Values Survey*, Institute of Policy Studies, Lee Kuan Yew School of Public Policy, 2021. As of August 29, 2022: https://lkyspp.nus.edu.sg/docs/default-source/ips/ips-exchange-series-17.pdf

Matthews, Ron, and Nellie Zhang Yan, "Small Country 'Total Defence': A Case Study of Singapore," *Defence Studies*, Vol. 7, No. 3, September 2007.

Mazarr, Michael J., Jonah Blank, Samuel Charap, Benjamin N. Harris, Timothy R. Heath, Niklas Helwig, Jeffrey W. Hornung, Lyle J. Morris, Ashley L. Rhoades, Ariane M. Tabatabai, and Sean M. Zeigler, *Understanding the Emerging Era of International Competition Through the Eyes of Others: Country Perspectives*, RAND Corporation, RR-2726/1-AF, 2022. As of August 24, 2022: https://www.rand.org/pubs/research_reports/RR2726z1.html

Mazarr, Michael J., Bryan Frederick, John J. Drennan, Emily Ellinger, Kelly Eusebi, Bryan Rooney, Andrew Stravers, and Emily Yoder, *Understanding Influence in the Strategic Competition with China*, RAND Corporation, RR-A290-1, 2021. As of May 23, 2023: https://www.rand.org/pubs/research_reports/RRA290-1.html

Mazarr, Michael J., Derek Grossman, Jeffrey W. Hornung, Jennifer D. P. Moroney, Shawn Cochran, Ashley L. Rhoades, and Andrew Stravers, *U.S. Major Combat Operations in the Indo-Pacific: Partner and Ally Views*, RAND Corporation, RR-A967-2, 2023. As of May 23, 2023: https://www.rand.org/pubs/research_reports/RRA967-2.html

McCurry, Justin, "Okinawa Rejects New US Military Base but Abe Vows to Push On," *The Guardian*, February 24, 2019.

McLaurin, John P., III, *US Use of Philippine Military Bases*, Army War College, 1990.

McMeekin, Sean, *July 1914: Countdown to War*, Basic Books, 2013.

McNerney, Michael J., Jonah Blank, Becca Wasser, Jeremy Boback, and Alexander Stephenson, *Improving Implementation of the Department of Defense Leahy Law*, RAND Corporation, RR-1737-OSD, 2017. As of August 02, 2022: https://www.rand.org/pubs/research_reports/RR1737.html

Mearsheimer, John J., "The False Promise of International Institutions," *International Security*, Vol. 19, No. 3, 1994–1995.

Mediansky, F. A., "The U.S. Military Facilities in the Philippines," *Contemporary Southeast Asia*, Vol. 8, No. 4, March 1987.

Mehta, Aaron, "Esper Calls for New Basing Investments in the Pacific," *Defense News*, August 27, 2019.

Memorandum of Understanding (MOU) Regarding United States Use of Facilities in Singapore, 1990.

Menon, Shivshankar, "Security Strategies for India as an Emerging Regional Power with Global Ambitions," lecture, United Service Institution of India, December 5, 2018.

Miglani, Sanjeev, "India Set to Approve Military Communications Deal with U.S.—Indian Defence Sources," Reuters, September 5, 2018.

Miglani, Sanjeev, and Nigam Prusty, "India Says to Sign Military Agreement with U.S. on Sharing of Satellite Data," Reuters, October 26, 2020.

Ministry of Defence, Singapore, "Overseas Operations: Notable SAF Deployments over the Years," webpage, undated. As of May 30, 2023:
https://www.mindef.gov.sg/web/portal/mindef/defence-matters/exercises-and-operations/exercises-and-operations-detail/overseas-operations

Ministry of Defence, Singapore, "Factsheet—The Strategic Framework Agreement," press release, July 12, 2005. As of August 26, 2022:
https://www.nas.gov.sg/archivesonline/data/pdfdoc/MINDEF_20050712001/MINDEF_20050712003.pdf

Ministry of Defence, Singapore, "Fact Sheet: 2019 Protocol of Amendment to the 1990 Memorandum of Understanding," fact sheet, September 24, 2019a. As of August 26, 2022:
https://www.mindef.gov.sg/web/portal/mindef/news-and-events/latest-releases/article-detail/2019/September/24sep19_fs

Ministry of Defence, Singapore, "Singapore and the US Renew Memorandum of Understanding," press release, September 24, 2019b.

Ministry of Defence, Singapore, "Cyber Defence," webpage, May 10, 2021. As of August 29, 2022:
https://www.mindef.gov.sg/web/portal/mindef/defence-matters/defence-topic/defence-topic-detail/cyber-defence

Ministry of Defence, Singapore, "Overseas Operations," webpage, March 8, 2022. As of August 26, 2022:
https://www.mindef.gov.sg/web/portal/mindef/defence-matters/exercises-and-operations/exercises-and-operations-detail/overseas-operations

Ministry of Foreign Affairs of Japan, "Exchange of Notes on the Implementation of Article VI of the Treaty" ["条約第六条の実施に関する交換公文"], January 19, 1960.

Ministry of Foreign Affairs of Japan, "The Signing of the Japan-Australia Acquisition and Cross-Servicing Agreement (ACSA)," webpage, May 19, 2010. As of April 25, 2022:
https://www.mofa.go.jp/announce/announce/2010/5/0519_02.html

Ministry of Foreign Affairs of Japan, "Japan-Philippines Summit Meeting," June 4, 2015.

Ministry of Foreign Affairs of Japan, "G7 Leaders' Statement," Berlin, Germany, March 11, 2022.

Ministry of Foreign Affairs of Japan, "Japan-China Relations (Basic Data)," webpage, February 24, 2022. As of March 16, 2022:
https://www.mofa.go.jp/region/asia-paci/china/data.html

Ministry of Foreign Affairs, Singapore, "International Peacekeeping," webpage, undated-a. As of August 29, 2022:
https://www.mfa.gov.sg/SINGAPORES-FOREIGN-POLICY/International-Issues/International-Peacekeeping

Ministry of Foreign Affairs, Singapore, "National Service Obligation," webpage, undated-b. As of September 19, 2022:
https://www.mfa.gov.sg/Overseas-Mission/Chennai/Consular-Services/National-Service-Obligation

Ministry of Foreign Affairs, Singapore, "MFA Spokesman's Comments on the Ruling of the Arbitral Tribunal in the Philippines v China Case Under Annex VII to the 1982 United Nations Convention on the Law of the Sea (UNCLOS)," July 12, 2016. As of August 29, 2022:
https://www.mfa.gov.sg/Newsroom/Press-Statements-Transcripts-and-Photos/2016/07/MFA-Spokesmans-Comments-on-the-ruling-of-the-Arbitral-Tribunal-in-the-Philippines-v-China-case-under

Ministry of Foreign Affairs of the Republic of Indonesia, "Indonesian FM Presents the Diplomacy Priorities 2019–2024 to the House of Representatives," November 14, 2019.

Ministry of Foreign Affairs, Republic of Korea. "First Korea-Indonesia Foreign and Defense (2+2) Senior Officials' Meeting," webpage, August 27, 2021. As of August 3, 2022:
https://www.mofa.go.kr/eng/brd/m_5676/view.do?seq=321820

Mintz, Alex, and Chi Huang, "Guns Versus Butter: The Indirect Link," *American Journal of Political Science*, Vol. 35, No. 3, August 1991.

Misalucha, Charmaine G., Julio S. Amador III, "U.S.-Philippines Security Ties: Building New Foundations?" *Asian Politics & Policy*, Vol. 8, No. 1, January 2016.

Mitrasca, Marcel, *Moldova: A Romanian Province Under Russian Rule: Diplomatic History from the Archives of the Great Powers*, Algora Publishing, 2002.

Montanelli, Indro, and Mario Cervi, *Italy of the Years of Mud*, Rizzoli, 1993.

Montolalu, Reynaldo Rudy Kristian, and Anak Agung Banyu Perwita, "Philippine–US Defense Cooperation: The Implementation of 'The Enhanced Defense Cooperation Agreement' to Respond China's Assertiveness in the South China Sea (2010–2016)," *Journal Asia Pacific Studies*, Vol. 3, No. 1, January–June 2019.

Morey, Daniel S., "Military Coalitions and the Outcome of Interstate Wars," *Foreign Policy Analysis*, Vol. 12, No. 4, October 2016.

Moriyasu, Ken, "Abe Leads Charge for Japan to Boost Defense Spending to 2% of GDP," *NikkeiAsia*, April 22, 2022.

Morris, Lyle J., and Giacomo Persi Paoli, *A Preliminary Assessment of Indonesia's Maritime Security Threats and Capabilities*, RAND Corporation, RR-2469-RC, 2018. As of August 19, 2022:
https://www.rand.org/pubs/research_reports/RR2469.html

Morrow, James D., "Alliances: Why Write Them Down?" *Annual Review of Political Science*, Vol. 3, 2000.

Mukherjee, Andy, "Singapore's Tougher Stay-at-Home Rules for the Superrich," Bloomberg, May 5, 2022.

Murphy, Sean D., "The Role of Bilateral Defense Agreements in Maintaining the European Security Equilibrium," *Cornell International Law Journal*, Vol. 24, No. 3, 1991.

Nepomuceno, Priam, "EDCA to Allow PH, US to Respond to Regional Security Challenges," Philippine News Agency, April 18, 2018.

Nieman, Mark David, Carla Martinez Machain, Olga V. Chyzh, and Sam R. Bell, "An International Game of Risk: Troop Placement and Major Power Competition," *Journal of Politics*, Vol. 83, No. 4, 2021.

Niksch, Larry, *Indonesia: U.S. Relations with the Indonesian Military*, Congressional Research Service, August 10, 1998.

Nohara, Yoshiaki, "Japan Flags Vulnerability to China Supply Chain Constraints," Bloomberg, February 3, 2022.

Norrlof, Carla, and William C. Wohlforth, "Is U.S. Grand Strategy Self-Defeating? Deep Engagement, Military Spending and Sovereign Debt," *Conflict Management and Peace Science*, Vol. 36, No. 3, 2019.

Nye, Joseph S., Jr., "The Changing Nature of World Power," *Political Science Quarterly*, Vol. 105, No. 2, Summer 1990.

Obama, Barack, and Benigno Aquino III, "Remarks by President Obama and President Benigno Aquino III of the Philippines in Joint Press Conference," transcript, White House, Office of the Press Secretary, April 28, 2014.

Observatory of Economic Complexity, "India/China," webpage, undated-a. As of July 13, 2023: https://oec.world/en/profile/bilateral-country/chn/partner/ind

Observatory of Economic Complexity, "Indonesia," webpage, undated-b. As of May 3, 2022: https://oec.world/en/profile/country/idn

Observatory of Economic Complexity, "Indonesia/China," webpage, undated-c. As of July 13, 2023: https://oec.world/en/profile/bilateral-country/chn/partner/idn

Observatory of Economic Complexity, "Japan/China," webpage, undated-d. As of September 23, 2020: https://oec.world/en/profile/bilateral-country/jpn/partner/chn

Observatory of Economic Complexity, "Philippines/China," webpage, undated-e. As of May 25, 2023: https://oec.world/en/profile/bilateral-country/phl/partner/chn

Observatory of Economic Complexity, "Singapore/China," webpage, undated-f. As of May 25, 2023: https://oec.world/en/profile/bilateral-country/sgp/partner/chn

OEC—*See* Observatory of Economic Complexity.

Office for National Statistics, "UK Trade: Monthly Trade in Goods," database, United Kingdom, September 2022. As of July 12, 2023: https://www.ons.gov.uk/economy/nationalaccounts/balanceofpayments/bulletins/uktrade/september2022

Office of the Secretary of Defense, *Annual Report to Congress: Military and Security Developments Involving the People's Republic of China 2018*, May 16, 2018.

Office of the U.S. Trade Representative, "Indonesia," webpage, undated-a. As of August 3, 2022: https://ustr.gov/countries-regions/southeast-asia-pacific/indonesia

Office of the U.S. Trade Representative, "Philippines," webpage, undated-b. As of May 25, 2023: https://ustr.gov/countries-regions/southeast-asia-pacific/philippines

Oliver, Steven, and Kai Ostwald, "Explaining Elections in Singapore," *Journal of East Asian Studies*, Vol. 18, No. 2, July 11, 2018.

Olson, Mancur, Jr., and Richard Zeckhauser, "An Economic Theory of Alliances," *Review of Economics and Statistics*, Vol. 48, No. 3, August 1966.

Ordaniel, Jeffrey, and Collin Koh, "Pragmatic and Principled—U.S.-Singapore Relations as a Model Partnership in the Indo-Pacific," in Jeffrey Ordaniel and Ariel Stenek, eds., *The United States and Singapore: Indo-Pacific Partners*, Pacific Forum, 2021.

Ordaniel, Jeffrey, and Ariel Stenek, eds., *The United States and Singapore: Indo-Pacific Partners*, Pacific Forum, 2021.

Organisation for Economic Co-operation and Development, "Data: Outward FDI Flows by Partner Country," webpage, 2021. As of June 9, 2022: https://data.oecd.org/fdi/outward-fdi-flows-by-partner-country.htm

Otterman, Sharon, "Saudi Arabia: Withdrawal of U.S. Forces," Council on Foreign Relations, February 7, 2005. As of September 13, 2022:
https://www.cfr.org/backgrounder/saudi-arabia-withdrawl-us-forces

Pacific Air Forces Public Affairs, "US, Indonesian Air Forces to Conduct Cope West 22 Exercise," June 6, 2022.

Pager, Tyler, "Biden Nominates Top National Security Staffer as ASEAN Ambassador," *Washington Post*, May 13, 2022.

Panda, Ankit, "Singapore: A Small Asian Heavyweight," Council on Foreign Relations, April 16, 2020.

Pant, Harsh V., "India, Australia, and the Indo-Pacific," Australia India Institute, April 14, 2022.

Pant, Harsh V., Prithvi Iyer, Nivedita Kapoor, Aarshi Tirkey, and Kartik Bommakanti, *The ORF Foreign Policy Survey 2021: Young India and the World*, Observer Research Foundation, 2021.

Pant, Harsh V., and Shashank Mattoo, "The Rising Sun in India-Japan Relations," *The Hindu*, May 1, 2022.

Park, Jae-Jeok, "A Comparative Case Study of the US-Philippines Alliance in the 1990s and the US-South Korea Alliance Between 1998 and 2008: Alliance (Dis) Continuation," *Asian Survey*, Vol. 51, No. 2, March/April 2011.

Park, Johann, and Valentina Bali, "International Terrorism and the Political Survival of Leaders," *Journal of Conflict Resolution*, Vol. 61, No. 7, 2017.

Park, Susan, *International Organisations and Global Problems: Theories and Explanations*, Cambridge University Press, 2018.

"Participation in the Nuclear Ban Treaty Greatly Exceeds Non-Participation by 59%" ["核禁条約参加を, 59% 不参加を大きく上回る"], *Asahi Shimbun*, November 17, 2020.

Paul, T. V., Deborah Welch Larson, and William C. Wohlforth, *Status in World Politics*, Cambridge University Press, 2014.

Pettyjohn, Stacie L., and Jennifer Kavanagh, *Access Granted: Political Challenges to U.S. Overseas Military Presence, 1945–2014*, RAND Corporation, RR-1339-AF, 2016. As of August 25, 2022:
https://www.rand.org/pubs/research_reports/RR1339.html

Peuch, Jean-Christophe, "Turkey: U.S. Plan to Oust Saddam Leaves Ankara Between Iraq and a Hard Place," Radio Free Europe/Radio Liberty, August 8, 2002.

Pew Research Center, "Global Indicators Database," webpage, undated. As of May 30, 2023:
https://www.pewresearch.org/global/database/

Pew Research Center for the People and the Press, *What the World Thinks in 2002*, December 4, 2002. As of May 18, 2023:
https://www.pewresearch.org/global/2002/12/04/what-the-world-thinks-in-2002/

Pew Research Center, "Spring 2019 Global Attitudes Survey: Topline Questionnaire," December 5, 2019. As of August 29, 2022:
https://www.pewresearch.org/global/2019/12/05/chinas-economic-growth-mostly-welcomed-in-emerging-markets-but-neighbors-wary-of-its-influence/

Philippines Department of Tourism, "Tourist Arrivals in the Philippines by Country of Residence, January–December 2019," table, February 12, 2020. As of May 30, 2023:
http://www.tourism.gov.ph/Tourism_demand/Arrivals2019.pdf

"Philippines, China to Discuss Fishing Rights in South China Sea, Marcos Says," Reuters, May 1, 2023.

"Philippines Seeks New Markets Amid Sea Dispute with China," Reuters, May 17, 2012.

Phillips, Kristine, "Philippines's Duterte Vows Not to Come to the U.S.: 'I've Seen America, and It's Lousy," Washington Post, July 22, 2017.

Piiparinen, Anni, "China's Secret Weapon in the South China Sea: Cyber Attacks," The Diplomat, July 22, 2016.

Plourde, Aimée M., "The Origins of Prestige Goods as Honest Signals of Skill and Knowledge," Human Nature, Vol. 19, No. 4, December 2008.

Poling, Gregory, and Conor Cronin, "The Dangers of Allowing U.S.-Philippine Defense Cooperation to Languish," War on the Rocks, May 17, 2018.

Poushter, Jacob, and Caldwell Bishop, "People in the Philippines Still Favor U.S. Over China, but Gap Is Narrowing," Pew Research Center, September 21, 2017.

Prasirtsuk, Kitti, "An Ally at the Crossroads: Thailand in the US Alliance System," in Michael Wesley, ed., Global Allies: Comparing US Alliances in the 21st Century, Australian National University Press, 2017.

Price, Gareth, "Ukraine War: Why India Abstained on UN Vote Against Russia," Chatham House, March 25, 2022.

Prime Minister of Japan [Kishida Fumio], "Press Conference by the Prime Minister Regarding Japan-U.S. Video Conference Summit Meeting," Speeches and Statements by the Prime Minister, webpage, January 21, 2022. As of August 25, 2022: https://japan.kantei.go.jp/101_kishida/statement/202201/_00012.html

Pu, Xiaoyu, Rebranding China: Contested Status Signaling in the Changing Global Order, Stanford University Press, 2019.

Purba, Kornelius, "Will Jokowi's Decree on Natuna Change the Equation?" Jakarta Post, April 18, 2022.

Putnam, Robert D., "Diplomacy and Domestic Politics: The Logic of Two-Level Games," International Organization, Vol. 42, No. 3, Summer 1988.

Quinlivan, James T., "Coup-Proofing: Its Practice and Consequences in the Middle East," International Security, Vol. 24, No. 2, Fall 1999.

Radin, Andrew, Andrew Scobell, Elina Treyger, J. D. Williams, Logan Ma, Howard J. Shatz, Sean M. Zeigler, Eugeniu Han, and Clint Reach, China-Russia Cooperation: Determining Factors, Future Trajectories, Implications for the United States, RAND Corporation, RR-3067-A, 2021. As of August 29, 2022: https://www.rand.org/pubs/research_reports/RR3067.html

Rahman, Christopher, "Singapore: Forward Operating Site," in Carnes Lord and Andrew Erickson, eds., Rebalancing U.S. Forces: Basing and Forward Presence in the Asia-Pacific, Naval Institute Press, 2014.

Rajagopalan, Rajeswari Pillai, "Logistics Pact with U.S.: Why LEMOA Is Significant for India," Observer Research Foundation, August 31, 2016.

Rajagopalan, Rajeswari Pillai, "India's Military Outreach: Military Logistics Agreements," The Diplomat, September 9, 2021.

Randolph, R. Sean, *The United States and Thailand: Alliance Dynamics, 1950–1985*, Institute of East Asian Studies, University of California, Berkeley, 1986.

Rapp-Hooper, Mira, *Shields of the Republic: The Triumph and Peril of America's Alliances*, Harvard University Press, 2020.

Rassbach, Elsa, "Protesting U.S. Military Bases in Germany," *Peace Review*, Vol. 22, No. 2, 2010.

Reed, Stanley, "Burned by Russia, Poland Turns to U.S. for Natural Gas and Energy Security," *New York Times*, February 26, 2019.

"Regime in Italy Falls Amid Furor," United Press International via *South Florida Sun Sentinel*, October 18, 1985.

Rehberg, Carl, and Mark Gunzinger, *Air and Missile Defense at a Crossroads: New Concepts and Technologies to Defend America's Overseas Bases*, Center for Strategic and Budgetary Assessments, 2018.

Reiter, Dan, "Security Commitments and Nuclear Proliferation," *Foreign Policy Analysis*, Vol. 10, No. 1, January 2014.

Reiter, Dan, and Paul Poast, "The Truth About Tripwires: Why Small Force Deployments Do Not Deter Aggression," *Texas National Security Review*, Vol. 4, No. 3, Summer 2021.

Reyes, Sebastian, "Singapore's Stubborn Authoritarianism," *Harvard Political Review*, September 29, 2015.

Riedel, Bruce, "Kennedy's Almost Quagmire Was Far from Cuba," *Politico*, November 29, 2015.

Riedel, Bruce, *JFK's Forgotten Crisis: Tibet, the CIA, and the Sino-Indian War*, Brookings Institution, 2017.

Rivas, Ralf, and Sofia Tomacruz, "How Duterte's Love Affair with China Shaped the PH Economy," Rappler, July 21, 2021.

Rosen, Mark, and Douglas Jackson, *The U.S. India Defense Relationship: Putting the Foundational Agreements in Perspective*, CNA, February 2017.

Ruby, Tomislav Z., and Douglas Gibler, "US Professional Military Education and Democratization Abroad," *European Journal of International Relations*, Vol. 16, No. 3, 2010.

"Rudolf: Swedish Steam Merchant," webpage, uboat.net, 2022. As of July 25, 2022: https://uboat.net/allies/merchants/ship/123.html

Russett, Bruce, "Defense Expenditures and National Well-Being," *American Political Science Review*, Vol. 76, No. 4, December 1982.

Sacks, David, *Enhancing U.S.-Japan Coordination for a Taiwan Conflict*, Council on Foreign Relations, Center for Preventative Action, January 18, 2022.

Saunders, Elizabeth N., *Leaders at War: How Presidents Shape Military Interventions*, Cornell University Press, 2011.

Schneider, Howard, "A Key Chinese Advantage Erodes," *Washington Post*, October 27, 2012.

Schultz, Kenneth A., "Perils of Polarization for U.S. Foreign Policy," *Washington Quarterly*, Vol. 40, No. 4, 2017.

Schwartz, Ben, "New Delhi Is Getting Serious About Its Defense Partnership with Washington," *In-Depth* blog, October 30, 2020.

Schweller, Randall L., "Bandwagoning for Profit: Bringing the Revisionist State Back In," *International Security*, Vol. 19, No. 1, Summer 1994.

Schweller, Randall L., "Unanswered Threats: A Neoclassical Realist Theory of Underbalancing," *International Security*, Vol. 29, No. 2, Fall 2004.

Seah, Sharon, Hong Thi Ha, Melinda Martinus, and Pham Thi Phuong Thao, *The State of Southeast Asia: 2021 Survey Report*, ISEAS–Yusof Ishak Institute, February 10, 2021.

Shugart, Thomas, and Javier Gonzalez, *First Strike: China's Missile Threat to U.S. Bases in Asia*, Center for a New American Security, 2017.

Silver, Laura, "China's International Image Remains Broadly Negative as Views of the U.S. Rebound," Pew Research Center, June 30, 2021.

Singh, Abhijit, "China's Military Base in Djibouti: Strategic Implications for India," War on the Rocks, August 21, 2017. As of August 29, 2022: https://warontherocks.com/2017/08/chinas-military-base-in-djibouti-strategic-implications-for-india/

Singh, Anita, "Pakistan's Stability/Instability Complex: The Politics and Reverberations of the 2007 November Emergency," *Strategic Studies Quarterly*, Vol. 3, No. 4, Winter 2009.

Singh, Daljit, *Southeast Asia's Uneasy Position in America's Indo-Pacific Strategy*, ISEAS–Yusof Ishak Institute, 2018.

Slantchev, Branislav L., "How Initiators End Their Wars: The Duration of Warfare and the Terms of Peace," *American Journal of Political Science*, Vol. 48, No. 4, October 2004.

Snyder, Glenn H., "The Security Dilemma in Alliance Politics," *World Politics*, Vol. 36, No. 4, July 1984.

Snyder, Glenn H., *Alliance Politics*, Cornell University Press, 2007.

Solsten, Eric, *Portugal: A Country Study*, ed., Library of Congress, U.S. Government Printing Office, 1993.

Solsten, Eric, and Sandra W. Meditz, eds., *Spain: A Country Study*, Library of Congress, U.S. Government Printing Office, 1990.

"South China Sea Arbitration Case," Xinhua via *Global Times*, March 31, 2018.

Stach, Lukasz, "The Philippines Maritime Forces and Its Maritime Military Power Projection Capabilities: Unfulfilled Ambitions?" *Defense & Security Analysis*, Vol. 37, No. 4, 2021.

Statista, "Annual Flow of Foreign Direct Investments from China to Indonesia Between 2010 and 2020," Statista, January 4, 2022.

Stiles, Matt, "Upset over a U.S. Missile Defense System, China Hits South Korea Where It Hurts—in the Wallet," *Los Angeles Times*, February 28, 2018.

Storey, Ian, and William Choong, "Russia's Invasion of Ukraine: Southeast Asian Responses and Why the Conflict Matters to the Region," ISEAS–Yusof Ishak Institute, March 9, 2022.

Strangio, Sebastian, "Philippines Pledges to Back US if Ukraine Conflict Spreads to Asia," *The Diplomat*, March 11, 2022a.

Strangio, Sebastian, "Indonesian Public Opinion Ambivalent About Rising Geopolitical Tensions: Report," *The Diplomat*, April 5, 2022b.

Strangio, Sebastian, "Japan, Philippines Agree to Boost Security Cooperation," *The Diplomat*, April 8, 2022c.

Strategic Framework Agreement Between the United States of America and the Republic of Singapore for a Closer Cooperation Partnership in Defense and Security, July 12, 2005.

Stravers, Andrew, "Pork, Parties, and Priorities: Partisan Politics and Overseas Military Deployments," *Conflict Management and Peace Science*, Vol. 38, No. 2, 2021.

Stravers, Andrew, and Dana El Kurd, "Strategic Autocracy: American Military Forces and Regime Type," *Journal of Global Security Studies*, Vol. 5, No. 3, July 2020.

Sudduth, Jun Koga, "Coup Risk, Coup-Proofing and Leader Survival," *Journal of Peace Research*, Vol. 54, No. 1, January 2017.

Sulaiman, Yohanes, "Whither Indonesia's Indo-Pacific Strategy?" French Institute of International Relations, Center for Asian Studies, January 2019.

Suroyo, Gayatri, "China Agrees to Invest $3 Bln in Indonesia Sovereign Wealth Fund," Reuters, July 4, 2022.

Tago, Atsushi, "Why Do States Join US-Led Military Coalitions? The Compulsion of the Coalition's Missions and Legitimacy," *International Relations of the Asia-Pacific*, Vol. 7, No. 2, 2007.

Tan, Brenda, "Friend or Foe? Explaining the Philippines' China Policy in the South China Sea," E–International Relations, August 10, 2020.

Tan, Kenneth Paul, "The Ideology of Pragmatism: Neo-liberal Globalisation and Political Authoritarianism in Singapore," *Journal of Contemporary Asia*, Vol. 42, No. 1, 2012.

Tan, Kwan Wei Kevin, "Singapore's Expat Angst Forces Simmering Political Debate," Bloomberg, July 29, 2021.

Tan, See Seng, "Facilitating the US Rebalance: Challenges and Prospects for Singapore as America's Security Partner," *Security Challenges*, Vol. 12, No. 3, 2016.

Tan, See Seng, "(Still) Supporting the Indispensable Power: Singapore's Relations with the United States from Trump to Biden," *Asia Policy*, Vol. 16, No. 4, October 2021.

Tellis, Ashley J., "'What Is in Our Interest': India and the Ukraine War," Carnegie Endowment for International Peace, April 25, 2022.

Theohary, Catherine A., "Defense Primer: Information Operations," Congressional Research Service, IF10771, December 1, 2021.

Thomas, John T., "Bases, Places, and Faces: Operational Maneuver and Sustainment in the Indo-Pacific Region," *Journal of Indo-Pacific Affairs*, April 8, 2021.

Tiezzi, Shannon, "How Did Asian Countries Vote on the UN's Ukraine Resolution?" *The Diplomat*, March 3, 2022.

Tir, Jaroslav, "Territorial Diversion: Diversionary Theory of War and Territorial Conflict," *Journal of Politics*, Vol. 72, No. 2, April 2010.

Tomz, Michael, *Reputation and International Cooperation: Sovereign Debt Across Three Centuries*, Princeton University Press, 2008.

Torrey, Glenn E., *Romania and World War I: A Collection of Studies*, Histria Books, 1998.

Trajano, Julius Cesar, "US-Philippines: Resetting the Security Alliance?" commentary, S. Rajaratnam School of International Studies, February 24, 2021.

Treaty of Mutual Cooperation and Security Between Japan and the United States of America, January 19, 1960. As of June 2, 2023:
https://www.mofa.go.jp/region/n-america/us/q&a/ref/1.html

Trebon, Gregory L., *Libyan State Sponsored Terrorism—What Did Operation El Dorado Canyon Accomplish?* Air Command and Staff College, 1988.

Tremewan, Christopher, *The Political Economy of Social Control in Singapore*, Palgrave Macmillan, 1994.

TrendEconomy, "Japan | Imports and Exports | World | Compounds of Rare-Earth Metals, of Tritium or of Scandium or of Mixtures of These Metals," webpage, November 14, 2021. As of March 16, 2021:
https://trendeconomy.com/data/h2/Japan/2846

Turton, Shaun, "Beijing-Friendly Cambodia and Laos Pushed Out to ASEAN's Fringe," *Nikkei Asia*, November 13, 2020.

UN—*See* United Nations.

Unaydin, Solmaz, "Turkey's Policy Towards the Middle East and the Question of Iraq," *Turkish Policy Quarterly*, Vol. 1, No. 4, Winter 2002.

Ungku, Fathin, Bernadete Christina Munthe, and Tom Daly, "Freeport, Tsingshan Finalising $2.8 Billion Copper Smelter Next Week—Minister," Reuters, March 24, 2021.

United Nations, "UN Comtrade Database," webpage, undated. As of May 26, 2023:
https://comtradeplus.un.org/

United Nations Conference on Trade and Development, *World Investment Report*, 2022a. As of August 29, 2022:
https://unctad.org/topic/investment/world-investment-report

United Nations Conference on Trade and Development, "General Profile: Japan," webpage, UNCTADSTAT, October 20, 2022b. As of April 7, 2022:
http://unctadstat.unctad.org/countryprofile/generalprofile/en-gb/392/index.html

United Nations Statistics Division, "Countries and Areas: Japan," webpage, undated. As of July 12, 2023:
https://data.un.org/CountryProfile.aspx/_Docs/CountryProfile.aspx?crName=Japan

UN Security Council Resolution 678, on Iraq and Kuwait, November 29, 1990

UN Security Council Resolution 1441, on the situation between Iraq and Kuwait, November 8, 2002.

U.S. Agency for International Development, "Our Work: Philippines" webpage, August 10, 2022. As of July 12, 2023:
https://www.usaid.gov/philippines/our-work

USAID—See U.S. Agency for International Development.

U.S. Army Japan, homepage, undated. As of June 2, 2023:
https://www.usarj.army.mil/

U.S. Census Bureau, "U.S. Trade in Goods by Country," webpage, undated. As of September 23, 2022:
https://www.census.gov/foreign-trade/balance/index.html

U.S. Department of Defense, *Military and Security Developments Involving the People's Republic of China 2021: Annual Report to Congress*, November 3, 2021.

U.S. Department of Defense, "Philippines, U.S. Announce Four New EDCA Sites," press release, February 1, 2023.

U.S. Department of Defense and U.S. Department of State, *Foreign Military Training Report: Fiscal Years 2016 and 2017*, Vol. I, 2017.

U.S. Department of State, "Report on U.S. Policy Toward Spain," undated, in Charles S. Sampson and James E. Miller, eds., *Foreign Relations of the United States, 1961–1963*: Vol. 13, *Western Europe and Canada*, 1994. As of July 12, 2023: https://history.state.gov/historicaldocuments/frus1961-63v13/d375

U.S. Department of State, "U.S. Arms Sales and Defense Trade," fact sheet, January 20, 2021a.

U.S. Department of State, "U.S. Security Cooperation with India," fact sheet, January 20, 2021b.

U.S. Department of State, "Joint Vision for a 21st Century United States-Philippines Partnership," press release, November 16, 2021c.

U.S. Department of State, "Joint Statement of the U.S.-Japan Security Consultative Committee ('2+2')", press release, January 6, 2022a.

U.S. Department of State, "Fourth Annual U.S.-India 2+2 Ministerial Dialogue," press release, April 11, 2022b.

U.S. Department of State, "The United States–ASEAN Relationship," fact sheet, August 3, 2022c.

U.S. Embassy & Consulates in Indonesia, "U.S. Building Maritime Capacity in Southeast Asia," fact sheet, undated. As of August 19, 2022: https://id.usembassy.gov/our-relationship/policy-history/embassy-fact-sheets/fact-sheet-u-s-building-maritime-capacity-in-southeast-asia/

U.S. Embassy in the Philippines, "U.S. Provides Php269 Million in New COVID-19 Assistance, Total Aid Exceeds Php470 Million," press release, April 22, 2020.

U.S. Embassy in the Philippines, "U.S. Assistance for Typhoon Odette Tops PHP 1 Billion with New Major Announcement," press release, January 5, 2022.

U.S. Forces Japan, homepage, undated. As of June 2, 2023: https://www.usfj.mil/

U.S. Government Accountability Office, *Army Pacific Pathways: Comprehensive Assessment and Planning Needed to Capture Benefits Relative to Costs and Enhance Value for Participating Units*, GAO-17-126, November 2016.

U.S. Government Accountability Office, *DoD Should Improve Oversight and Seek Payment from Foreign Partners for Thousands of Orders It Identifies as Overdue*, GAO-20-309, March 2020.

U.S. Indo-Pacific Command, "U.S. Military Delivers Advanced Unmanned Aerial System to Philippine Air Force," press release, October 14, 2021. As of June 3, 2022: https://www.pacom.mil/Media/News/News-Article-View/Article/2811142/us-military-delivers-advanced-unmanned-aerial-system-to-philippine-air-force/

USINDOPACOM—*See* U.S. Indo-Pacific Command.

"U.S. Will Defend Philippines If Attacked in the South China Sea," Reuters via CNN, August 6, 2022.

Valencia, Mark, "Trying to Solve the Philippines' South China Sea Conundrum," *The Diplomat*, June 5, 2018.

Vann, Michael G., "When the World Came to Southeast Asia: Malacca and the Global Economy," *Maritime Asia*, Vol. 19, No. 2, Fall 2014.

Venzon, Cliff, "Duterte Struggles to Sell His China Pivot at Home" Nikkei Asia, October 9, 2019. As of August 29, 2022:
https://asia.nikkei.com/Spotlight/The-Big-Story/Duterte-struggles-to-sell-his-China-pivot-at-home

Viñas, Angel, "Negotiating the U.S.-Spanish Agreements, 1953–1988: A Spanish Perspective," *Jean Monnet/Robert Schuman Paper Series*, Vol. 3, No. 7, September 2003.

Vinogradov, Vladen N., "Romania in the First World War: The Years of Neutrality, 1914–1916," *International History Review*, Vol. 14, No. 3, August 1992.

Wada Haruki, *The Korean War: An International History*, Rowman & Littlefield, 2018.

Wagle, Ankush, "Analyzing U.S. Singapore Maritime Security Cooperation through the Indo-Pacific Lens," in Jeffrey Ordaniel and Ariel Stenek, eds., *The United States and Singapore: Indo-Pacific Partners*, Pacific Forum, December 2021.

Wagner, R. Harrison, "Bargaining, War, and Alliances," *Conflict Management and Peace Science*, Vol. 21, No. 3, 2004.

War Cabinet, Chiefs of Staff Committee, COS Secret Series of Memoranda, 271(S)–319(S), British National Archives, CAB 80/105, March 31–May 3, 1940a.

War Cabinet, Chiefs of Staff Committee, Plan R.4: Postponement. Note by the Secretary, British National Archives, CAB 80/105/3, April 3, 1940b.

"War in Brief: India: U.S. Planes Refuel for Gulf Missions," *Los Angeles Times*, January 29, 1991. August 29, 2022:
https://www.latimes.com/archives/la-xpm-1991-01-29-mn-408-story.html

War Office, Patrol and Road Reports: Usambara Railway, British National Archives, WO 158/455, 1914–1916.

Weatherbee, Donald E., "The Philippines and ASEAN: Options for Aquino," *Asian Survey*, Vol. 27, No. 12, December 1987.

Wei Hong [韦红] and Yin Nannan [尹楠楠], "The Choice of Strategic Pivotal States in Southeast Asia for '21st Century Maritime Silk Road'" ["'21 世纪海上丝绸之路' 东南亚战略支点国家 的选择"], *Socialism Studies* [社会主义研究], No. 6, 2017.

Werner, Ben, "Philippines Freezes Pull-Out From Visiting U.S. Forces Agreement," USNI News, June 8, 2020.

Wertheim, Stephen, *Tomorrow, the World: The Birth of U.S. Global Supremacy*, Harvard University Press, 2020.

White, Joshua T., *After the Foundational Agreements: An Agenda for U.S. India Defense and Security Cooperation*, Brookings Institution, January 2021.

White House, "Fact Sheet: Strengthening the U.S.-Singapore Strategic Partnership," press release, August 23, 2021.

White House, *Indo-Pacific Strategy of the United States*, February 2022. As of September 19, 2022:
https://www.whitehouse.gov/wp-content/uploads/2022/02/U.S.-Indo-Pacific-Strategy.pdf

Wike, Richard, Janell Fetterolf, Moira Fagan, and Sneha Gubbala, *International Attitudes Toward the U.S., NATO and Russia in a Time of Crisis*, Pew Research Center, 2022.

WITS—*See* World Integrated Trade Solutions.

Wolford, Scott, "Power, Preferences, and Balancing: The Durability of Coalitions and the Expansion of Conflict," *International Studies Quarterly*, Vol. 58, No. 1, March 2014.

Wong, Catherine "'Nothing More Than a Piece of Paper': Former Chinese Envoy Dismisses Upcoming Ruling on South China Sea Claims," *South China Morning Post*, July 6, 2016.

World Bank, "Foreign Direct Investment, Net Inflows (BoP, current US$)—Indonesia," webpage, undated-a. As of May 9, 2022:
https://data.worldbank.org/indicator/BX.KLT.DINV.CD.WD?locations=ID

World Bank, "GDP (current US$)—India," webpage, undated-b. As of June 9, 2022:
https://data.worldbank.org/indicator/NY.GDP.MKTP.CD?end=2020&locations=IN&start=2012

World Bank, "World Integrated Trade Solution," database, undated-c. As of July 12, 2023:
https://wits.worldbank.org/

Wright, Claudia, "Journey to Marrakesh: US-Moroccan Security Relations," *International Security*, Vol. 7, No. 4, Spring 1983.

Yap, Cecilia "Philippines Asks U.S. for Vaccine Help as China Tensions Grow," Bloomberg, April 11, 2021.

Yee, William Yuen, "Explaining China's Relationship with Indonesia, Its Gateway to Southeast Asia," China Project, December 2, 2021.

Yen Nee Lee, "Philippine President Duterte's China Pivot Hasn't Reduced Tensions in the South China Sea," CNBC, December 26, 2021. As of June 6, 2022:
https://www.cnbc.com/2021/12/27/philippine-president-dutertes-china-pivot-hasnt-reduced-south-china-sea-tensions.html

Yeo, Andrew, *Activists, Alliances, and Anti-US Base Protests*, Cambridge University Press, 2011.

Yeo, Andrew, "The Politics of Overseas Military Bases," *Perspectives on Politics*, Vol. 15, No. 1, 2017.

Yeo, Andrew, and Stacie Pettyjohn, "Bases of Empire? The Logic of Overseas U.S. Military Base Expansion, 1870–2016," *Comparative Strategy*, Vol. 40, No. 1, January 2021.

Yeo, Mike, "Australia and Japan to Strengthen Defence Cooperation," *Australian Defence Magazine*, December 2, 2021.

Yong, Charissa, "Singaporeans Should Be Aware of China's 'Influence Operations' to Manipulate Them, Says Retired Diplomat Bilahari," *Straits Times*, June 27, 2018.

Milton Keynes UK
Ingram Content Group UK Ltd.
UKHW051021030324
438619UK00003B/6

9 781977 412515